Coaching CHAMPS

Building a System of Support for All Teachers

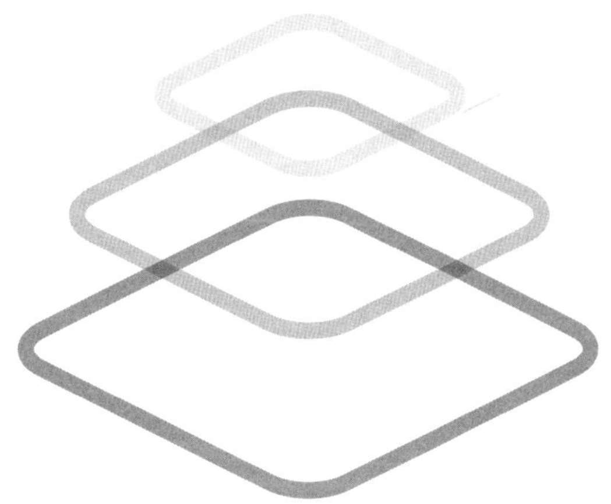

Tricia Skyles
Randy Sprick
Jim Knight

Published in the United States by
Ancora Publishing
21 West 6th Avenue
Eugene, Oregon 97401
ancorapublishing.com

ISBN: 978-1-59909-115-0
Cover and book design by Natalie Conaway

Any resources and website addresses are provided for reader convenience and were current at the time of publication. Report broken links to info@ancorapublishing.com.

Download Reproducible Materials
Go to download.ancorapublishing.com and enter access code 978-1-59909-115-0

TABLE OF CONTENTS

About the Authors . . . vii
Acknowledgments . . . ix

Introduction: A Context for Coaching . . . 1

Purpose of This Book . . . 3
Coaching Within MTSS . . . 3
Formalizing a Structure for Coaching . . . 5
The Improvement Cycle . . . 6
The CHAMPS Approach . . . 7
STOIC Framework . . . 8
Goals of Coaching for Equity . . . 9
Dispelling the Myth of "Magical" Classroom Management . . . 11

SECTION ONE

Coaching as a Universal Strategy for Teachers . . . 13

CHAPTER 1
Coaching to Lead Change . . . 15

The Rationale for Coaching . . . 18
Change Is a Process . . . 20
Drivers of Change . . . 25
Clarity of Shared Principles . . . 30

CHAPTER 2
Structure: Developing a Clear Vision . . . 33

Develop an Overall Vision . . . 35
Identify the Four Cornerstones . . . 37
Identify Coaches . . . 40
Select a Model for Classroom Management . . . 42
Define a Three-Part Target for Your Classroom Management Model . . . 47

CHAPTER 3
Teach: Professional Development for Effective Implementation . . . 53

Communicate Expectations and Your Three-Part Target to Staff . . . 54

Develop a Training Plan for Teachers 70
Clarify the Role of Coaches and Provide Training and Resources 77

CHAPTER 4
Observe: Data Collection to Inform Practice 105

The Role of the Evaluator in Data Collection 106
The Role of the Nonevaluative Coach in Data Collection 115
Conducting a Walk-Through Visit 120
Debriefing After a Walk-Through Visit 130
Self-Coaching Through Peer-to-Peer Learning Observations 136

CHAPTER 5
Interact Positively: Building Trust Through Communication and Partnership 145

Build Trust 146
Communicate Masterfully 148
Listen Authentically 152
Create Ongoing Regard 155
Partnership Principles 156

CHAPTER 6
Correct Fluently: Course Corrections and Collaboration 175

Identify Flags That Signal Need for Tier 2 Coaching Support 177
Establish a Process for Teachers to Request Tier 2 Coaching Support 182
Early-Stage Interventions: A Bridge Between Tier 1 and Tier 2 190
Caution 196

SECTION TWO
Coaching as Targeted Support for Teachers 203

CHAPTER 7
Coaching Through a Cycle of Continuous Improvement: Review ... 205

The Improvement Cycle 206
Step 1: Review 211
Basic 5 Observation Tool 220
Step 1 (10 Minutes) 221
Step 2 (5 Minutes) 222

Step 3 (5 Minutes) 223
Step 4 (5 Minutes) 224
Data Analysis 225

CHAPTER 8
Coaching Through a Cycle of Continuous Improvement: Prioritize 231
Step 2: Prioritize 231

CHAPTER 9
Coaching Through a Cycle of Continuous Improvement: Revise 239
Step 3: Revise 239
Identify Strategies 240
Explain Strategies 262
Model Strategies 265

CHAPTER 10
Coaching Through a Cycle of Continuous Improvement: Implement 269
Step 4: Implement 270
Monitor Implementation 270
Motivate Staff and Students 284
Ongoing Collaboration 286
Exit Strategy 288

CHAPTER 11
Planning Into Practice: The Improvement Cycle in Action 291
A Schedule of the Process 292
The Role of the Evaluator 299

SECTION THREE
Coaching as Intensive Support for Teachers 301

CHAPTER 12
A Formal Plan of Assistance 303
Research 305
Role of the Evaluator 307

Role of the Coach 307
Process of Accountability 308
Plan of Assistance 315
Troubleshooting Lack of Progress 325
Exit Strategy 326
Story of Hope 326
Conclusion 331

References 333
Appendix: The Research 345

ABOUT THE AUTHORS

Tricia McKale Skyles is a senior educational consultant with Randy Sprick's Safe & Civil Schools. After being a classroom teacher, Tricia served as an Instructional Coach with Dr. Jim Knight. Through her initial work with coaching, she assisted teachers in implementing CHAMPS classroom management. After moving into the role of Behavior Coach, she began to work extensively with the Safe & Civil Schools library of resources. She now works with Safe & Civil Schools to provide training, coaching, and consultation with district and campus leaders, classroom teachers, and paraprofessionals. A middle school teacher at heart, Tricia now resides in Rolla, Missouri, with her family when she isn't flying around the country in an aluminum tube.

Randy Sprick has worked as a paraprofessional, teacher, and teacher trainer at the elementary and secondary levels. Author of a number of widely read books on behavior and classroom management, Randy is former director of Safe & Civil Schools, a consulting company that provides inservice programs throughout the country. Although Randy is largely retired, his Safe & Civil Schools colleagues continue the work of helping large and small school districts improve student behavior and motivation. Efficacy of that work is documented in peer-reviewed research, and Safe & Civil Schools materials are listed on the National Registry of Evidence-Based Programs and Practices (NREPP). Randy was the recipient of the 2007 Council for Exceptional Children (CEC) Wallin Lifetime Achievement Award and was inducted into the Direct Instruction Hall of Fame, along with numerous other awards and honors.

Jim Knight, Founder and Senior Partner of Instructional Coaching Group (ICG), is also a research associate at the University of Kansas Center for Research on Learning. He has spent more than two decades studying professional learning and instructional coaching. Jim earned his Ph.D. in Education from the University of Kansas and has won several university teaching, innovation, and service awards.

The pioneering work Jim and his colleagues have conducted has led to many innovations that are now central to professional development in schools. Jim wrote the first major article about instructional coaching for the *Journal of Staff Development*, and his book *Instructional Coaching* (2007) offered the first extended description of instructional coaching. Jim's book *Focus on Teaching* (2014) was the first extended description of how video should be used for professional learning. Recently, writing with Ann Hoffman, Michelle Harris, and Sharon Thomas, Jim coauthored two books: *Instructional Playbooks* and *Evaluating Instructional Coaching.*

Jim has written or coauthored several books in addition to those described above, including *High-Impact Instruction* (2013), *Better Conversations* (2015), *The Impact Cycle* (2018), *The Instructional Playbook* (2020), *Evaluating Instructional Coaching* (2021), and *The Definitive Guide to Instructional Coaching* (2021). He also authored articles on instructional coaching and professional learning in publications such as *Educational Leadership*, *The Journal of Staff Development*, *Principal Leadership*, *The School Administrator*, and *Kappan*, and is also a columnist for *Educational Leadership*.

Through ICG, Knight conducts coaching workshops, hosts the podcast "Coaching Conversations," and provides consulting for educational organizations around the world.

ACKNOWLEDGMENTS

This book has, at its heart, been born of the belief that educators need advocacy. In the belief that we must create for them a system of support so they can, in turn, support our kids. We cannot say we care about kids without caring about teachers. And so, it is to all educators, veteran and new alike, that we dedicate this book. You truly fight the good fight every day.

This book would not have been possible without the work and inspiration of so many people. To Matt Sprick, editor extraordinaire, who helped shape this idea into its best version. It's not easy to be a boss, an editor, and a friend, let alone combine those roles. You made the writing process both a challenge and a joy.

To Cristy Coughlin, research expert and the smartest person in the room. If you want to make a book better, learn the phrase, "I'd like to defer to Cristy." How one person can have a perfectly cited and well-written analysis back to you before you even complete your question will forever be a mystery.

To Sara Ferris and Natalie Conaway, who made sense of any edits and designed a book to look and feel approachable, words cannot begin to express the level of gratitude you deserve. You see things where others can't and make the written words shine.

Elizabeth Winford, our Director of Professional Development: You talk us down off our metaphorical ledges from time to time, help us juggle any and all responsibilities, and make everyone you meet feel seen. Your light guides us and our clients so that projects like this are even possible.

To the exceptional behavioral consultants working to take the vast library of Safe & Civil Schools and make it meaningful to educators around the globe: Tricia Berg, Jacob Edwards, Kathy Hoes, Susan Isaacs, Jeremy Resnick, Karl Schleich, Pat Somers, Jessica Sprick, and Tom Stacho. All who have met you simply want to exist in your orbit. The world, let alone education, is simply better because you are a part of it.

A thank you to all our special contributors who provided the genesis for many of the ideas in this edition. Robert Profitt, Ryan Reeves, James Sparks, Brian Stevenson, and Cheri Stevenson of the Washington County School District in St. George, UT: You helped clarify what self-coaching looks through peer observation. Your story of hope regarding a teacher in need was incredibly inspiring and led to the creation of a Tier 3 for coaching. Angela Hernandez and Cheryl Boyland of Arlington ISD in Arlington, TX, illustrated a path for how educators could access additional support in Tier 2. Lisa Perez of Houston ISD in Houston, TX, developed a way to track trend data while keeping the confidentiality of the coaching relationship intact. And to Wendy Reinke and Lynn Barnes, coauthors of former editions of *Coaching Classroom Management*. Wendy's work on motivational interviewing and the Classroom Ecology Checklist were invaluable pieces to bring forward into this new edition. Lynn's work with authentic learning opportunities provided a tool to track how teachers spend time, helping teachers increase instructional minutes in the classroom. Thank you, all, for allowing your stories and ideas to aid in the construction of this comprehensive approach to teacher support.

A special thank you to Sara Wiebke, P-12 Literacy Coordinator for the Utah State Board of Education. If we could all have your articulate tenacity, we would have far fewer challenges in the field of education.

• • •

In my career, I've had three major points where preparation and sheer dumb luck have intersected. I'd like to thank Ron Wilson, who took a chance on putting a brand-new teacher in front of a bunch of middle school kids. Jim Knight asked me to take a complete leap of faith and come out of the classroom and into the world of coaching. Randy Sprick introduced me to the world of behavior as a critical piece of the instructional puzzle. You each opened the door for so many opportunities and allowed me to be a part of something so much bigger.

My family has always allowed me to do what I do, even when they may not know exactly what that is. My parents, Todd and Trudy Britt, and my sister and her family, Tammy and Clay Patterson, Aaron and Lora Patterson, and Andrew Patterson. And to Zach Patterson, who decided to pursue education with that same middle school teacher's heart.

And, especially, I'd like to thank my husband, Matt Skyles, for serving as my main IT department and taking care of things at home when I'm in front of the computer, alternately typing, pacing, and hyperventilating. I require a lot of snacks and encouragement, and you provided both in spades.

—Tricia Skyles

My entire career has been a series of fortunate accidents resulting in the opportunity to work with skilled professionals who taught me the life-changing benefits of effective teachers. I began as a teacher aide in the fall of 1971 at the Parkrose Project for Emotionally Disturbed Children, knowing literally NOTHING about students or teaching. I was mentored and supported (coached) every day by highly skilled, endlessly compassionate, and very funny educators. Beginning with those roots, this book represents fruit that has been nurtured by countless other colleagues—far too many to mention. I hope each of you knows that I am grateful for the gift of working with and learning from you. I have been coached by the best.

For the content of this book, thanks to Tricia Skyles, Jim Knight, and Wendy Reinke. Getting to develop professional and personal relationship with both of you is a gift beyond measure. For vision and content of this edition, Tricia Skyles (lead author) and Matt Sprick worked tirelessly to shape and polish this resource into something that is highly functional and very practical for coaches everywhere. For editing and design, I wish to thank Matt Sprick, Jessica Sprick, Sara Ferris, Natalie Conaway, and everyone else connected with the Ancora Publishing team, all of whom are family, friends, and colleagues.

As of this writing, Marilyn Sprick has been my partner in all things for 47 years—there are no words that come close to expressing, uh, everything.

—Randy Sprick

I am deeply grateful to Tricia Skyles, Randy Sprick, and Wendy Reinke, who have taught me more about data and classroom management than any other people in the world. Instructional coaching, as I describe it, would not look the way it does if I hadn't met these three brilliant people. I am also deeply grateful to everyone at our little organization, the Instructional Coaching Group. Each day we are moving closer to our vision of excellent instruction, every day, in every class, for every student, everywhere, and it is happening because of the commitment, smarts, creativity, and kind hearts of the good people at ICG. Lastly, I wouldn't be doing any of this work if wasn't for the nonstop support and inspiration I get from my business and life partner Jenny Ryschon Knight. The day Jenny said yes was the luckiest day of my life, and twenty years later, I'm truly more grateful now than ever. I love the life we live together.

—Jim Knight

INTRODUCTION

A Context for Coaching

When I was hired as a coach in Jim Knight's original project in Topeka, Kansas, I wasn't sure what I was walking into. As a middle school teacher, I hadn't had a coach. Coaching was a relatively new concept in the field of education. In fact, at the time the job position was "Instructional Collaborator." Coach wasn't even in the name. I was learning by doing. I also had access to my colleagues, expert coaches who were able to coach me in turn.

During my first 3 years as a coach, I was in a building that was facing incredible challenges. Leadership had become a revolving door, with almost every leadership position turning over more than once in that time frame. Because leadership was ever changing and expectations for students and staff seemingly shifted by the minute, students finally looked around and realized there were more of them than there were of us. And the students quickly took control, realizing that our standards for behavior were so inconsistent that there was a high probability most of them wouldn't be called out for any violations.

Jim Knight had been working to figure out how we as coaches could address behavior concurrently with providing instructional support. A colleague of his, Jodi King, had recommended Randy Sprick's work, specifically *CHAMPS*, a resource that provided tools and strategies for classroom management. Jim took the copy Jodi provided and read it on a plane ride home. He was convinced this was just the ticket we needed, as coaches, to bring to our teachers.

Susan Isaacs, now my colleague and friend, came to Topeka, Kansas, to provide a one-day overview with Jim, the coaches, building administrators, and some lead teachers. At the end of the day, the coaches and Jim debriefed. I'm not sure about my fellow coaches, but I was largely unconvinced. With the heart of a secondary teacher, I am typically skeptical of anything from an "expert." First of all, there was an acronym. Secondary teachers tend to shy away from acronyms, believing them to be so cute as to be ineffectual. I thought, "This will never work with *our* kids," again falling prey to the idea that our students are somehow averse to every research-based resource available.

I was convinced *CHAMPS* was another flash-in-the-pan, of-the-moment resource that would quickly fade. I didn't want to bring something to my teachers that I doubted would work and that would be one more thing added to their already overflowing plates. So I did what anyone in my position at the time might do—I set out to sabotage its implementation.

Jim had requested that we take a couple of things we'd learned and apply them with a couple of teachers. Just to get our feet wet. Just to get some experience and expanded learning on what the CHAMPS model could do. I took that directive straight to a teacher who'd already informed me she was quitting. At the time, I thought this was an excellent plan. "She's leaving anyway," I thought. "What harm will this do? She's not entirely bought in, I'm not entirely bought in, but when it fails and she leaves, I can tell the team, 'See, I told you it wouldn't work.'" No flaws in that plan, right?

She and I worked through two things together. We started by defining and teaching her expectations for teacher-guided instruction. We both shockingly realized there might be some ambiguity in her expectations for students. She made them explicitly clear through the process of applying the CHAMPS acronym. Then she asked, "Now what?" I said, "I don't know. I haven't read that far in the book." We figured it out together, creating a lesson plan that she delivered the next day.

Once we did that, we started collecting data on her interactions with students and thinking of ways to improve the amount and quality of attention she paid to students who were following her expectations. When I say that the impact was immediate, I'm not exaggerating. The climate of her classroom changed dramatically, though it was still far from perfect. She didn't leave the profession. She stuck with it, staying in the classroom because she knew how to start off better the next year.

It's probably one of the most authentic coaching experiences I've been a part of. It was a true partnership. I wasn't the expert—I was only slightly ahead of what we were learning. It was truly a reciprocal endeavor. While I wouldn't recommend that coaches always coach what they *don't* know, the experience helped me realize that coaching can be effective when you stop believing you have all the answers. I had a plan, but I still came to the table with an open mind. I was expecting it to fail, but willing to believe that it could succeed. And so was the teacher.

We were both shocked and thrilled that such simple steps, both powerful and easy, could make a difference. The difference could be felt—by both us and the students. I became a rabid believer in the potential for classroom management design to have a huge impact on student behavior and learning. I started training staff on the campus and in the district, working and learning right along with them. I was modeling lessons and being observed by my peers so they could provide feedback. They coached me so I could be a better coach to the teachers in my care.

—Tricia Skyles

PURPOSE OF THIS BOOK

This book is about building a schoolwide program for implementing proven, research-based classroom management practices through coaching—and seeing that plan through to success. This is not, nor is it intended to be, a general classroom management book; there are already many fine ones. In fact, the intended audience for this book is not the classroom teacher per se, but rather anyone charged with helping teachers—including principals, assistant principals, school psychologists, counselors, mentor teachers, behavior management coaches, and instructional coaches. If you're a coach or leader who has realized poor behavior management systems are getting in the way of your teachers being able to provide quality instruction, we believe this resource will be a game changer.

COACHING WITHIN MTSS

We've designed this book around the MTSS framework. MTSS (multi-tiered system of supports) is an effective framework that helps educators provide academic and behavioral support for all students. MTSS models often refer to levels of support in three tiers:

- Tier 1: Universal support (for everyone)
- Tier 2: Targeted support (for some)
- Tier 3: Intensive support (for a few)

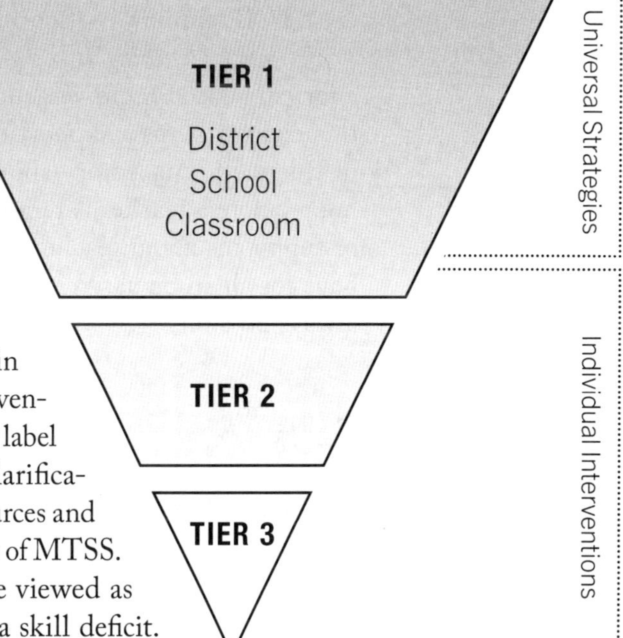

What we know about effective support for students in all tiers can be translated into a guide for supporting teachers. By creating tiers for educators, just as we do for students, we can adapt and modify professional development and coaching systems to meet both the collective and individual needs of all teachers.

Many districts and buildings are currently engaged in some process aligned with PBIS (positive behavior interventions and supports). Note that PBIS has become a popular label that is used in a variety of ways and so warrants some clarification. PBIS is simply the collection of evidence-based resources and research-based practices that would be included in all tiers of MTSS.

It is important to note that MTSS should never be viewed as a support system intended only for educators showing a skill deficit. Instead, MTSS should be viewed as a system of support that also fosters growth in teachers who are highly skilled and want to further hone their abilities. The intent for both groups is to increase the likelihood of teacher retention, which in turn increases the skill level of all educators. If the goal of classroom management is to develop a classroom of students who are responsible, motivated, and highly engaged in meaningful tasks, you need a large group of highly skilled educators who are also responsible, motivated, and highly engaged in meaningful tasks to ultimately hit this target. Coaching is a vital piece of this framework in all three tiers of support, and it's how we've organized this resource.

Section 1: Coaching as Universal Support for All Teachers. This section begins by outlining an effective system of support for the whole team, in this case classroom teachers. Administrators and coaches are guided in building a system of support for all staff to address behavior. This section discusses how to drive change effectively, how to choose a classroom management model, and how to prepare not only for initial implementation but also for ongoing professional development. Setting up a system of regular observations will help provide objective feedback to staff and identify and assist staff who may require more targeted coaching support.

Section 2: Coaching as Targeted Support for Teachers. This section discusses how to provide more formal, structured coaching support to teachers whose needs have not been met with Tier 1 universal supports. This coaching approach relies on the process of continuous improvement and a set of benchmarks (the Basic 5) that coaches can use to provide support to staff. Staff members identified in need of targeted support include those who are showing a skill deficit in behavior management practices as well as those who are continuing to build on an already exceptional skill set, whether for enriching their practice, becoming a model classroom, or working toward their own administrative degree. Additionally, this section embeds strategies for assisting teachers within the STOIC framework (see below).

Section 3: Coaching as Intensive Support for Teachers. This section focuses on building a formal plan of improvement. Again, built around the idea of the STOIC variables, this chapter helps a support team create an intentional plan of assistance. Included in this section is a story about hope. Tier 3 efforts should not be seen as the final hoop before a teacher is removed. On the contrary, building an effective Tier 3 level of support is about teacher retention. It hinges on the belief that we expect staff to have for all students: With enough support and the right resources, improvement is always possible.

REPRODUCIBLE FORMS

Throughout the three sections you'll find examples of reproducible forms that are provided as downloadable PDFs. These will make it easier to implement the supports outlined in each section and also ensure consistency in the coaching process. Purchasers of this book have permission to print and copy the forms as needed to use in their own coaching practice. To download all of the reproducible forms, go to download.ancorapublishing.com and enter access code 978-1-59909-115-0.

FORMALIZING A STRUCTURE FOR COACHING

Having those in leadership work together to build an effective coaching system is vital. And so, too, is the quality of the information and resources being used within that system. All tools and suggestions in this book are compatible with the research literature. More importantly, they are intended to enhance the flow of instruction, streamline every aspect of school functioning, cultivate partnership learning, stimulate new thinking, and replace misunderstanding with respectful dialogue. To succeed, any structure designed to support instructional and behavioral coaching must consider all these things.

Formalizing a structure within a school for collaborative coaching is a first step toward creating a positive climate and common purpose among staff and students. However, some of the processes for building and sustaining a positive, supportive schoolwide environment fall outside the scope of this book. Although many of the intervention techniques described here may help the behavior of individual students, the design of behavior support plans for students is a topic for another time. Nor will we focus on how coaching can facilitate improvement in schoolwide concerns such as dress code or behavior in halls and restrooms.

In this book, the Basic 5 Benchmarks are used to assess classroom teachers and determine the level of structured coaching support needed across all tiers. The Basic 5 get their name from the five categories of behavior, or benchmarks, that represent indicators of classroom functioning:

- *Opportunities to Respond*—chances given by the teacher for students to engage in teacher-directed instruction
- *Ratio of Interactions*—ratio of positive to corrective interactions between the teacher and students
- *Disruptions*—unwanted or inappropriate behaviors that interrupt the flow of instruction for the teacher or another student or students
- *On-Task Behavior*—amount of on-task behavior exhibited by students
- *Alignment with Expectations*—the daily reality of student behavior compared with posted expectations and classroom rules

The Basic 5 Benchmarks (Reproducible 3.5 on p. 66) and the Basic 5 Observation Tool (Reproducible 7.1 shown on pp. 209–210) helps coaches gather preliminary data about each of these benchmarks in the classroom. Based on observation data, each Basic 5 benchmark is categorized into one of three classifications:

- Level 1: Classroom skills are functioning at a high level, and the teacher should proceed with what they already have in practice.
- Level 2: Changing or augmenting current management techniques is recommended.
- Level 3: Immediate intervention is necessary to secure the learning environment of students.

If a teacher's performance falls into Level 3 on one benchmark, a coach can gather more specific data regarding this variable and work to help the teacher attain proficiency in that area. If the teacher's scores tend to fall into Level 2 overall, the coach and teacher might choose either to focus on one or two skills or to attack all of them directly, using the coach's discretion and relationship with the teacher as a guide.

These levels align somewhat with the idea of tiers, with Level 1 indicating a low need for support in the benchmark and Level 3 indicating a high need for support. While no professional is ever finished making finer distinctions within each benchmark, mastery of these five variables will put any teacher along the path to being an effective classroom manager.

THE IMPROVEMENT CYCLE

Structured coaching is about supporting teachers' continuous improvement. The most effective teachers are those who engage in the process of continuous improvement throughout each year and from year to year, continually refining and adjusting their practices to fit the needs of the students they are currently working with. They accomplish this by committing to the Improvement Cycle (Figure I.1), which involves reviewing data, prioritizing goals for improvement based on those data, revising aspects of their classroom management plan to address those goals, and implementing new plans while monitoring the efficacy of any changes. The Improvement Cycle is continuous because the process of evaluating how things are going in the classroom and adjusting plans is never finished.

Figure I.1 *Improvement Cycle*

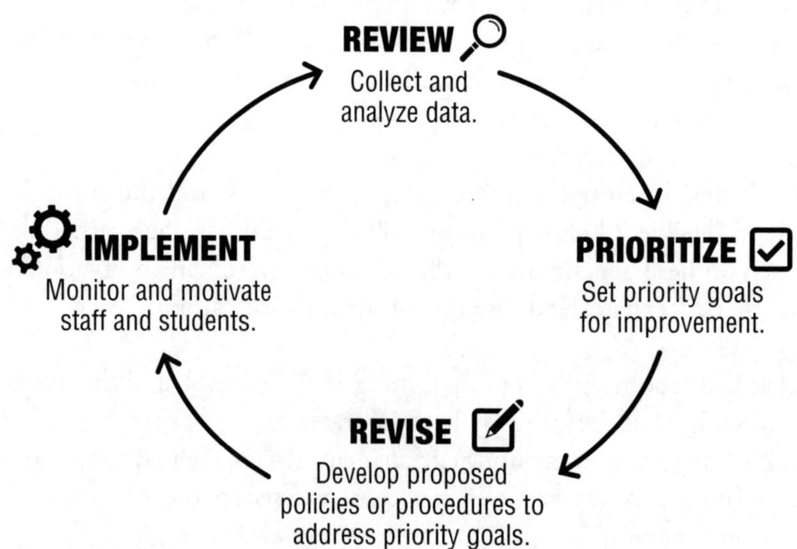

The Improvement Cycle also offers a way for coaches to use data to make meaningful decisions and support teachers in refining their classroom management practices. The cycle discussed in this book directly matches the Improvement Cycle introduced to teachers in *CHAMPS* as an ongoing cycle of reflection and growth in the classroom. In this book, the Improvement Cycle embeds the Basic 5 Benchmarks, providing coaches with a framework for defining measurable targets and delivering crucial feedback for teachers working to improve their classroom management skills. In the context of coaching, this format will allow coaches and teachers to work collaboratively yet efficiently to create classroom environments that help all students reach their highest potential.

THE CHAMPS APPROACH

In this book, the term *classroom management* encompasses classroom-based discipline and behavior support, classroom organization (as it relates to student behavior), and all practices designed to reduce student misbehavior, increase responsible behavior, or increase motivation.

This book draws many concepts and examples from the CHAMPS classroom management approach set forth in *CHAMPS: A Proactive and Positive Approach to Classroom Management* (3rd ed., Sprick, J., et al., 2021), for teachers of grades K–8, and *Discipline in the Secondary Classroom: A Positive Approach to Behavior Management* (4th ed., Sprick, R., et al., 2021), a CHAMPS-based approach for grades 9–12. (For brevity, these books will hereafter be referred to as *CHAMPS* and *DSC*.)

The conceptual framework that underpins the CHAMPS approach speaks directly to teaching expectations. CHAMPS addresses five categories in which expectations should be precisely taught for any given classroom activity:

C	**Conversation**	*Can students talk to each other? If so, with whom can they speak, about what, and for how long?*
H	**Help**	*How do students get their questions answered? How do they get your attention?*
A	**Activity**	*What is the task or objective? What is the end product?*
M	**Movement**	*Can students move about?*
P	**Participation**	*What does the expected student behavior look and sound like? How do students show they are fully participating?*
S	**Success**	*If students follow the CHAMPS expectations, they will be successful.*

Note About the CHAMPS Acronym

Some teachers use S to indicate Special instructions for a particular activity or transition.

For teachers of high school students who would prefer a more sophisticated mnemonic, *DSC* introduces a variant, ACHIEVE:

A	**Activity**	*What is the task or objective? What is the end product?*
C	**Conversation**	*Can students talk to each other? If so, with whom can they speak, about what, and for how long?*
H	**Help**	*How do students get their questions answered? How do they get your attention?*
I	**Integrity**	*What are your expectations regarding students doing their own work and avoiding copying work or plagiarizing sources? When is collaboration appropriate or inappropriate?*
E	**Effort**	*What does appropriate student work behavior during the activity look or sound like? How do students demonstrate their full participation?*
V	**Value**	*How will participation in this activity be of value to students? How will student efforts on this activity contribute to their success in your class?*
E	**Efficiency**	*What tips or suggestions can you give students for getting maximum benefit from this activity?*

The concepts represented in ACHIEVE can serve as a basis for teaching more complex or philosophical classroom expectations to mature students.

STOIC FRAMEWORK

The best behavior management strategies address five areas of behavioral intervention: prevention, teaching expectations, monitoring, encouragement, and correction. To bring these variables more easily to mind, we have encapsulated them in the acronym STOIC:

- *Structure* for success.
- *Teach* expectations.
- *Observe* and monitor.
- *Interact* positively.
- *Correct* fluently.

Teachers *structure for success* by organizing classrooms and class activities to discourage misbehavior and encourage student engagement and motivation. In this context, *structure* encompasses both physical and logistical considerations. Teachers may also assign to each class a customized level of structure, depending on the students' prevailing age, maturity, independence, and self-motivation.

Teachers *teach expectations* for how to function successfully within that structure. To be successful, students need to know the teacher's clear expectations for all major instructional activities and transitions. No two teachers have exactly the same expectations and no two students have had exactly the same experience with teachers, which is why attending to expectations early and often reaps dividends of reclaimed time and productivity.

Teachers *observe and monitor* by circulating throughout their classroom unpredictably and scanning frequently, remaining physically and visually aware of what's going on in the room at all times. They use proximity to nip early-stage misbehavior in the bud. When appropriate, they collect observational data on student behavior to spot trends and patterns and inform interventions.

Teachers *interact positively* by providing both contingent praise and feedback and noncontingent positive attention. Students will always behave better and work harder for someone who they perceive values them and cares about their success.

Teachers *correct fluently* by responding to undesired behavior calmly, consistently, briefly, and immediately. They precorrect anticipated misbehavior beforehand and re-teach appropriate behavior afterward. A fluent correction does not disrupt the flow of instruction. Gentle corrections by exceptionally fluent teachers "fly under the radar," often going unnoticed by students other than the one targeted.

Together, the STOIC variables represent five essential aspects of any classroom management plan. Teachers who excel at managing their classrooms tend to accomplish the feat in their own individual and unique (and often unconscious) ways. Consequently, while many variables that influence student behavior are known, legitimate means of addressing them vary as widely as teachers themselves. Do not fall victim to the promise of a canned, one-size-fits-all solution. Were there such a quick fix, the smorgasbord of coaching, mentoring, and professional development options we have would hardly be in demand. Using the CHAMPS approach and STOIC framework, you can craft effective, research-based classroom management plans as individual as the classes they are designed for.

GOALS OF COACHING FOR EQUITY

Coaching for equity involves helping teachers identify and take concrete actions to ensure that each child receives whatever they need to develop to their full academic and social potential. Coaching for equity includes encouraging educators to analyze existing practices, reveal hidden norms, identify gaps, and consider meaningful supports for students who might otherwise fall through the cracks of the schooling system.

Teachers are primary agents of change toward achieving more equitable educational environments. Teachers' daily interactions with students and decisions about instructional practices exert a major influence over the trajectories of their students' education. The responsibility to provide equitable access to classroom instruction goes beyond the teacher's skill in delivering content through best instructional practices. Teachers must actively work to avoid equity traps, which McKenzie and Scheurich (2004) define as "ways of thinking or assumptions that prevent educators from believing their students of color can be successful" (pp. 601–602). Teachers fall into equity traps when they hold assumptions, stereotypes, and deficit thinking patterns about students and families of color.

Many schools and districts have begun important work around diversity, equity, and inclusion. Many have developed a cultural competency lens. While this is not specifically a book on coaching for equity, we believe this resource and *CHAMPS* can support the work of diversity, equity, and inclusion. Safe & Civil Schools fully supports and encourages this difficult and important work and recommends that you read seminal texts in this area, such as *Coaching for Equity: Conversations that Change Practice* by Elena Aguilar (2020).

As a decision-making framework designed to help teachers create a classroom where all students can thrive, this book and *CHAMPS* can support the implementation of best practices focused on diversity, equity, and inclusion. These resources promote a continuous improvement process where teachers have the ability to adapt their systems if they are not meeting the needs of their students. Teachers can apply cultural competency training by taking into account the varied cultures within their classroom.

Changing the mindset of teachers not only to recognize the inequity of certain practices, but also to become someone willing to act as an agent of change is a challenging task. However, working with teachers to collect data on how classroom practice impacts students, examine these data to understand if students or groups of students are not finding success, and replace problematic practices with those that are more equitable can meaningfully transform classrooms into environments that are culturally safe for students, make students feel more empowered and less threatened, and increase the likelihood that each child will realize their full potential (Lawrence & Tatum, 1997; Voltz et al., 2003).

Coaching for equity involves helping teachers:

- Examine whether their classroom rules and expectations are meeting the needs of all of their students. Do the rules meet the needs of all students? Are rules explicitly taught so all students understand how to be successful in the classroom?
- Are there hidden norms? Does the teacher need to reevaluate their classroom expectations because the expectations are not actually aligned with the expectations that have been taught to students? Has the teacher actually taught the posted classroom rules?

- Is the teacher actively and positively engaged with every student? Is the teacher inadvertently using more corrective interactions with certain racial groups, for example?
- Are there individual students who are struggling more than others? If so, are the numbers disproportionate based on race or ethnicity?

These are the questions we can't shy away from when engaged in a true dialogue centered around the collaborative exploration of data. Again, we repeat, this is not a book about coaching for equity, but it is a book centered on data collection. And we cannot collect data without having the willingness to confront sometimes uncomfortable realities. This is a book about partnership. And through true partnership, any conversation is possible.

DISPELLING THE MYTH OF "MAGICAL" CLASSROOM MANAGEMENT

Often, the myth of "magical" classroom management is what leads to a teacher needing the more targeted support provided in Tiers 2 and 3. One disservice done to preservice educators is to have them student-teach with master teachers after the school year is already in progress. They don't get to see what happens during the first 2 weeks of school. They don't see all the preplanning or the hoops a master teacher jumps through to set up a successful classroom. Once in place, such a system is often so effective as to be nearly invisible to an inexperienced outside observer. Many new teachers enter the field believing these two myths: 1) good classroom management is a magical thing that either happens or doesn't, and 2) whether a class is well behaved or unruly depends on the kind of kids assigned to it.

For teachers who have bought into these fallacies, coaches are an integral resource at any level. When classroom management mastery doesn't magically occur, coaches will be equipped to bring resources to bear and break down complex phenomena into a series of manageable tasks and a well-thought-out system that affords all students the opportunity to be successful.

SECTION 1

Coaching as a Universal Strategy for Teachers

The current educational system has real barriers to implementing and sustaining an effective classroom management model. While there are many varied and valid reasons for this, we must focus on what we *can* do to increase efficacy. Pairing professional development with an effective coaching program has been shown to be a highly powerful tool in increasing both the rate and quality of implementation.

You don't need to be an expert coach or have all the answers to begin building an effective Tier 1 system for coaching. Coaching within this tier serves as a powerful vehicle for closing the gap between teacher knowledge and practice. Section 1 describes the distinct components necessary to provide highly effective coaching attached to classroom management. This section provides some critical guidelines for setting up successful universal support for staff to engage in the robust implementation of an effective classroom management model. Those of you familiar with the Safe & Civil Schools Library will notice we divide this section according to the STOIC variables, providing a chapter on each one.

Chapter 1, "Coaching to Lead Change" provides an overview of the success factors and barriers to long-term viability and success in implementing and sustaining new practice. This chapter discusses concrete components that leadership teams can provide to make change more likely. Addressing any potential barriers in the beginning will help guide your decision-making process for all other aspects of implementing an effective classroom management model.

Chapter 2, "Structure: Developing a Clear Vision" guides you in creating an overall vision for your school, choosing a classroom management model, and identifying all those who can serve as coaches in your model. This chapter also helps you define clear and attainable expectations for implementation.

Chapter 3, "Teach: Professional Development for Effective Implementation" helps you identify the components necessary to launch the model, introduce and explain expectations to staff, and craft professional development to assure their success. This chapter includes a look at both initial and ongoing professional development.

Chapter 4, "Observe: Data Collection to Inform Practice" looks at both the role of the evaluator and of coaches in the data collection process. A section on peer-to-peer learning observations is also included, especially helpful for those schools that might not have full-time coaches on staff.

Chapter 5, "Interact Positively: Building Trust through Communication and Partnership" looks at the nature of different coaching relationships and how to engage in effective coaching conversations. Partnership Principles are explored to respond compassionately to the needs of staff.

Chapter 6, "Correct Fluently: Course Corrections and Collaboration" looks at creating a very clear pathway to Tier 2 coaching support. This support is provided not only for teachers in need but also to those striving teachers who may wish to engage in a more formal process. We also offer interventions to help teachers avoid Tier 2 support if that's not in their perceived best interest.

CHAPTER 1

Coaching to Lead Change

> *Each person holds so much power within themselves that needs to be let out. Sometimes they just need a little nudge, a little direction, a little support, a little coaching, and the greatest things can happen.* —Pete Carroll

After being a classroom teacher, I had the opportunity to interview for a coaching position on a middle school campus in a different, much larger district. I accepted the job on a complete whim—I was prepared to be back in the classroom facing a new group of seventh graders ready to tackle language arts and world history. But instead of following the plan I thought I had in place, I took a complete leap of faith. And I became a coach by doing the dumbest thing possible. I took over the position from a very much beloved, aspirational, and inspirational human being who had been a steadfast part of the campus network for years. Everyone loved her. Through a variety of circumstances, she relocated to a new school and here I was, stepping into shoes that I would never be able to fill.

I spent my first few weeks as a coach wandering around the building, first trying to find an open office space of any kind and then trying to connect with people who were still grieving the loss of the coach they adored. And I was grieving in my own way, mourning the loss of connection to a group I still adore, middle schoolers, and grappling with the very real possibility I had made a giant mistake.

It turned out to be, still, one of the best decisions I've ever made in my life. I had to earn my place, forge real connections, and learn on the fly what my role should look like. Separate from the coach they had, I had to be an entirely different person who could still support and honor the teachers with whom I had been gifted. It was truly trial by fire, and I was burned far more often than I care to admit. But I learned *so* much. First, what not to do, then, slowly, what should be done. I realized teachers need advocates who will cheer them on and support them in keeping often multiple plates spinning in the air. Campus leaders need partners who will help move the school forward while empowering staff to make autonomous decisions about how to adopt and adapt best practice. I learned coaching isn't just one way to do business. Coaching is *the* way to do business.

Take Pete Carroll, for instance, whose quote is referenced above. Pete Carroll knows what effective coaching can do. With six bowl game wins and a BCS National Championship under his belt before becoming a head coach in the NFL, he has mastered the art of coaching student-athletes to be their best selves. Multimillion-dollar companies have long used coaching to help employees become as effective and efficient in their jobs as possible, with employees seeing the assignment of a coach as a mark of value. And within the last two decades, education has championed coaching as a way to advocate for and support educators in the classroom.

Coaching can be a complex process, and building an effective coaching system can often seem daunting. Coaches assigned to help educators improve instructional techniques often find general classroom management may get in the way of effective teaching. Teachers may lose precious instructional minutes dealing with challenging behaviors, both minor and severe. Coaches find themselves serving dual roles—working concurrently in both instruction and behavior. How do campuses, then, help teachers build a strong classroom management plan to begin with? And how should coaches be deployed to step in and provide support when behavior management becomes an issue?

This book is not intended to help campuses create an overall coaching program. Many fine books out there can assist with the process of setting up an initial coaching program. This book focuses on building a strong system of support for staff specifically in relation to classroom management. We fully expect, and believe, schools will be working concurrently on instructional support for staff. Behavior and instruction overlap and impact one another, so staff need to be able to access support in both areas to be as effective and efficient as they can.

While athletes spend about 95% of their time being coached and 5% of their time in exhibitions of skill, the numbers are flipped for educators. Only about 5% of their time is spent in professional learning and 95% of their time is spent in front of the classroom demonstrating skills. Having access to a coach who can often assist in real time can maximize these performances. As noted in the quote from Coach Carroll earlier, each person has so much power within themselves that sometimes they just need a little coaching for the greatest things to happen.

Skilled classroom management is a key indicator of students' academic success. But without a solid knowledge of classroom and behavior management strategies, inexperienced and unskilled teachers are often frustrated by misbehavior. Nearly half of new teachers leave the profession within 5 years, citing discipline problems and lack of administrative support for dealing with discipline issues as the two most common reasons. Professional development and other teacher training methods improve teacher skills, but one-shot training alone may not always lead to the lasting impact school and district leaders hope to accomplish.

In school athletics, a skilled coach is critical in helping young athletes improve their abilities. The coach must teach and re-teach fundamental skills, build team unity, inspire and exhort players to stretch themselves, and provide plenty of feedback, both positive and corrective. Before the game, the coach prepares for every contingency, scouts the opposition, reviews video, designs plays, confers with team captains, and trades notes with fellow coaches. After the game, there's more rallying, more review, more self-reflection, more practice, and lots more performance feedback. Coaching in the classroom is no less an assignment. Administrators and coaches must keep in mind how difficult it is for a teacher to change instinctual patterns of behavior. Teachers can learn new skills, but applying them comes in stages, which often tends to look like three steps forward, two steps back.

Based on years of research, a solid coaching model can have an unmistakable impact on teachers' skill levels. The very act of coaching exists to bring about change in practice, and literally anyone who interacts daily with teachers is a prospective coach. Across campuses, this broadens the scope of who can engage in coaching and how widely collaborative coaching can be used. When teachers have access to quality coaching, they have the opportunity to reflect and improve their capacity for dealing with classroom management and discipline.

The coaching experience itself does not happen in a vacuum. There is planning and intentionality in setting up a context for coaching that leads to sustained change. Both administrators and coaches must work together to design a climate and culture where staff see coaching as a resource to hone skills, regardless of the teacher's expertise. Building administrators must have a clearly defined idea of where they are headed. Both administrators and coaches must successfully address any barriers to change on both personal and organizational levels. The response of teachers to classroom coaching is largely contingent on how administrators and coaches frame this experience of change for them. For a coaching program to have any hope of leaving a lasting positive imprint on students' lives, these two groups must continually work together and in the same direction.

In this chapter, we will provide the rationale for using coaching as a keystone to increase both the rate and quality of effective classroom management implementation. Recognizing that change is a process, we will clearly identify potential barriers to engaging in this process. Through the unpacking of two drivers of change, we will identify leadership's role in leading the charge and how leadership teams (consisting of both administrators and all prospective coaches) can work together to plan for staff needs in advance. Finally, we will help you clarify the principles of an effective classroom management and coaching model. In doing this, you'll be able to create a framework for the adoption or improved implementation of a classroom management model with the support of coaches. Specifically, you will:

- Provide a rationale to staff for the use of coaches to support a robust classroom management model.
- Recognize that change is a process.

- Use drivers of change to plan for staff needs as you move into the selection of a classroom management model (Chapter 2) and the expectations for implementation (Chapter 3).
- Create a shared summary of principles for the campus.

In subsequent chapters in Section 1, we'll dive deeper into some of the components of the drivers of change, including developing a vision to help reach the desired outcomes, planning for successful implementation, the critical role administrators have in providing ongoing support for all staff, and basic standards of communication and partnership. In the Appendix, we also go into the research, proposing some additional suggestions for behavior support processes that administrators and coaches can foster within the school—specifically, schoolwide behavior support and organizational patterns for supporting individual students with severe and chronic behavioral problems.

THE RATIONALE FOR COACHING

For many years, while educators talked about the problem of classroom discipline, what to do about it fell largely to the whim of teachers, the best wishes of administrators, and the occasional armchair theorist. Twenty years ago, classroom management and discipline, not to mention coaching, simply didn't get the face time that instructional content did. Today, classroom management is a leading issue in education. But without coaching, getting consistent implementation of skillful behavior management can be problematic. Results in classrooms have been spotty, with disappointment often following initial high expectations.

Our purpose is to help you marshal a schoolwide program for implementing proven, research-based classroom management practices through coaching—and see that plan through to success. This is not, nor is it intended to be, a general classroom management book; there are already many fine ones. In fact, the intended audience for this book is not the classroom teacher per se, but rather anyone charged with helping teachers. We consider coaching to be the *keystone*—the final stone placed at the crown of an arch that gives it strength and stability. Without coaching, on-the-job learning by teachers can become scattershot. The effect of professional development may be muted, and the measure of successful implementation ill defined. The bottom line is that coaching enhances professional development, making it a far richer experience for teachers and fostering greater levels and quality of implementation.

Without coaching, teachers may struggle to fully implement effective behavior management and discipline practices in the classroom. There are at least two reasons for this. Teachers have to make so many instantaneous decisions that opportunities to savor the fruit of recent training are often lost in the barrage of minute-to-minute challenges they face. On top of that, student misbehavior has the potential to be perceived as extraordinarily threatening.

Let's take these reasons one at a time.

First, effective teaching requires that a teacher do many things at once and make many instantaneous decisions. Monitoring an independent work period, a "simple" activity to manage, requires the teacher to circulate, scan, answer students' questions, provide positive feedback, and keep students on task. If a student is not working on the assigned task and is distracting other students, the teacher needs to decide what to do. She cannot wait 5 minutes to think it through. She must take action now, while other students wait for her to help them with their assignment. There is no time to look this up in a book or go to the notes from the behavior support inservice she attended last month. She must decide *now* what she is going to do and then do it. Let's say she takes the very logical step of going to the student and reminding him that he needs to get back to work. If the student responds, "You can't make me," the teacher faces another instantaneous decision about what to do next—now with the added pressure of all the students who heard this interaction looking to see how she is going to respond to this direct challenge.

> *Effective teaching requires that a teacher do many things at once and make many instantaneous decisions.*

Therein lies the second difficulty. Misbehavior, particularly refusal to follow directions, poses a direct threat to the teacher's authority. Open defiance makes a difficult situation even more challenging and further reduces the likelihood that the teacher will execute steps learned in training. Confronted with this, many a trapped teacher has harbored panicky thoughts:

> *I have been hired to make these students engage in instructional tasks. This student is saying I can't make him. But I have to make him do this, or the other students will think I have no authority. And if the principal walks in right now, she will think I am not an effective teacher.*

While there is some debate in the scientific community about the specific pathways and processes that cause this effect, the following is a very basic explanation of what occurs in your brain when you experience fear, anxiety, or anger when students misbehave (Ferrara et al., 2020).

A region in the temporal lobe of the brain, called the amygdala, plays a significant role in emotions such as fear, anxiety, and anger. The information you receive from your senses converges in your amygdala. Then the amygdala sends messages to the systems involved with emotional reactions and physiological symptoms. If the experience is something you fear, you strongly dislike, or you know can hurt you, the amygdala triggers the systems that keep your body safe, such as the adrenal system. Your fight, flight, or freeze response is activated, which means your body rapidly mobilizes energy to deal with the danger. Your body gets ready to fight the threat, run from it, or hide from it.

A teacher in such a state, driven by the amygdala and forced to make an instantaneous decision about what to do, might be more likely to fall into past patterns than to try something picked up from a book or a workshop. The teacher clearly knows that even on her worst day, she probably shouldn't run screaming from the building, so her options are limited. What does her gut tell her when flight isn't an option? What do her instincts say? More than likely, they will tell her to fight back—to try to make the student do the thing he is refusing to do.

As in our athletic coaching scenario at the beginning of this chapter, this is where a classroom coach steps in to assist. In a true partnership coaching model, the coach helps the teacher review and self-reflect, supports the teacher through numerous practice attempts, and provides effective performance feedback. Coaches and teachers work together, step by step, to turn frustration into mastery.

CHANGE IS A PROCESS

Every change starts with someone making the decision to lead it. Dan and Chip Heath created an adept analogy for leaders or leadership teams to begin the process of change. In their book, *Switch: How to Change Things When Change is Hard* (2000), they identify three major points of focus. Leaders begin by "motivating the elephant," or engaging a person's emotional response to begin the journey. Appealing to staff with a strong rationale means nothing if it doesn't inspire change. The elephant loves a quick payoff; you must appeal to the core values of staff if you expect them to stay on the path for the long term. "Directing the rider" appeals to the rational side of staff. You need the driver to give direction to the massive elephant that, without a clear vision, simply meanders on and off the path and may never arrive at the destination. And you need not only a clear vision, but also a plan for implementing that vision by "shaping the path." Forward momentum is so much more likely for both the elephant and the rider when work is done at the beginning to remove the debris that may be in their path.

As agents of change, successful coaches adapt their approach. The previous analogy is just one way of thinking about how to adapt. At one point, a teacher might be most interested in data suggesting that a new practice be implemented (the elephant needs to be fed). Later, the teacher's interest might shift to managing implementation of the new practice (the driver needs assistance), and then to brainstorming how to modify the practice (clearing debris from the path). The process is fluid. There is no single "right" way through this organic process, and the support a coach provides must therefore be flexible and adaptable.

How do you convince a teacher that change is necessary or even worth considering? Some might argue that you don't. You can only gather and present data; the teacher is the ultimate arbiter of what is put into practice. When a teacher's perception of current reality is at odds with the data collected by a coach or administrator, the situation may appear impossible to change. In reality, the change process is most likely already at work. According to the transtheoretical model (TTM) of behavior change (Prochaska et al., 1994), the first of five stages of change is *precontemplation*—literally, unawareness. The second stage is *contemplation*—the teacher consciously begins to weigh the rewards of a change and the consequences of staying with the status quo. Only when the process has moved to the third, fourth, and fifth stages—*preparation*, *action*, and *maintenance*—will change be outwardly visible to an observer, though the change process likely will have been underway for some time.

Coaches and administrators alike provide a great service to teachers and schools by gathering data on current reality in classrooms. Whether it is a coach conducting a scheduled observation or a principal making an unannounced walk-through, if data indicate to a teacher that students' on-task behavior was 60%, those data may become a compelling reason for change. In advocating for pivotal change, coaches and administrators are equal partners. "Here are some things we *might* change" and "Something *must* change" are equally valid catalysts for improvement. Despite their inescapably different roles, coaches, teachers, and administrators should share the same goal—a better life for the students in their charge.

Organizational Barriers to Change

The personal experience of change for teachers is only one of the challenges administrators and coaches face. Perhaps the greater challenges are organizational barriers to change experienced in schools. If we want to have a lasting impact on instruction, we need to be aware of these obstacles and employ appropriate strategies to address them. The following is a summary of some of the most common barriers to change encountered in schools.

- The Attempt, Attack, Abandon Cycle
- Loss aversion
- Conflicting personalities and agendas
- Lack of coherent objectives

The Attempt, Attack, Abandon Cycle. Administrators, often the primary decision-makers on a campus, face a multitude of challenges as they try to meet the needs and expectations of students, teachers, the community, school board members, and politicians. Administrators often confront these demands with insufficient time or resources to respond to them effectively, faced with impatient constituents expecting quick results. For example, a school board might demand that office referrals in a district decrease immediately. Administrators pass that objective along to staff but lack the ability to provide any training on the skills necessary to respond effectively to misbehaviors. Now, instead of feeling like they have the ability to refer students who may be disrupting class, teachers simply stop writing referrals. The numbers drop, but misbehaviors are still present and impacting instructional time. Mix together haste, inadequate data, and insufficient processes for deliberation and reflection, and you have a recipe for making poor decisions.

We see examples of quick-fix or shortsighted decision-making every day in our work. In one school, a highly successful writing program was cut because the sixth-grade daughter of a senior administrator did not like the program teacher assigned to her. In another district, a half-million-dollar reading program was adopted even though everyone who reviewed the materials believed they were at the wrong reading level for students. Ineffective decision-making has serious implications for coaches and teachers who see the product of their hard work attacked or shelved and soon "learn" what kinds of effort are and are not likely to be rewarded.

The common thread is something we call the Attempt, Attack, Abandon Cycle (Figure 1.1), a vicious circle that ensures new teaching practices never get implemented effectively. Here is how the pattern plays out: Someone introduces a new practice into a school, and teachers make a halfhearted attempt to implement it. Before the practice has been given sufficient time to be implemented effectively, various individuals in the school or district begin to attack the program. As a result, many of the teachers tasked with implementing the program begin to lose their will to stick with it. Ultimately, even though the practice was never implemented well, leaders at the district or building level reject it as unsuccessful and abandon it, only to propose another program fated to be pulled into the self-defeating cycle, attacked and abandoned for another program, and on and on. Thus, schools continue on an unmerry-go-round of Attempt, Attack, Abandon that relegates promising practices to an ever-expanding litany of missed opportunities and failed attempts.

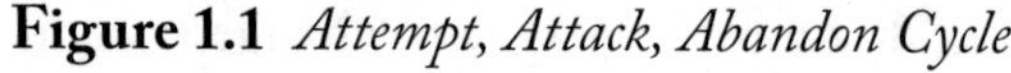

Figure 1.1 *Attempt, Attack, Abandon Cycle*

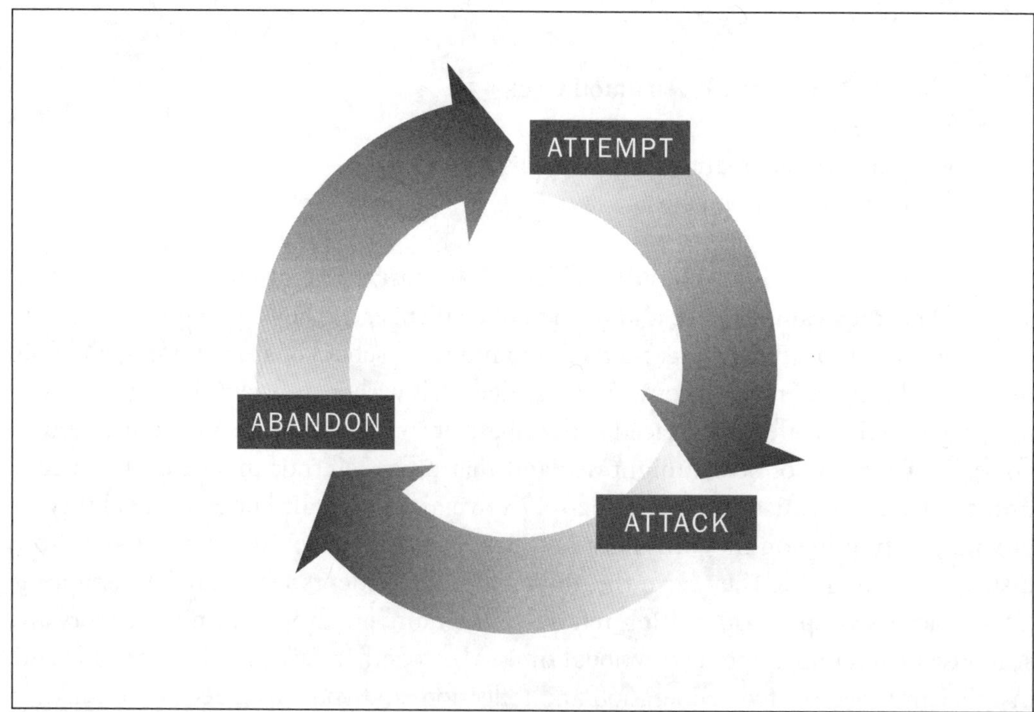

Loss aversion. In other cases, programs result in minimal improvement or, even worse, no improvement at all. Yet district and school leadership, as well as classroom teachers, may stick with it simply because that's "the way it's always been done." This is a tendency toward *loss aversion*, where people simply don't want to admit that time, energy, and other resources geared toward the initiative may have been a waste. At this point, they are simply trying not to lose as opposed to seeking actual gains.

PLAYING NOT TO LOSE

This issue of loss aversion arises not just in our districts, buildings, and classrooms. In Ori and Rom Brafman's book, *Sway: The Irresistible Pull of Irrational Behavior* (2009), they highlight the rise of the University of Florida's football program under the leadership of head coach Steve Spurrier. Up until his tenure, the teams in the SEC had been using a "war of attrition" game strategy, where the idea was to wage a defensive game by wearing out the opponent and running out the clock. In other words, the teams weren't playing to win; they were playing *not* to lose.

While this may avoid the inevitable work involved in seeking out a new resource, it certainly doesn't help staff and students grow. The idea of leaving behind the Attempt, Attack, Abandon Cycle isn't that you never let go of initiatives. The idea is that when you do move to another initiative, the move is intentional and based on real, objective data and not subjective insight, which can often be led by loss aversion.

Conflicting personalities and agendas. Over time in an organization, rivalries, jealousies, and empire building can become barriers to progress. Some school leaders struggle to embrace ideas that are introduced by staff members other than themselves. Others may be jealous of their colleagues' successes. We have seen districts where principals are unwilling to share promising innovations with other schools, even when their students stand to benefit.

Personality conflicts also arise. Some leaders simply do not get along. We have worked in schools where leaders deliberately sabotaged each other's efforts. One district leader forbade teachers to attend professional development sponsored by another district official. The reality is that personalities frequently come into play when meaningful change is promoted. To be effective, coaches and administrators need to be able to navigate the shoals of conflicting personalities.

Lack of coherent objectives. A final challenge educational leaders may face is the misalignment of objectives among classrooms, schools, districts, and states. Teaching attracts professionals who take great pride in autonomous action. This is both a blessing and a curse. Certainly, many of the most warmhearted and inspirational instructors are those who refuse to teach or lead within the restrictions of a prescribed curriculum. Indeed, by definition, professional practice is predicated on the ability of each professional to make the right decision at the right time. Doctors and pilots are just two of many professions that use checklists as a way to maintain minimum standards of practice, yet we don't expect our doctors to treat us without the ability to make decisions based on our unique needs. Neither should we expect this of our teachers.

At the same time, if everyone simply does their own thing in classrooms, schools, and districts, children inevitably suffer. A teacher who refuses to reinforce a schoolwide behavioral approach risks sending confusing mixed messages about school policy and acceptable personal behavior. Throughout this book, we will emphasize that as leaders of change, coaches and administrators must find ways of recognizing professional autonomy while at the same time guiding the adoption of practices that are aligned with the goals of research-based classroom management as well as the greater systems they operate within—school districts and states.

> *"As leaders of change, coaches and administrators must recognize professional autonomy while guiding the adoption of research-based practices."*

Teachers' Reluctance to Change

Teachers, like people in any other profession, often balk at the idea of adopting new ideas and practices to replace old, comfortable ones. People become set in their ways and find it easier to stick with practices they are familiar with, even if those practices are not totally effective. Change can make people feel vulnerable and out of control. Experienced teachers know exactly how they would handle a particular classroom situation and how the students are likely to respond. They may look less confident as they are learning and implementing new classroom practices. They may think that the new techniques may elicit unpredictable student responses, leading them to hesitate as they think about how to operate under the new program.

Implementing new teaching practices requires time and energy to learn the techniques, to teach students about changes in classroom management, and to assess and revise the new program as necessary. Even when teachers want to implement new ideas and practices, they may not have the time and energy to do so.

In addition, teachers may have had bad experiences in the past with new programs—not necessarily because of the programs themselves, but because of ineffective organization and implementation, resulting in the Attempt, Attack, Abandon Cycle described previously. Perhaps the professional developer charged with teaching the new program did not respect the teachers' professional autonomy, or the school did not provide enough quality training or support. Any of these factors may lead teachers to resist change in their classroom management plans.

BEEN THERE, DONE THAT

Imagine that you are a new teacher (for some of you that may be longer ago than others!). You are confident in your abilities, and for the most part you are quite adept in the classroom. You get high evaluations, and your students are fairly high achieving. Your administrator approaches you one day, gives you positive praise, and then asks you to serve on a committee that will be looking at classroom management because "you're so good at managing your own classroom." Thrilled at the prospect of taking on more responsibility that showcases your talent (and during your first year, no less!), you agree.

You serve on this committee for the next couple of years, but implementation is sporadic and you spend a lot of time defending the program to other teachers on the campus. After a couple of years, the principal who asked you to serve on the committee moves to another position in the district and the new principal scraps the program, and hence the committee, entirely. You're irritated that you spent 2 years on something that never got off the ground, but you're grateful that you don't have to argue with your colleagues anymore.

Two years later, another principal arrives on the campus and holds a staff meeting where she talks about a "new, amazing classroom management model." It's virtually the same one you spent 2 years working with staff to adopt, to no avail. She asks you to serve on the committee. You politely decline and, most likely, go on to vent in the teacher's lounge with your colleagues: "She must be crazy! Who has time to put this into practice?" The fact of the matter is not that most teachers are resistant to change, especially our veterans; it's that they've already done it—typically with limited resources and minimal support. They're resistant to changing *again*. Upholding the Attempt, Attack, Abandon Cycle mentioned earlier, they've fallen prey to a revolving door of programs and initiatives, and their ability to muster enthusiasm yet again has been entirely depleted.

DRIVERS OF CHANGE

It's easy to identify what gets in the way of effective change and to talk about leading change in the abstract. While our determination to overcome the aforementioned barriers may be strong, often our visions are so broad and the obstacles so obscure we settle for thinking about the change without ever getting it off the ground. For an effective classroom management model to be fully adopted and see success, we must take into consideration two concrete drivers of this change. First, the administrator must be a strong leader with the necessary skill set to create an environment where the model can succeed. (We'll go into further depth on how to create this context for coaching in subsequent chapters in this section.) Secondly, the administrator and leadership team, including coaches in charge of supporting the initiative, must preplan to address what staff will need to overcome any barriers and launch the change effectively.

The Principal as Leader

To establish a coaching program that produces clear and lasting improvement, educational leaders need to get on the same page, sometimes literally as well as figuratively, and collectively plan a few overarching strategies for success. Educational leaders, knowing they may get only one or two chances at massive systemwide improvement before the Attempt, Attack, Abandon Cycle kicks in, need to make those chances count. First, an administrator must set up a coaching staff for success by being the program's biggest supporter. Then the administrator must work with the coaching or leadership team and preplan to address staff needs to overcome inevitable resistance. To supplement the more detailed suggestions in upcoming chapters, we offer a few wide-view strategies that can improve outcomes for all educational leaders' efforts.

The one voice that carries the most weight in a school and carries furthest is the voice of the principal. The principal shapes the culture and guides the direction of a school. Consequently, when a principal vocally supports a coaching program, the likelihood of its success is enhanced. A hands-off stance toward coaching likewise has a chilling effect, making every coach's job more difficult.

Six Elements for Authentic Change

Charles Payne, author of *So Much Reform, So Little Change* (2008), determined through his extensive work with urban schools, and Chicago Public Schools in particular, that leadership is key to overcoming barriers, specifically as it relates to working together to plan for staff needs: "High-quality assistance from design teams significantly improved implementation and overall staff satisfaction" (p. 159).

In Figure 1.2 (shown on the next page), we introduce you to Peter Senge's Change Puzzle, six essential elements that, when combined, have the best chance of bringing about authentic change. This figure shows these elements: Trust, Vision, Skills, Resources, Payoff, and Action Plan. If any one (or often more) of these is not provided, staff will have a resulting action or feeling. For example, in looking at the figure, if trust is not in place, you may face sabotage from your implementers. If the vision is unclear, you will have confusion among staff. If skills aren't identified and taught, your staff may be filled with anxiety, and so on. While multiple versions of this puzzle, or matrix, exist, we find Senge's one of the most accessible. For leadership teams, addressing these six elements is how you provide quality assistance in meeting staff needs for implementation. Following are some questions to ask yourself about each of these elements as you begin rolling out a new classroom management model.

Trust. Do teachers have trust in leadership? Trust that this initiative will stick around for the long term? In many models this element is cropped from the page. Yet in all Safe & Civil Schools research, as well as work by researchers like Charles Payne, the evidence overwhelmingly supports the fact that trust is critical and "principal leadership [is] the most important indicator of the implementation level achieved" (Berends et al., 2002, p. 172). Earlier you saw a quote from Fullan that supports the idea that not only is leadership key, but intentionally building trust through forming authentic relationships is imperative to the success of any change. In addition, staff need reassurance that the initiative isn't simply one more attempt in the doomed Attempt, Attack, Abandon Cycle.

Vision. Do staff understand exactly what is expected of them? Do they understand that meeting these expectations will create an unmistakable impact on student behavior and achievement? Clarity of vision is so crucial to the success of an initiative that we mentioned it at the very beginning and devote the next chapter to its creation.

Skills. Have staff been trained in all the skills that will need to be employed for the successful implementation of the model? Have teachers been able to practice these skills and receive both positive and constructive feedback? Even the best classroom management model in the world suffers if skills are not taught and practiced by the very people who will be implementing these practices. These opportunities will be provided through initial and ongoing professional development and within the coaching experience, through both modeling and being observed when implementing new practice.

Resources. Do teachers have adequate resources to fully implement with efficacy? These resources include not only tangible materials and any accompanying professional development, but also intangibles like time, energy, and enthusiasm, two of which are very difficult to measure. Time is a critical resource to provide staff. Without a clear vision, staff may not manage their often-limited time wisely, spending more time on things that may not be a priority and running out of time to work on initiatives that would create unmistakable impact.

Payoff. Do staff see the inherent benefit to students if the model is implemented with efficacy? Will staff experience benefit to themselves when the model is fully implemented? If the vision is clear, all stakeholders should expect to see unmistakable benefits. Ideally, with an effective classroom management model like CHAMPS, students increase academic achievement, becoming better consumers of content in a well-designed classroom. Staff should see an increase in satisfaction with their positions, having freed up more mental capacity to focus on instruction because they aren't having to regularly respond to misbehavior. Instructional minutes should be gained, which benefits all parties. Staff should experience these identified payoffs rather quickly upon implementation to avoid losing momentum.

Action Plan. Do staff understand exactly what they need to do step by step to meet what's expected of them? Does the action plan move beyond an amorphous idea of better classroom management to include concrete steps to put the model into action? Without

Figure 1.2 *Change Puzzle Developed by Peter Senge (1993)*

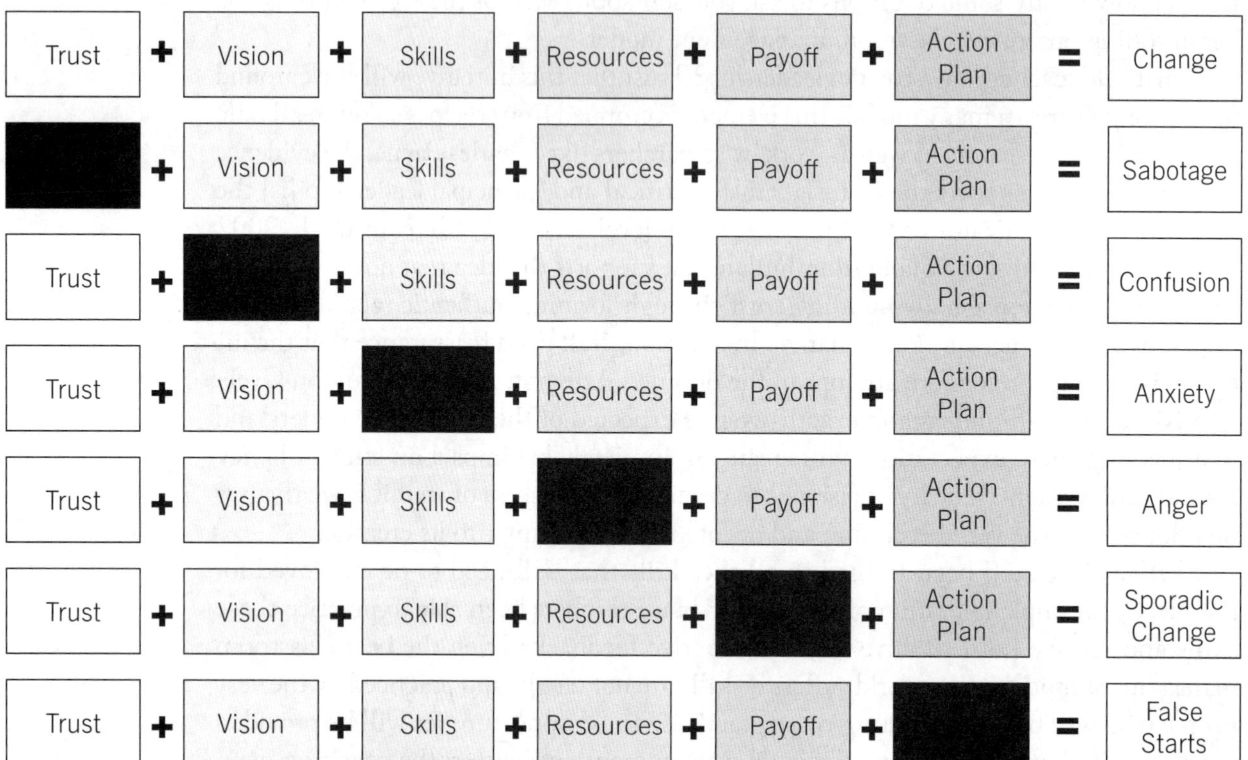

a solid action plan, staff may want to implement change but don't know where to start. This phenomenon is referred to widely as *choice paralysis*. When faced with too many options, you often can't make any decision at all. Identifying minimum expectations for implementation as well as a proposed timeline can take the burden off staff to sift through information to identify a starting place.

With all elements within the matrix provided for support, teachers will be more likely to implement a new approach to classroom management when the resource is powerful and the plan makes it easy to implement. To ensure that a model will have a powerful positive impact on student behavior and the overall school climate, it should be chosen carefully. The quality of research that supports the practices within the model should be considered, along with school achievement and behavior data to address the specific needs of the students in your school.

Along with the initial training workshops, follow-up support such as model lessons, coaching, and feedback should be provided. Teachers find it easier to put new ideas into practice when the approach is presented to them clearly and step by step, when they can see demonstrations of the teaching techniques, and when all the needed teaching materials are provided. Teaching demonstrations and model lessons, in addition to offering opportunities to experiment with the new practices, provide teachers with experiences

BOX 1.1

No Turning Back

A few years ago, my friends thought it would be a good idea to take a vacation to an all-inclusive resort in Puerto Vallarta. Sitting on a beach sipping tiny drinks under a big umbrella sounded mighty fine to me. However, these friends also decided to book an excursion to something called Extreme Adventure.

If you have ever met me, I don't think you would naturally pair me up with something that had either the word "extreme" or "adventure" in it. Yet, I also have a healthy fear of missing out, so I agreed to participate.

As part of this excursion, you go ziplining, rappelling, riding around in ATVs, etc. The adventure included a one-mile-long zip line at a speed of 60 miles per hour aptly named The Superman. Largely against my will, I did it. It was thrilling, it was exhilarating, it was everything they promised! I was not only surviving—I was thriving! And, at that moment, I had accumulated what I can only describe as misplaced confidence.

The next step was climbing a net ladder up 40 feet in the air, where more life-threatening adventure would ensue. Before we started the climb, they explained to each group that we needed to be sure we could complete the climb. While we would be strapped into safety equipment, the equipment was not designed to lower us back to the ground or raise us to the top. It was only there to stop us if we fell.

Remember what I said about misplaced confidence? This looked like no feat at all after that monster zipline, so upwards I began! And about 15 feet into that climb I realized I had made a huge mistake. I had not anticipated that grip strength would be required, and I was rapidly losing the ability to hold on. I was having to put my arms completely through the net to climb as my fingers became useless.

At one point, I just put my head down and let out a little cry, my only thought how stupid I was going to look on the news back home as the only woman who'd ever had to be rescued from a net. Then I got a grip on myself (not the net), and said, "You better get it together." Remember, the only way out of this was to climb because that equipment could not lower me down and it could not raise me up.

I'd love to say it was a moment straight out of Rocky when I reached the top of the net amid swelling music and cheers from the gallery, but it was more along the lines of people trying to get my helmet off so I didn't suffer heat stroke. At the top, surrounded by people in charge of the excursion, I slapped my husband's leg. "I get it," I panted, "I get it—school reform." While my husband thought for sure something was wrong, I truly had had an epiphany.

If you want to move people forward, you have to make it impossible to go back.

While I'm not sure it's even possible to prevent backsliding from time to time when it comes to school reform efforts, I do think we can make it more difficult to revert to prior practice. We make it more difficult to revert to prior practice when we provide what staff need when they need it so they can experience success early on. This includes understanding the drivers of change and not just appreciating them in theory but providing for them in practice.

that demonstrate that the new approach works. Seeing is believing, and teachers who believe that students will benefit from the new program will be more likely to implement the change.

Finally, the coach and professional developer need to respect teachers and value their opinions. Teachers will be more likely to embrace new ways of teaching if they have some freedom to choose how and what new practices they implement, and to adapt the new ideas to fit their and their students' particular needs.

Change feels less threatening to teachers when it comes out from the shadows. Classroom teachers who are considering implementing new practices will be interested in knowing early on exactly what they will have to do—the nuts and bolts of changing their approach to behavior management. Leaders of change can and should be ready with clear explanations, prepared materials, and data to back up their assertions. Coaches should be ready to model in the classroom, observe teachers, and provide targeted, data-based feedback.

Without a plan for implementation, throwing initiatives haphazardly at staff becomes a recipe for early burnout. Attrition rates for beginning teachers who've not had strong teacher preparation programs are much higher than for better-prepared colleagues. A strong leader who vocalizes clear support for a robust, research-based classroom management model and a leadership team that addresses staff needs at the forefront will go a long way in creating a staff of well-prepared teachers able to take on today's challenges. Administrators, with the support of a leadership team, should prepare clear outcomes in advance that will guide the improvement of current classroom practice.

CLARITY OF SHARED PRINCIPLES

Seneca, the Roman philosopher, once said, "You must know for which harbor you are headed if you are to catch the right wind to take you there." If the administrators and coaches within a school do not have a shared perception of what they are trying to accomplish regarding classroom management and its support through a coaching model, any changes that are made will likely not be substantive, productive, or long lasting. Reproducible 1.1 is a summary of shared principles this book will be steering you toward. Think about the degree to which the statements in the list correspond to what you hope to see in your school. In Chapter 2, we'll guide you in creating a vision for your campus for effective classroom management. In subsequent chapters, you'll look at each of these points in turn and adjust them to fit your vision. Plan on having a conversation with administrators and coaches within your school (or perhaps with coaches throughout the district) about these principles. Use the discussion as a platform for developing a shared vision of classroom management and classroom management coaching.

After you know what changes you want to create within a building, you can begin the work of creating those changes. The best current models of change have real-life implications for coaches. Change is understood as a process rather than a discrete event. Effective coaches provide the right kind of support throughout the process of change. Successful administrators offer the right balance of support for the coaching process and leadership in creating ongoing professional development opportunities. No checklist of procedures or one-shot professional development alone can substitute for this.

Wrapping It Up CHAPTER 1 SUMMARY

We hope this information helps you, as the leadership team, begin to plan your course of action. Advance planning should be done to ensure critical pieces of an effective system within each tier are put into place and can be sustained across time. Not only will this make your coaching support stronger, it will also increase the likelihood of teacher success, thereby impacting student behavior and academic achievement.

What to Know

- Coaches should be used to support staff in all three tiers of an effective MTSS (multi-tiered system of support).
- Solid coaching models have an unmistakable impact on teachers' skill levels.
- Professional development with the support of coaches leads to increased implementation and sustainability.
- Change is a complex process in which potential barriers must be addressed.
- The principal must be a vocal and enthusiastic advocate for the classroom management model and the coaching program that will support it.

What to Do

- Identify any potential barriers to the adoption of a classroom management model and the utilization of coaches by staff.
- Adopt a matrix to plan for staff needs as you move to clarify a clear vision of your classroom management and coaching model (Chapter 2) and communicate expectations for implementation (Chapter 3).
- Create a summary of shared principles for the campus.

Reproducible 1.1 *Summary of Shared Principles*

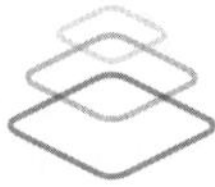

Summary of Shared Principles

1 Effective classroom management is a key component of effective instruction, regardless of grade level, subject, pedagogy, or curriculum.

2 Managing a classroom is part art and part science, conceptually simple enough to reduce to a handful of critical variables yet so intricate and complex that it is a lifelong learning task. Even the best and most experienced teachers must continually refine their classroom management plans.

3 The goal of effective classroom management is not creating "perfect" children, but providing the perfect environment for enhancing their growth, using research-based strategies that guide students toward increasingly responsible and motivated behavior.

4 Classroom management is never a one-size-fits-all or canned process. Experimentation and manipulation of classroom management variables, coupled with coaching feedback and the Improvement Cycle, give management plans their strength and effectiveness.

5 A well-managed classroom is one in which students are (a) meeting the teacher's procedural and behavioral (CHAMPS) expectations, (b) academically engaged in meaningful learning tasks, and (c) interacting respectfully with one another and with the teacher.

6 Adoption of a schoolwide or districtwide model for classroom management creates a common language that connects professional development, procedures, and problem-solving among teachers, coaches, and administrative staff.

7 The only absolute rule within the CHAMPS model is that all people should be treated with dignity and respect. Belittlement of students has no place in any teacher's repertoire.

8 Administrators must make clear what they expect to see when visiting classrooms and what support they will provide to help teachers meet those expectations (including coaching).

9 Administrators should provide clear feedback to teachers on what they see when visiting classrooms, including positive feedback and meeting with teachers individually when constructive feedback is necessary.

10 When observations or data collection reveal that a teacher needs to improve essential classroom management outcomes, the teacher should be made aware of the options for help available in the school and encouraged to seek assistance from a coach.

11 As many highly skilled and respected staff members as possible should be designated as classroom management coaches. In most cases, these will be instructional coaches who are assisting with classroom management as part of their efforts to assist teachers in implementing effective instructional practices. Ideally, their role should be nonevaluative and their work with teachers confidential.

12 Coaches should work within a multi-tiered framework to ensure that reliable data is collected within and across classrooms, and they should be well equipped with assessment aids and strategies. Coaches should know how to communicate effectively, what to look for when observing classrooms, and how to provide meaningful, ongoing support and follow-up.

REPRODUCIBLE 1.1

CHAPTER 2

Structure
Developing a Clear Vision

Vision without action is merely a dream.
Action without vision merely passes the time.
Vision with action can change the world.
—Joel A. Barker

Studies have been conducted that show we are actually happier when we are *planning* our vacations than when we are actually *on* them. I find this to be quite true as I have a habit of living all my vacations before they ever happen. The problem is that my visions of what will happen once we get there are too grandiose to ever be realized. And then I end up disappointed that I didn't get to swim under a waterfall beneath a rainbow as a sea turtle swam up to me to give me a kiss on the cheek on the Road to Hana. However, my husband is the opposite. He doesn't plan anything or have really clear expectations for how he wants vacation to go. He's never disappointed, but, to me, the experience can be rather lackluster. I'm convinced the key to a perfect vacation is the same key to creating a consciously inviting school climate for staff and students—a clear, attainable vision.

Joel Barker, quoted above, in 1975 began popularizing the concept of paradigm shifts in the corporate world by encouraging business leaders to craft and bring a vision into reality. Organizations in the private sector have been using coaching to change thinking and improve effectiveness for decades, and education, too, has taken a page from this playbook. Most campuses have in place, and often on a permanent plaque, the school's mission statement. Whether or not this mission is truly carried out on a daily basis is something addressed in whole school reform efforts. Underpinning the mission statement are all the initiatives, resources, strategies, and training efforts to keep this North Star in place. In this chapter, we'll look at how each single initiative, including the implementation of a comprehensive classroom management model, should have its own target in relation to the overall vision. This clarity will help guide staff not only in adopting new practice, but in helping them see how efforts all tie together to pull campus and staff toward the greater vision at large.

Effective classroom management starts with a clear vision crafted by building leaders that drives all staff, teachers and coaches alike, toward a common goal. While the term *leader* in this chapter most likely pertains to a principal or administrator, we do recognize that it may also include those in a nonevaluative role who are part of a leadership *team*, such as nonevaluative coaches, ancillary staff, and teacher leaders.

> "*A clear vision by building leaders drives all staff toward a common goal.*"

This chapter is intended for those on the campus in positions of leadership who are charged with establishing a clear vision. If leaders, by their words and actions, show an active interest in classroom management as part of this vision, staff will be more likely to follow suit. The converse is also true. If teachers perceive classroom management as low on the list of priorities, some teachers may not make the effort to evaluate and improve their classroom management skills, thereby never seeking out coaching as a way to make progress.

A principal or administrator charged with setting a vision for the campus and involved with the coaching process has a dual role: Administrators must provide staff with the information, training, and ongoing support they need to realize the vision, and must also see that staff meet the accountability standards that are set. Adding to an administrator's myriad duties is a balancing act—but one well worth it for the rewards leaders, teachers, and the student population will reap.

Bear in mind that as a campus leader, whether in an evaluative or nonevaluative capacity, you do not need to suddenly become an expert coach or have all the answers to every question and concern your teachers have. Over time, of course, leaders will accrue valuable knowledge and insight into classroom management coaching. But to begin your coaching program, this is what you'll do:

- Develop an overall vision for your school.
- Identify the four cornerstones that fulfill critical roles for implementing your classroom management model.
- Select a strategy-rich classroom management model that aligns with the overall vision.
- Identify all prospective coaches on the campus who have the time and ability to support teachers.
- Develop a three-part target for your model that you will use to communicate expectations for what staff will be expected to implement and how quality of the implementation will be assessed.

Understanding the thinking behind the ideas in this chapter will help you persuade teachers that these principles are well supported by the research literature and have led to success for educators who incorporate them. Background materials and a review of the supporting research for the ideas presented here are found in the Appendix. You should know the research literature well enough to communicate the importance of classroom management to your staff and why you or the district have chosen CHAMPS. CHAMPS works because it incorporates strategies that effective teachers use and that the past few decades of research support.

We know that skilled classroom management is a key indicator of students' academic success. The definition of skilled classroom management, however, has been somewhat murky in the past. When schools were initially built, the idea was to enact a factory model, treating students as products, churning them out at a rate fast enough to keep up with an industrialized world. In an actual factory, when products are below quality standards, you simply remove the product from the system. For many decades, therefore, when a student's behavior wasn't meeting staff expectations, the student was removed from the system. This doesn't align with what schools currently know to be best educational practices.

In the past few decades, many educational systems have adopted more customer service-oriented models. In these models, when a student is not meeting a benchmark of quality, the system is adjusted to meet the needs of the student. Customer service in this case does not mean the customer is always right—we do what is best for the student, but not always what the student wants. Customer service is also not the *absence* of a system; on the contrary, customer service models must have clear parameters in which to operate. Being able to provide effective customer service to both students and staff means we need to start with a clear vision of how a highly effective system is managed.

DEVELOP AN OVERALL VISION

An overall vision for your campus should be one in which staff feel empowered, and that empowerment begins by creating and clarifying what the campus will look like for both students and staff. An effective leader or leadership team should work to create a compelling, palpable vision of what students and staff can accomplish.

An overall vision consists of two ideas: emotionally compelling language paired with specific, measurable goals. Part of this vision includes items such as district and campus mission statements, staff beliefs, and campus Guidelines for Success. Put together, this is how an emotionally compelling environment is constructed. It's what gets educators out of bed in the morning. In addition to these pieces, a clear target related to both behavioral and academic achievement should be communicated to all stakeholders, including parents, staff, and students. These are the specific, measurable goals educators work toward to create the ideal overall environment. For lofty vision and mission statements, clear and direct targets are a critical component in ensuring these are reached.

Students can hit any achievement target that they can see and that will hold still for them. *—Richard Stiggins*

Think about it. If the teacher cannot create a compelling, palpable vision of what students are expected to accomplish and keep that expectation stable while students strive toward it, it is probably not a reasonable expectation.

The same should be said for teachers: They can hit the target (implementing research-based classroom management) if they can clearly see it—and if the target remains stable. Your job, then, is to furnish both the springboard and the stability for an effective classroom management model and the coach's role within that model.

When leaders, both administrators and leadership teams, work to develop a clear direction toward which to guide staff, it helps schools in two important ways. First, it helps ensure that staff behaviors, as well as decisions made by leadership, are goal directed. Secondly, it helps prevent behavior management practices from deteriorating over time—drifting away from a preventive, positive model and toward an ineffective, reactive approach (*Foundations*, Module F, 2014, p. 42).

In CHAMPS, a clear vision is already established. The goal of CHAMPS classroom management is to develop a classroom of students who are responsible, motivated, and highly engaged in meaningful tasks. Much like a mission statement, you must have a broad idea of what you are trying to accomplish over time. A vision such as the one CHAMPS provides helps educators with both planning and reflection on classroom management.

Even if it isn't immediately apparent that others want to share in your vision, the engagement and buy-in you need from parents and teachers will come when implementing a powerful classroom management model. When staff and parents see unmistakable impact on student behavior and achievement, buy-in becomes automatic. This won't always mean perfectly behaved children! Plenty of students are going to test the limits, and all students will have their bad days. (Teachers and administrators will, too.) Accordingly, the CHAMPS model includes building cooperative relationships with students, showing students more positive attention than corrective attention, and providing meaningful feedback. Misbehavior can be skillfully headed off, often before it occurs. When it does occur, correction should be fluent and effective.

Through the simple act of reading and thinking about classroom management, you are already forming the basis for the vision you will hold for your school. Envision a school where most misbehavior is prevented, where that which does occur is managed effectively, and where students are continually inspired to do their best. Always start with high expectations for teacher conduct and student behavior, knowing that one powerful common denominator among all human beings is the capacity for change and improvement. For students still developing in body and mind, that capacity for change, and its corresponding receptivity to encouragement, is magnified. Of course, you must remain realistic, but don't ever allow "realistic" to become a ceiling for improved student behavior.

Some students will come to school even as crises are occurring in their homes. Some may do only enough work to get by. Some may bully others. Some will act out impulsively. The goal of positive behavior support is not perfect children; rather, the goal should be creating the perfect *environment* for enhancing their growth. Tune the school environment to your students' needs—motivating them to be the best they can be, supporting them through personal crises, and ensuring their physical and emotional safety. That is the crux of an effective Tier 1 system within a multi-tiered system of support. To provide the customer service mentioned earlier, you must have a model that looks at the system as a whole and the people (students, staff, and leaders) within it.

If you cannot picture your school as that perfect setting for the students of your community and your staff as the group of people who create that setting, work on crafting a more positive mental image. Stay with your vision. Add to it each day. The ways and means for achieving a positive, effective setting vary from school to school. More often than you might think, the clear vision held by those in authority connects successful schools.

"A prime function of the leader," American reformer John Gardner once observed, "is to keep hope alive." This first task—vision—will never be complete. You must renew your vision continually and pump up your staff. "People often say that motivation doesn't last," says motivational speaker Zig Ziglar. "Well, neither does bathing—that is why we recommend both daily."

Peter Senge's change model, outlined in Chapter 1, shows the impact a lack of vision can wreak. Without this clear vision, you run the risk of a confused staff, unsure as to the purpose behind the implementation of the classroom management model. Vision is *the* vital part of a leadership team's role.

This first task—vision—will never be complete. You must renew your vision continually and pump up your staff.

IDENTIFY THE FOUR CORNERSTONES

Regardless of anyone's job description, the next step is to identify staff on campus who will fulfill four critical roles (Figure 2.1). For the implementation of any initiative to succeed, you need four groups of people on the ground coordinating services for the launch of your chosen classroom management model:

- Practitioners
- Trainers
- Support personnel
- Evaluators

Figure 2.1 *Four Cornerstones of Classroom Management Model*

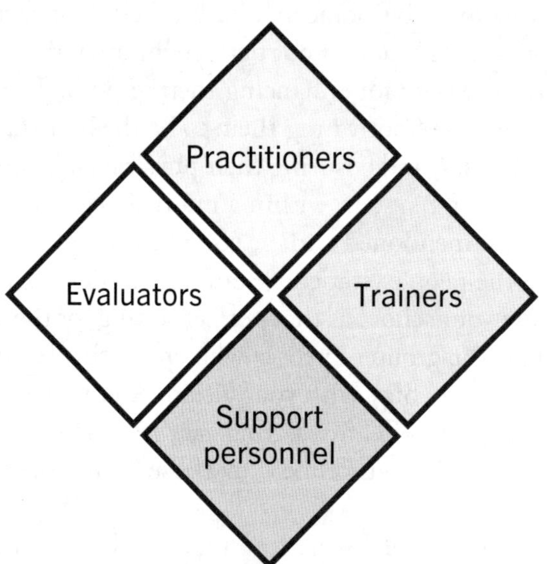

Practitioners. These are the people tasked with putting the actual initiative or resource into practice. The group that makes up the practitioners will vary depending on the goal of the initiative or the theme of the resource. For the CHAMPS model, the practitioners would be classroom teachers. For your coaching system, it would be any person identified as a coach. Often, when asked about the standards for implementation (the Do part of the target mentioned later in this chapter), administrators with a poorly developed plan will simply rely on voluntary implementation. In other words, there is not an intentional group of practitioners. It's much more difficult for the next group, the trainers, when forced to spend even more time "selling" staff with a compelling rationale to adopt a model. Letting practitioners know in advance who they are and reminding them of the overall vision will get staff more receptive to professional development around the chosen model.

Trainers. Often, this role is filled by someone outside of the district who is an expert in the adopted model. Based on the belief that it's often difficult to be a prophet in your own land, many districts and campuses employ expert outside consultants to come in and deliver content in rich and engaging ways. Ideally, trainers are well versed in the model. They have implemented the model themselves and are able to easily field a variety of questions that will crop up around the content. Quality professional development should include an overview of the model while breaking it down into easy-to-implement tasks. Trainings should include active engagement intended to give practitioners resources (to avoid anger) and work on skills (to avoid anxiety). While experts in the model, trainers should also be humble and compassionate with where practitioners are in the stages of change. Trainers should be able to tailor content based on conversations they have in advance with leaders about their vision as well as conversations with practitioners in the moment that reflect where they are.

This is not to say that district- and campus-based trainers cannot adequately provide professional development, especially in places where there is a designated team of professional developers on site. Just as it takes years and practice to become a highly skilled teacher, the same is true for any professional developer, or teacher of adults. Whether your trainers come from outside or within, ensure they know the content well enough to help practitioners launch the new initiative.

PRACTICE WHAT YOU TEACH

Historically, Safe & Civil Schools offered a Training of Trainers model for district and campus personnel to learn our material with the purpose of delivering content at their home sites. While there have certainly been some amazing trainers who completed this model to successfully train in their home district, we have often found the model to be inadequate in helping districts and campuses gain traction with implementation. Often, people participating in the model were not in a position to devote time to creating and presenting professional development or were brand-new to the content themselves. This would then frustrate district and campus leaders, who might forgo our library of resources when implementation was shoddy or sporadic. Safe & Civil Schools has realized that the best trainers, for any company, are the people who have been practitioners themselves. It is critical for trainers to adapt to varying professional development settings and answer deeper-level questions about content. For practitioners engaged in training, this adds validity to the model that's been chosen and increases the likelihood that implementation will be attempted with more understanding and enthusiasm.

Support personnel. Coaches, whether evaluative or nonevaluative, typically make up this group. Once the initial professional development has been offered, with your expert consultants often now off-site, you will need someone at the campus (and ideally, district) level to help lead any staff meetings or mini professional developments around the new model. Support personnel can answer questions, help troubleshoot, and work with teachers one-on-one or in smaller learning communities to continually review and revisit the model. Having support personnel on hand helps alleviate practitioners' frustrations. We've already established that practitioners will not retain all of the information heard in the first big wave of professional development. Support personnel can help explore and break down any forgotten content as well as assess the quality of implementation within any classroom. Ideally, support personnel are also well versed in the content, having received the same or additional professional development in the initiative, and possessed of a coaching mindset that helps practitioners persevere and master content.

Evaluators. Often district or building administrators, this group is well versed in the Measure part of the three-part target (discussed later in this chapter). They know how and when to measure preestablished benchmarks. They have practiced measuring objective data points and established interrater reliability to ensure data are valid. Without this group in action, practitioners, often overwhelmed with competing initiatives, may choose not to implement. Without accountability systems in place, time and money will have been wasted on expert trainers, and support personnel will struggle to justify why staff need to adopt these new practices. Think of your behavior behind the wheel of a car. On a nice sunny day, with little traffic and a wide-open highway, your speed might often surpass the posted limit. But when your GPS alerts you to a traffic camera ahead, many of you ease off the pedal. The same is true for staff. Behavior often changes when someone else is watching. This is not to say we are recommending "power over" and a message that practitioners will be in trouble if they don't implement. Rather, the purpose of evaluation is to make sure staff needs are being met, that there is some level of fidelity of implementation, and that this cornerstone group acts as the living reminder of the campus vision and the expectations for implementation.

Cornerstones are an important feature on which a particular thing depends. Without these cornerstones intentionally established in advance, your model is on shaky ground. The absence of any one of these cornerstones can lead to the toppling of even the most research-based effective classroom management model. With all cornerstones in place, the groundwork is now laid for a strong, lasting foundation.

IDENTIFY COACHES

We suggest that anyone who has regular contact with classroom teachers is potentially a coach. If you are reading this now, chances are you are already a coach in some capacity, and chances are also good that you, on occasion, benefit from the coaching of others. The untapped reserve of educators who can be coaches may be much greater than you think—certainly it's much deeper than many schools today make use of. Coaching that happens naturally, spontaneously, and unofficially has many great benefits. In advocating for more coaching and official channels in which coaches can work, we are *not* discounting the importance of spontaneous, informal discussion among colleagues. To the contrary, research and experience tell us that collegial discussion *and* coaching are pivotal in the development of a strong school culture that supports all its participants, both staff and students alike.

Show us someone who interacts daily with teachers, and we'll show you a prospective coach. These coaches can then be divided into two broad classifications: *evaluative* and *nonevaluative* coaches. Although coaching most frequently occurs in one-to-one interactions between a teacher and a nonevaluative coach, we recognize that administrators or ancillary staff may also act in the capacity of a coach, especially in smaller schools and schools that do not have a dedicated coaching position.

Evaluative coaches. By the nature of their position, the administrator-as-coach tends to be evaluative. Administrators have an important role in coaching, but because they are also involved in teacher evaluation, the nature of that role is distinctly different. The administrator must hold teachers to a high standard of accountability. The administrator's position and job description is one of authority relative to most teachers. When we refer to the administrator, we mean that person has some direct connection to teacher evaluation and is thus an *evaluative* coach.

We use the term *administrator* or *evaluator* to include principals, assistant principals, and other building administrators, except where specific reference is given. Different buildings have different norms for staffing administrative positions. Many small and midsize elementary schools have a single administrator, the principal. Larger elementary schools and most middle schools and high schools have a principal and one or more assistant or vice principals. We will assume that in schools with more than one administrator, their roles have been clearly defined—staff members understand who supervises whom, which administrator is in charge of what, and who is responsible for stepping in to deal with a severe disciplinary issue or behavioral emergency.

Nonevaluative coaches. The peer-as-coach is typically nonevaluative. Most (but not all) educational professionals invited to coach classroom management will be collaborative and nonevaluative—instructional and behavioral coaches, fellow teachers, standards coaches, reading specialists, new-teacher mentors, behavior specialists, department chairs, school counselors, psychologists, and so on. The common thread is that the nonevaluative coach's role is entirely to help teachers with behavior management; there should be no direct reporting to an administrator or link to teacher evaluation. In a later chapter, we will explore the need to keep some level of confidentiality between evaluators and nonevaluators, if at all possible, to protect candor in the coaching relationship.

As the leadership team starts to consider these two groups of coaches, both evaluative and nonevaluative, we recommend creating a list of these coaches, clearly differentiating between the two roles. The following criteria can be useful in determining which staff members can be considered as potential coaches:

- *Administrators.* Administrators will serve as the evaluative coaching team. This type of evaluative coaching includes administrators who are able to collect data and have one-on-one conversations on a *regular* and *ongoing basis* with staff. Working with staff, both collectively and individually, must be a function of the evaluative coach. If an administrator will not have the capacity to work with teachers one-on-one, we recommend that they not be included on the list of potential coaches.
- *Full-time coaches* are staff members hired with the primary directive of coaching (behavior coach, instructional coach, etc.), with no other job responsibilities as a classroom teacher or other member of the support staff (counselors, school psychologists, etc.).
- *Part-time coaches* include any staff member who serves as a coach part-time and has other duties (classroom teachers, counselors, school psychologists, etc.). This type of part-time coaching must include dedicated time *during the instructional day* to provide support.

CAUTION

Full-time classroom teachers and other full-time support staff members do not have dedicated time during the instructional day to provide a high level of one-on-one support. These staff members can provide spontaneous, unofficial, and informal coaching support. As stated earlier, while this type of coaching is beneficial, such coaches will not be able to provide the types of support outlined in these pages. They simply do not have the time to do so.

Instead of lengthy constructions such as *instructional coach* or *behavior support coach*, we will generally default to the shorthand *coach*, applying it universally in a nonevaluative sense. In similar fashion, we will refer to any and all incarnations of behavior support coaching simply as *coaching*. If your school uses different but analogous terms for certain concepts in this book, by all means go with the lingo you and your colleagues are accustomed to. Substitute the terminology you are comfortable with as you read and adapt documents in this book and in the downloadable materials.

There's a reason staff developers call anyone charged with helping teachers a *coach*. A coach teaches, models, inspires, and critiques (provides feedback), and continues in this relentlessly until mastery is achieved—and long afterward. You'd be hard pressed to name a top-caliber athlete who doesn't retain a coach. Likewise, the skills of a diligent music student may one day eclipse those of her teacher, but that doesn't mean the maestro has nothing more to offer. This continuous cycle of improvement is a theme we will return to again. Ongoing schoolwide gains in classroom management *can* be realized. Across the country, goals for student behavior are being attained and maintained, with the help of coaching programs. The role of the coach, and of coaching, never ends.

SELECT A MODEL FOR CLASSROOM MANAGEMENT

To translate your vision into action, you must provide staff with powerful strategies to manage their classrooms. Most readers of this book will have already chosen CHAMPS as their classroom management model. If you have not yet chosen a model, we highly recommend CHAMPS because it empowers teachers with an effective, research-based model that allows for a level of teacher autonomy in how to apply the various tools and strategies. This section will clarify your responsibilities to coaches and teachers in implementing CHAMPS and connect your vision to demonstrable results.

Two primary considerations should govern the choice of any effective classroom management approach. First, your model should be consistent with the findings of the best research—the school and teacher effectiveness literature as it relates to classroom management. Second, the model should provide plenty of how-to information. An administrator who tells teachers they need to have routines and procedures but does not provide information on the *why* and *how* is courting failure. By and large, teachers simply do not have the time to translate raw research into daily practice.

What the Research Says About Effective Classroom Management Practices

You don't have to sift through libraries of research because others have already done so. Studies have been aggregated and analyzed, and books written to report these findings. The resources in the Safe & Civil Schools Library bring together the most applicable research with practical, teacher-tested suggestions for applying it. Though it only skims the surface of a sea of literature, this book will explore well-researched concepts powerful enough to bring immediate and long-lasting results.

The school and teacher effectiveness literature has isolated characteristics shared by effective teachers (those whose students consistently achieve academic excellence) that are often lacking in ineffective teachers (those whose students consistently achieve poorly). Dr. Robert Marzano is a modern pioneer in the movement to translate research and theory into practical tools for K–12 teachers and administrators. Through his meta-analysis of the research on classroom management, Marzano has drawn together the findings of hundreds of research studies to lay out the parameters that most strongly influence behavior support for the classroom and the classroom management variables that have the greatest effect on student achievement (Marzano et al., 2003).

Marzano's recommendations include:

1. Establish clear rules and procedures for:
    - General classroom behavior
    - Beginning and ending of day or class period
    - Transitions and interruptions
    - Use of materials and equipment
    - Group work
    - Seatwork
    - Teacher-led activities

2. Use strategies to discourage misbehavior and encourage appropriate behavior, including:
    - Corrective consequences for problematic behavior
    - Positive consequences for appropriate behavior

3. Build supportive teacher-student relationships through:
    - Exhibiting assertive behavior
    - Establishing clear learning goals
    - Providing flexible learning goals
    - Taking a personal interest in students
    - Using equitable and positive classroom behaviors
    - Responding appropriately to students' incorrect responses

4. Cultivate a present, aware, and controlled mental set by:
    - Exhibiting Withitness, or being aware of what's going on around you and being able to perceive the needs of your students with accuracy and care
    - Maintaining emotional objectivity, or the ability to enforce rules and maintain high expectations without taking student misbehavior personally

Another excellent summary of classroom management research literature was conducted by Simonsen and colleagues (2008). They identified twenty practices that in general are supported by the research and have sufficient evidence to recommend their adoption to support classroom behavior. The practices were then grouped into five evidence-based critical features of classroom management:

1. Maximize structure and predictability (including using a physical arrangement that minimizes distraction).
2. Post, teach, review, monitor, and reinforce expectations (and provide active supervision).
3. Actively engage students in observable ways.
4. Use a continuum of strategies to respond to appropriate behaviors (including specific and/or contingent praise, classwide group contingencies, behavioral contracting, and token economy strategies).
5. Use a continuum of strategies to respond to inappropriate behaviors (including error corrections, performance feedback, differential reinforcement, planned ignoring plus praise and/or instruction of classroom rules, response cost, and timeout from reinforcement strategies).

Both Marzano's and Simonsen's research supports CHAMPS as an effective approach to classroom management.

Some of your staff may want a system that guarantees as little mental expenditure as possible and results in docile, compliant children. As nice as this would be, it is not possible. Research-based change is a measured, deliberate process. Be skeptical of any miracle cure based on piecemeal or partial data that change from year to year.

No one says it will be easy. Effective classroom management is inherently difficult, requiring preplanning and then frequent split-second decisions about how to handle different situations as they arise. No one in the business world expects that managing 20 to 40 employees will be simple or easy—and that applies to supposedly mature, responsible adults who are paid to be there! Managing 20, 30, or 40 children, some who do not want to be there and none who are being paid, is never going to be simple. Classroom management, like effective instruction, is a lifelong learning task. While not always easy, it can be dependably effective. The CHAMPS approach to classroom management, when implemented well, results in improved student behavior, enhanced teacher confidence, and a more functional school culture and climate over time.

Teacher effectiveness literature does not dictate exactly what a teacher must do. Research is, by definition, an observational tool, descriptive rather than prescriptive. It is broadly and generally effective in identifying which methods effective teachers use that ineffective teachers do not use. Try seeing yourself as a researcher, a careful observer of trends and norms within your own school. You are in the best position to be the expert on what is working in your school.

CHAMPS, *Discipline in the Secondary Classroom*, *Early-Stage Interventions*, and other books in the Safe & Civil Schools Library from Ancora Publishing (ancorapublishing.com) help bridge the gap between research and implementation. Teachers are encouraged to use principles of effective classroom management to create their own plan, identify decisions they need to make about their plan, and then follow logical steps to implementation. As an example, the research literature indicates that effective teachers have efficient routines and procedures. CHAMPS breaks this down into practical tasks: "Develop routines for beginning and ending class." These are further broken down into the discrete elements of an efficient beginning routine: "Students should be actively engaged with a meaningful task while the teacher takes attendance." Going still further, CHAMPS gives examples of how a teacher might incorporate these practices. Yet for all its suggestions, it remains up to each teacher to decide exactly how to develop a routine for beginning class.

> *"To communicate CHAMPS as your classroom management model compellingly, you have to know it well enough to describe what effective implementation looks and sounds like."*

To communicate CHAMPS as your classroom management model compellingly, you have to know it well enough to describe what effective implementation looks and sounds like. Keep STOIC in mind, which offers a framework for communicating the variables that are essential to any effective classroom management approach:

S **Structure** involves organizing classrooms to prevent misbehavior and encourage student engagement.

T **Teaching** expectations involves clarifying for students how to function successfully within that structure and fostering student success with practice, repetition, and a healthy dose of inspiration.

O **Observation** involves continuously circulating throughout the classroom and periodically collecting observational data on student behavior to uncover trends and identify areas for improvement.

I **Interacting** positively involves building positive relationships with students and providing age-appropriate positive feedback.

C **Correction** is, of course, a necessary component of any effective classroom management system, which should offer guidelines for responding to undesired behavior calmly, consistently, immediately, and as briefly as possible, in a manner that teaches and re-teaches appropriate behavior.

AUTONOMY WITHIN THE MODEL

We may highlight what the literature has found to be true of effective teachers in general, but we cannot replace the judgment or experience of any individual teacher. Respect the right of your teachers to employ techniques and tactics that work for them so long as their chosen approach remains consistent with the research literature on effective teaching. Respect your teachers' intelligence and their capacity for self-monitoring. Likewise, encourage teachers to respect their students' intelligence and capacity for self-governance. The steps and suggestions in this chapter should not be construed as commands. You can and should set standards of accountability for your teachers, but this accountability will be based largely on results: Are students actively engaged in instruction? Are they behaving in a respectful manner?

This book is about giving teachers the tools, resources, and support to attain the standards you set. But there's little to be gained by trying to force a teacher to follow a predetermined path or canned approach to classroom management mastery. Daniel Pink, in *Drive* (2011), clearly outlines the three drivers of true motivation: autonomy, mastery, and purpose. The more someone is told exactly what to do, the less of all three that person has. Teachers were hired for their ability to think, not for the sole purpose of implementing a lockstep approach to managing their classrooms. Independently and of their own volition, effective teachers make sound decisions that creatively address CHAMPS expectations and STOIC variables. Respect for the autonomy and competence of your teachers demonstrates commitment to the philosophical underpinnings of the classroom management model you have adopted. Lead by example. As often as you speak about your vision, let your example speak for you.

Moving Away From Ineffective Models

What if you currently have in place an ineffective model? What if teachers prefer a non-research-based, punitive model of classroom management? Some teachers appreciate a particular approach to classroom management because it allows them to send a student out of class any time the student's behavior is bothersome. If such a model is in place in your school, ask yourself the following questions:

1. Are students frequently missing out on instruction because they are being sent out of the classroom (to the office, the hall, or another classroom)?
2. Are the same "banished" students sent from the room over and over?
3. Are you committed to implementing research-based practices in your building?

If the answer to all three of these questions is yes, you need to provide the leadership to change the current approach and staff beliefs. Staff may not like the change because the current procedure can be very reinforcing—they can get rid of the problem any time they want. However, if you are committed to instruction (and to raising academic achievement), removing students from class ensures only that they are *not* participating. Besides, if this procedure were effective, it would change behavior and so would not have to be used with any degree of frequency. Because your answer to the second question above is yes, it must not be working. If you are going to change the model, follow the suggestions in this chapter carefully. In fact, it might be a good idea to get several influential teachers to work through this chapter with you so that you and a group of highly respected teacher peers present the case for the CHAMPS model to the whole staff.

Also keep in mind that a model that looks at only one aspect of behavior management, such as focusing solely on relationships or responding effectively to student misbehavior, will also be ineffective over time. While these programs may be a great way to support an already robust system, they will be inadequate in creating a comprehensive management plan that addresses all aspects of the STOIC framework.

DEFINE A THREE-PART TARGET FOR YOUR CLASSROOM MANAGEMENT MODEL

To bring your overall vision into greater focus, your next task is to develop clear expectations for your staff about implementation of your classroom management model. One of the central tenets of CHAMPS is that students should be taught how they are expected to behave—they should never have to guess what they are expected to do. Misbehavior should not be a function of ignorance. Principals and administrators owe no less to their teaching staff. We propose creating a three-part target for the model. Unless you clearly communicate your own expectations for classroom management, it is not reasonable to assume your staff will be able to meet them. And, without a clear target, there may be no clear reason for teachers to seek coaching for improvement at all.

You can't hit a target you cannot use, and you cannot see a target you do not have. *—Zig Ziglar*

A three-part target entails clarifying three major categories of expectation for teachers' individual classroom management plans:

- What practitioners should know
- What practitioners should do
- How implementation will be measured

Figure 2.2 *Three-Part Target for Classroom Management Model*

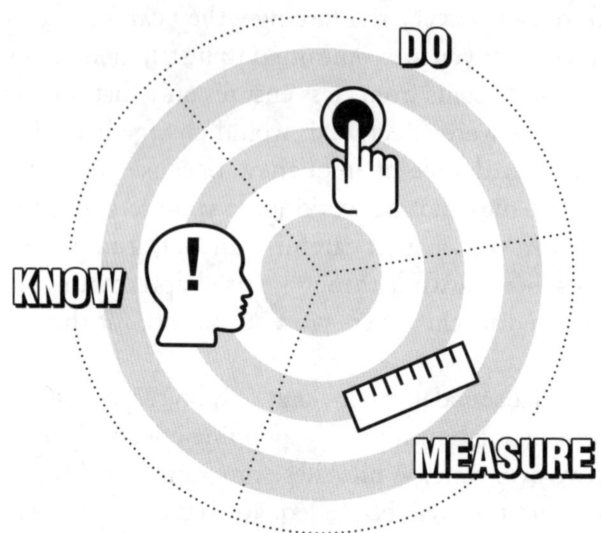

Give some thought to how you will introduce your classroom management model to staff and describe your expectations for successful implementation. In the next chapter, you will refine this three-part target and use it to communicate expectations to staff.

Know

What Do You Want Your Practitioners to Know About the Model?

Plan to introduce the model and explain how it was chosen. This part of the target helps leadership identify those critical pieces that you want your practitioners to learn first and retain the longest. Consider:

- What are the major goals and purposes of the model?
- Provide your staff with information on the who, what, when, and why of the model:
    - *Who* adopted the model—is it a districtwide or schoolwide initiative, and *what* is it all about?
    - The *when* should include some information on the history of CHAMPS use—is this the first year or third year? Has the program (or one like it) been used before in the building or district?
    - The *why* should address the rationale: *Why* do we need a schoolwide model for classroom management, and why do we need coaches?
- How is the model compatible with research?

Chapter 3 provides sample exhibits and talking points that you can share with staff to describe key features of CHAMPS.

Do

What Do You Want Your Practitioners to Implement From the Model?

In addition to explaining CHAMPS as the adopted model of classroom management, you will want to be sure that your teachers know what you expect them to do with this knowledge. This part of the target looks for congruence between teacher's implementation and the model itself. This includes what work you want teachers to turn in to you and what you expect to see when you go into classrooms for observations and formal evaluations. Consider:

- What will teachers be expected to do throughout the school year with regard to their classroom management practices?
- What are the minimum expectations for implementing the model?
- How will teachers know whether their implementation is in congruence with the model?

In the next chapter, exhibits and talking points for communicating this part of the target are organized around the STOIC acronym to make your expectations easy for your staff to remember and to connect with CHAMPS and your schoolwide vision of classroom management.

Measure

What Will Be Used to Measure the Effectiveness of Implementation?

Two thirds of the work is making sure practitioners know the content of the CHAMPS model and the minimum requirements for implementation. The third part of the target, the way by which effectiveness will be measured, is vital to creating a level of consistency on your campus. Consider:

- How will key features and outcomes of the model's implementation be measured?
- What data will routinely be used to assess the effectiveness of implementation?

In this book, we rely on the Basic 5 Behavior Benchmarks to measure a practitioner's application of essential features of your classroom management model. The Basic 5 Benchmarks provide general guidance for the minimum standard that should be met in any classroom. These benchmarks allow teachers, coaches, and administrators to analyze classroom data with clear goals in mind.

The Basic 5 Behavior Benchmarks are:

- *Opportunities to Respond*—chances given by the teacher for students to engage in teacher-directed instruction.
- *Ratio of Interactions*—the ratio of positive to corrective interactions between the teacher and students.
- *Disruptions*—unwanted or inappropriate behaviors that interrupt the flow of instruction for the teacher or another student or students.
- *On-Task Behavior*—the amount of on-task behavior exhibited by students. (Strictly speaking, *on-task* is one metric of academic engagement; for simplicity's sake we will use them synonymously.)
- *Alignment With Expectations*—the daily reality of student behavior compared with posted expectations and classroom rules.

These benchmarks allow a teacher to analyze classroom data with clear goals in mind, such as maintaining at least a 3:1 ratio of positive to corrective interactions, providing more than forty opportunities to respond during teacher-directed instruction, having fewer than five disruptions in a 10-minute period, having students on task at least 90%–100% of the time, and having at least 90% of students in alignment with behavioral expectations during any instructional activity. If data are collected that show staff are reaching these goals, remember that the broader goal is always continuous improvement, tweaking classroom management practices to continue maximizing student success.

Exhibits and talking points are provided in Chapter 3 to help you provide staff with more in-depth descriptions of how implementation and staff adherence to the model will be measured.

Wrapping It Up

CHAPTER 2 SUMMARY

Skilled teachers' words and deeds bring out the best in their students. Likewise, the sincerity of leadership should inspire excellence in staff. By following the ideas in this chapter, leaders will demonstrate a clear vision for the school and communicate high expectations that teachers can and should effectively manage behavior and motivate their students.

What to Know

- An effective leader or leadership team should work to create a compelling, palpable vision of what students and staff can accomplish. This vision should make staff feel empowered.
- The four cornerstones of practitioners, trainers, support personnel, and evaluators are critical to ensuring model implementation and sustainability.
- A research-based, strategy-rich classroom management model, like CHAMPS, should always move the campus in the direction of the overall vision developed.
- An effective classroom management model is one that supports the overall vision of a campus, is positive and proactive, and is research based.
- Clear expectations should be communicated to staff on how the CHAMPS model will be implemented and assessed.

What to Do

- Develop an overall vision for your campus.
- Identify the four cornerstone roles for implementing your classroom management model.
- Identify all prospective coaches on the campus who have the time and ability to support teachers.
- Adopt CHAMPS as a research-based, strategy-rich classroom management model.
- Clarify a three-part target for your model that you will use to communicate expectations for what staff will be expected to implement and how quality of the implementation will be assessed.

Notes

CHAPTER 3

Teach
Professional Development for Effective Implementation

Life as a teacher begins the day you realize you are always a learner. —Robert John Meehan

Knowledge is not power; implementation is power. —Garrison Wynn

There was a meme I recently came across online. It said, "I hate when I think I'm buying organic vegetables, but when I get home, I discover they're regular donuts." How many times have we created goals for ourselves (in this case, to eat more vegetables) and come up with a plan of action (make a healthier grocery list, source recipes), even going so far as to bring the vegetables home and put them in the crisper drawer? We *know* how to eat healthier, but what we *do* often doesn't align with that information.

I think about that quote all the time now when designing professional development or working with teams who in turn provide information to staff. We have been aware of the disconnect between knowledge and implementation for millennia. This knowing-doing gap can take the clearest vision and simply make it words on a page, lacking real meaning to impact both staff and students. Implementation doesn't stop with the initial professional development. To maximize the likelihood that implementation will occur and continue to enhance practice, campuses must plan beyond those first few hours of training. To close this gap, leaders and coaches must work together to intentionally build a system of ongoing support to relentlessly drive implementation forward.

Once your leadership team of coaches and administrators has created a plan for overcoming initial barriers to adopting new practice, chosen a classroom management model, and communicated expectations to your staff, you can begin to build your implementation plan and further define your coaching program to support your classroom management model. As part of this planning, you will:

- Communicate expectations for the three-part target.
- Develop a training plan for the classroom management model.
  - Schedule training sessions and mini professional developments.
  - Assign or ask for volunteers to teach the different aspects of the model and lead discussion sessions.
  - Plan for new teacher orientation to the classroom management model.
- Clarify the role of the coach and train coaches on how best to support the classroom management model within all three tiers.

COMMUNICATE EXPECTATIONS AND YOUR THREE-PART TARGET TO STAFF

In Chapter 2, you began thinking about how you will use a three-part target to introduce your classroom management model to staff and clarify your expectations for its successful implementation. As a reminder, a three-part target includes clarifying three major categories of expectations for teachers' individual classroom management plans:

- What practitioners should know
- What practitioners should do
- How implementation will be measured

For each of these categories (Know, Do, Measure), we supply a sample exhibit to share with teachers and a more detailed rationale with talking points you can use when presenting the material to staff.

Know

What do you want your practitioners to know about the model?

Introduce the model, explain how it was chosen, and identify those critical pieces that you want your practitioners to learn first and retain the longest. Reproducibles 3.1 and 3.2 (pp. 55 and 56, respectively) are sample handouts you can use or adapt to introduce key concepts to your staff. If using these reproducibles, schedule at least 60 to 90 minutes to go over each one. This will allow time for you to present key information

Reproducible 3.1 *Key Concepts of the CHAMPS Model*

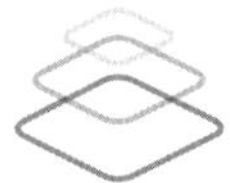

Key Concepts of the CHAMPS Model

1. Our model for classroom and behavior management is the CHAMPS approach.
2. What is the CHAMPS approach?
   A. The CHAMPS approach is not a canned discipline plan.
   B. CHAMPS is a decision-making template.
   C. CHAMPS walks teachers through the process of developing a comprehensive classroom management plan.
   D. As you build or revise your management plan, take into account the following factors:
      1. Your personal style
      2. Your students' need for support (high, medium, or low)
      3. The school and teacher effectiveness literature (CHAMPS has done this for you—everything in CHAMPS is based on the research literature)
3. The CHAMPS approach encourages you to experiment with five major categories of procedures—variables that can be easily remembered with the acronym STOIC.
   - *Structure* for success.
   - *Teach* expectations.
   - *Observe* and monitor.
   - *Interact positively.*
   - *Correct fluently*—respond to misbehavior calmly, consistently, briefly, and immediately.
4. The only absolute rule within the CHAMPS approach is this: All people should be treated with dignity and respect. Techniques such as humiliation or belittlement of students should never be part of any educator's repertoire.
5. All teachers are expected to read *CHAMPS: A Proactive and Positive Approach to Classroom Management* (3rd ed.) or, for high school staff, *Discipline in the Secondary Classroom* (4th ed.). Teachers are also expected to participate in professional development activities to learn the CHAMPS approach. A schedule of training opportunities will be provided.

Reproducible 3.2 *Introduction to the STOIC Framework*

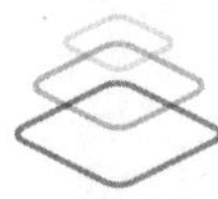

Introduction to the STOIC Framework

sto•ic Someone admired for patience and endurance in the face of adversity.

The five variables of STOIC provide a compact summary of the methods used by effective classroom managers to encourage responsible behavior. Teachers can adapt these variables to build or revise their classroom management plan.

S

Structure for Success

Identify any changes in physical arrangements, scheduling, procedures, supervision patterns, and so on that may have a positive effect on behavior.

T

Teach Expectations

Identify a plan to teach students to function successfully in the structure you have created. This can be as simple as a goal discussion or as involved as daily modeling and rehearsal of responsible behavior. The intervention plan must address when, where, and how positive expectations will be taught to the student.

Observe and Monitor

- Short term—circulate through and scan the room continually.
- Long term—collect data to determine progress (or lack thereof) across time.

I

Interact Positively

- Provide noncontingent attention by greeting and showing an interest in the student.
- Provide contingent attention in the form of frequent positive feedback on behavioral and academic effort. When students are meeting your expectations, following your procedures, and engaging appropriately in academic tasks, provide age-appropriate positive feedback. This can be verbal, written, or (to a limited extent) nonverbal. Your positive feedback should be specific, contingent, and nonembarrassing. In particular, look for opportunities to praise students for exhibiting the expectations that have been taught.
- Maintain at least a 3:1 ratio of positive to corrective interactions. Be sure that students are getting, on average, at least three times more attention when engaged and exhibiting expected behaviors than when off task and violating expectations.

Correct Fluently

Respond to misbehavior calmly, consistently, briefly, and immediately. Always correct respectfully. Determine how you will react to each type of misbehavior that may be related to this problem. Your goal is to be on "automatic pilot" when correcting any chronic misbehavior so you can keep your focus on instruction and on building positive relationships with targeted and nontargeted students.

 REPRODUCIBLE 3.2

and for questions and discussion. The content of the memos could be discussed together as part of a staff development or early-release day. Alternatively, they could be presented as the primary agenda items during successive staff meetings. Plan to revisit on an ongoing basis key parts of the model that staff must know.

The talking points that follow will help you present and explain each of the concepts in the handouts.

Professional Development Note

Please note that these reproducibles and corresponding talking points do not take the place of quality professional development. Later in this chapter, we discuss possible training sequences. What's included here is simply to help introduce CHAMPS and the expectations for staff, who will be trained through a much more comprehensive implementation model.

Talking Points for the CHAMPS Introduction *(Reproducible 3.1)*

Introduce the model and explain how it was chosen:

> *As we've outlined, effective classroom management is integral to student achievement. Research literature clearly shows what effective teachers do to manage classes that less effective or struggling teachers tend not to do.*

1 Our model for classroom and behavior management is the CHAMPS approach.

Provide your staff with information on the who, what, when, and why of the model. *Who* adopted the model? Is it a districtwide or schoolwide initiative? *What* is it all about? The *when* should include some information on the history of CHAMPS use. Is this the first year or third year? Has the program (or one like it) been used before in the building or district? The *why* should address the importance of having a common language, a shared way of looking at classroom management to ensure consistency of communication, philosophy, and training. For any kind of coaching support to work, a common classroom management model that all educators can reference and use as a baseline must exist.

2 What is CHAMPS?

This section describes what CHAMPS is and is not. It gives staff who are unfamiliar with CHAMPS a preliminary understanding of the model and a sense of the direction in which they will be heading.

A. CHAMPS is not a canned discipline plan.

Let staff know that they will not be required to implement a set of procedures. Some may be worried that they will have to establish a token economy or correct misbehaviors in preestablished ways. Reassure them that nothing could be further from the truth—they will not be compelled to follow canned procedures.

B. *CHAMPS is a decision-making template.*

CHAMPS is designed to guide the teacher in creating or revising a classroom management plan to address everything included in the plans of the most effective teachers. Experienced teachers will find that they are already effectively implementing many of the techniques specified within CHAMPS. However, even the most experienced teacher can develop ideas for improving. For example, one of the tasks within CHAMPS is to implement an effective and efficient end-of-class routine, specifying the goals or outcomes the routine will accomplish. If a teacher's current ending routine accomplishes those goals, the teacher need not make any changes. However, if any of the ending-routine goals are not being met, the teacher can change the routine to accomplish those particular goals—which leads to the following:

C. *Any time student behavior is a problem, experiment with one or more aspects of your CHAMPS classroom management plan.*

Because CHAMPS is not a canned system of steps but rather a problem-solving model, when issues with student behavior occur, the CHAMPS approach can help teachers identify variables they can manipulate to affect student behavior in a positive way. (This is not manipulation in the sense of manipulating students to get what you want, but rather of manipulating or tweaking the conditions over which you do have some control in a school environment to bring about better results from your students. CHAMPS is built on a commonsense acknowledgment that you can no more control your students than you can a spouse or sibling.) Make one or more adjustments, observe what happens, and then analyze the results. If the first "experiment" doesn't work, you can always experiment with other variables.

This concept of experimentation can be a major stress reducer for teachers facing daily challenges in class. One big factor in all people's feelings of stress (not just teachers) is the degree of control they have over a situation. Studies in business, for example, have shown that secretaries experience more stress on average than bosses because they have less control over the decisions that are made. Faced with students who misbehave, a teacher who has little knowledge of classroom management may get angry or perhaps even resort to yelling at the students. If this doesn't work (and there is very low probability that it will), the teacher may embark on a "more-of-the-same" cycle of escalation, getting louder and angrier as the weeks go by. (To see this is to be reminded of Albert Einstein's definition of insanity: doing the same thing over and over again and expecting different results.)

With the CHAMPS approach, you can let teachers know that you do not expect them to "control" student behavior. Instead, you will expect them to try manipulating some of the variables within CHAMPS. If one experiment does not improve the situation, they should try something different.

D. *As you build or revise your management plan, take into account your personal style, your students' need for structure, and the school and teacher effectiveness literature.*

As you talk with your teachers about this section, let them know that, as they make decisions about their management plan, they should take into account their own personal style. Some teachers like a very quiet classroom while other teachers can tolerate higher levels of noise. Let your staff know that as long as the noise does not bother neighboring classrooms, the level of noise is entirely each teacher's professional choice. Likewise, the amount of movement in the room factors into personal style; some teachers like to allow a lot of movement while others have less tolerance for movement. These choices will be up to the teacher.

In addition to the teacher's personal style, the needs of the students must be considered. Each group of students has a personality all its own. Some groups can function responsibly in a classroom that has relatively little structure—a room with lots of noise, lots of movement, and only moderate amounts of teacher orchestration. Other groups are comparatively immature. If excess noise or movement is present, such groups will tend to escalate to even more noise and movement that may border on or cross into aggression. Consequently, with this group of students the teacher will need to structure more tightly (for example, choose activities that have less potential for students to get overly excited) and orchestrate activities more carefully. The teacher will have to teach expectations more precisely and with more repetition, observe more carefully, and provide both positive interactions and calm, consistent corrections more frequently.

The third variable that teachers should take into account as they design their plan is how teacher effectiveness literature relates to behavior management. If you've adopted the CHAMPS model, you have ensured that teachers who work through the *CHAMPS* or *DSC* book will be guided to make choices that conform to the research literature. For staff members who are interested, point them to this book's Appendix or to original research studies that synthesize findings from the teacher effectiveness literature (e.g., Marzano et al., 2003).

CHAMPS encourages you to experiment with five major categories of procedures (STOIC).

This item identifies the broad variables that teachers can manipulate to build or revise their classroom management plan. The five all-encompassing variables of STOIC provide a compact summary of the methods used by effective classroom managers to encourage responsible behavior. As you share this concept with the staff, note that effective classroom management is conceptually simple (only five variables) yet incredibly complex (a lifelong learning task). Reproducible 3.2 introduces the STOIC variables.

Use of the STOIC acronym creates a common language among staff members. This shared conceptual framework is the beginning of enhanced communication and comprehension. Educators attuned to the nuances of this language can clearly identify any aspect of a classroom dynamic and quickly zero in on the variables they might manipulate or experiment with to have a positive effect on student behavior. As teachers participate in professional development, solve problems, and set personal improvement goals, encourage them to use the STOIC variables as a guide for thinking and talking about student behavior.

The only absolute rule within CHAMPS is this: All people should be treated with dignity and respect. Techniques such as humiliation or belittlement of students should never be part of any educator's repertoire.

This is included to allow you to inform staff that while CHAMPS encourages experimentation with different techniques and strategies—variables, in other words—one category is off limits: disrespecting students. While the vast majority of teachers do not need to be reminded of this, a few may (consciously or unconsciously) berate and belittle students, publicly embarrass students, or engage in destructive sarcasm. Emphasize unequivocally that disrespectful interactions are an abuse of the teacher's inherent power position and a destroyer of student self-esteem and motivation—and not just of the targeted student. A mean-spirited or hurtful comment affects not only the student to whom it is addressed, but all students who hear it. It's worth sharing the following quote by Haim Ginott with your staff as you discuss this foundational concept:

> *I've come to the frightening conclusion that I am the decisive element in the classroom. It is my personal approach that creates the climate. It's my daily mood that makes the weather. As a teacher, I possess a tremendous power to make a child's life miserable or joyous. I can be a tool of torture or an instrument of inspiration. I can humiliate or humor, hurt or heal. In all situations, it is my response that decides whether a crisis will be escalated or de-escalated and a child humanized or dehumanized.*

Sarcasm is a gray area. Some teachers think that sarcasm is a reasonable way to interact with students. This may be the case if the teacher is skillful, sensitive, and humane. As a rule of thumb, effective humor brings people closer together while ineffective humor creates greater distance between people. In sports, the inspirational basketball coach may use sarcasm occasionally to tease players. That same coach will be sensitive enough to know that when team members are discouraged or a particular player appears despondent in practice, the time is not right for sarcastic comments; more encouraging techniques are warranted. Let your staff know that if they are going to use sarcasm, they should be consciously aware of what they are doing, avoid overusing it, and kid around only with students who are cognitively and linguistically sophisticated enough to know that they are not being insulted or demeaned in any way.

All teachers are expected to read *CHAMPS: A Proactive and Positive Approach to Classroom Management* (3rd ed.), or for high school staff, *Discipline in the Secondary Classroom* (4th ed.), and participate in professional development activities to learn the CHAMPS approach. A schedule of training opportunities will be provided.

Let your staff know you want them to participate actively during professional development and training sessions, not because you think they are bad managers of their classes but because you expect that all staff, no matter how experienced, will continually strive to become more effective in their classroom management. Two hallmarks of professionalism are professional autonomy and continual improvement. Promote the first and expect the second. Think of it this way: None of us wants to visit a physician who stopped learning and refining their craft a decade ago.

Do

What Do You Want Your Practitioners to Implement From the Model?

In addition to explaining CHAMPS as the adopted classroom management model, you want to be sure that your teachers know what you expect them to do with this knowledge. Communicating this part of the target clarifies what work you want teachers to turn in to you and what you expect to see when you go into classrooms for observations and formal evaluations. Reproducibles 3.3 (for grades K–8, shown on p. 62) and 3.4 (for grades 9–12, available to download) are one-page handouts you can provide to supply information regarding the minimum expectations for implementation.

NOTE: In this section of the target (Do), be mindful to explicitly state how something is to be implemented if you are aiming for a standard of consistency. For example, if you expect all teachers to use the CHAMPS acronym when posting and teaching expectations, let them know in advance. In this example, if you determine that teachers must post a visual of CHAMPS expectations, you may end up with some teachers creating elaborate laminated posters displayed at the front of the room while other teachers print out an 8.5" x 11" sheet of paper and thumbtack it haphazardly on a bulletin board partially hidden by a filing cabinet. While the third part of the target, the measurements, will certainly speak to creating consistency between classrooms while allowing teacher autonomy, if you have standard specifications in mind, communicate them here.

Reproducible 3.3 *CHAMPS Implementation Requirements*

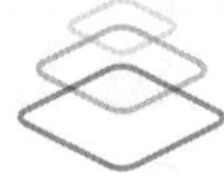

CHAMPS
Implementation Requirements (Grades K–8)

What you need to do ◀ ▶ What I hope to see

1. ***Structure*** your classroom for success (*CHAMPS* [3rd ed.], Chapters 2 and 3).
    - ▶ Complete your Classroom Management Plan (Reproducible 1.1, Chapter 1, Task 3).
2. ***Teach*** your expectations—clarify and communicate them to students (Chapter 4).
    - A. Post expectations for each major instructional activity as it occurs, including teacher-directed instruction, independent seatwork, cooperative groups, and tests.
    - B. Reinforce your expectations in a variety of ways:
        - ▶ Posters on permanent display
        - ▶ CHAMPS display on screen
        - ▶ CHAMPS wall chart
        - ▶ Flip chart
        - ▶ Other
3. ***Observe*** and monitor student behavior (Chapters 5 and 10).
    - A. Physically circulate.
    - B. Visually scan.
    - C. Collect and analyze data.
4. ***Interact*** positively by providing praise and noncontingent attention (Chapters 6 and 7).
    - A. Strive to create a positive classroom climate and positive relationships with students.
    - B. Supply positive feedback, intermittent celebrations of success, and (as needed) structured reward systems.
    - C. Maintain at least a 3:1 ratio of attention to positive behavior to attention to negative behavior. (Note that this is an average; there is nothing inherently wrong with a short interval in which the ratio is skewed to the corrective side.)
5. ***Correct*** misbehavior fluently (Chapter 8).
    - A. Get back to instruction as quickly and as seamlessly as possible.
    - B. Be calm, consistent, brief, and immediate.

NOTE: The goal is positive student behavior. As long as students are respectful and actively engaged in your instructional activities, you are implementing the CHAMPS approach successfully.

 REPRODUCIBLE 3.3

Talking Points for CHAMPS Implementation *(Reproducibles 3.3, 3.4)*

Reproducibles 3.3 and 3.4 are organized around the STOIC acronym to make your expectations easy for your staff to remember and to connect with CHAMPS and your schoolwide vision of classroom management. These are our recommendations to maximize effectiveness.

1 **Structure your classroom for success.**

When required to complete a personalized classroom management plan, teachers will have to make basic decisions about their classroom rules, procedures for managing student work, how they will monitor student behavior, and so on. Staff should be encouraged to read and refer to *CHAMPS* or *DSC* as they are completing these documents. Ask teachers to hand in the completed document to you at the beginning of the year.

2 **Teach your expectations—clarify and communicate them to students.**

Chapters 2 and 3 of *CHAMPS* and *DSC* are devoted to the essential tasks of clarifying in detail how the teacher wants students to behave during instructional activities and transitions. By completing the CHAMPS worksheets in these chapters, the teacher is forced to make decisions about exactly what they want from students. We often hear from experienced teachers that completing the CHAMPS worksheets helped them identify assumptions they had unwittingly been making about what students should know regarding how to behave.

By posting expectations, the teacher clarifies them not just to students but to you and other classroom observers. A principal, administrator, or coach cannot tell if students are meeting the teacher's expectations without knowing what those expectations are. Remember that CHAMPS allows a lot of flexibility for teachers to design their classroom plans around their own style and the needs of their students. This means that, for example, in one teacher's classroom students may be required to raise their hand and wait to be called on, while in another teacher's classroom they can speak up as long as they do not interrupt another speaker. Unless these expectations are posted, you as an observer will not know whether student behavior is acceptable or not.

3 **Observe and monitor student behavior.**

If teachers are systematically observing student behavior, they can make informed choices about when and how to provide positive feedback and when and how to correct misbehavior. If the teacher is not systematically observing, hundreds of opportunities to notice positive student behavior are missed. This could result in students developing an attitude of "Why should I bother to do what the teacher wants me to? They never even notice if I do." Without observation, students will learn that their minor misbehaviors are not noticed. For some students, this will accelerate quickly into major misbehavior.

In addition, the teacher who systematically observes by visually scanning and physically circulating throughout the room prompts students to behave responsibly. (While driving, for example, we all travel the speed limit when a police car is in view. We also all remember the teacher with whom we could not get away with anything—"she had eyes in the back of her head.") Frequent and careful observing is an essential classroom management skill. Let teachers know that you expect them to be consciously aware of everything that is going on in all parts of the room, regardless of the type of activity taking place at the time.

Another benefit to teachers of consciously observing is gaining a more objective view of progress in the classroom. That is the reason that you will occasionally assign self-assessment tools (*CHAMPS* or *DSC* Chapter 10) as described in Chapter 4 of this book, or tools revolving around the Basic 5 Benchmarks, as described in Chapter 7.

4 **Interact positively by providing praise and noncontingent attention.**

Teachers are expected to strive to interact with students more frequently when students are behaving well than when they are misbehaving. Even excellent teachers can fall into patterns of paying more attention to misbehavior than to positive behavior. With this item, you are alerting staff to the fact that you expect them to strive for a 3:1 ratio of interactions (or better). That is, the teacher should be engaging in at least three positive interactions (noncontingent attention and attention to appropriate behavior) for every reprimand or correction given to inappropriate behavior.

Emphasize that correcting students is not bad or wrong—in fact, to be consistent, it is essential. Correctives are a problem only if they exceed the positives, because students may learn that the easiest way to get adult attention (for which some students are desperate) is to do something that annoys the adult.

A final reason to emphasize positive interactions is that the way the teacher interacts with the students is the defining variable in whether a classroom is a positive and motivating setting or an oppressive and negative one.

5 **Correct misbehavior fluently.**

What is done to correct misbehavior is actually of less importance than that *something* is done in a manner that allows instruction to continue. For example, if during teacher-directed instruction, a student makes a disrespectful comment and the teacher matter-of-factly states, "That was disrespectful—I would like to speak to you after class. Now, class, the next paragraph states . . .," the flow of the lesson is maintained. On the other hand, if the teacher immediately takes the student into the hall or gets into an argument about assigning detention, the flow of the lesson is lost.

If teachers strive for fluency, they will find that they are less likely to get into power struggles with students and also that the momentum of a lesson can frequently reduce and eliminate most misbehavior.

This section also provides tips for striving to be immediate (nip the problem in the bud), brief (we frequently talk too much), respectful (never belittle students), calm (naked emotion from the teacher can ruin instructional flow and may be reinforcing to some students), and consistent ("getting away with it" is inherently reinforcing and fun).

Measure

What Will Be Used to Measure the Effectiveness of Implementation?

The Basic 5 Behavior Benchmarks (Reproducible 3.5) provide general guidance for the minimum standard that should be met in any classroom. These benchmarks allow teachers, coaches, and administrators to analyze classroom data with clear goals in mind.

An expanded explanation of the Basic 5 and additional strategies to increase each benchmark are discussed in the Tier 2 section of the book, in Chapter 7. Communicating these standards at the beginning of the year will give your staff a standard bar of measurement while allowing for autonomy from classroom to classroom.

Without a standard set of benchmarks, we often set up a culture of mediocrity. There are times teachers are assessed stylistically, that is, in relation to how their evaluator would conduct whatever activity is being observed. When a teacher has the same teaching style as the evaluator, that teacher may receive high evaluations that aren't necessarily grounded in objective effectiveness data. At other times, teachers are evaluated comparatively to one another. As long as the teacher is perceived as being better in practice than other teachers at the same grade level, in the same field, or even across the hall, they, too, receive high evaluations. Being evaluated either stylistically or comparatively can set teachers up in a state of mediocrity. They may even avoid seeking coaching to improve performance because it does not truly measure if their practice is effective or not.

Setting concrete benchmarks also protects the teacher's autonomy to engage in professional decision-making. If a teacher is hitting a predetermined objective benchmark and students are academically achieving, that teacher should be free to set up the classroom in whatever way is best for their personality, the unique needs of their students, the content or grade level they teach, and even the time of day in which they are providing instruction. The autonomy to make decisions based on these considerations is crucial for professionals; the consistency of an objective benchmark is what ensures everyone is striving to hit a shared standard for a highly successful classroom.

Reproducible 3.5 *Basic 5 Behavior Benchmarks*

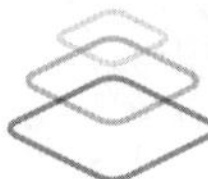

Basic 5 Behavior Benchmarks

Level 3 = Stop (do something different)
Level 2 = Caution (intervention recommended)
Level 1 = Keep going (keep doing what you're doing)

BENCHMARK	LEVEL 3	LEVEL 2	LEVEL 1	DATA COLLECTION TOOL
Ratio of Interactions (positive to corrective)	Less than 1:1 or less than 1 interaction per minute	At least 1:1 consistently	At least 3:1 consistently	Ratio of Interactions Monitoring Form (Reproducible 10.1) • 30-minute recording time • Any activity • Use for individual or classwide monitoring
Opportunities to Respond (per 10-minute interval)	Fewer than 10	10 to 40	More than 40	Opportunities to Respond Observation Sheet (Reproducible 10.2) • 10-minute recording time • Use during teacher-guided instruction • Use for individual or classwide monitoring
Disruptions (per 10-minute interval)	More than 10	5 to 10	Fewer than 5	Misbehavior Recording Sheets (Reproducibles 10.3A and 10.3B) • Use for duration of one activity or entire period • Any activity • Use for classwide monitoring
On-Task Behavior	Less than 80%	80% to 89%	90% to 100%	On-Task Behavior Observation Sheet (Reproducible 10.4) • 5-minute recording time • Any independent work time • Use for classwide monitoring
Alignment with Expectations	Less than 80%	80% to 89%	90% to 100%	CHAMPS Versus Daily Reality Scale (Reproducible 10.6) • Use for duration of one activity or entire period • Any activity • Use for classwide monitoring

 REPRODUCIBLE 3.5

Talking Points for CHAMPS Assessment *(Reproducible 3.6)*

While your benchmarks will be defined at the district or campus level, these are our recommendations based on the effective schools literature. Reproducible 3.6, Basic 5 at a Glance, summarizes each of these benchmarks for easy reference by classroom observers.

If data are collected and a teacher is already reaching these goals, remember that the broader goal is continuous improvement. Educators should continue to look for ways to tweak classroom management practices to continue maximizing student success.

Ratio of Interactions

Along with proactively teaching expectations, the single most effective step teachers can take to connect with their students and improve overall classroom climate is to increase the number of positive interactions they have with each student relative to corrective interactions—their *ratio of interactions*. A teacher who is fixated too much on misbehavior could be inadvertently perpetuating it. Positive interactions are defined as *both noncontingent positive interactions and contingent positive praise that draws attention to students' positive behaviors*. Teachers should strive to maintain a 3:1 ratio of positive to corrective interactions.

2 Opportunities to Respond

Increasing students' opportunities to respond academically correlates to an increase in on-task behavior as well as opportunities for the teacher to provide positive feedback. An opportunity to respond (OTR) is defined as *an instructional question, statement, or gesture made by the teacher seeking a verbal, written, or action-based response from students*. Measured during teacher-guided instruction, the goal is to offer approximately 40 or more OTRs per 10-minute block of instruction. This number may be decreased based on the types of responses a teacher provides for students and if a higher level of questioning is being used. For example, a turn-and-talk to grapple with a higher-level question may result in high engagement (another benchmark) while offering fewer OTRs. Generally speaking, if OTRs are measured between 10–39, as long as students are engaged and achievement is high we would consider this measurement adequate for effective instruction.

3 Disruptions

Disruptive behavior can be defined as *a statement or action by one or more students that interferes with an ongoing class activity*. As a general starting point, a disruption is any behavior that causes the teacher to pause or stop the flow of instruction in order to respond. A disruption would also include any behavior that gets another student off task. Disruptions cost teachers valuable instructional minutes. Per 10-minute instructional block, we would hope to see 5 or fewer disruptions.

Reproducible 3.6 *Basic 5 at a Glance*

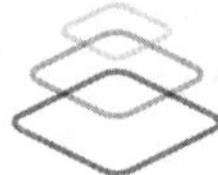

Basic 5 at a Glance

1. **Ratio of Interactions**

   Positive interactions are defined as *both noncontingent positive interactions and contingent positive feedback that draws attention to students' positive behaviors.* Teachers should strive to maintain a 3:1 ratio of positive to corrective interactions. Corrective interactions include any response that draws attention to students' inappropriate behaviors. Note that interactions are considered positive or corrective based on the student's behavior at the time the teacher attends to them.

2. **Opportunities to Respond**

   An opportunity to respond (OTR) is defined as *an instructional question, statement, or gesture made by the teacher seeking a verbal, written, or action-based response from students.* Measured during teacher-guided instruction, the goal is to offer approximately 40+ OTRs per 10-minute block of instruction. This number may be decreased based on the types of responses a teacher provides for students and if a higher level of questioning is being used. Generally speaking, if OTRs are measured between 10–39, as long as students are engaged and achievement is high, we would consider this measurement adequate for effective instruction.

3. **Disruptions**

   Disruptive behavior can be defined as *a statement or action by one or more students that interferes with an ongoing class activity.* As a general starting point, a disruption is any behavior that causes the teacher to pause or stop the flow of instruction in order to respond. A disruption would also include any behavior that gets another student off task. Per 10-minute instructional block, we would hope to see 5 or fewer disruptions.

4. **On-Task Behavior**

   On-task behavior is defined as *a student being academically engaged in the current task of the instructional activity.* During any given activity, the goal for this benchmark should be 90% or more of students actively on task.

5. **Alignment With Expectations**

   This measurement is defined as *the degree to which students have met the teacher's posted expectations.* During any given activity, the goal for this benchmark should be 90% or more of students in alignment with posted expectations.

 REPRODUCIBLE 3.6

4 On-Task Behavior

Every teacher's preferred personal style is respected in CHAMPS, meaning that what's appropriate engagement for one class may be considered off task in another. On-task behavior is defined as *a student being academically engaged in the current task of the instructional activity.* During independent instruction, this may be a student working on their own to complete an assignment, read a text or book, or complete a hands-on project. During teacher-guided instruction, this could look like a student raising their hand, answering a teacher's question, or engaging in an on-topic conversation with a group or partner to answer a given prompt. During any given activity, the goal for this benchmark should be 90% or more of students actively on task.

5 Alignment With Expectations

The need for clear expectations is critical to managing any classroom effectively. This measurement is defined as *the degree to which students have met the teacher's posted expectations.*

While this measures behavioral compliance, expectations should be designed with the intent to maximize instructional minutes. Clearly defined behavioral expectations, when followed, should lead to a greater likelihood for students to engage and be successful in relation to instructional content. During any given activity, the goal for this benchmark should be 90% or more of students in alignment with posted expectations.

Doug Reeves (2006) once stated, "The size and prettiness of the plan is inversely related to the quality of action and the impact on student learning." The three-part target is designed to capture your vision with an intentional summary to help teachers avoid choice paralysis and give coaches a clear starting point when engaging in goal setting with staff. However, don't let a clear target (the science of teaching) distract from the innate ability of many of your teachers to engage in autonomous best practice (the art of teaching).

Let your teachers know that you are not going to be visiting their classrooms with detailed checklists of CHAMPS procedures they must be implementing. Rather, you will observe whether the students are actively and respectfully participating in the lesson. If the activity is teacher directed, you will evaluate whether students are participating in the instruction. If the activity is student directed—say, working on study questions—you will evaluate whether they are on task. If the activity is cooperative groups, you will be looking to see if they are working on the assigned task and interacting respectfully with one another.

You do not want your staff to think of CHAMPS as "one more thing we *have* to do." Rather, they should see it as a way to achieve active and respectful student participation. If a teacher is accomplishing that, make sure they know that you are satisfied with this success—if it isn't broken, you are not going to suggest it be fixed. Keep in mind that the goal of all classroom management models should be to develop a classroom of students who are responsible, motivated, and highly engaged in meaningful tasks. When a teacher has met that standard, celebrate the success of your staff and the unmistakable impact on student achievement.

DEVELOP A TRAINING PLAN FOR TEACHERS

There can be no implementing the CHAMPS approach (or any other model) without quality training for your teachers, the practitioners for the classroom management model. A strong initial introduction and regularly scheduled follow-up professional development sessions will yield better results than a one-time workshop. When combined with coaching from support personnel, results from training will be greatly enhanced. This initial training with ongoing maintenance distributed over time creates opportunities for practitioners to share ideas and work with products such as drafts of schedules and room arrangements. It gives practitioners a chance to try out new techniques and later discuss what worked and what did not.

Initial Training Sessions

Initial training sessions should introduce core components of the classroom management model with additional follow-up sessions to maximize both the rate and effectiveness of implementation. We have tied this recommendation to the model presented in *CHAMPS* and *Discipline in the Secondary Classroom* to serve as concrete examples. These initial and ongoing professional development sessions for *CHAMPS* and *DSC* should be led by qualified consultants from Safe & Civil Schools.

One or two days of training in the summer preceding implementation, with full-day follow-ups. This model can be offered at the building level for an entire faculty, or it can be a district offering for participating teachers from different schools. Teachers are introduced during the summer to tasks that are most essential for setting up their management plan for the first day of school. The focus is on establishing the classroom structure and creating lessons to teach expectations to students. This would emphasize Chapters 2 and 3 in both *CHAMPS* and *DSC*.

In mid-autumn, participants meet to discuss what has worked well and what has not, with new content taught on increasing student motivation (*CHAMPS* and *DSC* Chapters 6 and 7). In midwinter, the group gets back together for another day of discussion with new content on addressing chronic misbehavior (*CHAMPS* and *DSC* Chapter 8). In the spring, the group rejoins to discuss strategies for wrapping up the year and how chronic problems that occurred this year might be used to plan better structure and more detailed lessons for next year.

One or two days of training after the start of the school year, with full-day follow-ups after a few weeks of implementation. This model is very similar to the one described above but considers the more limited time for reflection and the immediacy of putting tasks into practice. Teachers are introduced to the tasks most essential for building their classroom management model in the moment (similar to building an airplane as it's being flown). The focus is on procedures, clarifying and teaching expectations, and building relationships with students. In addition, Safe & Civil Schools consultants work with campuses to identify tasks and suggestions to address any specific needs. Follow-up sessions as described above happen approximately 6–8 weeks from the initial training to allow staff to refine practice and learn new content.

Ongoing Maintenance

Ongoing maintenance and support for the classroom management model should be provided for practitioners throughout the year as part of an effective Tier 1. This part of the training plan should include encouraging teachers to complete periodic self-assessments about their classroom management practices and scheduling brief discussion and practice opportunities in staff meetings to further support training. Ongoing maintenance can be led by district or building personnel with a comprehensive understanding and background in *CHAMPS* and *DSC*.

Monthly faculty study on a particular chapter. This model can be a building-level offering for an entire faculty or a districtwide offering for teachers from different schools. Focusing on a chapter or two each time, the peer discussion tasks are used to emphasize and expand learning from the initial training sessions. These meetings could be conducted on early-release days. Participation by the entire faculty increases the likelihood that the training will favorably affect the culture and climate of the school. Distributing chapters throughout the year allows information to be covered so staff is not overwhelmed with too much content too quickly.

Voluntary study group that meets regularly. Rather than a whole faculty session, this model requires only a small group of motivated staff who can work through the material. Structured presentations are not necessary. Each week, a different participant can be responsible for bringing some snacks and guiding the discussion. These sessions can be conducted weekly, biweekly, or monthly, depending on what the participants find most useful. To guide these sessions, we recommend using the Peer Discussion Worksheets in Chapter 10 (Task 3) of both *CHAMPS* and *DSC*.

Self-assessment. Encourage teachers to self-monitor and reflect on their efficacy periodically. Self-assessments such as Reproducible 3.7, Checklist of Classroom Management Practices, can help teachers judge the degree to which their current management plan and level of structure are working. These data collection tools can be used to get a handle on how instruction is going. If a peer-to-peer coaching model is being used on campus, peers can assist each other in this data collection process and offer coaching assistance to one another.

Reproducible 3.7 *Checklist of Classroom Management Practices (pp. 1–2 of 4)*

Checklist of Classroom Management Practices (p. 1 of 4)

Thanks to Sherry Rogowski and the Guilford County (NC) Public Schools for developing and sharing this checklist.

STOIC VARIABLES		CLASSROOM MANAGEMENT PRACTICES	Y / N	COMMENTS, NOTES, EVIDENCE
Structure your classroom for success	Physical Arrangement	1. I have arranged the room so I can get from any part of the room to any other part relatively efficiently.	☐ ☐	
		2. My students and I can access all materials, work spaces, and the pencil sharpener without disturbing others.	☐ ☐	
	Schedule	3. My schedule provides the appropriate consistency, variety, and physical activity to meet the needs of my students and the academic content.	☐ ☐	
	Attention Signal	4. I have chosen an attention signal that has both a visual and an auditory component and can be used in all settings inside and outside the classroom.	☐ ☐	
	Classroom Rules	5. I have identified three to five specific, observable, and positively stated classroom rules that do not have regular expectations. I have aligned these rules with our schoolwide or classroom expectations (e.g., Guidelines for Success).	☐ ☐	
		6. I have posted my classroom rules in my classroom.	☐ ☐	
		7. I have identified my teacher responses to classroom rule violations.	☐ ☐	

Checklist of Classroom Management Practices (p. 2 of 4)

STOIC VARIABLES		CLASSROOM MANAGEMENT PRACTICES	Y / N	COMMENTS, NOTES, EVIDENCE
Teach students how to be successful in your classroom	Lesson Plans	11. I have created lessons on my classroom rules and explicitly taught them to my class. I have taught students how these rules align with schoolwide or classroom expectations (e.g., Guidelines for Success).	☐ ☐	
		12. I have created lessons for my procedures and routines, and explicitly taught them to the class.	☐ ☐	
		13. I have created lessons for my major expectations for classroom acivities (e.g., teacher-directed instruction, cooperative groups, independent seat work, etc.) and explicitly taught them to the class.	☐ ☐	
		14. I have created lessons and established time expectations (e.g., how long it should take students to move into cooperative groups) for major within-class transitions.	☐ ☐	
	Teaching and Reviewing	15. I have created a schedule of when I will teach and review my attention signal, classroom rules, procedures, routines, and CHAMPS (or ACHIEVE) expectations.	☐ ☐	
		16. I have taught (and reviewed when needed) until at least 90% of students routinely comply with my expectations every day.	☐ ☐	
Observe student behavior	Active Supervision	17. I circulate and scan frequently as a means of observing and monitoring student behavior as it relates to my expectations.	☐ ☐	
	Positive Supervision	18. I model friendly, respectful behavior while monitoring the classroom.	☐ ☐	
	Collecting Data	19. I periodically collect data (e.g., CHAMPS vs. Daily Reality Rating Scale, Ratio of Interactions Monitoring, etc.) to judge what is going well and what needs improvement in my classroom management plan.	☐ ☐	

REPRODUCIBLE 3.7

Reproducible 3.7 (cont.) *Checklist of Classroom Management Practices (pp. 3–4 of 4)*

Checklist of Classroom Management Practices (p. 3 of 4)

STOIC VARIABLES		CLASSROOM MANAGEMENT PRACTICES	Y / N	COMMENTS, NOTES, EVIDENCE
Interact positively	Noncontingent Attention	20. I have a plan for when and how to interact with all of my students in a friendly manner (e.g., stand at the door every day to greet each student, speak to each student at lunch, etc.).	☐ ☐	
		21. I interact frequently with every student in a welcoming manner (e.g., say hello, greet at door, use student's name, talk with students at every opportunity, etc.).	☐ ☐	
	Positive Feedback	22. I frequently use effective positive feedback (i.e., specific, descriptive, accurate, contingent, immediate, age appropriate).	☐ ☐	
	Intermittent Celebrations	23. I have a plan for using intermittent celebrations with individual students and the entire class.	☐ ☐	
		24. I have a plan to use classwide motivation systems when needed.	☐ ☐	

Checklist of Classroom Management Practices (p. 4 of 4)

STOIC VARIABLES		CLASSROOM MANAGEMENT PRACTICES	Y / N	COMMENTS, NOTES, EVIDENCE
Correct fluently	Respond Fluently	26. I correct student misbehavior consistently.	☐ ☐	
		27. I correct student misbehavior calmly.	☐ ☐	
		28. I correct student misbehavior immediately.	☐ ☐	
		29. I correct student misbehavior briefly.	☐ ☐	
		30. I correct student misbehavior respectfully by using appropriate tone of voice, nonverbal communication, personal space, etc.	☐ ☐	
		31. I understand how to recognize and avoid power struggles.	☐ ☐	
		32. I understand and use graceful exits (e.g., take a personal timeout) when I find myself in a power struggle with a student.	☐ ☐	
	Preplanned Responses	33. I have a menu of in-class teacher responses that can be applied to a variety of early-stage misbehavior not covered by my rules.	☐ ☐	
		34. I have a plan for how to respond to different types of misbehavior fluently.	☐ ☐	
		35. I develop and implement behavior intervention plans when necessary for a student who displays chronic misbehavior.	☐ ☐	
		36. I understand teacher-managed versus office-managed behavior as defined by my school.	☐ ☐	
		37. I understand and follow the procedures defined by my school for documenting minor misbehavior (teacher managed) in my classroom.	☐ ☐	
		38. I understand and follow the procedures defined by my school for referring students to the office for major misbehaviors.	☐ ☐	

REPRODUCIBLE 3.7

Encourage staff to incorporate these self-assessments into their planning calendars. Plan to remind staff by sending memos to conduct self-assessments or add in agenda prompts to debrief these activities during a meeting. Staff members who are struggling can receive additional coaching support on request without waiting for an extrinsic evaluator to assess classroom practice.

Mini professional development sessions. In addition to providing ongoing guidance in implementing the CHAMPS approach, scheduling mini PD (professional development) sessions will offer periodic discussion and practice opportunities to give staff members a chance to apply what they've learned. This chapter provides 22 examples of discussion topics and situational practice opportunities that can be addressed at any point during the school year. These include guided discussion topics that link to content in *CHAMPS*, discussion of self-assessment activities, and hypothetical classroom situations with guided tasks and questions. These mini PDs do not take the place of initial and ongoing training provided by a highly qualified professional developer. Instead, they serve as reminders of critical elements of best practice.

Mini PDs are helpful for several reasons. First, they serve to notify staff that classroom management is important and worth thinking about on a regular basis. Conducting the sessions communicates that those who are leading implementation recognize that classroom management is complicated, with few right or wrong answers, and that by discussing and learning together, the professional staff can learn a lot from one another. The act of exploring the relative efficacy of alternative approaches as a group gives these short agenda items their strength. Instead of right answers, the sessions create opportunities to remind staff that all students must be treated with dignity and respect. They also serve as regular reminders that administrators, as the evaluative cornerstone, will be looking at classroom management issues when conducting walk-throughs and that coaches are available to help with any and all difficulties, from classwide management issues to individual behavior plans.

These activities can be as brief as 5- to 10-minute agenda items. They can occur during staff meetings or in grade-level or departmental meetings as infrequently as once per quarter or as frequently as once a week. The advantage of conducting them during staff meetings is that the agenda can be controlled by those leading the discussion, which ensures that these agenda items will be discussed—and that they won't drag on too long. Disadvantages, perhaps, are the competition with so much other business that must be discussed during staff meetings and the difficulty of keeping a large staff actively involved.

Grade-level or departmental meetings come with a different set of trade-offs. More people will have a chance to participate actively, but administrators and coaches won't be able to attend every meeting. As a result, staff might not get around to the discussion and practice sessions. Ensuring that the management ideas generated are those administration can support also becomes a greater challenge.

If the school has scheduled early-release structures for regular inservice and planning, mini professional development can be a highly productive part of these sessions. Even if the scheduled topic is on instruction or curriculum, a 10-minute discussion can be a great way to create variety and link instruction to classroom management. Remember that a strong positive correlation exists between effective classroom management and increased student achievement. As a campus works to enhance instruction, every extra minute that can be wrung from the schedule, every set of student eyes and ears that can be redirected to the teacher, is a point scored for academic achievement.

Consider sharing responsibility for the discussion. If the administrator chairs the first session, assign subsequent discussions to members of grade-level or department teams. In an elementary school, for instance, each of the grade levels could be assigned two topics per year. The specialists (PE, music, library, technology, and so forth) could be assigned two topics, and the special education teachers could take two more. This would cover anywhere from 14–18 of the topics listed. In a large secondary school, each major department could be assigned three topics, with those further divided among sub-teams so that everyone on staff eventually participates. The built-in advantage is that when everyone has a leadership role, everyone has more of an investment in making the process work.

Discussions should be kept fun and active. Encourage this by asking participants to show interest and engage the session leader.

Following are 22 possible topic titles for classroom management discussions, enough to anchor mini PD throughout the entire school year.

Mini PD Forms

Reproducible handouts for each topic are shown on pages 77–98 and provided for download as both PDFs and Word documents that you can customize (see p. 4 for download directions).

1. Finalizing Your Classroom Management Plan
2. Is Your Classroom Management Plan Structured Enough?
3. Making Positive Family Contact
4. Refusal to Follow Directions
5. Monitoring Ratios of Interactions*
6. Brainstorming Interventions for a Class That Is Not Responding to the Attention Signal
7. Recording Misbehavior*
8. When and When Not to Use a Disciplinary Referral
9. Grade Book Analysis*
10. Introducing a Rule After the Start of the School Year
11. Re-Teaching Expectations Throughout the Year
12. Welcoming a New Student to the Classroom
13. A Well-Behaved Class Misbehaves With a Guest Speaker
14. Brainstorming Interventions for a Target of Chronic Teasing
15. Self-Evaluation of Teacher-Directed Instruction*
16. Responding to an Emotional Outburst From a New Student
17. Recording On-Task Behavior*
18. Responding to the Class Clown
19. How to Respond to a Student Who Is Sleeping in Class

20. Would a Student Be Likely to Report a Serious Problem to an Adult?
21. Maintaining Student Motivation During the Last Month of School
22. Family or Student Satisfaction Survey*

*Data collection tools from Chapter 10 in *CHAMPS* or *DSC* correspond to these topics. Prior to the mini PD session, ask teachers or grade-level or content area teams to complete the appropriate tool in advance of the whole staff session.

You can follow these topics linearly or select pertinent ones based on data analysis. Keep in mind that these are only ideas, and we encourage leadership teams and smaller learning communities to consider this format when addressing other issues that may arise during the year. Each mini PD follows a fairly simple lesson plan format. While variations of these formats are apparent within each inservice, leadership teams should feel free to use or adjust these components at will. Mini PD sessions that ask for staff involvement are a useful tool to solve problems for which staff input would be helpful.

The administrator, who will most likely be the evaluator, is responsible for ensuring that training is available and that participants actually participate and implement the assignments in their classrooms. One of the best ways to do this is to drop in on training sessions. If this approach is new to an administrator, the administrator should plan to participate actively in all the training sessions and go into classrooms to try out the assignments firsthand.

Orientation for New Teachers

After the training program is up and running, you will need to develop a plan for teaching the CHAMPS model to new staff members who missed the initial training sessions. If the district has made a commitment to the CHAMPS approach, a districtwide plan for new teacher induction may already be in place. If not, develop an orientation plan for new teachers to introduce CHAMPS and offer ongoing training. An orientation plan should also provide guidance for coaches in how to support and mentor new staff. Mentoring first-year and relocated teachers makes a demonstrable difference to any school's long-term success.

If only a few new teachers have joined the staff, encourage them to read *CHAMPS* or *DSC* and meet regularly with a coach or mentor to help with implementation. If more than a few teachers have come onboard, it may be worthwhile to bring a qualified consultant in again, mirroring the training full staff received during the first year of implementation.

Finally, the self-assessment assignments and mini PDs at staff meetings discussed earlier can be modified to maintain an ongoing dialogue about classroom management and discipline issues. Discussions and thought exercises can help new staff become familiar with the classroom management model adopted for your school or district.

Creating an intentional long-term training plan for practitioners is critical. Regardless of the research behind the CHAMPS approach (or any other model), teachers tasked

Reproducible 3.8A *Finalizing Your Classroom Management Plan*

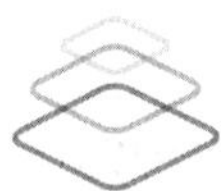

Finalizing Your Classroom Management Plan

CLASSROOM MANAGEMENT MINI-INSERVICE

Objectives

1. To encourage reflection on strengths of your current management plan.
2. To learn ideas from colleagues about their strengths.
3. To "brag" a bit about our great colleagues.

Reflection (2 minutes)

Following is a list of topics from the CHAMPS Classroom Management Plan. Identify one that you believe to be a major strength in your plan and make some notes about your methods with regard to that topic. Prepare to report about this strength—what you have developed or what you do with students.

- Guidelines for Success
- Posted rules
- Attention signal
- Expectations for classroom activities and transitions
- Procedures for family contact
- Procedures for managing student assignments
- Procedures for managing student technology use
- Long-range goal
- Procedures for interacting with and encouraging students
- Correction procedures for misbehavior

Small group exchange (5 minutes)

Have teachers divide into groups of six to eight staff members, most of whom they do not work with regularly. Each person will briefly summarize their procedure or idea.

Optional large group report (3 minutes)

If you learned a great idea from a colleague or are planning to visit a colleague's classroom, let the whole group know this. (For example, "Brad has incorporated his CHAMPS expectations into his first literature theme and has a bulletin board in the room that he said I could come and see after this meeting.")

REMINDER Coaches are available within the building to serve as a sounding board, conduct demo lessons, help with data collection, observe, and provide collaborative, nonevaluative feedback.

 REPRODUCIBLE 3.8A

Reproducible 3.8B *Is Your Classroom Management Plan Structured Enough?*

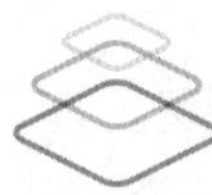

Is Your Classroom Management Plan Structured Enough?

CLASSROOM MANAGEMENT MINI-INSERVICE

Objectives

1. To encourage reflection on your current management plan.
2. To explore ideas about re-teaching expectations and increasing the structure.

Reflection

Consider whether your current classroom management plan is working the way you expected. Consider the frequency and intensity of any misbehavior. Think about how well the class as a whole participates in teacher-directed lessons. Ask yourself how well the class stays on task during independent work periods and cooperative groups.

Large group brainstorming (5 minutes)

Improving a problem class: Without sharing personal reflections about your class, help others by sharing ideas about how to improve a class's behavior at this point in the school year. Remember the rules of brainstorming: We will not evaluate any ideas, but anyone can ask a "Could you explain that some more?" type of question.

Large group brainstorming (5 minutes)

Improving the behavior of one student: Without sharing personal reflections about their class, ask teachers to help others by sharing any ideas about what a teacher might do to help one student improve their behavior if the rest of the class is highly responsible.

Optional large group brainstorming (3 minutes)

Encourage a highly responsible class: Without sharing personal reflections about their class, have teachers share any ideas about how to thank a responsible class and help them learn to take pride in the fine job they are doing.

REMINDER Coaches are available within the building to serve as a sounding board, conduct demo lessons, help with data collection, observe, and provide collaborative, nonevaluative feedback.

 REPRODUCIBLE 3.8B

Reproducible 3.8C *Making Positive Family Contact*

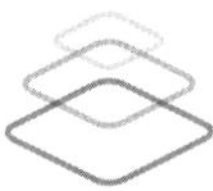

Making Positive Family Contact

CLASSROOM MANAGEMENT MINI-INSERVICE

Objectives

1. To encourage staff to build positive relationships with students' families* by making early contact with them at the beginning of the year.
2. To remind staff to make regular contact throughout the year.

Situation

You are preparing initial contact with your students' families. You want to emphasize the importance of two-way communication, and you want to treat families as equal partners in the collaborative process of educating students. You want this correspondence to be presented in a way that consciously invites families to bring their questions or provide additional ideas or insights that might be beneficial.

Small group discussion (3 minutes)

With two to four colleagues:

1. Identify at least two different ways that a teacher might make initial contact with families.
2. Identify at least two different ways that a teacher might maintain ongoing contact with families.

Large group debrief (3 minutes)

Groups report an idea for making initial contact and maintaining ongoing contact. The purpose of these discussions is to identify common characteristics for positive communication with families.

Optional large group discussion (3 minutes)

Positive family contacts are especially important when a teacher has a large number of students with high need for support. Because it's also possible that contact will be more difficult to achieve with families of students that have high needs, stress that the greater the needs of the students, the greater the need for teachers to establish and maintain positive contact with families. Discuss what a teacher might do if unable to easily make contact with a family.

* More students than ever live in one-parent households, in foster care, with grandparents, and in other circumstances. It is often inaccurate to refer to the student's *parents*, and it is cumbersome to continually refer to the student's *parent(s)*, *grandparent(s)*, or *guardian(s)*. Therefore, in most cases the term *student's family* will be used when referring to a student's primary caregivers.

REMINDER Coaches are available within the building to serve as a sounding board, conduct demo lessons, help with data collection, observe, and provide collaborative, nonevaluative feedback.

 REPRODUCIBLE 3.8C

Reproducible 3.8D *Refusal to Follow Directions*

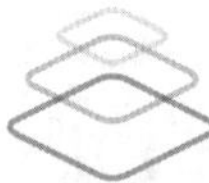

Refusal to Follow Directions

CLASSROOM MANAGEMENT MINI-INSERVICE

Objectives

1. To explore intervention options for a student who refuses to work.
2. To remind staff that responses to misbehavior should treat students with respect and maintain the flow of the instructional activity.

Situation

In your class, a student of average academic ability is fairly quiet, though she answers any questions you pose directly to her. She has completed all assignments and is achieving average grades. She participates in class if asked to, but rarely volunteers answers. During an independent work period, you notice that the student is not working and is staring into space. You go to the student and quietly remind her to get back to work. She looks at you and calmly states, "You can't make me."

Small group discussion (3 minutes)

With two to four colleagues:

1. Identify at least two different ways that a teacher might skillfully handle this immediate sitaution.
2. Identify at least two different ways that a teacher might be unskillful in responding to this situation.

Large group debrief (3 minutes)

Groups report what they've identified. The purpose of these discussions is not to identify how best to handle this scenario, but to recognize that multiple skillful ways exist for handling other such situations and to remind staff that an unskillful response stands a fair chance of drawing other students off task or coming across as disrespectful.

Optional large group discussion (3 minutes)

Discuss what a teacher might do if the event with the student repeats itself on each of the next 2 days. Ideas could include how to respond immediately but should also identify other interventions (such as contacting the student's family).

Self-reflection questions

Would your immediate reaction to the stiuation have been different if the student had been identified as male? Or if the student had been identified as being of a particular race or ethnicity? Would your responses or long-term interventions have been different?

REMINDER Coaches are available within the building to serve as a sounding board, conduct demo lessons, help with data collection, observe, and provide collaborative, nonevaluative feedback.

 REPRODUCIBLE 3.8D

Reproducible 3.8E *Monitoring Ratios of Interactions*

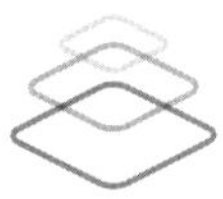

Monitoring Ratios of Interactions

CLASSROOM MANAGEMENT MINI-INSERVICE

Instructions to the team presenting this inservice to the staff

One or two weeks prior to the staff meeting, copy and distribute the Ratio of Interactions Monitoring Form (*CHAMPS* Chapter 10, Tool 2; *DSC* Chapter 10, Tool 2) to all teachers. This tool will allow teachers to self-assess whether they are providing more attention to positive student behavior or to negative behavior. Include a cover note requesting that each teacher follow the instructions, collect data, and analyze the data prior to the next staff meeting. Give the date of the staff meeting in which this will be discussed.

At the staff meeting

Step 1 (2 minutes)

Have someone from your team provide an overview of the importance of striving to maintain positive interactions. Ask teachers to look at the analysis of the collected data and identify one positive thing about their interactions with students and one thing they would like to improve about interactions with students.

Step 2 (1 minute)

Have teachers divide into groups of four to six. Arrange this so that teachers are in groups that are different from the groups they are usually with for department or grade-level meetings.

Step 3 • Small group discussion (7 minutes)

Ask teachers to discuss the positive aspects of their student interactions and the things they would like to improve. Encourage them to share ideas with each other about how to maintain high ratios of positive to corrective attention.

REMINDER Coaches are available within the building to serve as a sounding board, conduct demo lessons, help with data collection, observe, and provide collaborative, nonevaluative feedback.

 REPRODUCIBLE 3.8E

Reproducible 3.8F *Brainstorming Interventions*

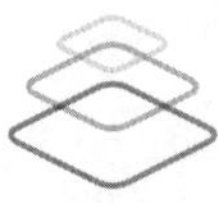

Brainstorming Interventions

for a Class That Is Not Responding to the Attention Signal

CLASSROOM MANAGEMENT MINI-INSERVICE

Objectives

1. To explore ideas for getting students to comply with the teacher's attention signal.
2. To encourage teachers to assess whether students are responding promptly enough to their signal.

Situation

The class responded reasonably well to your signal at the beginning of the year, but you now realize that you must repeat the signal several times and wait much longer than 5 seconds between giving the signal and gaining the class's attention.

Small group discussion (3 minutes)

With two to four colleagues, discuss what might be done to improve the class's responsiveness to the signal. Agree on at least two recommendations.

Large group debrief (5 minutes)

Identify the person who will record these ideas on chart paper or a whiteboard and send a memo listing all the ideas to the staff within a couple of days. Small groups should report their top two ideas, after which any additional suggestions can be added to the list.

Large group reminder (1 minute)

Encourage teachers to think about their attention signal and to observe their classes for a couple of days to determine how much time passes between giving the signal and gaining student attention. If students are responding to the signal within 5 seconds, provide positive feedback to the class, letting them know that their cooperation is appreciated. If, on average, more than 5 seconds elapse before student attention is acquired, plan to implement some of the suggested ideas until students are responding consistently to the signal.

REMINDER Coaches are available within the building to serve as a sounding board, conduct demo lessons, help with data collection, observe, and provide collaborative, nonevaluative feedback.

 REPRODUCIBLE 3.8F

Reproducible 3.8G *Recording Misbehavior*

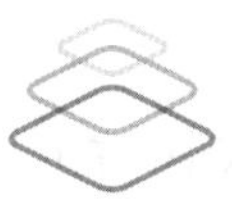

Recording Misbehavior

CLASSROOM MANAGEMENT MINI-INSERVICE

Instructions to the team presenting this inservice to the staff

One or two weeks prior to the staff meeting, copy and distribute the Misbehavior Recording Sheet (*CHAMPS* Chapter 10, Tool 3; *DSC* Chapter 10, Tool 3) to all teachers. This tool will allow each teacher to keep an objective record of all misbehavior during a particular time period. This record will allow the teacher to reflect on whether the frequency and intensity of the misbehaviors is significant enough to warrant modifying the current structure of the Classroom Management Plan. Include a cover note requesting that each teacher follow the instructions, collect data, and analyze the data prior to the next staff meeting. Include the date of the staff meeting at which this will be discussed.

At the staff meeting

Step 1 (2 minutes)

Have someone from your team go over the importance of occasionally collecting objective data on the frequency of misbehavior and the fresh perspective that is gained by taking the time to examine what is going on in the classroom. Ask each teacher to look at their analysis of the collected data and determine whether the Classroom Management Plan needs to be modified.

Step 2 • Large group discussion (8 minutes)

Reducing misbehavior: Without sharing personal reflections or data about their class, ask teachers to help others by sharing ideas about how to improve a class's behavior at this point in the school year. Remember the rules of brainstorming: We will not evaluate any ideas, but anyone can ask a "Could you explain that some more?" type of question. If needed, get the brainstorming rolling by suggesting "re-teach expectations" and "institute a classwide reward system."

Optional • Large group discussion (3 minutes)

Reducing structure for a highly responsible class: Without sharing personal reflections about their class, have teachers share ideas about how to reduce the structure of a classroom (one in which little misbehavior occurs) and ways to help the students learn to take pride in the fine job they are doing.

REMINDER Coaches are available within the building to serve as a sounding board, conduct demo lessons, help with data collection, observe, and provide collaborative, nonevaluative feedback.

 REPRODUCIBLE 3.8G

Reproducible 3.8H *When and When Not to Use a Disciplinary Referral*

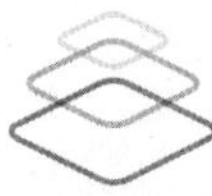

When and When Not to Use a Disciplinary Referral

CLASSROOM MANAGEMENT MINI-INSERVICE

Objectives

1. To help staff identify which situations warrant sending students to the office and which should be handled in the classroom.
2. To know how to write an effective disciplinary referral.

Instructions to the team presenting this inservice to the staff

For the meeting, prepare chart paper for each grade-level or department team. The chart paper should be divided into three sections, with numbers 1, 2, and 3 written in large bold print. Post them around the room. Assign each team to one chart paper.

At the staff meeting

Step 1 (1 minute)

Have someone from your team emphasize that a teacher must know the expectations of the administrator in charge of discipline about what types of behaviors should be handled in the classroom and what types should be handled through the use of an office disciplinary referral. This activity is to determine if staff are on the same page.

Step 2 (2 minutes)

Have each team identify which behaviors should always be handled by the classroom teacher. Give teams 2 minutes to brainstorm those behaviors and list them in Section 1 of the chart paper.

Step 3 (2 minutes)

Have each team identify which behaviors should never be handled by the adult in the classroom. These are the behaviors that should be handled immediately by the office. Give teams 2 minutes to brainstorm those behaviors and list them in Section 3 of the chart paper.

Step 4 (2 minutes)

Have each team determine what qualifies as a Level 2. Are there qualifiers for the behaviors in this level? If these behaviors require some level of outside support that doesn't include the administrator, to whom should these behaviors be reported?

Step 5 (3 minutes)

Have each team quickly report on one thought generated by the activity.

After the staff meeting

The leadership team collects the chart papers to compare. Are staff on the same page? Do expectations for what is and is not an office referral need to be more clearly defined or communicated?

REMINDER Coaches are available within the building to serve as a sounding board, conduct demo lessons, help with data collection, observe, and provide collaborative, nonevaluative feedback.

 REPRODUCIBLE 3.8H

Reproducible 3.8I *Grade Book Analysis*

Grade Book Analysis

CLASSROOM MANAGEMENT MINI-INSERVICE

Instructions to the team presenting this session to the staff

One or two weeks prior to the staff meeting, copy and distribute the Grade Book Analysis Worksheet (*CHAMPS* Chapter 10, Tool 4; *DSC* Chapter 10, Tool 4) to all teachers. This tool will allow teachers to identify strengths and areas of improvement in student academic behavior—percentage of students completing assignments, percentage of student handing in homework, current grade status, and so on. This is still early enough in the year that changes in classroom management can affect students' success or failure in the class. Attach a cover note requesting that each teacher follow the instructions for summarizing data from the grade book and analyze the data prior to the next staff meeting. Include the date of the staff meeting in which this will be discussed.

For the meeting, prepare chart paper with each of the following items written in large bold print. Post them around the room.

- Punctuality
- Attendance
- Work Completion
- Work Quality

At the staff meeting

Step 1 (2 minutes)

Have someone from your team provide an overview of the importance of using the grade book as a source of data for identifying whether changes could be made in a teacher's Classroom Management Plan that may help some students be more successful in class. Ask each teacher to look at their analysis of the collected data and identify one area that needs improvement.

Step 2 (2 minutes)

Have teachers go to the poster for the issue they would like to spend some time working on—punctuality, attendance, work completion, or work quality.

Step 3 (2 minutes)

Have each group brainstorm and write on the chart paper ideas that might have a positive impact on the issue discussed. Let them know that each group should be prepared to report any ideas generated to the large group.

Step 4 (2 minutes)

Have each group quickly report on the ideas listed on the chart paper.

Step 5 (3 minutes)

Have someone type up the ideas from each group and distribute to staff via email or a memo in each staff member's mailbox.

REMINDER Coaches are available within the building to serve as a sounding board, conduct demo lessons, help with data collection, observe, and provide collaborative, nonevaluative feedback.

 REPRODUCIBLE 3.8I

Reproducible 3.8J *Introducing a Rule After the Start of the Year*

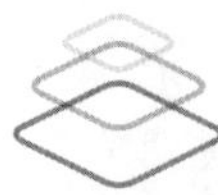

Introducing a Rule After the Start of the Year

CLASSROOM MANAGEMENT MINI-INSERVICE

Objectives

1. To help staff introduce a rule that may be needed for the classroom to function in a safe and effective way.
2. To remind staff to enforce rules once they are in place.

Reflection (2 minutes)

Following are a list of criteria from CHAMPS that are recommended when creating your classroom rules. Determine if your current classroom rules reflect these criteria:

- Rules should be stated positively.
- Rules should be specific and refer to observable behaviors.
- Rules must be applicable throughout the entire class period during all activities and transitions.
- Rules should be posted in a prominent, visible location.

Small group discussion (3 minutes)

With two to four colleagues:

1. Identify if class behavior indicates that a new classroom rule must be introduced.
2. Create the rule using the criteria above.

Large group debrief (3 minutes)

Groups report an idea for teaching students the new rule. The best way to help students understand the rules is to demonstrate specific examples of following and not following the rules. Plan to teach the new rule each day for at least 5–10 days until students are proficient at following the rule.

Optional large group discussion (3 minutes)

Once students fully understand your rules, including new ones that are introduced, you will use a range of corrective consequence strategies that allow you to respond consistently, unemotionally, and quickly to any rule violations. If you do not plan your likely response to common misbehaviors in advance, the probability is high that you might inadvertently reinforce misbehavior by giving it too much attention. Reflect on or add to the menu of corrective consequences you currently use and what you might use when responding to a violation of the new rule.

REMINDER Coaches are available within the building to serve as a sounding board, conduct demo lessons, help with data collection, observe, and provide collaborative, nonevaluative feedback.

 REPRODUCIBLE 3.8J

Reproducible 3.8K *Re-Teaching Expectations Throughout the Year*

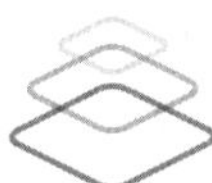

Re-Teaching Expectations Throughout the Year

CLASSROOM MANAGEMENT MINI-INSERVICE

Objectives

1. To help staff clarify and teach expectations for any activities or transitions during which student behavior has become problematic.
2. To remind staff to teach expectations, observe student behavior during activities and transitions, and give students feedback about their implementation of the expectations.

Small group discussion (3 minutes)

With two to four colleagues:

1. Identify if the visual currently being used is effective in helping prompt appropriate behavior.
2. Identify two ways a teacher could re-teach and reinforce expectations.

Large group debrief (3 minutes)

Groups report an idea for re-teaching and reinforcing expectations. The purpose of this discussion is not to identify the one best way to teach expectations, but to emphasize that the plan for how expectations are taught should be based on the complexity of a teacher's expectations, the teacher's teaching style, the age and sophistication of the teacher's students, and the level of structure and support that has been established in the classroom.

Optional large group discussion (3 minutes)

Observing student behavior and giving students effective feedback is critical in helping students meet clearly communicated expectations. Have staff reflect on the quality of both positive and constructive feedback they provide. Have staff share examples of what effective, positive feedback should sound like and how constructive feedback should be delivered when students are not meeting expectations.

REMINDER Coaches are available within the building to serve as a sounding board, conduct demo lessons, help with data collection, observe, and provide collaborative, nonevaluative feedback.

Reproducible 3.8L *Welcoming a New Student to the Classroom*

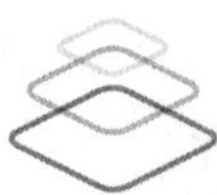

Welcoming a New Student to the Classroom

CLASSROOM MANAGEMENT MINI-INSERVICE

Objectives

1. To help staff make the process of joining a class as comfortable as possible for a new student.
2. To explore ways a teacher might help a new student learn to navigate a new classroom and set of procedures and routines.

Reflection (2 minutes)

The first 2 weeks of school are the most important time for teaching behavioral expectations and classroom routines. However, most teachers experience some degree of flux in the student population over the course of the year. Have teachers reflect on whether they have some form of orientation in place. Have teachers list what they already do to make students feel welcome in their classrooms.

Small group discussion (3 minutes)

With two to four colleagues:

1. Identify two ways a teacher could make a conscious effort to welcome both the student and family.
2. Identify two ways a teacher could teach classroom expectations and procedures to the new student.

Large group debrief (3 minutes)

Groups report what they've identified. The purpose of this discussion is not to identify the one best way to welcome students and teach expectations and procedures, but to emphasize that some form of orientation (similar to what teachers provide for all teachers during the first 2 weeks of school) will be essential to get the student off to a successful start.

Optional large group discussion (3 minutes)

The higher you expect your student mobility rate to be, the more prepared staff need to be to teach expectations to new students. Discuss the typical and current mobility rate of the campus. Determine how the mobility rate impacts the level of structure and planning that might go into an orientation plan.

REMINDER Coaches are available within the building to serve as a sounding board, conduct demo lessons, help with data collection, observe, and provide collaborative, nonevaluative feedback.

 REPRODUCIBLE 3.8L

Reproducible 3.8M *A Well-Behaved Class Misbehaves With a Guest Speaker*

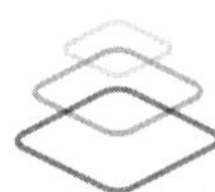

A Well-Behaved Class Misbehaves With a Guest Speaker

CLASSROOM MANAGEMENT MINI-INSERVICE

Objectives

1. To explore intervention options for a classroom that becomes silly and disrespectful with a guest speaker.
2. To remind staff that responses to misbehavior should treat students with respect and maintain the flow of the instructional activity.

Situation

Your class is a responsible and respectful group of students. Because of their collective maturity, you can generally be somewhat unstructured in your management plan. You allow class discussions to be somewhat freewheeling and spirited, and students have handled this well.

As a guest speaker poses questions to the class, several students begin chiming in minor putdowns to the responses of other students. This progresses until many students are engaged in disrespectful humor and showing off for each other. You realize that you should have intervened earlier, but you didn't because you were surprised by this behavior from this group of students. The guest speaker is scheduled to be with the class for another 7 minutes.

Small group discussion (3 minutes)

With two to four colleagues:

1. Identify at least two different ways that a teacher might skillfully handle this immediate situation.
2. Identify at least two different ways that a teacher might be unskillful in responding to this situation.

Large group debrief (3 minutes)

Groups report what they've identified. The purpose of these discussions is not to identify the best way to handle this situation, but to explore multiple skillful ways to handle such situations and to remind staff that an unskillful response may further disrupt the flow of instruction or be perceived as disrespectful.

Optional large group discussion (3 minutes)

1. Once the immediate crisis is past, what—if anything—might the teacher do after the guest speaker has left the classroom?
2. What expectations should be taught or reviewed prior to guest speakers (or any special events)?

REMINDER Coaches are available within the building to serve as a sounding board, conduct demo lessons, help with data collection, observe, and provide collaborative, nonevaluative feedback.

 REPRODUCIBLE 3.8M

Reproducible 3.8N *Brainstorming Interventions*

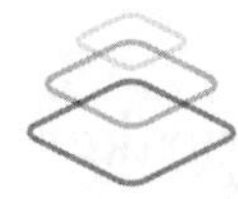

Brainstorming Interventions
for a Target of Chronic Teasing

CLASSROOM MANAGEMENT MINI-INSERVICE

Objectives

1. To explore intervention options for a student who is socially isolated and may be chronically teased by other students.
2. To remind staff that responses to misbehavior should treat students with respect and maintain the flow of the instructional activity.

Situation

One of your students does not seem to be part of a peer group. In unstructured settings, this student spends time alone. You suspect the student is being teased by other students, but you have no firsthand information—the student has not complained, and you have not observed direct harassment. This student is making adequate academic progress.

Small group discussion (5 minutes)

With two to four colleagues, discuss what you might do to determine whether your concerns are warranted. Assume you discover that this student is being teased by many different students. Should you intervene with this student, the rest of the class, or both? Keep in mind that intervening with the rest of the class could risk isolating this student even more. What actions might you take next? What interventions could you try? Identify at what point you should seek guidance from the school counselor or school psychologist.

Large group debrief (4 minutes)

Groups report what they've identified. The purpose of these discussions is not to identify the best way to handle such situations, but to explore the multiple skillful ways of handling such interventions.

Large group reminder (1 minute)

When even a shred of evidence indicates that a student is at risk of harming themself or others, immediately report your suspicions to the principal or counselor so a threat assessment can be conducted. Do not attempt to diagnose the seriousness of a threat on your own.

REMINDER Coaches are available within the building to serve as a sounding board, conduct demo lessons, help with data collection, observe, and provide collaborative, nonevaluative feedback.

 REPRODUCIBLE 3.8N

Reproducible 3.8O *Self-Evaluation of Teacher-Directed Instruction*

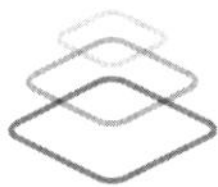

Self-Evaluation of Teacher-Directed Instruction

CLASSROOM MANAGEMENT MINI-INSERVICE

Instructions to the team presenting this session to the staff

One or two weeks prior to the staff meeting, copy and distribute the Opportunities to Respond Observation Sheet (*CHAMPS* Chapter 10, Tool 6; *DSC* Chapter 10, Tool 6) to all teachers. This tool will allow teachers to determine whether they are conducting teacher-directed lessons in a manner that actively engages students and provides students with sufficient opportunities to participate in the lesson. Attach a cover note requesting that each teacher follow the instructions, collect data, and analyze the data prior to the next staff meeting. Include the date of the staff meeting in which this will be discussed.

At the staff meeting

Step 1 (2 minutes)

Have someone from your team discuss the importance of providing opportunities for students to be active participants in lessons. Ask each teacher to look at the analysis of the data collected and identify whether they are satisfied with the number and variety of opportunities to respond that were created within the lesson.

Step 2 • Large group brainstorming (8 minutes)

Without sharing personal reflections or data about their class, ask teachers to help others by sharing possible ways to create opportunities to respond within teacher-directed lessons. Remember the rules of brainstorming: Ideas will not be evaluated, but anyone can ask a "Could you explain that some more?" type of question. If necessary, get the brainstorming rolling by suggesting that teachers could tell students to "stand up for true, stay seated for false" in response to true/false questions.

Optional • Encourage classroom visits (3 minutes)

Encourage teachers to ask another teacher (who shared ideas during the brainstorming) if they can come to their room to observe 5 minutes of a teacher-directed lesson to learn some ways of creating opportunities to respond.

REMINDER Coaches are available within the building to serve as a sounding board, conduct demo lessons, help with data collection, observe, and provide collaborative, nonevaluative feedback.

 REPRODUCIBLE 3.8O

Reproducible 3.8P *Responding to an Emotional Outburst*

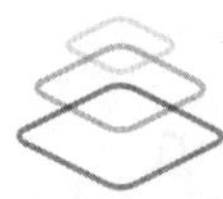

Responding to an Emotional Outburst
from a New Student

CLASSROOM MANAGEMENT MINI-INSERVICE

Objectives

1. To explore intervention options for a student who exhibits an unexpected emotional outburst.
2. To remind staff that responses to misbehavior should treat students with respect and maintain the flow of the instructional activity.

Situation

A new student moves to your school from out of state. No records arrive with the student, who is placed in your general education classroom. At the end of the first day, you have a nagging suspicion that the student might be a problem, but this reaction puzzles you because he followed any and all directions and seemed academically able, but not so high-performing that enrichment materials were necessary. Upon reflection, you identify your concern: the student was emotionally flat all day—no smiles, frowns, little eye contact, a monotone voice, and so on. On Day 2, it's the same pattern, even in response to other students—just flat.

On Day 3, during an independent work period, you approach the student, who is engaged in classwork, and quietly compliment him for his on-task behavior. He responds loudly and with hostility, "Yeah, right, like you care!"

Small group discussion (4 minutes)

With two to four colleagues:

1. Identify at least two different ways that a teacher might skillfully handle this immediate situation.
2. Identify at least two different ways that a teacher might be unskillful in responding to this situation.

Large group debrief (3 minutes)

Groups report what they've identified. The purpose of these discussions is not to identify the best way to handle this situation, but to explore the multiple skillful ways of handling such situations and to remind staff that unskillful responses may be disrespectful or may draw other students off task.

Large group reminder (1 minute)

Once the immediate crisis is past, what—if anything—might you do before the end of the day? Should you contact the parents about this one-time occurrence?

Self-reflection questions

Would your immediate reaction to this situation have been different if the student were identified as female? Or if you knew the student had been identified as having an emotional or behavioral disorder?

REMINDER Coaches are available within the building to serve as a sounding board, conduct demo lessons, help with data collection, observe, and provide collaborative, nonevaluative feedback.

 REPRODUCIBLE 3.8P

Reproducible 3.8Q *Recording On-Task Behavior*

Recording On-Task Behavior

CLASSROOM MANAGEMENT MINI-INSERVICE

Instructions to the team presenting this session to the staff

One or two weeks prior to the staff meeting, copy and distribute the On-Task Behavior Observation Sheet (*CHAMPS* Chapter 10, Tool 5; *DSC* Chapter 10, Tool 5) to all teachers. This tool will allow teachers to determine the percentage of on-task behavior exhibited by their students during independent seatwork. Attach a cover note requesting that each teacher follow the instructions, collect data, and analyze the data prior to the next staff meeting. Include the date of the staff meeting in which this will be discussed.

At the staff meeting

Step 1 (2 minutes)

Have someone from your team go over the importance of helping students stay academically engaged during independent seatwork, noting that a way of gauging this is to measure the percentage of time on task (academically engaged or on-task behavior). Ask each teacher to look at their analysis of the data collected and identify whether they are satisfied with the percentage of on-task behavior during the recording period. Encourage teachers to reflect on whether the recording period was indicative of a typical work period or whether student behavior was better or worse than usual during the recording period.

Step 2 • Large group brainstorming (8 minutes)

Without sharing personal reflections or data about their class, ask teachers to help others by sharing possible ways to improve students' on-task behavior. Remember the rules of brainstorming: Ideas will not be evaluated, but anyone can ask a "Could you explain that some more?" type of question. If necessary, get the brainstorming rolling by suggesting re-teaching of expectations or making sure the work is appropriate for students' level.

REMINDER Coaches are available within the building to serve as a sounding board, conduct demo lessons, help with data collection, observe, and provide collaborative, nonevaluative feedback.

 REPRODUCIBLE 3.8Q

Reproducible 3.8R *Responding to the Class Clown*

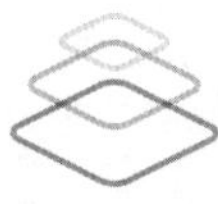

Responding to the Class Clown

CLASSROOM MANAGEMENT MINI-INSERVICE

Objectives

1. To explore intervention options for a student who chronically and disruptively jokes and gets the class to laugh at their antics.
2. To remind staff that responses to misbehavior should treat students with respect and maintain the flow of the instructional activity.

Situation

A bright student in your class fills the role of class clown. Although not hugely popular with other students, he is reasonably well liked. When he is disruptive, other students laugh at his actions or comments. You have to admit that he is often very funny, and even you sometimes laugh. However, the behavior seems to be increasing in frequency and intensity, becoming intrusive to instructional flow. What was funny at first is becoming grating and annoying.

You have tried reprimands and neutral-time discussions in which you appealed to his sense of cooperation. You have also spoken to his parents, who basically defended him and implied you should probably just lighten up.

Small group discussion (5 minutes)

With two to four colleagues, discuss whether your major intervention should be with this individual student, the rest of the class, or both. Identify different options the teacher might try next. Consider the concept of STOIC interventions and generate ideas to affect structure, teaching of expectations, observing, interacting positively, and correcting fluently.

Large group debrief (4 minutes)

Groups report what they've identified. The purpose of these discussions is not to identify the best way to handle this situation per se, but to explore the multiple skillful ways of handling chronic misbehavior.

Self-reflection questions

Would your intervention be different if the student's behavior were likable and charming (instead of grating and annoying), but was nonetheless disruptive to the flow of instruction?

REMINDER Coaches are available within the building to serve as a sounding board, conduct demo lessons, help with data collection, observe, and provide collaborative, nonevaluative feedback.

 REPRODUCIBLE 3.8R

Reproducible 3.8S *How to Respond to a Student Who Is Sleeping in Class*

How to Respond to a Student Who Is Sleeping in Class

CLASSROOM MANAGEMENT MINI-INSERVICE

Objectives

1. To explore intervention options for a student who is sleeping.
2. To remind staff that responses to misbehavior should treat students with respect and maintain the flow of the instructional activity.

Situation

You are presenting a whole-group lesson to the class when you notice that a student has her head down and is clearly asleep—not just resting. Other students around this student notice and are quietly laughing and looking to see if you notice.

Small group discussion (4 minutes)

With two to four colleagues:

1. Identify at least two different ways that a teacher might skillfully handle this immediate situation.
2. Identify at least two different ways that a teacher might be unskillful in responding to this situation.
3. What policies or procedures previously discussed by staff or shared with the student body might shed light on how such behavior should be handled?

Large group debrief (4 minutes)

Groups report what they've identified. The purpose of these discussions is not to identify the best way to handle this situation, but to explore the multiple skillful ways of handling situations like this and to remind staff that an unskillful response may draw other students off task or be perceived as disrespectful.

Optional large group discussion (3 minutes)

Would your immediate reaction to the situation have been different if you knew the student was experiencing major problems at home? If your answer is yes, is the different response fair to other students? Is it fair to this student?

REMINDER Coaches are available within the building to serve as a sounding board, conduct demo lessons, help with data collection, observe, and provide collaborative, nonevaluative feedback.

 REPRODUCIBLE 3.8S

Reproducible 3.8T *Would a Student Be Likely to Report . . .*

Would a Student Be Likely to Report a Serious Problem to an Adult?

CLASSROOM MANAGEMENT MINI-INSERVICE

Objectives

1. To explore staff perceptions about the likelihood of students' willingness to report a serious problem to an adult.
2. To brainstorm actions staff might take to encourage self-reporting.

Situation

Investigations of school shootings, student suicides, and peer and gang violence have demonstrated that students who were not directly involved in the occurrences frequently had prior information about the intent of the students involved. Imagine that a student in your class heard that another student (in or out of your class) was thinking of doing harm to themself or to others.

Large group discussion (9 minutes)

- Do you think the student would be likely to share that information with you or another adult? Does this vary by grade level?
- Do you think students have an understanding of the difference between tattling and social responsibility?
- What can individual teachers do to increase the likelihood that students report knowledge of another student's intent to do physical harm?
- What measures can be taken schoolwide to address this issue? That is, what might administrators or a leadership team do?
- How can we undertake these measures without needlessly raising students' and parents' anxiety about safety at school?
- If late in the school year, should any action be taken, or should school leaders wait until the next school year?

Large group reminder (1 minute)

Any time even a shred of evidence indicates that a student is at risk of harming themself or others, immediately report your suspicions to the principal or counselor so a threat assessment can be conducted. Do not attempt to diagnose the seriousness of a threat on your own.

REPRODUCIBLE 3.8T

Reproducible 3.8U *Maintaining Student Motivation*

CLASSROOM MANAGEMENT MINI-INSERVICE

Objective

To explore ideas for maintaining student motivation during the last month of school.

Situation

During the last month of school, students lose focus, resulting in increased discipline problems and decreased academic output.

Small group discussion (3 minutes)

With two to four colleagues, discuss what might be done to keep students engaged, excited, and behaving responsibly. Be prepared to share at least two specific suggestions with the entire staff.

Large group debrief (5 minutes)

Identify someone who will record ideas on chart paper or a smartboard and send a memo to the staff in about a week with all the ideas listed. Each group should report two ideas its members generated, after which groups can add additional items to the list.

Large group reminder (1 minute)

Encourage each teacher to identify one or two things they will do starting the next day, and one or two things they will do after receiving the memo in about a week.

REMINDER Coaches are available within the building to serve as a sounding board, conduct demo lessons, help with data collection, observe, and provide collaborative, nonevaluative feedback.

 REPRODUCIBLE 3.8U

Reproducible 3.8V *Family or Student Satisfaction Survey*

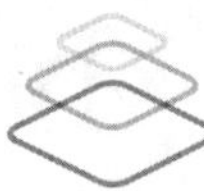

Family or Student Satisfaction Survey

CLASSROOM MANAGEMENT MINI-INSERVICE

Instructions to the team presenting this session to the staff

One or two weeks prior to the staff meeting, copy and distribute a family or student satisfaction survey (*CHAMPS* Chapter 10, Tool 7; *DSC* Chapter 10, Tool 7) to all teachers. This tool allows teachers to garner feedback from parents or directly from students, particularly those in middle or high school. Attach a cover note requesting that each teacher follow the instructions, collect data, and analyze the data prior to the next staff meeting. Include the date of the staff meeting in which this will be discussed.

At the staff meeting

Step 1 (2 minutes)

Have someone from your team provide an overview of the importance of continuous improvement, emphasizing that one way to accomplish this is to get feedback from parents or students. Stress that these data are only an indication of perception, not reality, but those perceptions may give teachers information on strengths and areas they could improve on through professional development. Ask each teacher to look at their analysis of the data collected and identify one positive thing they noticed about interactions with students and one thing that could be improved regarding interactions with students.

Step 2 (1 minute)

Have teachers get into groups of four to six. Group composition should be distributed differently from the groups in which they usually convene for department or grade-level meetings.

Step 3 (7 minutes)

Have teachers discuss their most positive interactions and the types of interactions they would like to improve. Encourage them to share ideas with one another about how they will use this information as they get ready for a new school year.

REMINDER Coaches are available within the building to serve as a sounding board, conduct demo lessons, help with data collection, observe, and provide collaborative, nonevaluative feedback.

 REPRODUCIBLE 3.8V

with implementation need and deserve quality, ongoing professional development. Giving practitioners time to practice new methods and strategies and providing opportunities to discuss implementation with colleagues over time will yield far greater results than any one-shot professional development. The learning from a one-and-done professional development, no matter how knowledgeable or charismatic the trainer, can be vastly improved by providing opportunities for practitioners to authentically collaborate on practice and by providing coaches to assist one-on-one in the classroom.

The great aim of education is not knowledge, but action. —Herbert Spencer

Coaching is the bridge between knowledge and action.

CLARIFY THE ROLE OF COACHES AND PROVIDE TRAINING AND RESOURCES

Once a model has been chosen, a target has been established, practitioners have been identified, and trainers have been booked to launch both initial and ongoing professional development, support personnel must be identified and trained. For classroom management at the campus level, the cornerstone of support is made up specifically of coaches.

Administrators, as evaluators of the model, should be familiar with research and understand how its findings can be applied in day-to-day classroom situations. However, administrators won't, and simply *don't,* need to have the answers to every teaching challenge that arises. That is the work of coaches. Coaches supply a vital link in the feedback circuit as objective, third-party observers. By witnessing a few of the hundreds of transactions that occur among teachers and students each day, coaches are invaluable in linking the "neural network" of a school, and for that reason they can be great allies to administrators and teachers alike.

When a behavior issue has a teacher feeling stymied, a coach can break the impasse with strategies, tips, and techniques for the teacher to try. When a teacher implements an intervention, a well-prepared coach is in the best position to give the teacher immediate feedback on its effects. The well-coached teacher is freed to divert more mental energy to instruction.

In another sense, a coach helps to validate (and perhaps propagate) the hard work that teachers put in on classroom management by serving as a conduit for communicating their progress and success.

The more coaching help, the better—this includes instructional coaches, content area specialists, counselors, psychologists, mentors, and others whose professional duties intersect with those of teachers in a primarily nonevaluative way. There is good reason for asking as many colleagues as possible to be available as coaches. First, a teacher who wants assistance can get it quickly while the need is greatest and before unnecessary damage is done. Second, teachers can select and work with a coach with whom they are comfortable. If a teacher does not expect to communicate well with the standards coach, they can ask for help from the school counselor. Third, the hard work of teaching most often occurs in relative isolation, with teachers physically separated from their colleagues in other classrooms. Given a rich menu of coaching options that includes colleagues they respect, teachers will feel empowered instead of marooned.

One caveat, however, is that a teacher should be involved with one or, at most, two coaches at any time. When streams of input from several coaches run together, positive correlation from any single intervention will be more difficult to verify. Moreover, teachers may become overwhelmed with competing suggestions—*too* much information. As in life, successful coaching usually comes down to relationships. With help pouring in from all sides, the personal touch tends to get diluted.

Clarify the Role of Coaches

The predominant coaching model involves nonevaluative coaches. These coaches may be full-time behavioral or instructional coaches or part-time coaches with another primary role on campus. All involved staff should know whether the coach is expected to report about a working relationship to administrators on the campus. The coach's role should be kept independent from the evaluation process. Except under exceptional circumstances (and then only with the full knowledge of everyone involved), the coach should not have to report confidential conversations or data specific to any one teacher to those in an evaluative position.

Peer-to-peer coaching is often used as a primary model, many times in smaller schools that don't have anyone to offer full-time or part-time coaching support. It can also be used in conjunction with more formal coaching models. Peers should assist one another with a commitment that any data collected remains between the peers. If multiple sets of peer coaches meet periodically, via PLC (professional learning community), grade level, or content teams, peers may opt to share data to look at trends collectively and identify goals.

There are also campuses where the evaluator is the only available coach. In this case, administrators must clearly define when they are acting in the capacity of evaluator or in the capacity of nonevaluator. While in the eyes of teachers administrators can never truly separate themselves from an evaluative role, they can certainly inform staff transparently when they are engaged in formative assessment versus summative assessment of skills.

After you create a list of coaches, identify the type of help that each coach can provide. Who can help with implementation of the classroom management model? Who can assist in designing and implementing interventions for individual students? Can some help with both?

Define Availability of Coaches

Quantities of time should be clearly allocated to coaches. How available should they be for working with teachers? For being present in classrooms? What proportion of their time should be devoted to coaching relative to their other duties? Obviously, a school counselor will have less time available for coaching than a designated literacy coach who already spends time in classrooms. The principal or leadership team should get as specific as possible in penciling out coaches' responsibilities on a day-by-day basis. Coaches should be brought together to sketch out sample calendars for a typical day, from before the first bell to after school lets out.

In addition to how much time will be spent on coaching, the percentage of that time that should be spent in classrooms should be spelled out. It is easy for coaches to fall into a pattern of spending all their time in meetings or preparing materials. Coaches will have to balance competing appeals for their time. Both full-time coaches and part-time coaches (those in the building with another primary position) should be given clear direction on how much of their coaching time can be allocated to working with teachers in their natural habitat, the classroom.

Clarify How Teachers Can Access Coaching Supports

After compiling this information, summarize it in a table such as that shown in Reproducible 3.9, Coaching Availability Chart. This should be shared with teachers as part of the process of relaying to staff the expectations and information about the support available for helping them meet those expectations. Be sure to identify whether any prospective coach's role is evaluative (administrative) or nonevaluative (collaborative). This summary should also be posted where teachers congregate—physical locations such as the faculty room and digitally via email or through the school's internal network. A teacher who wants assistance should have the option of contacting any of the identified coaches. The list of coaching options, created by the administrator or leadership team, should be as inclusive as possible to stimulate the free flow of ideas across disciplines and among varying personal styles. From this cross-pollination of ideas grow the best solutions.

Provide Resources for Coaches

Teachers are expected to practice fluent and ever-improving classroom management. The administrator, as the evaluator, is in a position of putting demands on teachers and holding them accountable for meeting these demands. Together, the classroom management model selected and the coaching network established provide safety valves for teachers, a way for them to know where they are going and that they will never have to go it alone.

Reproducible 3.9 *Coaching Availability Chart*

Coaching Availability Chart

Person/Role	Nonevaluation or evaluative (peer or administrative)?	Type of coach (behavioral or academic/curriculum)?	Involved with CHAMPS coaching?	Available to help with classroom management or individual students?	Time available for being in classrooms?

Key: **E** = Evaluative
NE = Nonevaluate
B = Behavioral
A = Academic/Curriculum

 REPRODUCIBLE 3.9

It stands to reason that coaches within the system will need a comparable safety valve. An outlet should be created by facilitating training and networking opportunities for coaches. A study and support group is a good idea. The staff members who are designated as coaches should be encouraged to get together at least once a month (more frequently is even better) to discuss process and progress. These meetings would be good opportunities to convene coaches from different schools to share their experiences and insights. During these times, coaches can alternately function as a study group, support group, and self-marketing group.

As a study group, they could draw on the chapters in this book to prepare discussions on which ideas are proving useful, which are not, and why. They might recount what has worked, what hasn't, and what has made the difference. Before moving on to the next topic, they might brainstorm what could be done to make their approach more effective. By working through the material together, they create their own accountability for expanding their skill as behavior coaches. Just as teachers need to be lifelong learners about classroom management and effective instruction, coaches need to be lifelong learners about the art and the science of being a resource to teachers.

As a support group, coaches can commiserate with each other about how difficult and potentially lonely it can be to function essentially as peers to classroom teachers who, at least initially, may view them with skepticism. They can share case scenarios while maintaining the confidentiality of individual teachers and gather ideas from their colleagues about how to proceed.

As a self-marketing group, they can periodically develop and implement strategies to remind teachers about the service they can provide. Without occasional reminders, teachers can get so busy in their classrooms that they forget that nonevaluative help is available to all.

If there is a bit of salesmanship detected here, that's right. Coaches are part public relations professionals, promoting their "product"—their services—to fellow professionals. In one sense, a coach is only as good as what they can sell to the teaching team. The voluntary and nonevaluative nature of the working relationship between a teacher and coach means that coaches will have to compete for teachers' minds—and hearts—in the marketplace of ideas. One might say that their effectiveness as coaches is directly related to their effectiveness as marketers of their own coaching prowess.

Administrators can take a lower profile with this group than with the teaching faculty. Administrators can demonstrate support by joining some of these meetings and inquiring about how meetings are proceeding, being cognizant of the coaches' need to speak freely in a nonevaluative context. An administrator might supply snacks for one of their regularly scheduled meetings and enjoy a snack with them before they start their business while letting them know how much their assistance and expertise are appreciated. With a little practice, administrators will settle into being a coach to the coaches in the mode that's most comfortable. Leaders should have confidence that, given time and opportunity, campus coaches will find their stride.

Wrapping It Up

CHAPTER 3 SUMMARY

Prepare your teachers and coaches for success.

What to Know

- Quality ongoing training yields better results than one-time workshops.
- The coaches' roles in supporting implementation should be clearly defined and communicated to staff.
- Coaches also need support in order to support staff effectively.

What to Do

- Communicate expectations for the three-part model.
- Develop an ongoing training plan for the classroom management model.
  - Schedule introductory training sessions and ongoing mini PDs (professional developments).
  - Assign or ask for volunteers to teach the different aspects of the model and lead discussion sessions.
  - Plan for new teacher orientation to the classroom management model.
- Train identified coaches on how best to support the classroom management model within the first tier.
- Provide a list of coaching resources to all teachers and post the list where teachers congregate—physical locations such as the faculty work room and digitally via email or through the campus internal network.

CHAPTER 4

Observe
Data Collection to Inform Practice

You can't improve what you don't measure. —Michael Hyatt

Without data, you're just another person with an opinion. —W. Edwards Deming

Imagine going to the hospital with life-threatening symptoms. Instead of running medical tests and thoughtfully reviewing the scientific data, the doctors stand around your hospital bed sharing what they think may be putting your life in jeopardy, basing their diagnoses on what they have seen and experienced in the past. Not only would your symptoms not improve, they likely would get even worse and potentially prove fatal. It is doubtful any doctor using that approach would still be in practice. Yet, rather than accurately assessing the situation with data, educators too often rely on what some refer to as the educator's cardiac assessment—"In my heart, I feel the students are behaving better." Or, for some, use of the gut assessment when we feel as if things are getting worse.

Accurate data to inform classroom management practice is no less critical to the life of a teacher. Using only what's felt in the heart (and gut) to guide us can amplify existing issues. And for some teachers, it may prove fatal to their careers. After the classroom management model has been chosen and the vision of the approach has been clarified to staff, the next step is to monitor how well teachers are implementing the model in their classrooms. This provides teachers invaluable and actionable information to inform practice and gives the leadership team the information needed to drive decision-making on the campus.

Both evaluative and nonevaluative coaches should conduct classroom walk-throughs to monitor how well teachers are implementing the model. In this chapter, we will look at the role of both in creating effective walk-through practices. This is the Observe piece of STOIC. Research demonstrates that student behavior is more responsible and motivated when adults are actively observing. The same is true for staff. (See Box 4.1.)

Walk-through visits are where "the rubber meets the road." To extend the metaphor, you can have a great vehicle (the CHAMPS model), a great destination in mind (cooperative and highly motivated students engaged in meaningful instruction), and a great road system (your school) that connects where you are (students with all their strengths and challenges) with the destination. However, if the drivers—teachers—keep the vehicle parked, head in the wrong direction, drive unsafely, forget to purchase gas, or neglect periodic maintenance, they will never reach the destination.

A walk-through is nothing more than a 3- to 5-minute drop-in visit—yet it can be a great deal more. In each walk-through you conduct, you will probably observe both instructional and behavior management issues. This can seem like a lot to do in such a short time, but with a good mental game plan, you can gather a great deal of information in a brief visit.

In this chapter, we explore the power of observation within the roles of evaluators, nonevaluative coaches, and peers. In this chapter, you will learn how to:

- Define the role of the evaluator in collecting data and establishing accountability to reach the three-part target.
- Define the role of nonevaluative coaches in collecting data and providing assistance.
- Conduct a walk-through visit.
- Debrief after a walk-through visit (evaluators).
- Set up a system of peer-to-peer learning observations.

THE ROLE OF THE EVALUATOR IN DATA COLLECTION

In Chapter 2, we outlined the four cornerstones necessary to create a solid foundation for implementation. The role of the evaluator is critical. In the classroom, as in any workplace, an employee who works largely alone, no matter how self-sufficient or self-motivated, tends to pick up the pace a little when others are around to watch. That is human nature.

In the simplest terms, keep three questions in mind when conducting classroom observations:

1. Are students academically engaged at least 90% of the time? (student engagement)
2. Are interactions between the teacher and students respectful? (teacher behavior)
3. Does student behavior meet the teacher's expectations? (student behavior)

BOX 4.1

Power Over Versus Power With

I have to admit, I don't always follow the clearly posted expectations that have been taught to me when I'm behind the wheel of my own car. I tend to do the Midwest rolling stop, speed up just a bit to get through yellow lights, and rarely, if ever, go the speed limit. Even if it's one or two miles over the posted expectation, I feel a sense of saving myself precious time.

I now have a built-in GPS in my car and typically have it turned on at all times so I can access it when needed. I may be speeding or prepared to roll through that yellow light, but the minute my GPS informs me that traffic cameras may be observing me, my behavior immediately changes. I'm the most law-abiding driver out there. I'm sitting up straighter, my hands are suddenly at 9 and 3, and my tires may actually stop rotating when I reach a stop sign. When I'm being observed, my behavior changes for the better. This is something described as "power over." While it may seem powerful, it's based on coercion and control, and, unfortunately, it's very short lived. While this observational tactic may have the power to punish my actions, it has no power when it's not there. In other words, my behavior is affected for a very short time. I may even feel resentful that I'm being observed in that moment and simply want it to pass.

Now my father, he sees speeding as a deep character flaw. He believes that when you're speeding, you're communicating that you may not care about others on the road or simply that you're inefficient in how you manage your time. My father has no power over me. He can't affect my behavior through punitive consequences: he can't ground me, he can't give me a ticket, he can't take away my car. But here's what he can do. He can look at my speedometer when I'm driving. He can sigh and shake his head. And then he can say this, "I just worry about you. I worry about how fast you drive, and I worry you'll get hurt or you'll hurt someone else. I just want you to be safe. I'd hate to get a call telling me something has happened to you." In other words, he's communicating he's on my side. He's observing my behavior and letting me know that the purpose of his observation is to give me feedback that's in my best interest. While some of you may think this is simply the power of a guilt trip, the difference is in the relationship. This is "power with," shared power that grows out of relationships built on respect and mutual support. When my dad is with me, I don't speed (or, let's be real, certainly not as much). And my behavior changes for much longer. I hear his voice in my head, and I know we have a shared goal—to keep me safe.

It's vital for the evaluator to communicate a sense of "power with," a sense of empowerment and collaboration. This puts the evaluator in the role of the "warm demander," expecting excellence from staff and believing in their autonomy—that once given the proper feedback and support through the coaching model, teachers can reach any target provided.

If the answer to each question is yes, the teacher has a good working classroom management plan. If the answer to any question is no, the teacher should be advised that they need to adjust their classroom management plan to address the problem. Keep in mind that as an evaluator, you do not have to know how to fix the problems, but you do need to ensure that helpful resources are available to teachers. You don't have to be an expert in classroom management; you are simply evaluating whether the teacher's plan is or is not working based on the three criteria listed above. You should be able to identify that a problem exists and set a goal for improvement. You should ensure that coaches are available to observe, model, co-teach, and provide feedback.

Administrators with training in clinical supervision know the common format of having a preconference prior to the observation, observing at a specified time for a specific period (usually 20 to 40 minutes), and holding a scheduled post-conference. Walk-through visits are different. Walk-throughs do not occur on a schedule, they may or may not have a post-conference, and other than discussion in a staff meeting or professional development, there will be no preconference. They can also be quite brief.

Some administrators may feel they don't have time to take data or learn new ways of evaluating a teacher. If that describes you, start slowly. Read through the following material and incorporate the strategies gradually. You will soon internalize the procedures, and your observations will become more and more informative and helpful for the teachers.

Your role as an evaluator consists of the following:

- Create a game plan for observations and prepare staff for walk-through visits.
- Regularly conduct and keep track of walk-through visits.
- Debrief with teachers after walk-through visits.
- Emphasize the importance and availability of coaching resources.
- Collaborate with nonevaluative coaches to analyze trend data and identify professional development needs.
- Create a culture of continuous improvement.

ALTERNATIVE DATA MEASURES

Some districts, through negotiated agreements, may not allow informal administrative walk-throughs. If this is the case on your campus, we recommend disregarding the suggestions in this section. Work with campus staff on what data measures might be used to assist teachers in accessing additional support. Data measures such as office discipline referrals, academic assessment data, and attendance can be used, as well as things like injury reports, number of student referrals to Tier 2 teams and special education, and the number of referred students who don't qualify for additional support. Without formative data walk-throughs, campuses must choose other extrinsic data measures that an administrator can use to make inferences and provide teachers with the support they may need.

Create a Game Plan for Observations and Prepare Staff for Walk-Through Visits

As an evaluator, think about which behaviors you are most interested in looking for. These are summarized for you in Figure 4.1, which is provided as a PDF in the reproducible downloads. Download the PDF (see p. 4) to your phone or tablet and carry it with you for easy referencing.

1. *Student behavior.* You want to see students on task, respectful, and meeting the posted expectations.
2. *Student engagement.* Get a sense of students' connection with instruction. In particular, look at opportunities to respond and the percentage of correct academic responses.
3. *Teacher behavior.* A teacher should be observing student behavior (physically circulating and visually scanning the classroom), maintaining a healthy ratio of positive to corrective interactions, and providing fluent corrections.

Figure 4.1 *CHAMPS Game Plan for Walk-Through Visits*

CHAMPS Game Plan for Walk-Through Visits

1. **Observe student behavior.** Are students . . .
   a) Actively observing (circulating and scanning)?
   b) Behaving respectfully toward one another and toward the teacher (at least 95%)?
   c) Complying with the teacher's posted expectations (at least 95%)?

   If the answer to all of these questions is yes, focus the rest of the observation on students' connection with instruction (Step 2). If the answer to any of the questions is no, divide the remainder of your time between Steps 2 and 3.
2. **Observe student engagement.** Look at . . .
   a) Opportunities to respond (estimate OTRs per minute).
   b) Percentage of correct responses (PCR).
   c) Any instructional variables that have been a focus of staff development.
3. **Observe teacher behavior.** Is the teacher . . .
   a) Actively observing (circulating and scanning)?
   b) Using praise effectively (at least a 3:1 ratio of positive to corrective interactions)?
   c) Correcting misbehavior fluently (calmly, consistently, briefly, and immediately)?

When creating a game plan for walk-throughs, think about what you are likely to see if you are visiting the classroom of one of your best teachers. Think about how it contrasts with the classroom of a struggling teacher. Comparing these teachers will help you simplify the task of observing other teachers. For example, to evaluate whether students are engaged in the instructional activity, think of the outstanding teacher whose students are totally in touch with the lesson—100% engagement. By way of contrast, the ineffective teacher may have lots of misbehavior in the classroom, with only about half the students doing anything even remotely connected with the lesson. You'll discover that most teachers rate somewhere in between. While the Basic 5 Behavior Benchmarks remind us not to evaluate based on purely subjective and comparative data, by keeping the outliers of the spectrum in mind, particularly on the positive end, you can know when you need to encourage a teacher to work more toward achieving what a master teacher achieves consistently.

The decision on what you will look for will always be up to you, the administrator. You may choose to go into a classroom and follow the recommended guidance for conducting a walk-through visit that is presented later in this chapter. Other times, you may choose to have all evaluators and nonevaluative coaches collect the same data point (e.g., "This week, coaches will be looking solely at Ratio of Interactions"). Remember the Measure part of your three-part target and select data sources that will help you assess the effectiveness of your Tier 1 classroom management model. The data to collect may be determined because you see a need and want to know if your concern is valid, or it may be a simply a good time of year to measure a particular data point.

At times you will let the staff know what is being collected, such as Ratio of Interactions. Letting staff know in advance will make you into a visual reminder when you walk in—they should be reminded to engage in that practice when they see you. At other times, you may let staff know that you will be observing but will not be telling them what data points will be collected. This serves to get you, often, a more accurate picture of staff members' overall management skills.

You can also let your staff know ahead of time, even at the beginning of the year, that walk-throughs and post-observation conferences will take place. Stress that your goal is for teachers to be highly effective when measured through a formal, summative assessment. To do that, you must provide brief, frequent walk-throughs and plug teachers into resources early on. Just as you do for students, you want struggling teachers to get support quickly when needed. Reproducible 4.1 is an example of a handout you could share with staff to prepare them for your walk-through visits.

Regularly Conduct and Keep Track of Walk-Throughs

If classroom management as a focus of your walk-through visits is new to you, plan to visit the classrooms of your most skillful teachers first. You might let a few teachers know (privately) that you want to try your hand at collecting data in their rooms first, as this will allow you to practice your skills and gather baseline information on what data look like in the classroom of an excellent teacher *before* you start using your skills to help other teachers make improvements.

Set a goal for the number of walk-throughs you hope to complete each week. It is easy to get so busy with meetings, paperwork, disciplinary referrals, and other essential tasks that months can slip by before you realize you're falling well short of your goal.

Reproducible 4.1 *Memo to Staff in Preparation for Walk-Through Visits*

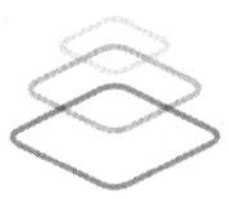

Memo to Staff in Preparation for Walk-Through Visits

Date ________________

Memo to staff:

My goal is to visit all classrooms as frequently as possible. When I drop in unannounced, I will stay for about 3 to 5 minutes. I have no specific agenda and will be looking at quality of instruction and classroom management.

Plan to carry on as if I were not in the room. Let your students know in advance that when I (or any other visitor) visit the classroom, they should simply stay focused on the lesson or task.

Following is a list of classroom management variables I will be looking at.

1. ***Student behavior.*** Are students ...
    - Actively engaged in the lesson?
    - Behaving respectfully toward one another and toward you?
    - Complying with your posted expectations?
2. ***Students' connection with instruction.*** I will be looking at ...
    - Opportunities to respond (OTRs).
    - Percentage of correct academic responses (PCR).
    - Other instructional variables that have been a focus of staff development.
3. ***Teacher behavior.*** Are you ...
    - Actively observing (circulating and scanning)?
    - Using attention effectively (at least a 3:1 ratio of positive to corrective interactions)?
    - Correcting misbehavior fluently (calmly, consistently, briefly, and immediately)?

I will obviously not be able to observe all these things at each visit. If at any point you disagree with feedback I provide, please discuss it with me—the walk-throughs are mainly a way for us to create a dialogue about how best to approach and implement effective classroom management practices.

 REPRODUCIBLE 4.1

By setting a reasonable goal for the number of classroom visits and keeping a record of how many you complete, you can create accountability for yourself.

Reproducible 4.2 offers an example of how to keep a record that will allow you to scan a few pages and know what classrooms you have visited recently and when. If you enter teachers' names alphabetically or by grade and then make multiple copies, you can record several months' worth of walk-throughs. By entering the time of the observation, you can avoid always visiting a particular classroom at the same point in its schedule. In some cases, you may want to visit a classroom at the *same* time over several days to determine whether a particular activity or transition is improving. You can also create a similar record on an Excel spreadsheet.

This record also reveals whether you have missed any classrooms or whether you are visiting any particular classrooms with excessive frequency. Once you feel comfortable gauging behaviors in your most successful classrooms, you should make an effort to visit all classrooms proportionately. Without some kind of record, you may find it too easy to visit only those classrooms that are the most fun—or perhaps those in which the teacher is most welcoming and appreciative of your presence.

Debrief With Teachers After Walk-Through Visits

You do not have to conduct a post-conference with every teacher after every visit, but you should do so if you observed major problems during a walk-through. For those teachers without major issues, a post-conference after every third visit is probably sufficient, but don't assume that your best teachers don't ever need post-conferences; they want to know what you think, and most appreciate hearing that they are doing a good job and enjoy talking over what they might do to improve. And when teachers do make improvements, celebrate the successes! Whenever you follow up a walk-through visit with a teacher conference, indicate this with a "C" on your record of visits (Reproducible 4.2) to keep track of how frequently you are debriefing. Guidance for debriefing is provided later in this chapter.

Emphasize the Importance and Availability of Coaching Resources

If you are following the suggestions in previous chapters, hopefully you have assembled a group of trusted instructional coaches and other staff members in your building who can assist teachers with classroom management. This precious resource will go underutilized if you do not emphasize the importance of coaching when talking with your staff. Remind teachers that coaches who help with behavior management do not report to you; their visits to classrooms are entirely confidential, and information is shared between the coach and the teacher only.

Reproducible 4.2 *Record of Walk-Through Visits*

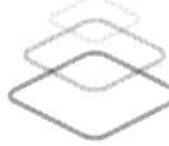

Record of Walk-Through Visits

Directions: List teacher names alphabetically or by grade. For each walk-through, record the date and time of the observation. Whenever you follow up on a walk-through visit with a teacher conference, include a "C" on the record.

DATE ▸	3/2	3/3	3/4	3/5	3/6	3/9	3/10	3/11	3/12	3/13	3/16	3/17	3/18	3/19	3/20	3/23	3/24	3/25	3/26	3/27
TEACHER	M	T	W	TH	F	M	T	W	TH	F	M	T	W	TH	F	M	T	W	TH	F
K. Edwards		9:00		10:30		1:00C		2:15					9:00	9:00C				1:00	1:00	
K. Warren	10:15		9:00			1:15C		2:00			9:00	9:00C				1:00	1:00			
1st Lee	10:00		9:15			1:30C		1:45					9:15	9:15C				1:15	1:15	
1st Jackson		9:15		9:45C		1:45		1:30C			9:15	9:15				1:15C	1:15			
2nd Sparks				9:30	9:00C	2:00		1:15		1:30C			9:30	9:30	9:30C			1:30	1:30	1:30C
2nd Matthews	9:45		10:00C			2:15		1:00C			9:30	9:30				1:30C	1:30			
3rd Powell	9:30		10:15C				1:00		2:15				9:45C	9:45				1:45	1:45C	
3rd Kennedy		9:30		10:15C			1:15		2:00		9:45C	9:45				1:45	1:45C			
4th Beamer				10:00	9:15C		1:30		1:45	1:00C			10:00	10:00	10:00C			2:00	2:00	2:00C
4th Shaw	9:15		9:45C				1:45		1:30		10:00C	10:00				2:00	2:00C			
5th Coleman				9:15	9:30C		2:00		1:15	1:15C			10:15	10:15	10:15C			2:15	2:15	2:15C
5th Rice		9:45		9:00C			2:15		1:00		10:15C	10:45				2:15	2:15C			
5th Chavez*	9:00		9:30C					10:00					10:30					9:00C		
*Morning only—afternoons at middle school																				

 REPRODUCIBLE 4.2

In addition to suggesting coaching when you notice problems, try to "sell" your teachers on the idea of having a coach help them develop plans for improving the behavior of a particular student, collect data on any aspect of classroom management, or, for teachers already engaged in effective classroom management practices, further hone their skills. Be sure to remind staff that these coaches do not report to you. Their visits to classrooms are entirely confidential and are between the coach and the teacher only.

Whenever you notice that a teacher is having trouble with some aspect of classroom management, be proactive. Let the teacher know, in a clear but supportive way, that the problem needs to be addressed. Set specific goals. Help identify ways to resolve the problem. And use the power of your vision for schoolwide classroom management and the cumulative expertise of your coaching program to break down tough classroom management issues and build up strong supports for sustainable improvement.

Collaborate With Nonevaluative Coaches to Analyze Trend Data and Identify Professional Development Needs

Observational data gathered during walk-through visits are essential to identifying staff needs and guiding professional development planning. While official staff development is often planned well in advance, staff meetings and professional learning communities also give opportunities to help teachers grow.

Once data are collected, the leadership team should meet, including both the administrator (as the evaluator) and nonevaluative coaches. If data from walk-through visits indicate that more than 20% of staff are struggling to hit the same benchmark or are experiencing the same inappropriate behaviors from students, you and your leadership team should first reflect to see what may be missing from the rollout plan. If everything is accounted for, a professional development should be planned for the whole staff. Another option would be to offer different professional development based on multiple staff needs reflected in the data. Data-based decision-making is at the heart of what we choose to provide for students. The same should be true for staff.

Create a Culture of Continuous Improvement

As a principal or building administrator, you wear many hats in shaping classroom management. You develop a vision for your school, choose a management model, arrange training in that model, inform staff what is expected, monitor implementation (especially in terms of student behavior), provide feedback to staff, and encourage teachers to seek out coaches. Your role in this continuous cycle of improvement is never complete—there will always be more proactive, more positive, more instructional strategies to manage classrooms than the ones you and your staff are currently using. Your staff should become increasingly collaborative over time. No one should expect any single person—be it an administrator, coach, or teacher—to have all the answers to complex problems or for the answers to remain changeless in the shifting winds of student behavior. Every staff member should recognize that they are never in it alone, that their colleagues are available to help, and that all are empowered to help in a system that recognizes and values the contributions of each individual.

“*As a principal or building administrator, you wear many hats in shaping classroom management.*”

THE ROLE OF THE NONEVALUATIVE COACH IN DATA COLLECTION

While some of the processes outlined for evaluators will also be used for nonevaluative coaches, the biggest difference is in how any data gathered in these walk-throughs are wielded. The main role of nonevaluative coaches is to be a visible resource on campus for teachers, your practitioners, to assist with troubleshooting any challenges to effective implementation.

As a nonevaluative coach, you should also be able to help the evaluator analyze trend data and assist in planning the appropriate professional development for staff as a whole. You should also act as the teachers' advocate, reporting any systemwide challenges or concerns from staff while protecting the confidentiality of individual teachers.

In this section, we'll look more in-depth into each piece of your role.

- Help collect trend data and data related to the three-part target.
- Collect data to support teachers' personal growth.
- Analyze trend data with leadership, including evaluators.
- Advocate for staff in reporting systemwide challenges or concerns.
- Protect the confidentiality of individual teachers.

Help Collect Trend Data

Brief walk-throughs offer nonevaluative coaches a chance to observe how classrooms are operating, to determine whether any classroom management issues are evident, and to help corroborate evaluator observations. However, as a nonevaluative coach, the intent of your walk-through visit will differ from a walk-through conducted by an evaluator. At Tier 1, unless the teacher has requested an informal coaching conversation, walk-through visits don't require you to debrief on data collected or provide positive and corrective feedback. You will simply collect data in the classroom to identify trends in practices and areas to highlight for additional support. In a 3–5 minute walk-through, you will be looking at student behavior, student engagement, and teacher behavior. Sometimes it will be your decision on what to look for. At other times, what to look for may be predetermined by a leadership team (e.g., "This week, coaches will be looking solely at Ratio of Interactions"). If the administrator is seeing the same trends, this gives a good indication that your data collection methods are calibrated reasonably well and that you have a fairly accurate picture of what staff need in terms of overall support (see Box 4.2 on the next page). Note that, in the role of a nonevaluative coach, you will not report data on individual teachers to the evaluators. This is critical to the health of a coaching relationship. The administrator should be aware of the limitations on the data you share—averages among staff, as well as both the high and low points, should be reported but not connected to any individual.

BOX 4.2

Comparing Trend Data: Calibrating the Data Collection Process

As a teacher specialist at the district level, Lisa Perez from Houston Independent School District often visits a campus collecting trend data to help leadership teams make informed decisions. She needed a quick format for looking at both the implementation of CHAMPS as the classroom management model and the quality of implementation. Reproducible 4.3, Trend Data Collection Form, offers another observation tool that can be used by both evaluators and support personnel. This modification of Ms. Perez's original form keeps the identity of teachers cloaked while observers look for the same evidence and data points within each classroom. These look-fors include evidence of the implementation of certain tasks as well as some of the same data points introduced in Reproducible 4.6, the Drop-In Observation (CHAMPS Game Plan) form shown later in this chapter (p. 128). This format provides an easy way to quickly share trends without breaking confidentiality.

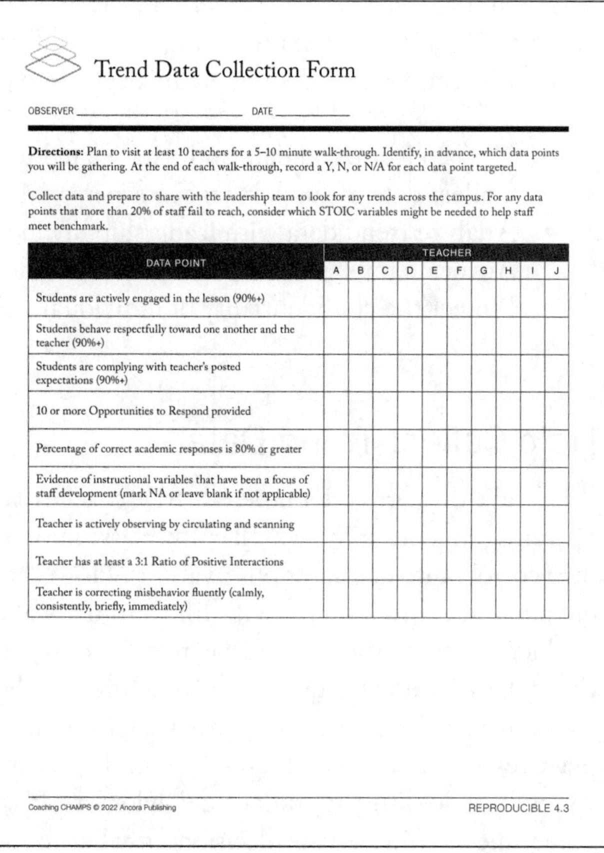

Trend Data Collection Form

OBSERVER ____________________ DATE __________

Directions: Plan to visit at least 10 teachers for a 5–10 minute walk-through. Identify, in advance, which data points you will be gathering. At the end of each walk-through, record a Y, N, or N/A for each data point targeted.

Collect data and prepare to share with the leadership team to look for any trends across the campus. For any data points that more than 20% of staff fail to reach, consider which STOIC variables might be needed to help staff meet benchmark.

DATA POINT	TEACHER									
	A	B	C	D	E	F	G	H	I	J
Students are actively engaged in the lesson (90%+)										
Students behave respectfully toward one another and the teacher (90%+)										
Students are complying with teacher's posted expectations (90%+)										
10 or more Opportunities to Respond provided										
Percentage of correct academic responses is 80% or greater										
Evidence of instructional variables that have been a focus of staff development (mark NA or leave blank if not applicable)										
Teacher is actively observing by circulating and scanning										
Teacher has at least a 3:1 Ratio of Positive Interactions										
Teacher is correcting misbehavior fluently (calmly, consistently, briefly, immediately)										

 REPRODUCIBLE 4.3

Comparing trend data with others will help to see if you are calibrated. If trends are not in reasonable alignment, it may be time for leadership teams, including administrators and nonevaluative coaches, to practice calibrating the data collection process. Calibration is essential within a campus and, ideally, within a district. When the people who collect data are not in agreement on how to measure for specific benchmarks, it invalidates the data and erodes trust with teachers.

If my coach comes into my classroom and continually measures on-task behavior at a rate of 89% but my administrator continually measures it at a rate of 61%, I know the data are invalid. And whose data will I most likely uphold? The measure that puts me closer to the benchmark. I'll start to think these walk-throughs are a joke, with luck being the biggest indicator of where I will fall in relation to the target. Occasionally, all data collectors should let staff know they will be coming into classrooms to practice data calibration. They will collect data together in the same classroom for the sole purpose of improving their practice, not to evaluate the teachers in any way.

Collect Data to Support Teachers' Personal Growth

Teachers often want to collect data to assist with their own personal growth. Both *CHAMPS* and *Discipline in the Secondary Classroom* include different data tools teachers can use to gather objective information about how well their classroom is functioning across a variety of dimensions, including student behavior, student engagement, and teacher behavior. Practitioners may ask you to gather data using any of those tools, or they may ask you to share the findings from your walk-through visit for the purpose of engaging in organic collaboration outside of the formal coaching process or an administrator's main directive. You are there to help all teachers—teachers who are struggling and teachers who are looking to further improve an already impressive skill set. You are the visual reminder to staff of the model's target. When they see you, they should be motivated to self-reflect and put these often newly learned skills into practice. You're their cheerleader; they should know, beyond a shadow of a doubt, that your sole purpose is to offer any assistance when needed and advocate on their behalf when challenges arise.

Analyze Trend Data With Leadership, Including Evaluators

After collecting walk-through data, nonevaluative coaches should meet with the administrator to share their observations. A coach's job is to provide trend data (e.g., "I was in twenty classrooms this week for 5-minute walk-throughs measuring Ratio of Interactions. The highest measure was 8:1 positive to corrective interactions and the lowest was 0:7. The average for all was 3:5. Did your data reflect this as well?"). While administrators may choose to share individual teacher data, we recommend that coaches do not confirm or invalidate these measurements. Coaches may also suggest areas to target for additional professional development and coaching support that may benefit teachers.

Advocate for Staff in Reporting Systemwide Challenges or Concerns

During the data collection process, inevitably systemwide challenges or concerns will arise. This will either be evident within the objective data measurements or through more informal measures, such as teachers who request to preconference with you. I've often found the most authentic descriptions of challenges and concerns aren't uncovered in any staff meetings, but in staff restrooms, teacher lounges, and the school parking lot. When doing walk-throughs and engaging in conversations with teachers, pay careful attention to trends that indicate a breakdown has happened somewhere within the system provided for staff. For instance, if it becomes obvious that a high percentage of staff have failed to comply with a directive from the Do part of the target (the expectations for implementation), that may indicate a need was not met for them.

Let's say you notice that over half of the teachers have not posted their behavioral expectations. In talking with staff, you learn their biggest complaint is they didn't have time to do them. Perhaps professional development was offered in August, only a few days before school started, and with everything else on their plates, this requirement for implementation simply didn't happen. Reporting back to leadership that over 50% of the staff feel like they didn't have the time to create a visual prompt of their expectations should give leadership pause. According to the Change Puzzle in Chapter 1 (Figure 1.2), when time, a resource, is not provided, inevitably you will experience anger from your staff. At the next opportunity for staff to meet, you may want to offer them time to spend creating these visuals.

When coaching is done right, through a partnership model, teachers will see you as an advocate, one who will be able to report challenges and concerns without any fear of reprisal. We'd like to think all administrators have the social emotional skillset to receive constructive feedback, but even the most highly skilled often struggle to respond well. Coaches can act as a safe liaison between evaluators and practitioners.

Protect the Confidentiality of Individual Teachers

Being available to staff opens you up to being a confidante of many a staff member. With great trust comes great responsibility. You are often walking a fine line between the leadership team and staff. Earlier in this section, we recommended refraining from sharing individual data on teachers. (See Box 4.3 for more on confidentiality.) There are certain exceptions to this rule:

- **Practitioners give permission to share data with others.** When given permission, you can certainly share objective data. This may happen because a highly effective staff member would like to proudly share their data to validate their practice. It may also happen because a teacher in Tier 2 or Tier 3 support trusts you to report individual data that may help with their support plan or show growth.
- **Sharing data is part of your formal job description.** For example, if you are involved in collecting data that may be used as part of a formal plan of assistance for teachers (see Chapter 12), you might be asked to collect objective data about teacher practices and report to the administrator. If this is a possibility, be upfront with teachers. Clarify with your administrator on what occasions you must share data. Every time data is collected? Only from walk-throughs? During formal coaching cycles? Having this information in advance will lend transparency to the process and help sustain trust between coaches and staff. In some instances, you may choose to collect data and give them directly to the teacher to share with the evaluator. If allowed, this is often the best option when you are required to share data.

BOX 4.3

Confidentiality

The first time a coach works one-on-one with a teacher in any capacity within any tier, we recommend the use of a confidentiality agreement. Early on in my coaching career, when working for Pathways to Success in Topeka, Kansas, we provided a Statement on Confidentiality (Figure 4.2) that was signed by both the coach and each staff member they coached. We gave them the original and kept a copy for ourselves. There was many a time when I reminded an administrator that I had signed a confidentiality agreement. My hands were tied in the best way possible. This engendered trust between me and the teachers and went a long way in convincing some staff members to finally (finally!) work with me. I learned so much from that experience, but what I learned most was that if staff doesn't trust you, if staff sees you as an arm of the administration, your coaching relationship may be over before it ever begins.

Some coaches have asked me over the years whether I think it's OK to report incidents they see in the classrooms. When I ask about those incidents, they often come down to a violation of Safe & Civil Schools's one absolute rule: There is no room for the belittlement or humiliation of children. "The teacher is so mean to students." I've stood firm in my response. You may report anything you see that is truly unethical, such as a teacher taking bribes for grades, or illegal, such as sexual exploitation, physical abuse, drug and alcohol abuse, etc. Mandatory reporting will always take precedence over confidentiality. If it's simply that you vehemently disagree with the teacher's practice, that's not for you to report. You report objective trend data only. If the administrator is engaging in frequent walk-throughs, they will recognize the violation of best teaching practices. While you may take exception to this, keep in mind that once you "tell" on that teacher, every teacher in the building knows that you have the capacity to break confidentiality.

Figure 4.2 *Sample Confidentiality Agreement*

Date:

Teacher-Coach Confidentiality Agreement

In my day-to-day coaching activities, I may gather information either for research purposes or as an aspect of our own collaboration. My policy, and the policy of the entire staff, is that any information I collect in your classroom is confidential. Our work together is just between us—any data gathered during our collaboration will only be shared anonymously.

In my role as an instructional coach, I am not in any way an evaluator. I am a partner, and I fully expect you will teach me as much or more than I teach you.

I look forward to establishing an ongoing positive collaboration with you.

Signature: ____________________

Signature: ____________________

A good litmus test for whether you are perceived as an evaluator is what I call "The Teachers' Lounge Challenge." When the teachers' lounge is full and an administrator walks in, regardless of the topic of conversation, what happens? Conversation falters or stops, at least briefly. If you are a nonevaluative coach, wait until the teachers' lounge fills up. Walk in. See what happens. If conversation quiets, you may be seen as breaking confidentiality. It's something to consider when building coaching relationships with the practitioners you hope to support.

While the role of the evaluator is to provide gentle pressure (the administrator as a warm demander), the role of nonevaluative coaches is to provide assistance to meet that pressure. All staff should feel a sense of urgency and enthusiasm about hitting the objective benchmarks. These benchmarks inform practice and move staff ever closer to the overall vision for your campus.

CONDUCTING A WALK-THROUGH VISIT

This section provides procedural guidance for conducting a walk-through visit for both evaluators and nonevaluative coaches who plan to visit and observe a teacher's classroom.

Choose an unobtrusive location to position yourself. When conducting a walk-through, enter the class as unobtrusively as possible. If the activity underway is teacher directed, move to a place in the classroom where you will be able to observe both teacher and student behavior—perhaps off to the side, but not all the way in the back of the room. If it is a cooperative group activity, you should probably choose not to be stationary; move around the room, listening to the group conversations to determine students' level of on-task behavior (time on task) and whether they are interacting successfully with the curriculum, as measured by the percentage of correct responses.

If the activity is independent seatwork or if the teacher is working with a small group while others work at their desks, you can decide whether to circulate and observe or watch from a stationary position. The advantage of moving about is that you can monitor the quality of student work and examine PCR (percentage of correct responses). The disadvantage is that your presence (proximity) may prompt greater levels of on-task behavior and thus create a slightly skewed picture. If your goal is to determine how smoothly the teacher circulates and how well students stay on task, a stationary spot at the side of the room is probably better.

Keep the focus on the class. During an observation, some teachers might try to divert attention from themselves by engaging you in an activity or dialogue. The teacher may ask you to help a particular student, stop a lesson so students can demonstrate something to you, or try and draw you into discussion about a parent. All these can be ways a nervous teacher may prevent you from observing a lesson or collecting data on students. If this occurs, you need to decide whether you will immediately ask the teacher to continue with the lesson or whether you will go along with this diversion and talk to the teacher later about the importance of simply carrying on with the schedule. If immediately redirecting the teacher can be done without embarrassing the teacher in front of their students, do so. However, if there is a chance the teacher will feel publicly reprimanded, go along with the teacher and discuss your expectation later. When you reconvene, make it clear that the next time you drop in, you want the teacher to carry on as if you were not in the room.

A more difficult decision is how to handle students who want to interact with you. Many students like having contact with school leaders and may want to show you their work or ask questions. However, if you reinforce this, your presence can actually become a destabilizing influence and prevent you from getting a clear picture of what is really occurring in the classroom. Ask your teachers to make students aware that when a visitor enters, they should just keep working as if no one were visiting. Also, have teachers let students know that you (or other visitors) may ask them questions or ask to see their work, but unless the adult talks to them, students should just carry on as normal.

Start by focusing on student behavior and engagement. Are at least 90% of students engaged in the lesson? Do a quick scan around the room and identify any students who appear to be off task. If the activity is teacher directed, evaluate whether students seem to be paying attention: Are they responding when the teacher presents a task, and are they following directions? If the activity is independent work, are they reading or writing? If the activity is a cooperative task, are the groups talking about the assigned task? On your observation form, record the number of students on task and the total number of students in the room at the time. This is a simple way to measure academic engagement. You can determine the exact percentage of on-task behavior later by dividing the number of on-task students by the total number of students. (For example, if 28 students are in the room and 6 students are off task, you know immediately that the percentage of on-task behavior is significantly less than 90%. Later you can determine that the exact percentage on task is 78.6%.) If the percentage of on-task behavior is less than 90%, you may choose to focus on this issue with the teacher, overlooking the subsequent observation questions and instead continuing to watch on- and off-task behavior to see if the number of off-task students increases or decreases during the remainder of your time in the classroom.

Are at least 95% of students behaving respectfully toward one another and toward the teacher? This is a somewhat subjective judgment. You might think of it like this: If the superintendent of schools were standing next to you now, would you be embarrassed to have the superintendent witness any of the behaviors you are observing? One student in the class may exhibit chronic patterns of disrespect, and over time you may want to help the teacher develop strategies to help this student, but if more than one student in a class is behaving disrespectfully, you will want the teacher to work actively to change this. Even if most of the students are engaged in the lesson, disrespectful behavior—if not addressed by the teacher—tends to be slightly contagious, infecting an increasing number of nearby students. A problem with disrespect may be a major feature in your feedback; you may wish to spend the rest of your walk-through time focusing on this issue, thinking of some positive things to relate to the teacher as well.

Are at least 95% of students complying with the teacher's posted expectations? This issue is less important than the preceding questions and should be a focus only if the answer to those questions is positive—that is, if students are engaged and respectful. If students are not engaged, you already know that they are not meeting the teacher's expectations, so you can largely disregard this question. If they are engaged and respectful, look for behavioral congruence—the students' alignment with the teacher's posted expectations. For example, if the activity underway is a discussion and the teacher expects students to raise their hands and wait to be called on before they speak, but several students are not doing this, make a note of the discrepancy. If students are expected to stay seated during teacher-directed instruction but several students are moving around the room—handing papers in, getting a drink of water, and so forth—note the discrepancy. If students are not following the teacher's procedures, it sets a precedent that they can choose which expectations to follow. You can point out these discrepancies to the teacher so expectations can be re-taught (or modified if the teacher does not deem them problematic). You are not telling teachers how to structure their rooms; rather, you are merely observing whether students are consistently meeting the posted expectations.

While more objective and reliable ways of measuring the following benchmarks are provided in Tier 2, a rough estimate based on what you observe during a few drop-in visits should suffice to give you a sense of how the teacher is guiding students' connection with instruction:

- *Opportunities to respond.* This observation is useful during teacher-directed instruction. Is the teacher creating opportunities for the students to *do* something, not just be passive recipients? The worst-case scenario is the teacher who lectures at length without asking questions or giving students tasks or activities in which to engage. The best-case scenario is a teacher who frequently intersperses questions that engage all students ("Everyone prepare an answer for the following question, and I will call on one of you"), activities ("Stand up if you believe the following statement to be true"), and tasks ("Copy this list in your notes—you will need it to study for the test").
- *Percentage of correct responses.* Keep a tally of each academic question asked or task assigned and whether the students respond correctly or incorrectly. The goal is for students to be responding correctly at least 90% of the time. You can collect these data during teacher-directed tasks by making a tally mark for each correct response and a minus sign for each incorrect response. After the observation, you can determine the percentage of correct responses by dividing the correct academic responses by the total of the correct and incorrect responses. You can also do this during independent seatwork by walking around, examining students' work, and making the same marks. During cooperative activities, your observation will probably be more subjective, but if you notice that two out of six groups are way off base (not off task, just conceptually wrong) in their discussion of the assigned task, for example, you would share that information with the teacher.
- *Other instructional variables that have been a focus of staff development.* If student behavior is engaged and respectful, and if students have opportunities to respond and most are responding correctly, observe any other instructional variables as time allows.

Observe teacher behavior. If most students (90% or more) are respectful and actively engaged in the lesson, you can spend the remainder of the visit focusing on the teacher's methods of instruction. If more than a couple of students are misbehaving or off task, spend the remaining minutes watching the teacher's classroom management skills.

Is the teacher actively observing student behavior by circulating and scanning? Determine whether the teacher is aware of what is going on in the classroom. Does the teacher notice misbehavior in the early stages and move to correct it? Does the teacher notice when students need assistance and provide it quickly? Does the teacher make eye contact with students, regardless of the instructional activity? This last consideration is an effective way for teachers to make connections with students. Again, think about your outstanding teachers, how they connect with their classes and are completely tuned in to every student all the time.

Is the teacher being positive (maintaining at least a 3:1 ratio of positive to corrective interactions)? These data can be collected in an objective way. Each time you hear the teacher correct a misbehavior, make a tally mark in the corrective column—this does not indicate that the teacher was negative, rather that the teacher paid attention to negative behavior. This teacher behavior is not bad or wrong—to the contrary, it is essential. The goal is not to eliminate attention to misbehavior, but for teachers to strive to provide, overall, about three times more attention to every student engaged in positive behavior.

Every time the teacher compliments a student or group of students exhibiting positive behavior, make a mark in the positive column. Every time a teacher provides noncontingent attention to a student who is behaving responsibly, mark that interaction as positive. So if a student is working on an assigned task at her desk and the teacher asks, "How are you doing, Tamika?" in passing, count it as a positive interaction—this teacher provided positive affirmation by noticing the student while she was engaged in responsible behavior.

The ratio of interactions is important because, in every classroom, some students are starved for attention. If the teacher is, on average, paying more attention to negative behavior than to desired behavior, students may learn that it is easier to get attention by annoying the teacher than by trying to meet the teacher's expectations.

If the teacher compliments the entire class, count this as one positive. On the other hand, if the teacher singles out a group of four students, saying "All four of you are doing a great job," count this as four positive interactions. Likewise, if the teacher has to remind a group of four students to get back to the assigned task, count this as four corrective interactions.

You may find it a bit tricky to determine whether certain interactions are positive or corrective. When in doubt, ask yourself if the student was meeting the teacher's behavioral expectation *at the time of the interaction*. For example, a student is staring out the window instead of meeting the expectation of working on her lab activity. The teacher approaches the student, looks at her lab book, and says in a pleasant way, "Emily, you have a great start here. Keep going or you're not going to be done by the end of the period." The tendency is to mark this as a positive interaction, but in accordance with the guidelines, because the student is engaged in a negative behavior at the time of the interaction, the interaction should be marked in the corrective column. Again, remember that this does not indicate that the teacher did something wrong—in fact, this is a great technique—but it should still be coded as a corrective interaction.

Another type of interaction that is difficult to tally is an academic correction, due in part to its similarity to behavioral correction. For example, the teacher is circulating while students are working on a math assignment. He notices a student has made some errors, and he says, "Jake, I see that in a couple of problems here you have . . . " The tendency may be to mark this as corrective, but remember that the criteria is to ask whether the student was meeting the teacher's *behavioral* expectations at the time of the interaction. In this case, the student was doing his work, so even this would be counted as a positive interaction. The very act of correcting the error at that moment demonstrates to the student that he does not have to misbehave in order to be noticed by the teacher. Note that though your criteria may be different when looking at *instructional* expectations, for the purposes of classroom management, instructional correction and instructional praise will be counted as positive *if the student is behaving responsibly at the time the interaction takes place.*

The 3:1 ratio is an average across time. If fairly frequent misbehavior occurs during a particular 5-minute period you witness, the ratio may be skewed toward the corrective. If a teacher's ratios have been positive through three walk-throughs but on the fourth are skewed 1:4 on the corrective side, be sure to let the teacher know that you do not view this as a problem so long as the teacher *on average* settles back into the positive ratio as soon as possible.

When a teacher's ratio is consistently 3:1 or better, you can begin enriching your observations with additional data. Is the positive feedback to students specific (targeted and descriptive) or general? Are praise statements and reprimands nonembarrassing to students? Is the teacher correcting misbehavior fluently (calmly, consistently, briefly, and immediately)? A fluent correction is a calm correction. If the teacher gets visibly upset with a student's misbehavior, this is likely to lead other students off task, focusing on the far more dramatic interchange between the teacher and the misbehaving student rather than on instruction. Another problem with emotional responses to misbehavior is that they may give the errant student a sense of power: "Look how mad I can make the teacher!"

Consistency is essential. The teacher should strive to correct every instance of any particular misbehavior. If the teacher corrects one student for blurting out without raising their hand to speak but responds to what other students say when they blurt out answers, this is truly not fair. If you notice this kind of inconsistency during a walk-through, make a note and plan to address it with the teacher later.

Brevity is also important. The key concept is that when misbehavior occurs, the teacher's attempt to correct the misbehavior does not make the situation worse. In brief, the teacher should avoid talking too much. Let's look at a couple of examples. If a student makes a disrespectful comment to the teacher during a teacher-directed lesson and the teacher responds by saying, "Michael, that was disrespectful; I will speak to you about it after class," and then proceeds with the lesson, the brief interaction would be considered fluent. If the student claims he is being treated unfairly and the teacher says, "As I said, I will speak to you after class," and resumes the lesson, the exchange would still be fluent; the momentum of the lesson is being maintained. On the other hand, if at either the initial disruption or the attempt to argue, the teacher were to enter into a debate over respect or fairness, it would not be considered fluent, because the teacher's focus on the misbehavior would draw other students' attention away from the lesson and toward the corrective interchange.

Consider another example. A teacher is circulating while students are working on an assignment at their seats. The teacher notices that a student is not working on her assignment; he stops at the student's desk to give a gentle reminder: "Megan, you need to get to work." So far, this is a fluent correction. Now assume that the student says to the teacher, "You can't make me." If the teacher argues with the student or in any way attempts to threaten her, you will probably notice more and more students in the room start to watch the gathering drama. This correction is not fluent because it draws other students off task and does not successfully engage the offending student. What if, instead, the teacher quietly replies, "Megan, you are right, I can't make you. I hope you will get to work because this is a useful assignment. I'll come back in a minute and see if you have any questions," and then moves off to help another student or praise students who are on task. This would be a fluent correction. Whether or not Megan gets to work is one thing, but by avoiding a power struggle or long argument, at least the teacher did not distract others from their work.

In combination with the first three characteristics, immediacy is the mark of a fluent correction. The correction should happen as soon as the misbehavior is noticed by the teacher—not later. Note that in some cases, the teacher may deal with a problem immediately by telling the student that the behavior is unacceptable and that further discussion with the student or imposition of consequences may occur later. The misbehaving student and all students in the room know immediately that the behavior is unacceptable. It would not be immediate for the teacher to ignore the misbehavior altogether and then try to talk to the student after class about the issue. By the end of class, the student may not even remember what was said, let alone grasp that the teacher thought it was unacceptable.

Finally, one common thread through all fluent corrections is respect. No behavior reprimand should ever involve belittlement or ridicule of a student. The most effective corrections are matter-of-fact statements: what the misbehavior consisted of and the fact that such behavior is unacceptable. If the behavior has a prearranged consequence, the teacher should also remind the student of the consequence. ("Valerie, that was disruptive, and as you know, each disruption costs 30 seconds after class.")

Use forms to guide observation and feedback. Observation and feedback forms can be used to track your observations, demonstrate the frequency of your walk-throughs, and enhance the quality of the feedback you provide to staff. Look over the forms on the following pages (Reproducibles 4.4–4.7) and decide which will work for you.

NOTE: Some concepts on these forms are explained in greater detail in Chapter 7.

Reproducibles 4.4–4.7

These forms are provided as PDF files. Tailor them to fit your needs. Once you know which combination of forms you will use regularly, you can decide if these forms will be archived electronically or on paper.

Reproducible 4.4 *Drop-In Observation (General)*

Blank versions of all forms are available to download (see p. 4 for directions).

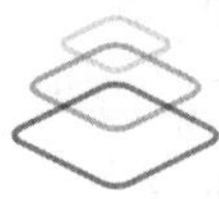

Drop-In Observation (General)

This form is open ended and can be used to provide positive or corrective feedback, to make notes of observation for further discussion with the teacher, and for other general purposes.

Teacher ____________________ Date/Time __________

Lesson/Activity ______________________________

Notes:

Observer ____________________

 REPRODUCIBLE 4.4

Reproducible 4.5 *Drop-In Observation (Academic)*

Drop-In Observation (Academic)

Use to provide feedback about student engagement within academic activities. At the bottom of the form, make notes on the type of work students are being required to do: Is it relevant? Is it age appropriate? Does it conform to district and state standards?

Teacher ______________________ Date/Time ____________

Subject/Lesson/Activity ____

Active student engagement:

TOT (Time on Task—percentage of students engaged and on task) _____

OTR (Opportunities to Respond) _____

PCR (Percentage of Correct Responses) _____

Meaningful student work:

Observer ______________________

 REPRODUCIBLE 4.5

Reproducible 4.6 *Drop-In Observation (Classroom Management)*

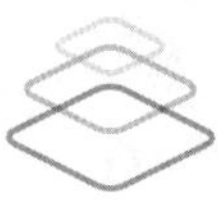

Drop-In Observation (Classroom Management)

This form focuses specifically on essential classroom management behaviors of the teacher. When noting posted expectations, answer basic questions regarding them: Are they understandable? Age appropriate? Stated positively? Are they used by the teacher in correcting misbehavior?

Teacher ______________________ Date/Time ____________

Posted expectations:

Ratio of Interactions

+	−

Fluent corrections:

Observer ______________________

REPRODUCIBLE 4.6

Reproducible 4.7 *Drop-In Observation (CHAMPS Game Plan)*

Drop-In Observation (CHAMPS Game Plan)

This is the most comprehensive of the drop-in observation forms. It directly parallels the items on the CHAMPS Game Plan for Walk-Through Visits (Figure 4.1) and provides space to elaborate on student behavior, connection to instruction, and teacher conduct.

Teacher ____________________ Class/Activity ____________________ Date/Time ______________

1. ***Observe student behavior.*** Are students . . .
   a) Actively engaged in the lesson (at least 90%)? ________%
   b) Behaving respectfully toward one another and toward the teacher (at least 95%)? ________%
   c) Complying with the teacher's posted expectations (at least 95%)? ________%

Notes:

2. ***Observe student engagement.***
   a) Opportunities to Respond. Estimated OTR per minute ________%
   b) Percentage of correct academic responses. Estimated PCR ________%
   c) Any other instructional variables that have been a focus of staff development:

   ____

Notes:

3. ***Observe teacher behavior.*** Is the teacher . . .
   a) Actively observing (circulating and scanning)? Yes/No ________%
   b) Being positive (at least a 3:1 ratio of positive to corrective interactions)? Estimated ROI ____:____
   c) Correcting misbehavior fluently (calmly, consistently, briefly, immediately)? Yes/No ________%

Notes:

Observer ____________________

 REPRODUCIBLE 4.7

The general Drop-In Observation form (Reproducible 4.4) is open ended and can be used to provide positive or corrective feedback and make notes of observations and questions you would like to discuss with the teacher.

The academic Drop-In Observation form (Reproducible 4.5) can be used when you want to gauge and provide feedback on student engagement within academic activities. Describe the overall level of student engagement. Use the separate sections to record time on task, opportunities to respond, and percentage of correct academic responses. At the bottom of the form, note the type of work in which students are engaged. Is it relevant? Age appropriate? Does it conform to district and state standards?

The classroom management Drop-In Observation form (Reproducible 4.6) focuses on essential classroom management behaviors of the teacher. You can count ratios of interactions and make notes about whether expectations are posted and about the content of those expectations. Are they understandable? Age appropriate? Are they used by the teacher in correcting misbehavior? You can also note how the teacher corrects. Are corrections calm, consistent, brief, and immediate? Is the teacher respectful?

Finally, the Drop-In Observation form based on the CHAMPS game plan (Reproducible 4.7) puts the content of the CHAMPS game plan in an easy-to-complete form directly parallel in organization to Figure 4.1. It provides space for you to note any aspects of student behavior, student engagement, and teacher behavior that catch your eye.

DEBRIEFING AFTER A WALK-THROUGH VISIT

This section provides guidance for evaluators debriefing after a walk-through visit. In most cases, nonevaluative coaches will not be providing formal feedback to teachers at this stage of the coaching process. If teachers have asked for data or requested an informal coaching conversation, coaches can review these suggestions and the recommendations in Chapter 7, which provides more formal coaching guidance around reviewing collected data as part of Tier 2 coaching supports.

Prioritize Providing Positive Feedback to Teachers

While observing, strive to identify several strengths or positive aspects of the teacher's behavior. Effective use of positive feedback will help your teachers become even better teachers. Your positive feedback will let teachers know that they are implementing strategies to achieve your building's vision of classroom management: classes in which students are respectful, responsible, and highly engaged. Without positive feedback, an insecure or new teacher, even if running a successful classroom, may not be aware of all the successful strategies they are using. A highly experienced teacher may know exactly what strategies are making their classroom work but cannot know whether you are aware of those things unless you discuss them with the teacher.

For example, imagine that you enter a room during a math lesson. For the first 4 minutes of your 5-minute visit, the teacher is re-teaching his expectations for how students should behave during independent work periods. He presents his expectations, discusses some types of misbehavior that have occurred recently, and then asks students to identify whether each of a series of behaviors he models are positive or negative examples of being on task. He then gives the assignment and asks students to begin work. As you leave the room, the teacher may wonder whether you approve of his methods or whether you think he wasted 4 minutes of the math lesson by discussing behavior, not math. If you recognize that by re-teaching expectations this teacher will actually increase student engaged time, you need to let the teacher know this. You might write the following feedback on one of the observation forms:

> *Mr. Warren, nice job of clarifying expectations. While you were presenting, you had at least 97% on-task behavior. The one time a student was off task, you issued a brief, immediate, calm reminder (to Alex) to look at you while you are presenting. Your ratio of interactions during the time I was there was one corrective (the reminder to Alex) to seven positives (one of which was to Alex, letting him know he was now on target). This re-teaching is very likely to result in a great independent work period—bravo!*

Plan to provide positive feedback to teachers after a walk-through visit in the same way that you want staff to provide positive feedback to students—with the opportunities to provide positives outweighing the times you deliver corrective or critical comments by three to one or better. See Box 4.5 for tips on positive feedback. Written and verbal feedback should be specific and descriptive, contingent (meaningful), and nonembarrassing.

- **Specific/descriptive feedback.** Specific feedback is laden with information—what was observed that merited a compliment: "While I was in the room, the students were on task at approximately a 95% level—great job of keeping your students engaged in an important instructional activity." By contrast, simply saying "Good job" provides no information about what was good or why the compliment is being given.
- **Contingent/meaningful feedback.** Comment about something important. Do not make a big deal out of something that is no big deal. Praise for trivialities can be insulting or diminishing. Plan to praise any demonstration of a new skill that has been emphasized. Note improvements in or mastery of a skill that has been the target of corrective feedback or goal setting. And praise any demonstration of a skill or accomplishment that you know the teacher is particularly proud of.
- **Nonembarrassing feedback.** We caution teachers about complimenting a student publicly in front of peers—youths on the receiving end of such compliments will likely be more concerned about what their friends are thinking than about the content of the feedback. Likewise, be cognizant of the setting in which you choose to issue positive feedback to your teachers, as they, too, may be concerned about the effect your comments are having on their colleagues. Avoid

BOX 4.5

Three Keys to Positive Feedback

Kegan and Lahey (2001) suggest that positive feedback is much more effective when it is direct, specific, and nonattributive. The first two characteristics are well known. Praise is more effective when it is given directly. Praise is more effective when it contains specific information rather than vague or general comments. Its third characteristic, nonattributive praise, is less well known. Put simply, rather than telling others about an attribute you observe in them, you simply report what you observed.

If we tell someone about an attribute they have, there is a good chance they will not agree with our assessment and consequently our comments will fall on deaf ears. It's a distinction easier to illustrate than to define. For example, if you watch Karl's class and say, "Karl, you're a patient man," Karl might nod appreciatively at the comment, but in his mind he might well be thinking, "Sure, you think I'm patient, but you should have seen me last Tuesday." A better approach is to avoid judgments of Karl and to simply tell him what you observed. Thus, rather than telling Karl that he's patient, you might say something like, "Karl, I noticed that when Isaiah struggled to answer a question, you gave him 10 seconds to find the right answer. When he got it and you told him he was right, he lit up like a Christmas tree."

You also need to avoid making negative judgments about teaching practices. If you inadvertently make a negative judgment that a teacher doesn't agree with, your comment can have a very negative impact on the relationship. Again, both evaluative and nonevaluative coaches are wise to simply report what they saw. Avoid pronouncements such as, "The reason your students are off task is that you didn't offer sufficient opportunities to respond." A better alternative might be to involve the teacher in a problem-solving dialogue about the data. You might, for example, simply report that the time on task was 73% and then collaboratively explore with the teacher possible strategies that might increase time on task.

Your goal during the collaborative exploration of data is to structure the conversation so that the coach and teacher work together as partners on this important and complicated business of increasing student learning. Avoid at all costs being perceived as someone who is there to "fix" the teacher. Instead, start the conversation by looking at data together with the teacher and then collaboratively generate strategies that might be employed to improve student learning. Not only will you increase the likelihood that teachers see themselves as equal partners in the coaching relationship, but because your approach involves your insights and the teacher's, it will often lead to better (and better implemented) plans to improve instruction than those generated solely by a coach.

verbal compliments that go on too long or are too effusive. Your positive feedback should never imply surprise—it would be insulting to the recipient if you acted shocked at the success. Simple, pleasant, matter-of-fact descriptions of the positive things you notice will be valued by teachers and will help reinforce those skills and procedures in their repertoire.

REFLECTIVE VERSUS EXPLICIT

Some models of coaching espouse an entirely reflective practice in which the administrator or coach merely stimulates a dialogue and teachers identify their own strengths and areas for improvement. Though this may be viable in some cases, it requires a highly knowledgeable teacher, and it may assume a model of coaching in which no objective measures of teacher effectiveness are used. We recommend a more explicit approach, one in which information is collected, shared, and jointly evaluated to confirm strengths and to set goals for improvement. In the case of classroom management, objective measures may include on-task behavior, opportunities to respond, percentage of correct responses, and ratios of interactions. These and other benchmarks will be laid out in Tier 2.

We understand that when engaging in a conference with a teacher, you will usually need to give both positive and constructive feedback. We encourage you to avoid the "feedback sandwich," wherein you give positive feedback, then constructive feedback, followed by positive feedback. Being on the receiving end of this sandwich often feels condescending, even if the intent was pure. It can feel inauthentic and insincere. Often the receiver may feel as if the constructive feedback is simply being buffered and won't know whether to trust the positive feedback given.

Similarly, we recommend you avoid data forms that record things like "three glows and a grow," "three strengths and a delta," "three stars and a black hole," etc. These are better used, and are intended, to frame self-reflection. They are often anecdotal and subjective in nature. Educators look only at one thing on those forms and it's most likely not the glow. In fact, when they receive this type of feedback, especially without any dialogue, teachers may not trust the positive things written. They often feel as if they are being buttered up for the blow to come.

Objective data will often be the best guiding point for dialogue. Dialogue with the use of effective communication skills in providing feedback will be appreciated and go far toward engendering trust within your staff. The next chapter will guide you through some of these skill sets.

Plan to keep your ratios of interactions skewed to the positive (3:1 or better) over time. Staff will learn that walk-through visits are not about trying to catch them doing something wrong; rather, you are interested in helping them build on their strengths. This is critical so that staff does not fear your visits or lose trust in you as a leader with their best interests at heart. Remember, you play for the same team! The recipient will be far more able to learn something from your corrective feedback if it is made in the context of what's going right—what skills, procedures, and interventions are being applied correctly.

You may have the chance to provide the positive feedback informally in the hall or the next time you chance upon the teacher. But make a point of visiting the teacher in their classroom on occasion. Visiting a teacher specifically to provide a compliment makes your feedback even more valuable.

Link Corrective Feedback to Coaching

When in the course of a classroom visit you notice a problem with student behavior, plan to point that out to the teacher as objectively as possible. With a few exceptions (described shortly), your corrective feedback will involve some aspect of student behavior that you hope the teacher will try to improve. The basic premise is, "If it isn't broken, don't try to fix it." If students are already meeting the following criteria, share the good news with the teacher and praise the teacher for doing a great job.

- At least 90% of students are on task and engaged in the lesson.
- At least 95% of students are behaving respectfully toward one another and toward the teacher.
- At least 95% of students are complying with the teacher's posted expectations.
- Students are given ample opportunities to respond.
- Students' PCR (percentage of correct responses) is better than 80% on new content and better than 90% on drill-and-practice material.

The one exception to the "if it isn't broken" rule is when student behavior is responsible but the teacher is not treating students respectfully. The only absolute rule within CHAMPS is that all people should be treated with dignity and respect. If the teacher is engaging in belittlement or ridicule, you must act to address the problem. However, provided that the teacher is treating students with respect and student behavior is on task, respectful, and successful, you need not ask the teacher to do anything differently. If, for example, student behavior is consistently fine and the teacher is respectful but perhaps not particularly fluent in correcting the few misbehaviors that do occur, your suggestion that the teacher change what they are doing has more potential to hurt than help.

Provide corrective feedback that is an objective description of the problem that you observe. "Nine out of 28 students, 32% of the class, were off task during my visit this morning" is an objective description. "Students are wasting too much time, and your room is chaotic" is not objective. Try to avoid labels or conclusions; just state the facts.

If the problem observed is relatively minor (85% of students on task with the goal being at least 90%), then leaving the teacher a note or a copy of one of the evaluation forms is probably fine—just be sure to mention some of the positive things you observed when you provide corrective feedback. Be sure to let the teacher know the target (in this case, 90% or more).

Whenever you observe major problems, such as only 68% on-task behavior, plan to meet with the teacher personally to discuss the problem. In person, you can explain that you have high expectations for the teacher, and you can describe in more detail the types of behavior you are seeing that you are interpreting as off task. Encourage the teacher to talk about the observed problem: Does the teacher perceive the problem? Was this 5 minutes an anomaly or the norm? Does the teacher have an idea of how to address the concern? If the teacher has reasonably sound ideas about how to address the problem, encourage them to experiment with these ideas and to let you know how it is going. In addition, let them know how long it will be before you are likely to return (will it be a few days or a few weeks?). Let the teacher know that you can be available for a walk-through if they want you to observe improvements; a specific time can be scheduled.

If a teacher is unsure how to fix a problem, remind that teacher where to go for help. You might suggest the teacher consult *CHAMPS*, do some brainstorming with other teachers, observe other teachers' methods, and work with coaches. How to attend to the problem should be the teacher's choice. Set a target date by which you expect to see improvement (for example, the students should be 75% on task within a week and 90% on task within 4 weeks).

Here's a simple format to follow when offering a teacher resources to address a challenge:

- Restate the gap.
- Offer (at least) 3 suggestions.
- Provide an incremental target.
- Set a date for your next walk-through.

As an evaluator, it may sound something like this, "Elizabeth, I've been in your classroom doing walk-throughs three times in the past 2 weeks. On average, the on-task behavior of students has been at 63%. Our target is 90%. I respect you as a professional, and I trust that you can close that gap. If you need support to do so, I have some suggestions you may want to consider. First, I have some books related to academic engagement that may help keep students on task: Anita Archer's *Explicit Instruction* and Jim Knight's *High-Impact Instruction*, among others. You are free to check them out of my professional library and see if there's anything in there that might interest and assist you. I also know there's a professional development coming up at the district office on engagement strategies. I'd be happy to help you secure a substitute teacher so you can attend. The third option is our campus coach, Jacob. Jacob attended the CHAMPS training earlier this year and is well versed in instructional practices. You can work with him, and he can collect more data as well as help you choose some strategies that are right for you. Now, you need to know that if you work with Jacob, I won't be asking him to pass on any information to me about what's happening in your classroom. This will allow you to speak candidly with each other. Honestly, how you fix this is up to you, but I do need you to work on this, and I trust you will. I'll be back in 3 weeks, and I need to see an increase in student engagement to at least 80%. We'll continue to watch its growth from there."

SELF-COACHING THROUGH PEER-TO-PEER LEARNING OBSERVATIONS

Often referred to as learning walks, these peer-to-peer observations occur as a brief classroom visit. These visits are accompanied by a research-based tool to provide participants with opportunities to reflect on what students are learning, learning strategies, student interaction with the content, and student engagement. Classroom observations are purely self-reflective and nonevaluative. The objective isn't to judge colleagues; it's to engage in reflection and consider adaptations to their own practice. Peer observers take data, including both objective data points and anecdotal notes. These data points will not be shared with the staff member being observed. The primary goal is to help the observers learn from their colleagues for the purpose of reflecting on their own classroom management plans.

Classroom observations should be short, approximately 15–20 minutes, and should allow time for discussion both immediately after the observation has occurred and at the conclusion of all learning observations. Whether you call them classroom observations or learning walks or peer-to-peer reflections, the goal should be the same: to normalize the process of both being observed and engaging in intentional reflection to inform practice.

Review the following recommendations for conducting peer-to-peer learning walks.

- **Design a structure for these learning observations.** Peer-to-peer observations are not done during typical isolated professional development dates on the calendar. For classroom observations to occur, they must be set up during times when students are on campus and engaged in learning. This may require substitute teachers to take the places of those observing. When and if substitute teachers run short in your district, staff can fill in for each other during planning times or by combining classes. We recommend this approach if staff are truly on board and recognize the benefit that these observations will have for them when it's their turn to go into the classrooms and watch.

  A sample schedule for these learning walks is included in Figure 4.3. This schedule, from Crimson Cliffs Middle School in St. George, Utah, shows how groups were created and a schedule set for all teachers to engage in both being the observer and being the observed.

Figure 4.3 *Sample Schedule of Learning Walks*

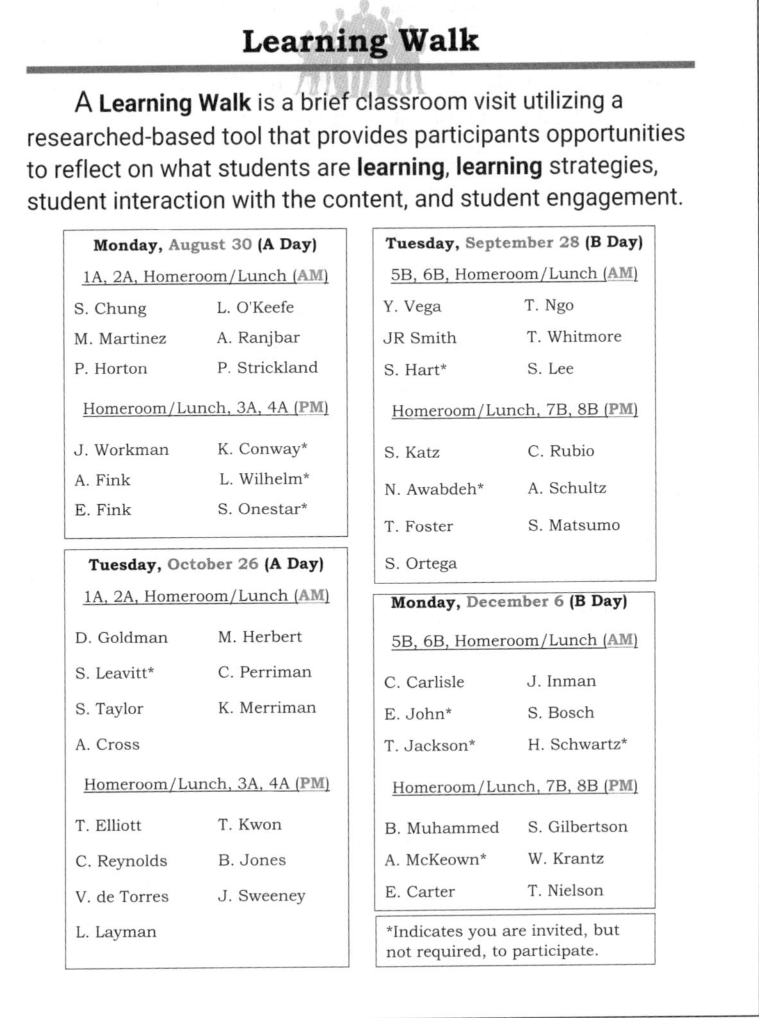

Learning Walk

A **Learning Walk** is a brief classroom visit utilizing a researched-based tool that provides participants opportunities to reflect on what students are **learning**, **learning** strategies, student interaction with the content, and student engagement.

Monday, August 30 (A Day)

1A, 2A, Homeroom/Lunch (AM)

S. Chung	L. O'Keefe
M. Martinez	A. Ranjbar
P. Horton	P. Strickland

Homeroom/Lunch, 3A, 4A (PM)

J. Workman	K. Conway*
A. Fink	L. Wilhelm*
E. Fink	S. Onestar*

Tuesday, September 28 (B Day)

5B, 6B, Homeroom/Lunch (AM)

Y. Vega	T. Ngo
JR Smith	T. Whitmore
S. Hart*	S. Lee

Homeroom/Lunch, 7B, 8B (PM)

S. Katz	C. Rubio
N. Awabdeh*	A. Schultz
T. Foster	S. Matsumo
S. Ortega	

Tuesday, October 26 (A Day)

1A, 2A, Homeroom/Lunch (AM)

D. Goldman	M. Herbert
S. Leavitt*	C. Perriman
S. Taylor	K. Merriman
A. Cross	

Homeroom/Lunch, 3A, 4A (PM)

T. Elliott	T. Kwon
C. Reynolds	B. Jones
V. de Torres	J. Sweeney
L. Layman	

Monday, December 6 (B Day)

5B, 6B, Homeroom/Lunch (AM)

C. Carlisle	J. Inman
E. John*	S. Bosch
T. Jackson*	H. Schwartz*

Homeroom/Lunch, 7B, 8B (PM)

B. Muhammed	S. Gilbertson
A. McKeown*	W. Krantz
E. Carter	T. Nielson

*Indicates you are invited, but not required, to participate.

- **Present teachers with a research-based tool for self-reflection.** Our colleagues in the Washington County School District, St. George, Utah, also shared the Peer Observation Form (Reproducible 4.8) they developed as part of their learning walks peer observation program.

  They modified the Basic 5 Observation Tool covered in Chapter 7 into a Peer Observation Form. This form acts as a way for staff both to learn from each other and to practice recording some of the same objective data points that are used to measure them in the classroom. This provides full transparency to the process of reaching the target and puts nonevaluative coaches in the spotlight as a resource for any teachers who would like to hone their skillset.

- **Train teachers to collect peer-to-peer data.** When collecting peer-to-peer data, observers should enter the classroom and go to the side. Ideally, observers are at an angle to see students' faces without being too obtrusive. Students should be given a heads-up in advance and prepared to see observers at any time.

  Observers should plan to stand or sit for the observation. Standing often yields the best look at data points. Classroom teachers may find it less obtrusive for observers to sit, however. While many classrooms lack additional chairs, the teacher may be able to provide seating arrangements prior to these learning observations. Defer to the classroom teacher on this decision.

  Once in position, peer observers will record data and any notes on the research-based tool provided, in this case the Peer Observation Form (Reproducible 4.8). If students are working, as opposed to being engaged in teacher-directed instruction, peers should be encouraged to ask students questions related to the observations.

Staff should be trained on how to collect data for ratio of interactions and opportunities to respond, as outlined in the section about conducting walk-through visits. A new data point, Disruptions, has been added to the observation. Disruptive behavior can be defined as *a statement or action by one or more students that interferes with an ongoing class activity.* As a general starting point, a disruption is any behavior that causes the teacher to pause or stop the flow of instruction in order to respond. A disruption would also include any behavior that gets another student off task. For instance, if two students are talking to each other and the teacher responds, this counts as one disruption. If one student is in the back of the room doing jumping jacks but the teacher is utilizing planned ignoring and has taught all students to ignore any misbehaviors, this does not count as a disruption. While you may disagree with this, this student's inappropriate behavior will show up in the next data point, On-Task Behavior. Disruptions are not synonymous with off-task behavior. For the off-task behavior to be a disruption, it must literally *disrupt* the focus of the teacher or other learners in the classroom. All three of these data points are collected simultaneously for the first 10 minutes of the observation.

On-task behavior is recorded slightly differently than in the 3–5 minute walk-throughs. This process is more time intensive but provides more accuracy in the actual percentage of on-task students. On-task behavior is defined as *a student being academically engaged in the current task of the instructional activity.* During independent instruction, this may be a student working on their own to complete an assignment, read a text or book, or complete a hands-on project. During teacher-guided instruction, this could look like a student raising their hand, answering a teacher's question, or engaging in an on-topic conversation with a group or partner to answer a given prompt. For this section, follow a set pattern to observe each student in turn for 5 minutes. Every 5 seconds, the observer glances up at the next student in the pattern and then looks back at the form. If the student appears engaged and on task at the moment the observer looks up, a + (plus) symbol is marked. If the student is not engaged or at least does not *appear* to be (remember, the reliability of this observation is built on the average of many time slices), a – (minus) is marked. After each mark is made, the observer waits for the remainder

Reproducible 4.8 *Peer Observation Form (p. 1 of 2)*

For a full description of how to collect data for Steps 1 and 2, see data collection instructions (pp. 224–224). For peer learning walks, campuses can use any of the walk-through forms (Repros 4.4–4.7) presented earlier in this chapter.

Peer Observation Form

TEACHER ______________________ DATE ______________

CLASS ______________ ACTIVITY ______________

STEP 1 During a 10-minute observation of teacher-guided instruction, record simple tally marks for each of the following behaviors. ***10 minutes***

BENCHMARK	OBSERVATION PERIOD		TOTAL
	Positive (Appropriate Behavior)	Corrective (Inappropriate Behavior)	
Ratio of Interactions			____:____ Positive:Corrective (3) (1)
Opportunities to Respond			
Disruptions			

STEP 2 **Benchmark: On-Task Behavior**

For the next 5 minutes, focus on a different student every 5 seconds. Record a "+" symbol to indicate on-task or engaged behavior and a "–" symbol to indicate off-task behavior. When each student has been observed, begin the progression again. Continue until 5 minutes has elapsed. ***5 minutes***

1	2	3	4	5	6	7	8	9	10	11	12
13	14	15	16	17	18	19	20	21	22	23	24
25	26	27	28	29	30	31	32	33	34	35	36
37	38	39	40	41	42	43	44	45	46	47	48
49	50	51	52	53	54	55	56	57	58	59	60

Divide the number of on-task (+) marks by the total number of marks (60).

Time on task (percentage of on-task behavior) = ______%.

 REPRODUCIBLE 4.8

Reproducible 4.8 (cont.) *Peer Observation Form (p. 2 of 2)*

Peer Observation Form (p. 2 of 2)

STEP 3

COMPONENT	DESCRIPTION	OBSERVED?	COMMENTS
Structure/Organize the classroom for success.	Is the room arranged so the teacher can get from any part of the room to any other part of the room relatively efficiently?	Y N N/A	
	Can the teacher and students access materials and the pencil sharpener without disturbing others?	Y N N/A	
Observe student behavior (supervise).	Does the teacher circulate and scan as a means of observing/monitoring student behavior?	Y N N/A	
	Does the teacher model friendly, respectful behavior while monitoring the classroom?	Y N N/A	
Interact positively with students.	Does the teacher interact with every student in a welcoming manner?	Y N N/A	
	Does the teacher provide age-appropriate, nonembarrassing feedback?	Y N N/A	
Correct irresponsible behavior fluently—that is, in a manner that does not interrupt the flow of instruction.	Does the teacher correct consistently?	Y N N/A	
	Does the teacher correct calmly?	Y N N/A	
	Does the teacher correct immediately?	Y N N/A	
	Does the teacher correct briefly?	Y N N/A	
	Does the teacher correct respectfully?	Y N N/A	

STEP 4 (Optional) Questions / Comments / Notes

 REPRODUCIBLE 4.8

of the 5 seconds and then looks up at the next student in the pattern. The number of + symbols is divided by the total number of marks (60) to arrive at a percentage for students' time on task.

In the third section of the observation form, peers are directed to look for specific evidence of the STOIC Framework being in place. Components that would be included in each piece of the framework are described through a question, which observers answer with a simple Yes, No, or Not Applicable to the learning environment at that time. Space for comments is provided. Observers can use this space to write specifics of what this looked like or questions they may want to discuss with other peers immediately after the observation. The information collected in this section may be helpful for the classroom teacher to aid in their own reflection.

The final section is purely anecdotal in nature. This may be optional, as time allows, but gives the observers space to jot down any questions or comments that arise. This is a great space to give room for peers to reflect on their own practices in the moment during the observation.

In initial learning observations, you may want observers to practice collecting only one or two data points. As these observations become more frequent and staff gain more confidence in the data collection process, peers may use the data collection tools in their entirety.

Clarify Expectations for Teachers to Debrief About Their Peer-To-Peer Observations

After data are collected, the opportunity to reflect with other peers is provided. If multiple peers are observing at the same time and/or in the same classroom, immediately after the observation, we recommend staff engage in a *hall talk*. These hall talks occur between observations and should include notes on what was observed, any questions that an observer might have had, and any clarifying information (e.g., "This was the first time this teacher asked students to engage in cooperative groups").

At the conclusion of all learning observations done that day, all teams that were deployed should meet back together and create a general list of what they observed. *At this point, ALL observation forms are collected and destroyed.* Observers should also receive a short evaluation of the learning observation process itself to complete immediately or by a later date.

Peer observers should avoid reflecting using evaluative and judgmental language in both hall talks and during general observations at the conclusion of the day. Statements such as the following should be avoided:

- "It was good when the teacher . . ."
- "I really liked . . ."
- "Well, everyone has a bad day sometimes . . ."
- "Wow! He/she is a great teacher!"

Peer observers should be directed to use statements such as:

- "When the teacher did (this), the students . . ."
- "I noticed/saw/observed . . ."
- "I wonder why . . .?"

This supports the objective that these observations are purely reflective and nonevaluative. The purpose of these classroom visits is for peer observers to consider adaptations to their own practice based on what they may learn from another colleague in their natural habitat, the classroom.

> *After I completed the learning walk this morning, I immediately made several changes based on what I had observed and implemented them beginning with my afternoon classes.*
>
> —M.B.

Wrapping It Up **CHAPTER 4 SUMMARY**

Whether through an evaluator, support personnel, or peers, observation is critical in the process of implementing and sustaining practice over time. Without observations, even teachers with the best intentions will slip into prior practice, into what's been comfortable in the past, believing this classroom management model is just another flash in the pan that will be replaced with the next big, shiny idea within a year or two. In other words, they believe, "This too shall pass." And data on school reform prove them right. Professional development that's not ongoing, supported by coaches, and actively observed will go by the wayside. This process erodes trust over time. To keep relationships intact and sustain momentum and enthusiasm for any initiative, you must give it life. Engaging in active observations helps keep the overall vision, and the target for reaching that vision, in sight at all times.

What to Know

- The role of the evaluator in engaging in intentional, ongoing walk-throughs is critical to keeping the pressure on, as a warm demander, to reach the intended target.
- The role of nonevaluative coaches is necessary in providing active assistance for staff to respond to the pressure of reaching the target.

- Staff should feel both a sense of urgency and enthusiasm to reach the target and should be willing and prepared for ongoing observations of classroom management practices.
- Peer-to-peer learning observations serve to build camaraderie and collaboration through the active reflection inherent in the process.

What to Do

- Prepare staff for visits from multiple observers: evaluators, nonevaluative coaches, and peers.
- Create or follow the game plan regarding data collection for walk-through visits.
- As evaluators, debrief after walk-through visits.
- Meet as evaluators and nonevaluative coaches to learn how to collect specific data.
- Practice data collection as evaluators and nonevaluative coaches for the purpose of calibration.
- Analyze trend data to provide for staff needs.
- Plan professional development based on trend data.
- Protect the confidentiality of practitioners within the coaching model.
- Set up a system of peer-to-peer learning observations.

Notes

STRUCTURE FOR SUCCESS · TEACH EXPECTATIONS
OBSERVE AND MONITOR · **INTERACT POSITIVELY** · CORRECT FLUENTLY

CHAPTER 5

Interact Positively
Building Trust Through Communication and Partnership

The biggest communication problem is we do not listen to understand. We listen to reply. —Stephen Covey

The words and actions of the leadership team have important symbolic connotations that overshadow even the selection of a classroom management model or launch of a coaching program. Although coaches are responsible for facilitating professional learning in a school, the principal is the instructional leader. They must empower their teachers to identify and collectively pursue a shared vision of instructional excellence.

Principals should also publicly support coaches. This encompasses support for both coaches' actions and their professional development. Support goes both ways. Coaches, by being supportive of their principal and, more generally, of the tough decisions that administrators have to make (even when unpopular), can strengthen their own ability to positively impact their school. Support demonstrates trust.

> *We have found that the single factor common to every successful change initiative is that relationships improve. If relationships improve, things get better. If they remain the same or get worse, ground is lost. Thus leaders must be consummate relationship builders with diverse people and groups—especially with people different than themselves. Effective leaders constantly foster purposeful interaction and problem-solving, and are wary of easy consensus.* —Michael Fullan

Building relational trust is a critical factor in moving schools forward. Fullan is correct—relationships *are* almost everything (2001, p. 74). The coach's job is more than simply sharing teaching practices. A coach should work to improve the culture of a school one conversation at a time.

This chapter outlines how to build these crucial relationships through coaching interactions. Specifically, you will:

- Identify the three qualities that build trust and the one that compromises it.
- Apply good listening skills to bolster communication.
- Think deeply about the principles needed to effectively partner with teachers.

Establishing a multi-tiered system of support for teachers through coaching requires careful and intentional action in establishing a supportive context for coaching. Although we discuss these principles in the context of establishing Tier 1 levels of support, they will be embedded and revisited within coaching interactions across all tiers of support.

BUILD TRUST

Trust is critical in any relationship, both personal and professional. The moment that trust begins to erode is often the demise of any relationship. Who among us hasn't left a job, a friendship, or possibly a relationship with a significant other because of the lack of trust? (And if you've never faced this issue, you are one of the lucky few.)

When I started my teaching career, I was hired by an administrator with whom I instantly connected. It had been my favorite building as a substitute teacher, and, as this was back in the day when teachers were plentiful and openings were not, I was hoping against hope that this building would take me in. I was hired after a year of substitute teaching as a seventh-grade language arts and social studies teacher and had the opportunity to work with a great leader and amazing colleagues, which is such a gift when you first enter the classroom. Unfortunately, this administrator was so good at his job that he was promoted and eventually went on to become a superintendent of schools in another district.

Over the course of the next 3 years, we had a few administrators try out the job, including an interim. By the time we landed on an administrator who decided to stay, trust between staff and leadership had eroded greatly. Everyone was jumpy, awaiting this leader's departure. We were certainly not on board to implement what we had begun to see as pet projects and, as in many unhealthy relationships, we were pushing away and against this person without even giving them a full chance.

I've thought about this a lot over the years. I've worked in two buildings as both a teacher and a full-time coach and in countless others as a district behavior coach and in my current role as a consultant. I jokingly say that out of all those administrators, I would still only work for one: my original principal. As I worked on this book and focused on how to improve interactions among all stakeholders, I reflected on this response I often give when people ask if I'd ever return to teaching full time. And it truly boils down to this: I trusted him. I believed he had my best interests and the best interests of our campus and students at heart. He didn't just know everyone as a professional, he was also a part of the community. He listened without judgment, and he trusted all of us to be the professionals he hired us to be. In other words, he was the epitome of the trust equation.

The Trust Equation

David Maister, Charles Green, and Robert Galford, in their book *The Trust Advisor* (2000), created a simple fraction to determine trust. It's been modified here using some adapted language to help coaches, both evaluative and nonevaluative, as they work to build and sustain trust across time:

$$\frac{\text{Credibility} + \text{Reliability} + \text{Warmth}}{\text{Self-Focus}} = \text{Trust}$$

Credibility, reliability, and warmth divided by self-focus. The larger the numerator and the smaller the denominator, the greater the trust. When you exhibit credibility, reliability, and warmth, and when you actively work to limit the focus on yourself, this builds relational trust. In all interactions with staff, coaches should be working to increase this number.

Credibility. Credibility "isn't just content expertise. It's content expertise plus presence, which refers to how we look, act, react, and talk about our content" (Maister et al., p. 71). It's asking if you know your stuff. In working to help practitioners implement the classroom management model, you should be well versed in the model. You should be able to answer questions related to content. Obviously, coaches may be just as new to the content as the teachers. Being honest with teachers that you are also in the learning process builds credibility. In other words, you're being honest that you don't know what you don't know. When you do know the content, you should be able to answer deeper-level questions, and when you don't have an answer, you should be upfront about that. Pretending to know content doesn't build credibility—it undermines both your role and the resource itself.

To build credibility within content knowledge, you should know at least slightly more than your teachers. Read the resource, take more notes during the initial professional development process, be willing to find answers to the things you don't know and retain that information for future reference. If you're there as the cornerstone of support personnel, you must have the content knowledge to, well, support.

Reliability. "Reliability is the repeated experience of links between promises and action" (Maister et al., p. 75). Simply put, you follow through on what you say you'll do.

In the early days of implementation, as you're building credibility, be aware of exactly what you can do in terms of support. Be aware of limitations on your content knowledge and your own time devoted to supporting the classroom management model. It is always better to underpromise and overdeliver than the reverse.

To build reliability, your word must be gold. The more you actively follow through on what you say you can provide to practitioners, the greater this number becomes. Breaking promises, however small or large they may be, breaks trust over time.

Warmth. Warmth "is about emotional closeness" (Maister et al., p. 77). This is about sharing your life with those you coach and them sharing their lives with you. As I stated in the example of my principal above, you are members of this community of stakeholders. You want to know them personally as well as professionally. It doesn't mean you have to become friends with every single person; it does mean you have to believe each person deserves a seat at the table and that you view them through a lens of curiosity as opposed to judgment.

Get to know each person by asking questions about family and interests. You don't have to dig deeply to find common ground. Learn enough so that you see this person as a whole human being, not just a cog in the wheel of implementation.

Self-focus. Each of these is divided by your amount of self-focus. Anything that keeps the focus on you detracts from focusing on those you support. This doesn't mean self-focus is zero. It's imperative that you are aware of your own limitations, that you set clear and definable boundaries of support, and that you are willing to share yourself to provide warmth. It simply means that the more you are concerned about your own issues, both personal and professional, that you may bring to the table, the less room you have to provide credibility, reliability, and warmth to others.

Reproducible 5.1 presents clear guidelines on how to engender trust within coaching interactions. Adapted from *Leadership in Behavior Support* (Sprick et al., 2016), these guidelines all fall under the idea that credibility, reliability, and warmth are the keys to building relational trust. Rank the traits listed on Reproducible 5.1, designating the trait that you consider your strongest as number 1 and the trait you consider your weakest as number 12. Prioritize working on your weakest traits first, and reevaluate periodically.

COMMUNICATE MASTERFULLY

To be a leader of change, you must communicate, and communicate masterfully. There is no substitute, no shortcut around it. Whatever the level of your leadership skills right now, the single most effective step you can take to bolster your capacity for school leadership is to work on and polish your ability to communicate clearly, empathetically, and without judgment or prejudice.

The ability of administrators and coaches to build successful relationships with teachers will largely determine whether a coaching program to support classroom management

Reproducible 5.1 *Leadership Traits That Engender Trust*

Leadership Traits That Engender Trust

Instructions: Rank the 12 traits below. Number 1 should be the one in which you consider yourself the strongest, and Number 12 is the one in which you consider yourself the weakest. Write the guideline that you ranked Number 12 on your planning calendar. For 2 weeks, try to focus on being more effective at that one trait. Then write the guideline ranked Number 11 on your calendar and focus on it for 2 weeks. Continue working on the guidelines in descending order until you have practiced each guideline you want to improve.

RANK	TRAIT	NOTES
	Manage space and materials efficiently.	
	Communicate expectations clearly.	
	Provide positive feedback.	
	Be genuine and honest.	
	Empathize with others by listening for understanding first.	
	Treat everyone with respect.	
	Be highly visible.	
	Respect confidentiality.	
	Treat all staff professionally.	
	Make a special effort to include noncertified staff.	
	Acknowledge past efforts before you suggest changes.	
	Build trust with parents and community members.	

 REPRODUCIBLE 5.1

will succeed. The empowerment that arises from open channels of communication among school staff is difficult to overstate.

The fact is that "perfect" communication does not exist, except as a worthy ideal toward which to strive. Part of what makes us human is the unique consciousness and perspective each of us brings to the discussion. When one person strives to communicate something important to another, the mental picture formed by the recipient will not be identical to the original notion. More often than we'd like to think, it is not even close. Communication breakdowns are a major impediment to strong relationships among school colleagues. This is not a school campus condition, it's a human condition—the answers are found in the greater sphere of human experience and apply equally to professionals in any discipline.

The words coaches use to describe their approach to communication are telling: compassionate, empathetic, understanding, patient. While these words may mean different things from one person to another, they point toward an underlying truth that becomes easier to discern as we reflect on them: The coach's first role is to build a strong, safe relationship with each teacher-collaborator, an oasis or garden in the path of a teacher's trek across the school year where assessment, observation, and feedback can freely take place and where psychic walls and barriers, defense mechanisms, and bunker mentalities can be safely let down.

It's that simple, and it's that tough. Coaching is relationship building. If you can't get past the guards at the gate, you will never see the person you came to help inside.

An important prerequisite to communicating effectively is recognizing the nature of different relationships.

Administrator-teacher relationship. The administrator-teacher relationship is inherently different from the teacher-coach relationship. A principal or administrator, no matter how nice, supportive, and collegial, is always in a superordinate position—the boss. The dynamics of communication are different in that situation than they would be for two colleagues on an equal footing speaking in a nonevaluative context.

Suppose a principal offers an observation about a teacher's behavior management technique. What does the teacher hear differently than she might were the same comment offered by a collaborating coach or fellow teacher? She may think the principal is telling her she needs to change the way she teaches. She may interpret the principal's interest as a prelude to evaluation. She may infer a great many things the principal did not intend—all of which would be completely rational in the context of their relationship; her status, pay, and future assignments depend, in some measure, on the principal's appraisal of her work. As cordial as their relationship may be, for many good and valid reasons she will likely not lay bare her innermost thoughts the way she might to a sympathetic third party.

The nature of the superior/subordinate relationship dictates to some degree the type of interactions an administrator can have with staff. If you are an administrator, do not mistake this necessary formality or "standing on ceremony" for anything more or less than it is—a simple function of your job description in relation to that of your teaching colleagues. What you hear from teachers may be shaded by self-protection, insecurity, or their own sense of professionalism. Likewise, what you say may fall with extra import on the ears of those who hear it. As an administrator, you need to be especially careful of what you say and to clarify what you mean when you say it—and then you must check to make sure you have been understood. Even if you want to, you cannot simultaneously be a buddy and a voice of authority to teachers.

> *"As an administrator, you need to be especially careful of what you say and to clarify what you mean when you say it."*

Coach-teacher relationship. The role of a coach in the coach-teacher relationship is (or at least should be) fundamentally different from that of an administrator in that a teacher can approach a coach in confidence and the coach can provide the teacher with nonevaluative support, keep their work together confidential, and protect the teacher's anonymity if necessary. Administrators and coaches should have clear agreements that coaches are not involved in teacher evaluation, that the teacher-coach relationship is confidential, and that teachers should have the choice of whether to work with coaches or not. This allows the role of coach to be entirely supportive and nonthreatening.

"Teachers know that if they tell me something, I won't get upset," says veteran coach Lynn Barnes. "I accept their opinions, and as a partnership, we are more accepting of each other. They're willing to share ideas; they're willing to meet with me, and they share their kids with me. They wouldn't share their kids if they didn't believe and trust me."

Coach-administrator relationship. In answering to a principal or administrator, the coach becomes a liaison between teachers and their supervisors. This quiet role is vitally important, for it completes the circle of accountability between teachers and administrators that exists in strong schools.

Good coaches knit the fabric of a school tighter with timely and reliable information about the needs of teachers and students. Without breaking confidentiality, they can advise administrators about challenges teachers face and how they are being met, areas of concern to address at the individual or schoolwide level, and success stories to be celebrated and perhaps replicated in other classrooms.

For example, a coach may suggest to the administrator that quite a few teachers (without specifying who) are tired and are having difficulty maintaining positive interactions with students. The coach and administrator could jointly decide on a fun team-building activity for a staff meeting, followed by a quick reminder about the benefits of a 3:1 ratio of positive to corrective interactions with students.

In *Better Conversations*, Jim Knight (2015) goes into detail about how to communicate in professional partnerships. He articulates the small skills that make up effective communication. These skills include listening with empathy, fostering dialogue, asking better questions, connecting, finding common ground, and redirecting toxic words and emotions. *Better Conversations* outlines the trust equation, introduced above, which is a culmination of applying all of these skills. Because the art of communication is so complex and requires ongoing self-reflection, we encourage you to study the art of communication in more depth. Like teaching and coaching, becoming an effective communicator is a lifelong learning task—no one will ever be such a gifted communicator that they cannot learn more. If you find a tip in this section useful, imagine it as the tip of a vast iceberg of knowledge, one that is continually being added to by effective communicators, and imagine that your discoveries along the way will someday become a part of it.

LISTEN AUTHENTICALLY

Open almost any book, including *Better Conversations*, on communication, personal growth, or leadership and you'll find a section on the importance of being a good listener. The writer Margaret Millar provided an astute observation about why many attempts at communication fail: "Most conversations are simply monologues delivered in the presence of witnesses" (1942). A good listener is more interested in what the other participant is saying than in what to say next. The coach who is a good listener talks less than the teacher, turns the focus of conversation back to the teacher, and in the event of disagreement, does not try to put their opinion across until hearing and understanding—and verifying that they understand—the teacher's position.

Listening is surprisingly difficult. Our opinions, beliefs, background, inclinations, impulses, and especially our memories all crowd for space in our consciousness. If it seems we too often cross signals when attempting to communicate, it helps to recognize how extraordinary it is that we understand each other as well as we do.

Some questions you ask will bring up anxiety for certain teachers. Other questions can draw out confidence and competence. Know that, as a coach or administrator, your job frequently requires you to bring up topics that pull teachers to both ends of this continuum. Your sensitivity in understanding this, in noticing subtle cues in the emotional undercurrent of your conversations, can make the difference between a successful collaboration and a missed opportunity. Listening is as much an act of will as it is a skill or art. Your attentiveness can be the decisive element that sways a collaboration for the better. When you listen, really listen.

> ***The secret of success is sincerity. Once you can fake that, you've got it made.*** *—Jean Giraudoux*

All kidding aside, if there's one secret to being a good listener, it's personal authenticity. Teachers can spot a phony a city block away. If you find yourself at a decision point between false sincerity or an honest shrug, choose authenticity. Your *intention* counts more than the behavior benchmarks you commit to memory, more even than the words you choose. The honesty you project will in time come to be mirrored by staff and ultimately by students. An old saying has it that you can't fake talent. You can't fake honesty, either. When you listen, know why you are listening. Listen because you're curious. Listen because you care. Authentic listening begins with honesty.

BUT OUT

Many years ago, before the advent of the iPad, I was in a bookstore in the Dallas Love Airport. I needed a book for the ride home, and I happened to pick up Ori and Rom Brafman's *Sway*, a book I've given away and repurchased countless times. For someone who works in school reform, the subtitle really drew me in: *The Irresistible Pull of Irrational Behavior*. "Oh, my goodness," I thought, rather smugly I might add, "I work with irrational people all the time!" Imagine my shock and horror at reading this book to discover that I, too, was absolutely irrational from time to time (less frequently than my husband would claim, but far more frequently than with what I was comfortable). I held on to beliefs and ideas for far longer than they served me well.

When I'm not ready to reconcile my beliefs with new data presented to me, I say the word *but*, and I say it a lot. I'll paraphrase the other person's thought ("Paraphrasing! Wow, I'm such a good listener," I would think), only to immediately follow with the word *but* and my own argument for why my belief or idea is better. I'll even start sentences with *but*! After reading *Sway*, I've become more aware and have worked to mostly eradicate that word from my vocabulary. At the very least, actively avoiding the word slows down my natural inclination to argue, and, I think, helps me to be a better listener. *But* is most often used to win others to our sides. When *but* is removed and the objective is no longer to "win," authentic listening and openness to new ideas are natural byproducts.

How do you develop interest, curiosity, and caring? "The more deeply you understand other people, the more you will appreciate them, the more reverent you will feel toward them," writes Stephen Covey, author and originator of *The 7 Habits of Highly Effective People* (1989). "To touch the soul of another is to walk on holy ground" (p. 258). The use of such words as *holy* and *reverent* by this master of professional development is not accidental. Truly effective communication occurs as a result of acts of *empathetic listening*—understanding the thoughts and feelings of another not just cognitively but emotionally, spiritually, personally, deeply. Empathy for another begins with humility. As you prepare to work with a teacher, check your ego and self-defense mechanisms at the door. Empathetic listening requires that you set aside your ego long enough to allow another's world view and perspective in. The suggestions you offer will be stronger for it and probably better received.

See Box 5.1 on the next page for more suggestions to help you become a better listener.

BOX 5.1 *Strategies for Better Listening*

What can you do strategically to become a better listener? Here are seven ideas to get you started.

❶ Develop inner silence.

Train yourself to silence thoughts that lead you to judge rather than simply experience the comments of others. When a colleague provokes a reaction in you that jars you out of your listening state, make a personal note to return to it and reflect on it later, and return to empathetic listening.

❷ Listen for what contradicts your assumptions.

People are attracted to messages that reinforce their beliefs and predispositions. You can push back against this bias by directing your brain to pay more attention to messages that contradict your assumptions.

❸ Clarify.

Paraphrase or mirror your partner; ask for elucidation or elaboration to ensure that you accurately understand what's being said. Used skillfully, this simple but often overlooked device can be integrated into the flow of conversation so that it disappears, and colleagues are unaware that you are using any listening strategy at all.

❹ Communicate your understanding.

Don't be such a good listener that you sit tongue tied, stone faced, and growing roots into your chair. Participate! Be demonstrative and energetic when the conversation demands it. Use the contrast between quiet moments and periods of levity or dynamism as an ally in creating a stimulating, rejuvenating conversation. You've worked hard to listen and to understand; don't stop the good work and drop your end of the conversation. Be animated, be passionate, but above all be yourself, providing as many verbal and nonverbal signals as you can think of to demonstrate that you're getting it, thus encouraging your speaker to keep talking.

❺ Practice every day.

Like any healthy habit or developed skill, your ability to listen should be practiced. Look for situations where you can work on your listening skills and set aside time to learn more about listening. Even time spent clipping school-themed comic strips or memorizing particularly clever work-related jokes is an opportunity to become a more involved participant in any collegial conversation—and a better listener.

❻ Practice with terrible listeners!

The teacher across from you is not ignoring you because they are stubborn—they're talking over you because they don't feel heard! Try telling yourself this even if at first you don't believe it. "Find the most stubborn person you know, the person who never seems to take in anything you say, the person who repeats himself or herself in every conversation you ever have—and listen . . . listen for feelings, like frustration or pride or fear, and acknowledge those feelings. See whether that person doesn't become a better listener after all" (Stone et al., 2000, p. 167).

❼ Develop a routine.

Memorize the pathways that your most successful conversations have traversed and make a mental note to try them again when the opportunity arises. Much of what you need to be an effective listener you already know! If you have engaged in a successful, productive dialogue in the past, you already have an inner template for what that looks, sounds, and feels like. Your task is to bring that knowledge to your awareness, to apply patterns consciously that may have happened spontaneously or unintentionally in the past. Map the course you envision for a successful listening conversation. It doesn't have to wind up there. As Oliver Wendell Holmes said, "I find the great thing in this world is not so much where we stand as in what direction we are moving. We must sail sometimes with the wind and sometimes against it—but we must sail and not drift, nor lie at anchor." When you listen, it matters less that you know where the conversation is headed than that you have a destination in mind.

CREATE ONGOING REGARD

Kegan and Lahey, the authors of *How the Way We Talk Can Change the Way We Work* (2001), created a language and script to create ongoing regard:

> *Ongoing regard is not about praising, stroking, or positively defining a person to herself or to others. We say it again: It is about enhancing the quality of a special kind of information. It is about informing the person about our experience of him or her.*

Ongoing regard involves a set of directives regarding the language you use when providing feedback to others. *Be direct* by delivering your message directly to the recipient—not to a room full of people. *Be specific* by describing the precise action for which you are thanking the person, excluding personal attributes. *Reveal the impact* that person's action had on you instead of generic phrases.

There is an accompanying script to the use of this language. *Greet* the person by saying their name correctly. *Express gratitude* and describe their action. *Discuss impact* by giving an example of why their action was valued. *Make reference* to how that action made you feel. And, finally, *give regards* again in closing.

Instead of this:

> *I'd like to thank Kathy for working so tirelessly on this project. She always does such a good job. Kathy, way to go.*

Imagine this:

> *Kathy, I wanted to thank you so much for working so tirelessly on this project. I know that you gave up time to get our new procedures in place for the students in the cafeteria. The time you sacrificed not only got it done more quickly, but it saved me and the other people on the team time as well. You really stepped in when others couldn't or wouldn't. I'm so glad to have you on the team. Thank you for all that you do.*

Ongoing regard provides a deeper understanding of the behavior or action being recognized. That recognition is apt to inspire more of that same behavior in the future. And it doesn't hurt that it tends to build morale for both parties. We would encourage you to use this language when building your 3:1 ratio with the staff you support. Recognition is a basic human need, and the specificity of this feedback makes those who receive it feel seen and heard.

PARTNERSHIP PRINCIPLES

The principles on which coaches base their actions might be as important as what they actually do when working with teachers. Simply put, if the coach approaches a teacher in a manner that's not conducive to a partnership, the coach may have a very difficult time leading change, no matter how much they know about effective classroom management. Good coaches think deeply about their philosophy, theory of action, and *principles* as they embark on the challenging and rewarding work of coaching. Underlying everything in this book is the principle that a coach-teacher relationship is first and foremost a partnership. This chapter discusses what partnership can mean to a coach and teacher.

Social scientist Riane Eisler (2000), in studying prehistoric cultures, came to see the *partnership model* of relationships as one of two possible ways of understanding life, the other being what she calls the *dominator model*. Author Peter Block suggests that the choice is between models of partnership and patriarchy, or the slightly less loaded word *parenting*. "Our difficulty with creating partnerships," he writes, "is that parenting—and its stronger cousin, patriarchy—is so deeply ingrained in our muscle memory and armature that we don't even realize we are doing it" (2013). We choose partnership as the basis for our model because anything else must involve an imbalance, a fundamental instability in professional relationships among educators that cannot help but be reflected in the relationship of teachers to their students, administrators to their staff, and the school to the outside community it serves.

Gandhi urged people to *be* the change they want to see in the world. As leaders of change, we must *be* the change we wish to see in our schools. By setting the example of partnership learning, we bring partnership and change into being. Seeing the world through partnership glasses reveals human relationships in new and unexpected ways. A philosophy of coaching may come from many perspectives—in particular, the principles of equality, voice, choice, dialogue, reflection, praxis, and reciprocity. These are subsets of one central principle: *Coaches and teachers must work together as partners.*

Knowing these Partnership Principles serves two purposes. First, the principles represent a foundation on which to base actions. When planning what to do and how to do it, you can stop and ask whether your actions are consistent with personal principles. Principles also function as a measuring stick for evaluating what worked and didn't work during professional learning. A coach who believes that a particular course of action hasn't been successful can go back to their core principles to, as often as not, discover that one or more have been violated.

Before adopting any principle as your own, reflect first on what it stands for. Requiring someone to adopt a predetermined set of principles would be completely inconsistent with the partnership approach. What matters is that coaches carefully consider their own philosophies. We lay out our vision of coaching as a partnership not for you to copy down and memorize, but as a point of departure for you to consider your own assumptions and discover your own guiding principles.

The sections that follow present a description of each Partnership Principle. In Reproducible 5.2, Partnership Principles—Reflection for Coaches, we place the questions from the end of each principle into a rubric for self-assessment. This tool reflects how well these principles are applied across the board in coaching conversations. You can also use this rubric to reflect on an individual coaching conversation. Simply replace the generic term *teacher* with the actual teacher's name as you answer each question.

In Reproducible 5.3, Partnership Principles—Assessment of the Coaching Conversation, we flip these questions slightly, phrasing them in such a way that a teacher who is being coached can assess the coaching interaction. We recommend periodically recording a coaching conversation. As a coach, rate yourself using Reproducible 5.2 and ask the individual teacher to rate the conversation using Reproducible 5.3. This is for your personal growth as a coach—to keep you aware of and help you build capacity in each of these principles.

Equality

Partnership springs from a quintessentially democratic ideal: the belief that all people are created equal and that everyone's voice counts, everyone has a say, everyone deserves an equal shot. Some presumption of equal status is prerequisite to any partnership. In a true partnership, one partner does not tell the other what to do; they discuss or debate issues as a team. The root of partner is *part*. Partners realize that they are only a part of the whole, and in healthy partnerships, people find that they make the best decisions when they listen to their partner and recognize their partner as an equal.

NON-EXAMPLE

Natalie, a first-year coach, was fuming. "What," she wondered, "is it going to take to get these teachers on board? Don't they realize they're hurting their kids by not using CHAMPS? I am so frustrated with their laziness and their resistance that I could just scream!" Natalie's frustration was understandable. She had been trying to get schoolwide buy-in for the last 8 months. The situation was all the more discomfiting because Natalie knew a lot about CHAMPS. She had read the book carefully, trained comprehensively, and attended additional workshops. Natalie was an expert and had clearly communicated her expertise to the teachers in her school when she arrived. Without blowing her horn too much, Natalie knew that her school was lucky to have her, and she really wanted to make a difference.

When she came in, Natalie couldn't wait to get started. She wanted everyone on board quickly, and she was prepared to do whatever it took to create a safer and more civil school. She had sent out a detailed memo to all staff explaining just how valuable CHAMPS was, scheduling three compulsory meetings at which she explained the power of CHAMPS and told everyone that she was there to make it happen.

Reproducible 5.2 *Partnership Principles—Reflection for Coaches*

Partnership Principles

Reflection for Coaches

Directions: Rate yourself on a scale of 1 to 5 on each question from the seven Partnership Principles. On which principle(s) did you rate yourself strongest? Which are most challenging? Choose one principle to improve as a goal.

	Strongly Disagree				Strongly Agree
Equality					
1. Do I really acknowledge teachers whose opinions are different than mine?	1	2	3	4	5
2. Do teachers believe that their knowledge and experience count when I work with them?	1	2	3	4	5
3. Do I believe that teachers bring important knowledge to the discussion?	1	2	3	4	5
Voice					
1. Do I listen with the intent to understand?	1	2	3	4	5
2. Do I fully understand what a teacher has to say before I voice my point of view?	1	2	3	4	5
3. Do I ask questions that encourage teachers to say what they really think?	1	2	3	4	5
Choice					
1. Do I allow teachers to make their own decisions about the feedback I present?	1	2	3	4	5
2. Do I respect their decisions if they differ from mine?	1	2	3	4	5
3. Do I recognize that teachers will need to adapt information for their individual needs?	1	2	3	4	5
Dialogue					
1. Do I speak less than 60% of the time when I talk with teachers?	1	2	3	4	5
2. Do teachers develop new ideas during our conversations?	1	2	3	4	5
3. Are our coaching conversations lively?	1	2	3	4	5
Reflection					
1. Am I able to accept teachers rejecting the views I offer?	1	2	3	4	5
2. Do I encourage reflection and discussion on ideas I share?	1	2	3	4	5
3. Do the suggestions I provide allow teachers to make their own decisions and adapt ideas to their needs?	1	2	3	4	5
Praxis					
1. Are teachers encouraged to explore ways they might use what I'm explaining?	1	2	3	4	5
2. Do teachers consider the practice implications of what I'm talking about?	1	2	3	4	5
3. Do I spend as much time with teachers planning action as talking about theory and practice?	1	2	3	4	5
Reciprocity					
1. Do I truly expect to learn from my teachers?	1	2	3	4	5
2. Am I open enough to all of my teachers to learn what they can teach me?	1	2	3	4	5
3. Am I energized by coaching interactions?	1	2	3	4	5

Principle to improve: ______________________________

Three ideas for improvement: ______________________________

____

____

____

 REPRODUCIBLE 5.2

Reproducible 5.3 *Partnership Principles—Assessment of the Coaching Conversation*

Partnership Principles

Assessment of the Coaching Conversation

Directions: Rate your coach on each question from the seven Partnership Principles. For any principle you are unsure about or feel does not apply, leave the assessment rating blank.

	Strongly Disagree				Strongly Agree
Equality					
1. Do you feel the coach really acknowledges your opinion when it differs from theirs?	1	2	3	4	5
2. Do you feel the coach belives that your knowledge and experience count when they work with you?	1	2	3	4	5
3. Do you feel the coach believes that you bring important knowledge to the school discussion?	1	2	3	4	5
Voice					
1. Does the coach listen with the intent to understand?	1	2	3	4	5
2. Does the coach fully understand what you have to say before they voice their point of view?	1	2	3	4	5
3. Does the coach ask questions that encourage you to say what you really think?	1	2	3	4	5
Choice					
1. Does the coach offer you real choices during your discussions?	1	2	3	4	5
2. Do you feel the coach allows you to make your own decision about the feedback they present?	1	2	3	4	5
3. Does the coach recognize that you will need to adapt materials for your own individual classroom?	1	2	3	4	5
Dialogue					
1. Does the coach speak less than 60% of the time during discussions with you?	1	2	3	4	5
2. Do you develop new ideas during a discussion with your coach?	1	2	3	4	5
3. Do you feel the coaching conversation is lively?	1	2	3	4	5
Reflection					
1. Does the coach accept when you reject the views they offer?	1	2	3	4	5
2. Does the coach encourage reflection and discussion on any content they share with you?	1	2	3	4	5
3. Does the coach provide suggestions that allow you to make your own decisions and adapt ideas to your classroom?	1	2	3	4	5
Praxis					
1. Does the coach encourage you to explore ways you might use what they are explaining?	1	2	3	4	5
2. Do you feel the coach encourages you to consider the practical applications of ideas you are discussing?	1	2	3	4	5
3. Does the coach spend as much time with you planning action as talking about theory and practice?	1	2	3	4	5
Reciprocity					
1. Do you feel the coach truly expects to learn from you as a collaborating teacher?	1	2	3	4	5
2. Do you feel the coach is open to learning what you can teach them?	1	2	3	4	5
3. Does your coach seem energized by what they learn during your coaching discussions?	1	2	3	4	5

REPRODUCIBLE 5.3

She described the expectations she thought were best for everyone. Natalie even said she'd be happy to come into classrooms and make sure the teachers were using CHAMPS correctly. However, the teachers didn't seem to want her help, regardless of how hard she pushed. Why wouldn't the teachers immediately do something that she had so clearly explained would be so beneficial to students? Natalie had to do something to prod them into action, but what?

• • •

When we look at this scenario, of course, it certainly seems plausible that the real reason teachers are choosing not to change has little to do with resistance or lack of interest and an awful lot to do with Natalie's approach. Well-meaning though her intentions may be, by violating the principle of equality (and perhaps some others as well), Natalie is acting as her own worst enemy.

For coaches, partnership is a fundamental belief that every participant should have a say in what decisions are made. Instead of coming from the top and cascading down through a school, decisions should be made in consultation with anyone and everyone affected by them. Of course, this is more easily typed on a memo than turned into actual practice in schools! Yet if we are committed to turning away from a dominance or parenting model, teachers must have a voice in decisions that affect their professional practice.

Allowing everyone to have a voice can seem messy, inefficient, and time consuming until you compare it with the opposite—providing no one with a say. A quote attributed to Winston Churchill puts it best: "No one pretends that democracy is perfect or all-wise. Indeed, it has been said that democracy is the *worst* form of government except all those other forms that have been tried from time to time."

Taking away teachers' equality engenders resentment that can destroy morale and diminish the likelihood of any meaningful change in schools. The principle of equality also has implications for one-on-one interactions between coaches and teachers. When coaches truly see teachers as partners, they stop seeing a teacher's resistance to change as stubbornness or point-blank refusal. Instead, the partnership approach lets the coach view resistance as a product of the *interaction* between coach and teacher.

GETTING *Real* • ***Questions for Administrators and Coaches***

- *Do I really acknowledge teachers whose opinions are different from mine?*
- *Do teachers believe that their knowledge and experience count when I work with them?*
- *Do I believe that teachers bring important knowledge to the coaching conversation?*

Coaches who embrace the principle of equality recognize that in a partnership the goal is not to win the teacher over to the "right" view, but to find a match between what the coach has to offer and what a teacher can use in the classroom. The first step is to understand the teacher's perspective. Coaches can get a better understanding of how to do that by considering the next principle: voice.

Voice

In the partnership approach to coaching, all individuals are given the opportunity to express their points of view—everyone gets a chance to learn from others. Because opinions will inevitably vary, coaches should encourage the expression of a variety of opinions.

POSITIVE EXAMPLE

When Chris, the coach, sat down with Dale Harimoto, he sensed right away that Dale was a little hesitant about collaborating. "Look," Dale said, "I'm interested in talking with you, but I don't have a lot of time. Have you really got anything in your bag of tricks that can help me reach more kids?" The teacher's words seemed like more of a statement than a question to Chris. Chris decided to start by asking simple questions. For about 30 minutes, Chris asked Dale about his classroom: What is the most rewarding part of your job? What hinders you from achieving your goals? What are your students' strengths and weaknesses? Chris listened with his mind and heart, empathizing with Dale's frustrations and following up with additional questions. In a few minutes, Dale had gone from frustrated to calm, and the two men agreed to meet again in a few days to discuss CHAMPS.

At that meeting, Chris laid out the general guidelines and asked Dale to list his most common classroom activities. Then Chris asked Dale what he thought the expectations should be for each activity. "It's your class," Chris told his colleague. "It needs to reflect your opinions; it needs to be right for your classroom." Over time, working together as partners, the coach and teacher created very clear expectations and Dale ably taught these to his students. By actively listening and empowering Dale to craft expectations that were uniquely appropriate for his class, Chris found a way to turn a potentially rocky relationship into a long-term learning partnership.

• • •

Chris was able to create a relationship with Dale because he respected and encouraged Dale's unique voice. If the coach and the teacher are on an equal footing, it stands to reason that the teacher should be free to say what they think and that their opinions count. Acknowledging the principle of voice means valuing both the content of what's said and the person saying it, the speech and the speaker. Learning for not only the teacher but the coach is significantly limited when the authentic voices of teachers are discouraged or silenced.

Coaches can do many things to encourage teachers to voice their opinions. They can focus conversations on teachers' needs, not the coach's ideas. Coaches can ask more questions and offer fewer prescriptive suggestions. They can encourage their collaborating teachers to shape the teaching practices to be used in the classroom. A coach who has adopted the principle of *voice* might decide to make sure the collaborating teacher gets the majority of speaking time during coaching conversations. When teachers are allowed to voice their concerns and ideas, the new practices are differentiated to fit the unique attributes of each classroom.

Providing the opportunity for voice is only the first half of the challenge. A good coach also provides a ready audience by listening authentically, empathetically, and with the intent to understand. The coach sees what the teacher sees, feels what the teacher feels. For a few vicarious moments, the coach looks out at the class through the eyes of the teacher.

Hearing the experiences and opinions of someone you value as an equal is an act of partnership and meets a fundamental human need to be seen and heard. When people believe they have been heard, it can be a deeply moving and meaningful experience.

GETTING *Real* • *Questions for Administrators and Coaches*

- *Do I listen with the intent to understand?*
- *Do I fully understand what a teacher has to say before I voice my point of view?*
- *Do I ask questions that encourage teachers to say what they really think?*

Choice

Partners *choose* to work together. People enter into a partnership as equals: Each has a hand in the direction of their endeavors, each can say yes and sometimes no, and each participates in making choices. A partnership without choice is no partnership at all.

 NON-EXAMPLE

When Principal Michelle Ryan walked by Jake Donnelly's class, she decided to stop in and see how the lesson was proceeding. The principal realized pretty quickly that things were not going at all well. Jake seemed tense and frustrated as he taught, and the students seemed to enjoy ruffling his feathers. One or two students kept tapping their desks, and Jake couldn't figure out who was making the noises, blurting out at the entire class that whoever it was "better stop it or everyone will get a second quiz on Friday!" Once the tapping stopped, however, the problems persisted. A couple of students had loud side conversations, and Jake loudly corrected them. Others were off task, a point Jake made several times to little effect. In all, Jake corrected nine students in the 5 minutes prior to the merciful ringing of the bell.

After class, Jake asked Michelle for some advice. "Jake, you'd better talk to our instructional coach, Alice. You need to change the way you correct your students. You need to praise them more. Alice will fix that right up. Please email me right away after the two of you get things straightened out in here." Jake promised he'd get right on it. On her way back to her office, Michelle happened upon Alice and asked her to get together with Jake right away. Alice did just that and after a little prodding set up a meeting.

Alice had always thought of Jake as a friendly colleague, but during the meeting she saw another side of him. "Just try to make this short," he said, "so I can get back to my real work here." Alice told Jake that Michelle had asked her to work with him on correcting students. She tried to open up the conversation, but Jake offered only monosyllabic answers. He fidgeted, checked his watch, sighed loudly, and eventually said, "I need to go. Just tell Michelle that I did what I had to do. If I need you, I'll call you." He stood up and walked out of the room. That was the beginning and the end of Alice's collaboration with Jake.

• • •

Why did Jake turn away from Alice and pass up an opportunity to learn from her? He may have resented not having a choice in the coaching or in who he would consult with. Picture a business partnership in which one partner makes all the decisions for the other. Imagine what would happen if one partner decided when and where to spend the profits, how to run the business, whom to hire, and so on. How would you feel if you were supposed to be a part of this partnership, yet your partner didn't consult you before acting, never asked your opinion, and never gave you a choice? Chances are you wouldn't feel like a partner at all.

One reason traditional professional development fails may be because teachers frequently have little choice in what they learn. When it comes to professional development, teachers often do not have a right to say no. Teachers are told to attend compulsory training sessions even if the sessions don't meet their needs or they've heard the speaker before. Or they are told that their school has adopted a new innovation and they are required to implement it, like it or not. Not surprisingly, many resist being forced to change.

Taking away the teachers' choice takes away their professionalism. Personal discretion is, in many ways, the heart of being a professional. Professionals are trusted to use their knowledge skillfully, artfully, and ethically. What makes people professional is not what they know, but their ability to choose correctly from among many options. When choice is not an option, teachers are reduced to being less than professionals.

Of course, choice is sometimes not an option for good reasons. For example, compulsory training can be necessary, unavoidable, and legally mandated. But be wary. A principal might decide that schoolwide implementation of CHAMPS would be better for students and staff than partial implementation, and therefore he may require that every teacher implement the CHAMPS approach. A coach might know that a teaching routine was used in a certain way during clinical study and may therefore want teachers to teach it only that way. But, even with no choice about their participation in training or in a teaching practice per se, teachers may still be allowed to choose where they might adapt instruction to suit the requirements, how they would like the training to be delivered, how frequently they want breaks during training, with whom they wish to work, and so on. Choice makes all the difference. The sunset of choice is the dawn of resistance. What is there for a teacher to resist when offered a free and honest choice?

Interestingly, many coaches find that offering teachers a choice actually increases their desire to teach with fidelity *and* increases the likelihood that they will implement suggested teaching practices.

Offering choices during professional learning does not mean that everything is up for grabs. Teachers are expected to strive for certain standards. Anyone who would be treated professionally must act professionally. Every meaningful choice is a step toward partnership.

GETTING *Real* • ***Questions for Administrators and Coaches***

- *Do I allow teachers to make their own decisions about the feedback I present?*
- *Do I respect their decisions if they differ from mine?*
- *Do I recognize that teachers will need to adapt information for their individual needs?*

Dialogue

When partners choose to come together as equals and feel free to voice their opinions, when they can act on the exhilarating belief that they are free to agree, disagree, and reflect on ideas as they choose, something marvelous happens. As conversations open up, ideas begin to zip around the room like balls in a pinball machine. In such interplay, it can be difficult to tell where one thought ends and another begins. When a group starts to think as one big mind, an exciting phase of partnership opens up: *dialogue.*

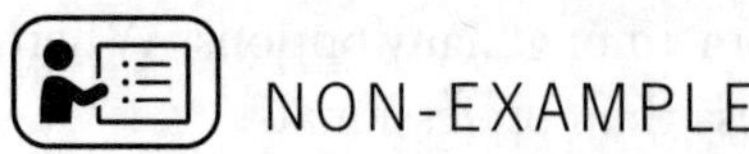
NON-EXAMPLE

Rafer, a new coach, was excited about his upcoming presentation to the staff. During several meetings, Rafer had persuaded his principal that the entire staff needed an overview of CHAMPS. Since this would be his one big chance to speak to the entire school, Rafer wanted to make sure he explained as much material as possible. He knew the material was important; he knew that it would make a difference. Rafer struggled to narrow down his topics, but he had much to share, and his ever-expanding PowerPoint presentation showed it. The trouble was that every time he added content, he had to remove another group activity. He decided to cut back on activities and focus on communicating the many good ideas.

The session started well, but after an hour Rafer could tell that participants were dragging. He picked up his pace, but the more he talked, the less interested they seemed. Smiles were turning into frowns.

The teachers were late returning from lunch, some as much as 30 minutes late. When Rafer resumed, he was further behind in his agenda. He apologized for rushing through the material and emphasized how important it was. Unfortunately, no one seemed to agree. At first passively and eventually vocally, teachers began criticizing the ideas Rafer presented. Soon the mood in the room turned pretty unpleasant.

At 2 p.m., Principal Wilson pulled the plug on the presentation. "Rafer," he said, "you've given us a lot to think about and I thank you, but now we'd better let the staff take some time to mull over all of your good ideas." Rafer had not explained even half of what he'd planned, but he realized his chance was over. Worse, he felt that rather than moving the school in the right direction, he had lost the staff. For months, he couldn't find anyone who wanted to talk with him about CHAMPS. It took Rafer a long time to repair the damage he'd done.

• • •

Professional learning does not have to be like Rafer's inservice. In a dialogue, one individual should not impose on, dominate, or control the discussion. Lecturing isolates people, but dialogue brings people together—learning, sharing, and exploring. Dialogue is not the same as debate, where little if any reflection is conducted on the assumptions that underlie the discussion.

Coaches who make dialogue their guiding principle build on equality and voice by avoiding any hint of manipulation, refusing to make winning their point the object of discussion. They facilitate open, robust, and freewheeling brainstorming sessions, and peek under the surface level of conversation to uncover the hidden assumptions beneath.

GETTING *Real* • ***Questions for Administrators and Coaches***

- *Do I speak less than 60% of the time when I talk with teachers?*
- *Do teachers develop new ideas during our coaching conversations?*
- *Are our coaching conversations lively?*

Reflection

Successful partnerships are built on respect and professionalism, where each partner is presented with enough information to reflect on its meaning and make the best decisions.

NON-EXAMPLE

Lynn, an experienced coach, was all about having the biggest impact possible in her school. She also believed in being efficient. Just as Lynn started working with first-year teacher Ana Jaramillo, she came upon a plan that she realized would save a lot of time and help Ana with a big issue.

Ana enjoyed her students, and her classroom was one of the livelier places in the school. This was a blessing and a curse. On the one hand, students seemed to have a lot of fun in Ana's class. On the other, disrespect flourished, and she frequently struggled to bring kids back on task. At times Ana would let problem behaviors go unchecked, hoping they would clear up, only to show flashes of temper when they didn't.

When Lynn and Ana met, Lynn suggested that they might explore the way Ana corrected students. Ana agreed. Lynn said she had a quick trick to help Ana. Ray Westberg, an experienced English teacher, had spent a great deal of time working with Lynn to create a list of consequences for problem behaviors and tuning it with students until it worked well. Lynn suggested that Ana could save a lot of time just by using Ray's list.

Ana was more than willing to try. After reading and memorizing Ray's list, Ana decided that from that day forth she was going to be consistent. She tried her best to correct the students consistently. She called kids on their misbehaviors. Yet her heart wasn't in it. Ana felt herself changing, and she didn't like the new Ana. She was constantly correcting students, even when she wasn't sure she wanted to.

Weeks passed. Even with Lynn's encouragement, Ana just couldn't put her heart into the corrections. "The fun's gone out of teaching," she confided to her mother. When she gave up her new plan after a semester of struggle, the students stopped trusting her. When the school year was over, Ana decided that teaching really wasn't for her.

• • •

Why didn't Lynn's plan work for Ana? One possible reason is that Ana wasn't given a chance to reflect on what she was doing and why. She wasn't encouraged to explore her own ways of approaching the problem. If coaches are creating a learning partnership, if teachers and coaches are equal, if teachers are free to speak their own minds and make real, meaningful choices, it follows that one of the most important choices they will make is how to make sense of what they are learning and use it in the classroom in an appropriate way.

Offering teachers the freedom to consider ideas before adopting them is central to the principle of reflection. Giving teachers the freedom to choose or reject ideas allows them time and space to reflect on what will or won't work in their classrooms. The reflective teacher makes decisions consciously and rationally.

Reflection is necessary for teacher learning because some of the most important parts of teaching are often automatic or instinctive. Skilled or artistic practitioners have a repertoire of competencies they may not even be able to identify. For that reason, becoming an effective teacher is as much about getting a feel for it as it is about learning specific skills. A teacher who is conscious of their teaching methods and tacit skills is better prepared to reflect on new techniques and introduce them in the classroom.

GETTING *Real* • ***Questions for Administrators and Coaches***

- *Am I able to accept it when teachers reject the views I offer?*
- *Do I encourage reflection and discussion on the content and ideas I share?*
- *Do the suggestions I provide allow teachers to make their own decisions and adapt ideas to their needs?*

Praxis

Praxis is a rich philosophical term for the practical application of learning. Simply put, it means *translating an idea into action.* Praxis describes the act of applying new ideas to our own lives. When we learn the primacy of expectations and then consider, develop, and refresh expectations to guide students, we are engaged in praxis. When a teacher learns about the importance of maintaining high rates of positive interactions, and then plans to increase how frequently they interact positively with students, the teacher is engaged in praxis. When a teacher learns about a new teaching practice, thinks about it deeply, and decides not to use it in their classes, the teacher is engaged in praxis. When we learn, reflect, and act, we are engaged in praxis.

Using the praxis principle, a coach provides the teacher with numerous structured activities that explore how an idea might work inside and outside the classroom. A teaching idea is moved along in its journey from theory to practice as it is considered and shaped, adapted and revised, and disassembled and rebuilt. Through that process, what began as a suggestion based on general principles and research-based practices becomes a personal instrument tailored by and for the teacher to address the needs of a unique group of students.

POSITIVE EXAMPLE

Teacher Mark Weldon didn't have a high opinion of professional development. "It's not much better than a root canal," he once said. Professional development was usually just some stranger talking about an idea that Mark would never be able to use in his classroom. Not surprisingly, he showed little enthusiasm when he first heard about having a coach in his classroom. However, Mark heard a lot of good things about the coach, LaVonne, as his fellow teachers sang her praises. He really took notice when a number of more experienced teachers, who he called the "Old Guard," joined the chorus. When Mark started to struggle with his seventh-hour class, he decided to see if LaVonne could offer any help. "It can't hurt," he said.

When Mark and LaVonne got together, the first thing that impressed him was the fact that she didn't try to talk him into anything. She told him she wanted them to work as partners, and she walked the talk. They threw around some ideas and together decided to start by writing up expectations for all the activities and transitions in Mark's class. When they next met, LaVonne wrote down Mark's ideas about his expectations for the class. LaVonne had some good questions and made suggestions, but she never told Mark what he should do. LaVonne even shared a little research data about expectations, but it was only in the context of a conversation about learning. When he checked his watch, Mark couldn't believe 2 hours had passed. It didn't seem to him that they had wasted a minute.

Over the next few weeks, LaVonne would sometimes model how the expectations might be taught. She also observed Mark in the classroom, and together they talked about what they'd seen when they observed each other. The whole experience was, Mark thought, pretty invigorating. It felt enjoyable and rewarding to be learning. Later, when a colleague remarked, "Mark, I thought you hated professional development," Mark responded, "I do. But this was useful, and it was time well spent. I'll take what LaVonne has to offer over another staff development any day."

• • •

What did Mark find so appealing about his experiences collaborating with LaVonne? Quite likely it was that he was fully engaged in applying what he was learning to his real-life experiences in the classroom. Mark didn't learn ideas in the abstract; rather, everything he learned was applied straightaway to his professional practice. What's more, he was able to shape what he learned to fit his classroom. In fact, he was rewriting his ideas all the time. He was the author of what he was learning.

When coaches work with teachers, they likely want an experience similar to LaVonne and Mark's. All education professionals want the people with whom they work to think about what they do, to change for the better, and to learn new ways of reaching students. All these practices are reflective. To encourage such reflective actions, a coach may give teachers many chances to consider how they might use new ideas. When a coach and teacher work together, they are a bit like children having fun with modeling clay, reshaping each new idea until they can see how it might look in the classroom.

PRAXIS IN ACTION

My son, now in his 20s, illustrated praxis in action as a growing teenage boy. Early in his teens, he began working toward his height of six feet plus and was eating every bit of food in the house in his attempt to get there. As a consultant with a behavioral company, I started working on a system of support. How could I help him as he grew while encouraging mindful eating habits? With that goal in mind, I started working on a plan centered on the STOIC Framework. I was going to teach expectations with the structure to support them.

At the time, he was eating a lot of empty calories. Now, I'm not against empty calories. Some of my best friends are empty calories. But I do understand that a lifetime of eating only empty calories can also negatively affect overall health. Because he was growing and could use some empty calories to burn, we worked on this expectation, as simply stated and as complex as it might be: Empty calories should be eaten in moderation as part of a healthy, balanced diet. Then I set out to create a system to support healthy moderation.

At the time he and I were crafting this expectation, he was very into s'mores. Specifically, melting marshmallows in the microwave and squishing that sweet goodness in between some chocolate and graham crackers. Each weekend, we went grocery shopping, and to structure for moderation for this specific treat, we decided to purchase the package of individually wrapped, smaller Hershey bars. Each package came with ten small fun-size Hershey bars for the week. Then he was given autonomy, or *choice* according to the Partnership Principles. He could use two bars and make five s'mores on Monday afternoon and be done. He could use double bars and enjoy one s'more per day. He could use single bars and make two s'mores per day. Many possibilities, one structure, all to meet the expectation. I then left to go on the road to train, really patting myself on the back for my clear and superior parenting skills.

Imagine my surprise when, during a training, I received a photo with just the caption, "HA HA HA." On my phone was a picture of a s'more in progress. Two open graham crackers, a marshmallow on one and very neatly lined chocolate chips that he had found in the cupboard on the other, all on a plate sitting in the sun. Now, let's think about what one needs to make a s'more with fidelity: graham crackers, marshmallows, chocolate, and heat. While two of those were not what I had expected (the chocolate in the form of those chips and the heat source as the sun versus the microwave), he was still making a s'more. The end game was the same. While he wasn't directly adhering to the structure I had intended, he was using praxis to adapt what he had been given to his own unique needs at the time.

During successful coaching, teachers have ample opportunity to think about and apply new ideas to their real-life practices.

The concept of praxis has many implications. Most important is the assumption that, if we are to apply new knowledge to our lives in some way, we need to have a clear understanding of our current reality. Educational theorist Paulo Freire suggested that praxis is a profound and important activity because it leads to truly analyzing our lives and the world in which we learn. For Freire, praxis is revolutionary: "It is reflection and action upon the world in order to transform it . . . . To speak a true word is to transform the world" (1970).

Praxis is not memorizing a new method of correcting students so that a teacher can use it in the classroom exactly as memorized. Praxis is not adopting someone else's plans for a class. Praxis is not coaching others so that the picture in their minds ends up identical to the coach's. Rather, praxis occurs when a teacher has a real chance to explore, prod, stretch, and re-create whatever is being studied.

Praxis happens between the deliberation and decision about what is to be done in a situation. In other words, if collaborating teachers plan to use what a coach is explaining, they'll need to make their own sense of it. They will have to be real partners who are welcomed to opt in or opt out, and who are—we hope—excited by the possibilities being offered.

GETTING *Real* • *Questions for Administrators and Coaches*

- *Are teachers encouraged to explore ways they might use what I'm explaining?*
- *Do teachers consider the practical implications of what I'm talking about?*
- *Do I spend as much time with teachers planning action as talking about theory and practice?*

Reciprocity

When coaches see themselves as partners, they recognize that they are learners as much as their collaborating teachers. Thus, coaches go into every interaction expecting to learn good ideas and to find each interaction satisfying and enriching.

 POSITIVE EXAMPLE

Instructional coach Ginger Phaneuf took a few minutes before leaving the school to write down her thoughts in her journal. A coach for 5 years, Ginger had made it a point to write a few lines each day before going home. Over such a long time, she had written about wonderful days and days she'd rather forget. Today was one of the best days.

Ginger told everyone that what she loved about being a coach was that, more than anything else, she was a learner. "I have the best job in school," she said, "because I get to see all the great things teachers are doing." And Ginger meant what she said. For her, each day was a chance to become a better coach and a better teacher.

Today was a great example of why Ginger loved coaching. In the second hour in Jim Paplinski's class, she learned a simple way to increase engagement by having students move images around on the SmartBoard. Following that, she observed Alison Percell and was blown away by how Alison encouraged a positive learning environment by prompting the students to graciously welcome their learning partner at the start of the class.

Ginger was most thankful, though, for the great coaching conversation she had with Sherrie Simmons. While she was talking with Sherrie, Ginger felt like they were truly thinking together. Ginger couldn't remember which ideas were hers and which ideas were Sherrie's. What she most remembered was that she felt incredibly energized by the conversation. "What I love the most about this job," Ginger wrote in her journal, "isn't just that I get to share great teaching practices. What I love is that coaching is a two-way street. I get back as much or more than I give. And that makes all the difference."

• • •

In a partnership, all participants benefit from the success, learning, or experience of others (Freire, 1970; Senge, 1990). All members are rewarded by what each individual contributes. When this principle is applied to coaching, it has some fairly obvious implications. Instructional coaches who operate from the Partnership Principles enter relationships with teachers believing that the knowledge and expertise of teachers are as important as the knowledge and expertise of the coach. By encouraging teachers' voices through dialogue and by observing teachers' reflections, coaches demonstrate faith in teachers' abilities to invent useful new applications for the content they are exploring. Coaches expect to learn from teachers, and they do. James A. Belasco, discussing executive coaching, succinctly describes the reciprocal nature of effective coaching:

Coaching is one of the deepest, mutually satisfying experiences a person can have. The coach helps the person being coached to learn and grow and realize their dreams. At the same time, the person being coached brings out the noblest sentiments and brings out the deepest gratification for the coach. Coaching is the quintessential win-win experience (Goldsmith, Lyons, & Freas, 2000, p. xiii).

Coaches learn about their collaborating teachers' classrooms and schools, and the strengths and the multiple perspectives on the content being presented when seen through the eyes of participants. The reward coaches reap for adopting the Partnership Principles is that they are continually learning from their collaborating teachers.

By acting on the principle of reciprocity, coaches also model for teachers the importance of continuous growth and development. Furthermore, by engaging in mutually enriching conversations, coaches find their work more satisfying and more fun. Coaches who act on the principle of reciprocity bring to life Robert Half's famous quotation: "When one teaches, two learn."

GETTING *Real* • *Questions for Administrators and Coaches*

- *Do I truly expect to learn from my collaborating teachers?*
- *Am I open enough to all of my teachers to learn what they can teach me?*
- *Am I energized during coaching conversations?*

PRINCIPLES GUIDE KNOWLEDGE

An Uber is cruising down a boulevard when it runs a red light.
"Hey!" the passenger shouts. "Be careful!"
"Don't worry," says the driver. "My brother does it all the time."
He barrels through the next red light, and the passenger screams, "Stop doing that!"
"I'm telling you, my brother does this all the time."
They approach the next light. Just when it turns green, the driver slams on the brakes. The confused passenger asks, "You just ran two red lights—why'd you stop at a green?"
"I had to," says the driver. "My brother might have been coming."

This joke is considered by *Reader's Digest* to be one of the best "dad jokes" ever. While the joke is funny, the point is quite impactful. The driver understands how to operate the car. He knows how to turn it on, how to steer, where the gas pedal and brakes are located, and even what the lights mean. But if the underlying principles that guide application of that knowledge are faulty, it will eventually lead to catastrophe. The same could be said for coaches. Coaches may know how to coach: the resource to use, how to help plan for and deliver professional development, what data to collect to measure effectiveness, and even what an effective coaching conversation should look like. But if the principles that guide actions are faulty, eventually it will lead to catastrophe in the form of broken trust and pushback from staff.

Wrapping It Up

CHAPTER 5 SUMMARY

Relationships are key to successful coaching. To create a supportive context for coaching, you will work to build trust, enhance communication, and incorporate Partnership Principles in your interactions with teachers.

What to Know

- Whatever the level of your leadership skills right now, the single most effective step you can take to bolster your capacity for school leadership is to work on and polish your ability to communicate clearly, empathetically, and without judgment or prejudice.
- Coaching is about relationship building.
- Listening is as much an act of will as it is a skill or art, and your attentiveness can be the decisive element that sways a collaboration for the better.
- Authentic listening means approaching each conversation with true interest, curiosity, and caring.
- Learning to listen involves a series of strategies to build skill.
- Ongoing regard provides for the basic human need of recognition.
- Seven Partnership Principles represent a foundation on which to base actions when working collaboratively.

What to Do

- Reflect on ways to build relational trust within your coaching role. Use Reproducible 5.1 to identify traits that come naturally and traits that you can work on to more easily build relational trust with others.
- Practice authentic listening with other members of the leadership team, with staff, and in other interpersonal relationships, incorporating the seven strategies for listening more effectively.
- Use the language of ongoing regard when striving to maintain a 3:1 ratio of interactions with staff.
- Encourage reflection on coaching conversations and the Partnership Principles. Use Reproducible 5.2 to self-reflect on how well Partnership Principles are applied across the board in coaching conversations. Ask others to use Reproducible 5.3 to assess the coaching conversation and provide feedback.

Notes

CHAPTER 6

Correct Fluently
Course Corrections and Collaboration

Every teacher needs to improve, not because they are not good enough, but because they can be even better. —Dylan William

It takes confident humility to admit that we are a work in progress. It shows that we care more about improving *ourselves than* proving *ourselves.* —Adam Grant

Constructive feedback is sometimes the hardest to receive. If you're anything like me, it's not the actual feedback that's been given, it's the embarrassment I often feel at needing it in the first place. There's no doubt many of us need improvement in various areas of our lives; however, knowing that and being prepared to hear about it are two very different things. I'm the type of person who would rather have constructive feedback delivered with no expectation that I respond to that feedback for at least 24 hours. This gives me time to get over the initial embarrassment I may feel, reconcile the information to my worldview, and think about how it might (or might not) inform my practice. The point is that course corrections can be fraught with peril in any relationship, personal and professional. However well intended it may be, some people are uncomfortable with being given data that show the need for growth.

If you are reading this chapter prior to the first five chapters in this section, we encourage you to reconsider. Just as we inform teachers when providing professional development in CHAMPS and the STOIC framework, the C is always the weakest variable at your disposal. Not only does it typically entail a withdrawal from the relational bank account, but it also hinges on the fact that something is already wrong and must be corrected, rather than on preventing the problem in the first place.

Even if you have read the chapters linearly to this point, we encourage everyone to reread the Communication and Partnership Principles sections in Chapter 5 just prior to entering a conversation that requires course correction. While active collaboration is inherent in this chapter and included as part of the process of course correction, it never hurts to have a refresher on how to engage in collaboration effectively during the coaching process.

At this point, you've worked to ensure that all the components necessary for change are in place. You've developed an overall vision and chosen a clear model for classroom management practices. You've prepared for implementation by identifying each of the four cornerstones and creating both an initial and an ongoing professional development plan. Data are now being collected on a regular basis through classroom observations, including the evaluators, nonevaluative coaches, and a peer-to-peer model. Relational trust between all stakeholders is increasing through effective communication and the use of Partnership Principles in authentic collaboration.

Now, we set our focus on providing course corrections for teachers who may be demonstrating a skill deficit *and* for staff who may be highly skilled and looking to further improve through a system of more targeted support. Tier 2 support that engages in a formal coaching cycle, known as the Improvement Cycle, along with the intentional implementation of certain tasks within the STOIC Framework and ongoing data collection, isn't just for those teachers who may be struggling with effective classroom management. Teachers who are simply looking to "be even better," as Dylan William suggests, can also receive Tier 2 support.

Think of it like this: When we engage in effective multi-tiered systems of support for students, we not only provide additional services for students who require specific supports to make adequate progress, we also provide services for gifted and talented students to work with teachers prepared to differentiate for their needs. If the purpose of this book is to create an effective MTSS model for staff needs in relation to behavior management, it makes sense to apply the same approach here for adults. This approach is also in the best interest of a campus that may be looking to create model classrooms or to increase a teacher's ability level to also act in the capacity of a peer coach. For teachers who are on the path to certification as an administrator, this level of support may also prove vital in building the skills necessary for them to one day help others through this same system.

In this chapter, we look at creating a very clear pathway to Tier 2 coaching support. This support will be provided both to teachers in need and to striving teachers who may wish to engage in a more formal process. We will even look at helping teachers avoid Tier 2 support if that's not in their perceived best interest. Specifically, you will construct a process to move teachers into targeted coaching support that includes:

- Identifying flags that will signal the need for Tier 2 coaching support
- Establishing a process for teachers to request Tier 2 coaching support
- Using a screener to assess implementation of the classroom management model
- Providing early-stage interventions to teachers who may wish to engage only in Tier 1 coaching support

IDENTIFY FLAGS THAT SIGNAL NEED FOR TIER 2 COACHING SUPPORT

In the first step of this process, you will want to replicate what is done for students. That is, identify a set of flags that signal to the system that Tier 2 support may be helpful. In effective MTSS for students, flags for students such as chronic absenteeism, failing two or more content areas, a certain number of office referrals in a certain period of time, and even teacher or parent request can signal to the system that a student may qualify for additional support. These flags should be clearly identified to staff, students, and parents and should be concrete and measurable. In this section, you'll work to develop a system of flags in much the same way for staff. These particular flags will be identified to staff only as an internal mechanism for growth and improvement.

Please keep in mind that these flags will also function to let you, as coaches, see any potential gaps in your Tier 1 system. For instance, going back to our student examples, if more than 20% of your students are chronically absent, that alone cannot stand as a singular flag. You cannot have more than 20% of your students in need of Tier 2 support. If, let's say, 40% of students are chronically absent, there's a gap in your attendance plan within the first tier of support. This would be true for any campus. Even if you are on a campus where 100% of your students require a high level of support, your Tier 1 policies and procedures to encourage certain behaviors (attendance, responsible behavior, adequate academic gains, etc.) might look very different from those at the school down the street, but still apply. You most likely lack the staffing and resources to provide more than 20% of the students in your system with individual interventions.

The same will be true for staff. If you set an expectation for staff that a teacher refer no more than 20% of their students to the office and then discover that 38% of your staff are sending large numbers of students for office referrals, that tells you there's a gap in the understanding or implementation of the initial classroom management model. Perhaps staff have poorly structured routines and procedures in their classrooms, the S in STOIC. Expectations may be unclear or have not been taught, the T. Or more than 20% of staff may not be engaging in a 3:1 ratio of positive interactions, the I. Perhaps staff have not been adequately trained in responding to misbehavior in a way that de-escalates the situation, the C in STOIC. It's your responsibility as a coach, whether evaluative or nonevaluative, to uncover any gaps by engaging in ongoing observations as outlined in Chapter 4. Any individual flag you set cannot net more than 20% of staff for Tier 2 assistance.

Figure 6.1 shows a flowchart of tiered coaching support. This is based on the work of the district PBIS team in Arlington ISD, a suburb of Dallas. Operating under Angela Hernandez and Cheryl Boyland, this team has created a system of processes and procedures that is recommended to all campuses to build consistency in the way that both building and district coaches are utilized. While the processes may be ever changing to respond to each year's unique challenges, many of the formats can carry over from one year to the next. The first item in this flowchart is the identification of need. Remember, this need could be teachers showing a deficit or it could be teachers who simply want a more formal context for growth.

Your campus may choose any of the following indicators to serve as flags for your system. You may also choose to disregard some of these flags or add your own. This is simply a springboard for discussion among your leadership team. Whatever you choose, these flags should be largely objective and measurable, and should be communicated to staff clearly at the beginning of the school year or whenever a tiered system of support is introduced on your campus.

Figure 6.1 *Flowchart of Tiered Coaching Support*

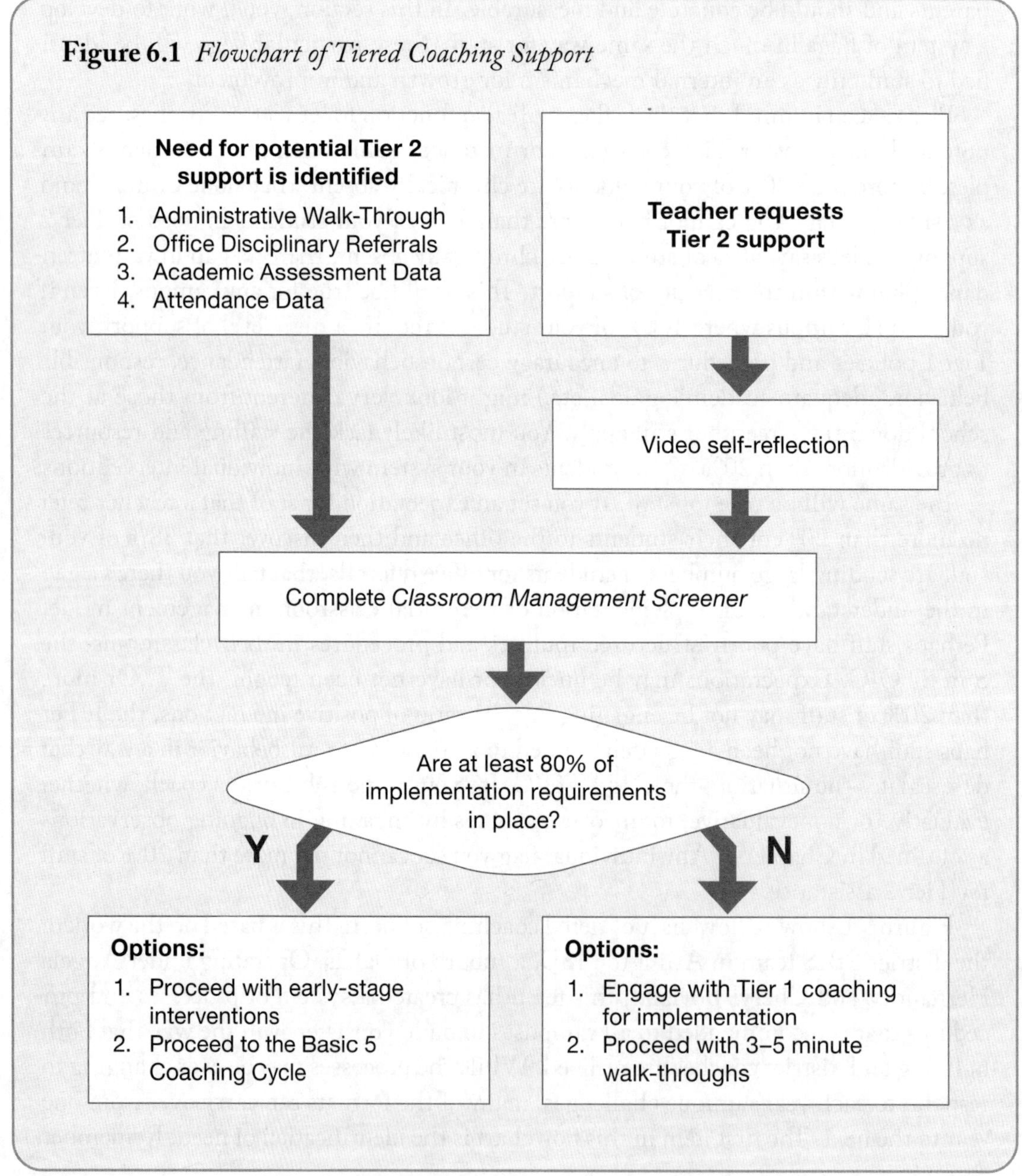

Administrator Walk-Through

In Chapter 4, we covered in depth what administrative walk-throughs should look and sound like. Administrators, as the primary evaluators of teacher effectiveness, have power that nonevaluative coaches simply do not. A nonevaluative coach cannot tell a teacher they may be headed for a more formal, targeted coaching cycle. This can only come from the person with the "teeth" on the campus. Yes, administrators serve as warm demanders, but they also serve to ensure that staff employ highly effective academic and engagement practices. To do so, they must be willing to identify when a teacher's needs aren't being served within the first tier of coaching support.

Administrators aren't just there to place those who struggle with classroom management into Tier 2. Administrators should also consider teachers who are doing so well that they may benefit from even greater support. Just as gifted and talented students have the capacity to perform at higher levels, teachers can also be tapped to further hone their skills into exceptionality.

For administrators, knowing when and how to refer a teacher to Tier 2 support rests largely on what is revealed within their 3–5 minute walk-throughs. If a teacher shows a clear deficit in one or more benchmarks during an initial walk-through, the evaluator should make a note to come into that teacher's classroom soon (within the next few days). If the deficit is still apparent, they should go in again within the next day or so. This provides three quick snapshots of staff practice. While these are quick snapshots, they may indicate a greater need for support, with more time attached—time that administrators simply do not have.

An administrator's goal should be to help teachers with any deficit quickly and efficiently. A conversation may sound like this:

> *Elizabeth, I've been in your classroom doing walk-throughs three times in the past 2 weeks. On average, the on-task behavior of students has been at 63%. Our target is 90%. I respect you as a professional, and I trust that you can close that gap. If you need support to do so, I have some suggestions you may want to consider.*
>
> *First, I have some books related to academic engagement that may help keep students on task: Anita Archer's* Explicit Instruction *and Jim Knight's* High-Impact Instruction, *among others. You are free to check them out of my professional library and see if there's anything in there that might interest and assist you. I also know there's a professional development coming up at the district office on engagement strategies. I'd be happy to help you secure a substitute teacher so you can attend.*
>
> *The third option is our campus coach, Jacob. Jacob attended the CHAMPS training earlier this year and is also well versed in instructional practices. You can work with him, and he can collect more data as well as help you choose some strategies that are right for you. Now, you need to know that if you work with Jacob, I won't be asking Jacob to pass on any information to me about what's happening in your classroom. This*

> *will allow you to speak candidly with each other. Honestly, how you fix this is up to you, but I do need you to work on this, and I trust you will. I'll be back in 3 weeks, and I need to see engagement increased to at least 80%. We'll continue to watch its growth from there.*

While obviously the conversation written here is much accelerated (and apparently one sided), the gist remains the same. Identify the gap, offer assistance, and then allow the teacher to make an autonomous professional decision about their own learning. If, when the administrator returns, growth has not occurred, this is the flag that should then signal to the system that additional Tier 2 support may be warranted. This flag then triggers a coach, either the administrator acting in the role or a nonevaluative coach, to assist the teacher in completing the STOIC Classroom Management Screener (Reproducible 6.3, discussed later in this chapter). From there, a decision on whether to initiate Tier 2 supports is made.

If a teacher is doing exceptionally well based on those snapshots, an administrator may choose to refer that teacher to Tier 2 support to continue positive growth. This conversation will look and sound different, and such teachers should always be given the choice to engage in Tier 2 coaching as a means of continuous improvement.

Office Discipline Referrals

This flag clearly identifies how many office referrals will signal to the system that a teacher may need additional Tier 2 support. Teachers should know this number in advance. It should be clearly communicated that the purpose of this flag is not that teachers keep students exhibiting referrable behavior in the classrooms and ignore the disruption to learning, but that the teacher is aware that the classroom management plan, designed around the STOIC framework, may have a gap somewhere in the variables. If the teacher is self-aware of the number of referrals and can work to identify and adjust the variable on their own, they can do so without the benefit of coaching support. If nothing changes and those referral numbers stay constant, it may be time that the system responds to assist that teacher.

The criteria for this flag could be written in a few different ways:

- A certain number of referrals within a certain time frame
- A certain percentage of students (typically 20% or more) who are referred within a certain time frame
- A certain number or percentage of the same behavior that is referred within a certain time frame

Please remember and communicate to staff that numbers of office referrals will not necessarily be used as a singular reason for Tier 2 support. For instance, there may be a teacher who never writes a referral, but that could mean that they are exceptional at tuning out referrable offenses, regardless of the disruption to the learning community.

Another teacher may be the only one following an outdated procedure in the staff handbook that directs teachers to write an office referral for every tardy a student acquires. An initial conversation with a coach or completion of the STOIC Classroom Management Screener (Reproducible 6.3) will identify any potential quick fixes with no need for targeted coaching support.

Academic Assessment Data

Low academic performance may also indicate to the system that a teacher is in need. If a certain number or percentage (again, typically 20% or more) of students are failing a class and/or failing to hit a district or campus benchmark of academic performance, this may indicate that classroom management is hindering instructional engagement. A coach may be deployed to assist the teacher in completing the STOIC Classroom Management Screener and have an initial conversation about moving into Tier 2 support.

If the screener shows an effective classroom management model has been implemented and academic performance is still below benchmark, consider these questions, among others:

- Does the curriculum match the assessment being used?
- Is there a deficit in the reading skills of students?
- Is there a need to increase the rigor of instruction?

If the answer is yes to any of these questions, plan to explore the campus's academic side of the MTSS framework further.

Attendance

Attendance has become a critical issue on many campuses across the country. "For students to be successful in school, they first have to be in school." With those simple words, Jessica Sprick and Randy Sprick (2018) launched a compelling case for prioritizing student attendance. If more than 20% of students on a campus are chronically absent, meaning they miss 5% to 10% or more of school, this should signal to the entire system that attendance must be looked at campuswide through a more proactive plan at the Tier 1 level. Don't be fooled by a high daily rate of attendance. For instance, if 20% or more of students have missed 2 days within the first 20 days of school, even if the daily rate of attendance is high, chronic absenteeism is a problem at the schoolwide level.

If a campus does not have an issue with chronic absenteeism, attendance at the classroom level could be a potential indicator of a teacher in need of assistance. If 20% or more of a classroom teacher's students are chronically absent, that should signal to the system that classroom management practices, as well as academic engagement strategies, may be ineffective.

ESTABLISH A PROCESS FOR TEACHERS TO REQUEST TIER 2 COACHING SUPPORT

Your process for initiating Tier 2 coaching support should allow teachers to specifically request additional coaching support. However, in an effort to save the limited number of support personnel some of their own resources (namely time, energy, and enthusiasm), we recommend putting a series of gates here. While we are not suggesting that a teacher's request simply be denied, we are suggesting that a teacher's request come with some professional self-reflection prior to the first coaching conversation.

> **_Exception for Gatekeeping_**
>
> 
>
> *If you are on a campus where very few teachers (less than 5%–10% of staff) ask for additional support, you may choose to ignore these caveats. These are only suggested as a way to build personal, professional reflection and help coaches use resources in the most efficient and effective way possible.*

Set Up Gates to Prepare Teachers for Tier 2 Coaching Support

Video self-reflection. The first gate, so to speak, should be that the teacher is willing to engage in the use of video for the purpose of self-reflection. A teacher may not have a clear picture of what teaching and learning looks and sounds like in their classroom because effective teaching requires a teacher to do many things at once and make many instantaneous decisions. Video helps make the unseen seen. Jim Knight's book *Focus on Teaching* (2014) walks coaches through the effective use of video to improve practice. He notes that one of the major reasons video is critical to staff is simply the busyness of teaching:

> *Anyone who spends even a short period of time in a classroom quickly realizes one big reason many teachers have an incomplete understanding of everything that occurs in their classroom: Teachers have too much to think about while teaching to be able to step back and oversee everything that is happening in their classes.* —Jim Knight (p. 6)

While we highly encourage the use of video self-reflection as an embedded part of a school's ongoing professional development, we recognize that might not always be easy to do. Video can be uncomfortable. As Jim Knight has stated more than once, no one typically looks at themselves on video and thinks they look younger or thinner than they are. Video, in some cases, has also been used not to coach teachers for improvement but as a way to gather "evidence" for removal. When that happens, trust is degraded and teachers may rightly shy away from video. Make sure that if you encourage teachers to participate in video self-reflection, whether as part of ongoing professional growth or to serve as a gate prior to requesting a coach, the methods and means are structured to create a safe environment for staff.

Video should be recorded on a staff's own personal device, over which they have total control. Video should be shared only of a staff member's own volition with whom and when they want. You may build a more structured system over time, especially for a teacher on a formal plan of assistance in Tier 3, but initially, ensure that control of the video, especially for the purpose of self-reflection, is in the hands of the person reflecting.

In Reproducible 6.1, Reflection on Teacher Practice, we outline several items that a teacher can look for when watching their own practice. Based on Jim Knight's work in *Focus on Teaching*, we've used a rubric of agreement that provides a less formal, more subjective look at teaching practices. Even an informal assessment paired with the power of video can serve to provide a clearer picture of the classroom. Reproducible 6.2, Reflection on Student Behavior, serves the same purpose, with the focus on what student learning looks and sounds like.

Whether a teacher feels that they lack skill or simply that they would benefit from continuous improvement, the teacher should agree to take a first look at practice through the use of video self-reflection. The insight gained, along with the perception data collected from the reproducibles, will be used to lead initial discussions with the coach prior to starting the more formal Improvement Cycle.

Classroom management screener. A second gate should be the use of a simple checklist from the Do part of the target. Has the teacher put into practice the minimum expectations from the classroom management model? The STOIC Classroom Management Screener, discussed in the next section of this chapter, can be used as an additional step for verifying the need for coaching support, especially when coaches are pulled in many different directions. Before requesting a coach's time, teachers should complete the screener concurrently with their video self-reflections.

If a teacher has not put into practice minimum expectations related to the model, they can either start by doing so or by identifying which expectations they have trouble implementing. The Checklist of Classroom Management Practices, found in Chapter 3 (Reproducible 3.7, pp. 72–73), can also be used as an expanded screener and to drive the conversation forward if the coach and teacher will be involved with implementation coaching.

The hard truth is this: If a teacher is not willing to engage in some level of self-reflection, ideally with the use of video, and is not willing to complete a checklist of minimum implementation requirements, it becomes more difficult to justify using a resource as precious as coaching in a more formal context. Coaches, especially those in a nonevaluative role, will be far more effective at moving the needle when working with teachers making first steps toward additional improvement. When these gates are not put into place or completed, often the cry for help is to simply put out a fire, usually one that focuses on a specific student who has triggered the staff member's amygdala. It simply may not be an effective use of time and resources if a coach is already stretched to the limit. The busier coaches are, the more useful these gates become.

Reproducible 6.1 *Video Reflection on Teacher Practice*

Video Reflection on Teacher Practice

Instructions:

1. Use the first viewing to get used to seeing yourself on film and to get a sense of the lesson.
2. Identify areas you'd like to focus on for the second viewing.
3. Identify where your practice lands according to the rubric provided.

TEACHER PRACTICE	3	2	1
Ratio of Interactions	Ratio of interactions was less than 1:1	Ratio of interactions was at least 1:1	Ratio of interactions was at least 3:1
Opportunities to Respond (during teacher-directed instruction in a 10-minute period)	Fewer than 10	10–40	More than 40
Expectations for Instructional Activities	Did not state or refer to expectations for activities	Directed students to follow expectations but did not explicitly state the expectations	Clearly explained expectations prior to each activity
Corrective Procedures	Responses tended to lead to power struggles	Responses showed a lack of calm or consistency from student to student	Corrections were calm, consistent, immediate, and based on a preplanned menu of responses
Types of Classroom Activities	Classroom activities used did not seem suitable to the content	Only one or two classroom activities were used	A variety of classroom activities were used
Understanding of Student Knowledge	Did not understand what most students know and don't know	Understood what some students know and don't know	Clearly understood what students know and don't know
Attention Signal	Multiple tries or types of attention signals were used to gain the attention of students	Attention signal effectively engaged the attention of 90% of students but took longer than 5 seconds	Attention signal effectively engaged the attention of 90% of students within 5 seconds
Physical Space	Some parts of the room cannot be accessed without significant difficulty	Some parts of the room are difficult to efficiently access	Can move around the room from any one place to any other place relatively efficiently

Primary areas of strength: ______________________________

____

____

____

Primary areas of concern: ______________________________

____

____

____

 REPRODUCIBLE 6.1

Reproducible 6.2 *Video Reflection on Student Behavior*

Video Reflection on Student Behavior

Instructions:

1. Use the first viewing to get used to seeing your class on film and to get a sense of the lesson.
2. Identify areas you'd like to focus on for the second viewing.
3. Identify where student behavior lands according to the rubric provided.

TEACHER PRACTICE	3	2	1
On-Task Behavior	Fewer than 80% of students were academically engaged in this activity	80%–89% of students were academically engaged in the activity	At least 90% of students were academically engaged in the activity
Alignment With Expectations	Fewer than 80% of students were following expectations for the classroom activity	80%–89% of students were following expectations for the classroom activity	At least 90% of students were following expectations for the classroom activity
Respectful Interactions	Fewer than 80% of students were respectful to each other and to the teacher	80%–89% of students were respectful to each other and to the teacher	At least 90% of students were respectful to each other and to the teacher
Disruptions (in a 10-minute time period)	More than 10 disruptions by students	5–10 disruptions by students	Fewer than 5 disruptions by students
Correct Academic Responses	New material: Less than 75% Drill and practice: Less than 80%	New material: 75%–80% Drill and practice: 80%–90%	New material: More than 80% Drill and practice: More than 90%
Routines and Procedures	Fewer than 80% of students were following expectations for routine and procedures	80%–89% of students were following expectations for routines and procedures	At least 90% of students following expectations for routines and procedures
Physical Space	Some parts of the room cannot be accessed without significant difficulty	Some parts of the room are difficult to efficiently access	Can move around the room from any one place to any other place relatively efficiently

Primary areas of strength: __________

Primary areas of concern: __________

 REPRODUCIBLE 6.2

Use a Screener to Verify Need for Tier 2 Coaching Support

Each person reading this book has, more than likely, been to a medical provider. Typically, you seek out medical care for a specific reason—an acute pain or injury or preventive services such as a health and wellness check. In each instance, a medical professional will start by asking you basic questions related to your health, such as height, weight, blood pressure, medications, and a description of current ailments. It may even feel redundant from time to time, for example, when you visit a doctor for a follow-up and already answered these questions during your last visit. However, these questions are necessary to ensure basic information is gathered that will give the doctor a baseline used to inform practice.

In much the same way, a screener prior to Tier 2 should be utilized with staff. In a screener, basic information is gathered about the teacher, such as years in the profession, different roles served, and a description of current challenges. The screener should also include a basic checklist related to the Do part of the target. Has each minimum expectation for implementation of the classroom management model been put into practice?

If minimum expectations have been put into place but challenges still exist, Tier 2 support with a more formal coaching cycle may be quite beneficial to the teacher. If the checklist shows considerable gaps in implementation, a less formal coaching cycle may be useful. A coach can work with a teacher on how to incorporate each item into current behavior strategies. The simple act of putting the classroom management model into place may prevent a teacher from needing further support in Tier 2.

If more than 20% of staff are failing to implement a certain classroom management practice, consider going back to the professional development section in Chapter 3 for more information on how to refine the campuswide training plan for all staff.

There will only ever be so many coaches on a campus. Even with the best ongoing professional development plans in place, multiple teachers will still need assistance. Knowing where to start can be overwhelming. If teachers know that they *must* put the Do part of the target in place first, it can save coaches on a campus precious time. It only makes sense to communicate to staff that Tier 2 support can be accessed only by putting Tier 1 systems into place first.

Choosing the Screener

Here, we have translated the Do part of the target, the minimum expectations for implementation, into a simple observation screener. Based off the suggestions offered in Reproducible 3.7, Checklist of Classroom Management Practices, the STOIC Classroom Management Screener (Reproducible 6.3) is a shorter version, providing a quick and efficient way to see evidence of implementation.

This screener will *not* speak to quality of implementation. For instance, in the Structure section of Reproducible 6.3, a teacher may have *expectations for classroom activities clearly defined and posted*, but that does not mean all students are following those expectations. Expectations Versus Daily Reality Rating Scale (Reproducible 10.6 on p. 283) will measure quality for that item on the screener. The screener's purpose is to simply identify whether expectations are clear and whether a visual has been created. If expectations are unclear and/or a visual has not been created, a coach may work with a teacher to more clearly define expectations, choose a visual, help make the visual, and/or determine best placement of the visual within the classroom itself. If expectations *have* been defined and a visual *has* been created, but alignment with expectations is still a challenge for the teacher, this *may* be a signal that Tier 2 support is the logical next step.

The screener should also *not* be used for evaluative purposes. In other words, a Yes does not indicate the teacher is highly effective, and a No doesn't mean the teacher is ineffective. For example, the S section of the screener asks if *the room is arranged so the teacher can get from any part of the room to any other part of the room relatively efficiently.* The answer might be No because the teacher has 30 students in a classroom built for 20 students, or because certain safety protocols are in place that the teacher could violate by moving from one space to another. The screener isn't intended to evaluate teacher performance. The screener exists to show where gaps in implementation might be and if those gaps are leading to ineffective classroom management.

A leadership team consisting of both evaluative and nonevaluative coaches should work together to determine if the STOIC Classroom Management Screener provided here is suitable for your campus. The team should feel free to adjust the screener accordingly if the Do part of your campus target differs from our CHAMPS implementation suggestions.

We provide two versions of Reproducible 6.3, STOIC Classroom Management Screener, for download (see p. 4 for directions). Reproducible 6.3A, shown on the next page, is an example of a screener in statement format. This screener can be used by an administrator or nonevaluative coach, as an outside observer, to look for evidence of implementation prior to a more formal coaching cycle.

Reproducible 6.3B (p. 189) is the same screener in the form of reflective questions. This format can be used by the classroom teacher concurrently with video self-reflection to determine what components of the model have and have not been put into practice.

Communicating the Screener

Whatever format the screener takes or content it contains, this tool should be clearly communicated to staff at the beginning of school or whenever the tiered system of support is introduced on a campus. Teachers should clearly know why the classroom management model was chosen, the three-part target related to the model, and the flags that signal to the system that Tier 2 support might be accessed. Teachers should also know that the screener will be used as the first step leading into Tier 2 coaching supports, regardless of whether additional supports are to be provided due to challenges or strengths.

The administrator should clearly communicate the expectation that staff implement what's offered to them in Tier 1. Even highly effective classroom teachers seeking Tier 2 support for advancement in their already exceptional skills will be asked to complete the screener. Keep in mind that highly effective classroom teachers may already have

Reproducible 6.3A *STOIC Classroom Management Screener (Coach)*

STOIC Classroom Management Screener (Coach)

TEACHER ____________ CURRENT ROLE ____________ YEARS EXPERIENCE ____ DATE __/__/__

Variables	Classroom Management Practice	Y / N	Comments
Structure your classroom for success	1. The room is arranged so the teacher can get from any part of the room to any other part relatively efficiently.	☐ ☐	
	2. Students can access all materials and work areas without disturbing others.	☐ ☐	
	3. The schedule adequately meets the needs of students and academic content.	☐ ☐	
	4. The teacher uses an audible, visual, and portable attention signal.	☐ ☐	
	5. Classroom rules are posted, applicable during all classroom activities, and aligned with classroom expectations.	☐ ☐	
	6. Responses to classroom rule violations are consistent.	☐ ☐	
	7. Classroom procedures, including beginning and ending routines, are in place.	☐ ☐	
	8. Expectations for classroom activities are clearly defined and posted.	☐ ☐	
	9. Expectations for classroom transitions are clearly defined and posted.	☐ ☐	
Teach students how to be successful in the classroom	1. The teacher has created lessons and explicitly taught classroom rules.	☐ ☐	
	2. The teacher has created lessons and explicitly taught procedures and routines.	☐ ☐	
	3. The teacher has created lessons and explicitly taught expectations for classroom activities.	☐ ☐	
	4. The teacher has created lessons and explicitly taught expectations for transitions.	☐ ☐	
Observe student behavior	1. The teacher circulates and scans as a means of observing and monitoring student behavior as it relates to classroom rules and expectations.	☐ ☐	
	2. The teacher models friendly, respectful behavior while monitoring the classroom.	☐ ☐	
	3. The teacher periodically collects data to make judgments about what is going well and what needs to be improved.	☐ ☐	
Interact positively	1. The teacher interacts with each of student in a welcoming and friendly manner.	☐ ☐	
	2. The teacher frequently uses effective positive feedback.	☐ ☐	
	3. The teacher uses intermittent celebrations with individual students and the entire class.	☐ ☐	
	4. The teacher uses classwide motivation systems when and if needed.	☐ ☐	
	5. The teacher strives to interact more frequently with every student when they are engaged in positive behavior than when they are engaged in misbehavior.	☐ ☐	
Correct fluently	1. The teacher corrects misbehavior consistently, calmly, immediately, and briefly.	☐ ☐	
	2. The teacher corrects misbehavior respectfully.	☐ ☐	
	3. The teacher understands how to recognize and avoid power struggles.	☐ ☐	
	4. The teacher uses graceful exits when they find themselves in a power struggle.	☐ ☐	
	5. The teacher has a menu of in-class responses that are applied to a variety of misbehaviors.	☐ ☐	
	6. The teacher has developed and implemented behavior intervention plans when necessary for a student engaged in chronic misbehavior.	☐ ☐	
	7. The teacher understands when and when not to use an office disciplinary referral.	☐ ☐	

 REPRODUCIBLE 6.3A

Reproducible 6.3B *STOIC Classroom Management Screener (Teacher)*

STOIC Classroom Management Screener (Teacher)

TEACHER ____________ CURRENT ROLE ____________ YEARS EXPERIENCE ____ DATE ___/___/___

Variables	Questions	Y / N	Comments
Structure your classroom for success	1. Is the room arranged so I can get from any part of the room to any other part relatively efficiently?	☐ ☐	
	2. Can student access all materials and work areas without disturbing others?	☐ ☐	
	3. Is my schedule adequately meeting the needs of my students and the academic content?	☐ ☐	
	4. Is my attention signal effective?	☐ ☐	
	5. Are my classroom rules posted, applicable during all classroom activities, and aligned with my classroom expectations?	☐ ☐	
	6. Are my responses to classroom rule violations consistent?	☐ ☐	
	7. Have I designed effective beginning and ending routines for my classroom?	☐ ☐	
	8. Have I defined expectations for transitions?	☐ ☐	
	9. Have I defined expectations for classroom activities?	☐ ☐	
Teach students how to be successful in the classroom	1. Have I created lessons and explicitly taught my classroom rules?	☐ ☐	
	2. Have I created lessons and explicitly taught my procedures and routines?	☐ ☐	
	3. Have I created lessons and explicitly taught my expectations for transitions?	☐ ☐	
	4. Have I created lessons and explicitly taught my expectations for classroom activities?	☐ ☐	
Observe student behavior	1. Do I circulate and scan as a means of observing and monitoring student behavior as it relates to classroom rules and expectations?	☐ ☐	
	2. Do I model friendly, respectful behavior while monitoring the classroom?	☐ ☐	
	3. Do I periodically collect data to make judgments about what is going well and what needs to be improved?	☐ ☐	
Interact positively	1. Do I strive to interact more frequently with every student when they are engaged in positive behavior than when they are engaged in misbehavior at a rate of 3:1?	☐ ☐	
	2. Do I have a plan for when and how to interact with my students using noncontingent attention?	☐ ☐	
	3. Do I use effective positive feedback when needed?	☐ ☐	
	4. Do I have a plan for using intermittent celebrations with individual students and the entire class?	☐ ☐	
	5. Do I have a plan to use classwide motivation systems when and if needed?	☐ ☐	
Correct fluently	1. Do I correct misbehavior consistently, calmly, immediately, and briefly?	☐ ☐	
	2. Do I correct misbehavior respectfully?	☐ ☐	
	3. Do I understand how to recognize and avoid power struggles?	☐ ☐	
	4. Do I understand and use graceful exits when I find myself in a power struggle?	☐ ☐	
	5. Do I have a menu of in-class responses that I can apply to a variety of misbehaviors?	☐ ☐	
	6. Have I developed and implemented behavior intervention plans when necessary for a student engaged in chronic misbehavior?	☐ ☐	
	7. Do I understand when and when not to use an office disciplinary referral?	☐ ☐	

REPRODUCIBLE 6.3B

everything in place on the checklist, even before a classroom management model, like CHAMPS, was introduced to their campus. The screener is simply an accumulation of best practices, and any classroom management model worth its salt should be as well.

Using the Screener

The screener can be used in a variety of ways. A campus doesn't have to land on one specific way to apply the screener. Our recommendation is that while the screener will always serve as a gate between Tier 1 and Tier 2, administrators and coaches can use the screener in other ways to help teachers reflect on current practice, such as:

- The screener can be used by individual teachers as reflections to complete at the beginning of each quarter and semester. You might advise staff to discuss these reflections in their smaller learning communities or use them to set goals for personal growth.
- The screener can be used prior to or during training, either when the classroom management model is initially introduced or during ongoing professional development. Partners or groups might use the screener to engage in real-time reflection during the session or turn them in anonymously after the session to help trainers plan for the next session based on the needs of the campus as a whole.

The screener is a reminder to all to take advantage of Tier 1 resources, a gate to Tier 2 access, and a way to plan for ongoing support of both teachers in need and teachers who simply want to continue to refine practice.

EARLY-STAGE INTERVENTIONS: A BRIDGE BETWEEN TIER 1 AND TIER 2

For teachers who implemented Tier 1 resources but are still experiencing a deficit in skill or for teachers who are heading toward the more formal support offered in Tier 2 due to lack of will, the use of a few solidly structured early-stage interventions can serve as an additional bridge between informal support and the additional rigor of the more formal Improvement Cycle. Interventions in *Early-Stage Interventions* (Sprick, et al., 2020), designed for students to serve as a bridge between Tier 1 and Tier 2, have been adapted here to fit the needs of staff.

The idea behind these early-stage interventions is that through slightly more formal interventions within Tier 1, some teachers may avoid the need for Tier 2 coaching support altogether. In other words, a campus can meet their needs through the resources and support personnel available to all.

These interventions can be used by either the administrator, acting in the capacity of an evaluator, or a nonevaluative coach. If there is any suspicion, based on anecdotal or objective data, that a skill deficit is due to lack of will on the teacher's part to engage in professional growth, these interventions may be more impactful coming from administration.

These interventions can also be omitted. A coach and teacher, having gone through the screener, may decide to jump right into the Improvement Cycle in Chapter 7 right away. These interventions simply serve as a bridge between levels of support when and if they are needed.

Planned Discussion

Planned discussion is when one or more of those charged with the support of a staff member meet with the staff member about a particular concern to develop an action plan for solving it. For the same reasons—ease and simplicity—that Planned Discussion is a great initial early-stage intervention, it is often overlooked. In the day-to-day working of a campus, 5-minute walk-throughs accompanied by a quick statement of praise or correction may get lost in the cacophony. While the use of fluent corrections given in a timely manner is certainly necessary, there may be some teachers who have built up a tolerance or resistance to constructive feedback, perhaps settling into the idea of, "This, too, shall pass." And the data prove them correct. Often, if a teacher is uninterested in the adoption of new practice, sometimes for very valid reasons, they can simply choose to ignore course corrections and continue along their current path. Meeting with a staff member in a one-on-one setting with time for extended collaboration to discuss issues and work together to address any problems may gain better and long-term results.

> *"Meeting in a one-on-one setting may gain better and long-term results."*

Planned Discussion is useful in the following situations:

- A teacher has not fully implemented the classroom management model, as indicated by the screener.
- A teacher has a minor, easy-to-fix deficit in hitting a specific benchmark.
- A teacher has a deficit in hitting a benchmark that they had been reaching regularly.
- A teacher has an ongoing issue with implementation or with the ability to hit one or more benchmarks, as part of the comprehensive plan of assistance in Tier 3.

Step-by-step instructions for implementing Planned Discussion are provided in Reproducible 6.4. This is a general template, and either a coach or administrator may find the need to add or omit steps. Also included is a Discussion Record (Reproducible 6.5, p. 193). This tool may be especially helpful as part of the documentation process for the intensive plan of support in Tier 3.

Reproducible 6.4 *Planned Discussion Step-by-Step Summary*

Planned Discussion
Step-by-Step Summary

Following is a summary of the steps involved in Planned Discussion. It is important to use professional judgment, adjusting procedures to meet the needs of the situation and the individual.

Step 1. Plan to meet with the teacher.

A. Schedule the discussion for a time convenient to both you and the teacher.
B. Determine a location where you can meet with the teacher one-on-one.
C. Identify a primary concern to discuss during the meeting.
D. Identify at least two teacher strengths using the language of ongoing regard (see Chapter 5).

Step 2. Meet with the teacher.

A. Ensure the teacher is comfortable and prepared to engage in the discussion.
B. Introduce your primary concern.
C. Describe the goal in relation to a measurable objective.
D. Develop a list of possible solutions.
E. Set up an action plan.
F. Schedule a follow-up meeting.
G. Conclude the discussion with ongoing regard.

Optional: Print a copy of Reproducible 6.5, Discussion Record, to document your discussion.

Step 3. Monitor progress.

A. Continue 3–5 minute walk-throughs to assess progress.
B. Acknowledge and encourage growth efforts.

Step 4. Meet with the teacher to follow-up.

A. At the follow-up meeting, determine what further action is necessary.
B. Document the effectiveness of the intervention.
C. Make determination about whether the teacher could benefit from Tier 2 support.

 REPRODUCIBLE 6.4

Reproducible 6.5 *Discussion Record*

Discussion Record

TEACHER ____________________ GRADE/CLASS ____________________

ADMINISTRATOR OR COACH ____________________ DATE AND TIME ____________________

1. Describe the area of concern.

2. Describe the goal.

3. Brainstorm a list of possible solutions.

4. Set up an action plan.

Schedule a follow-up meeting: Date ______________ Time ________

 REPRODUCIBLE 6.5

Data Collection and Debriefing

Collecting data helps the teacher better understand any problem and determine whether improvements are happening over time. Keeping a more structured, systematic record of teacher practice has the potential to directly affect the motivation of staff, as staff get more data to aid in decision-making about their own practice. Even if no improvement results from this intervention, subsequent interventions and more formal coaching cycles will build on the data collected.

As previously discussed in Chapter 4, *gathering data often solves the problem all by itself.* People tend to do their best when they're being observed by someone important to them, including a boss or mentor. It's part of human nature to shape up when we know we're being watched. Our houses are cleanest when company is coming over. Our driving habits are in top form when our GPS tells us we're being watched. We floss more often just before heading into the dentist's office. The act of being routinely monitored serves as a reminder to engage in what we know to be good practice.

Data Collection and Debriefing is useful in the following situations:

- A teacher has a minor, easy-to-fix deficit in hitting a specific benchmark.
- A teacher has a deficit in hitting a benchmark that they had been reaching regularly.
- A teacher has an ongoing issue with the ability to hit one or more benchmarks, as part of the comprehensive plan of support in Tier 3.

Step-by-step instructions for implementing Data Collection and Debriefing are provided in Reproducible 6.6. This is a general template, and either a coach or administrator may find the need to add or omit steps. While this data collection process is far less intensive than the Basic 5 Observation Form used for Tier 2 support, it extends Tier 1 walk-through and debriefing procedures described in Chapter 4.

Goal Setting

The process of goal setting helps teachers establish long- and short-term goals and identify specific, immediate actions they can take to work toward reaching those goals. Teachers struggling with professional growth may lack a sense of direction or purpose. They may have lacked support in the past when trying to establish new routines and practice. They may have experienced repeated failure without being able to determine why. Teachers may select goals that are too easy, which can lead to not experiencing pride in their growth. Or they may select goals that are so challenging they set themselves up for failure.

Goal Setting is useful in the following situations:

- A teacher has a minor, easy-to-fix deficit in hitting a specific benchmark.

Reproducible 6.6 *Data Collection and Debriefing Step-by-Step Summary*

Data Collection and Debriefing

Step-by-Step Summary

Following is a summary of the steps involved in Data Collection and Debriefing. It is important to use professional judgment, adjusting procedures to meet the needs of the situation and the individual. Engage in Planned Discussion concurrently or prior to the use of this intervention.

Step 1. Plan to meet with the teacher.

A. Schedule the discussion for a time convenient to both you and the teacher.

B. Determine a location where you can meet with the teacher one-on-one.

Step 2. Plan for the data collection process.

A. Review information gathered from previous interventions.

B. Identify at least two teacher strengths using the language of ongoing regard (see Chapter 5).

C. Identify target benchmarks on which to collect data.

D. Choose an objective data collection method from the tools and resources in Chapter 4 or Chapter 7.

E. Determine a schedule for when data collection will take place.

F. Plan to archive data.

G. Select a way to communicate the data back to the teacher.

Step 3. Meet with the teacher.

A. Introduce the concept of more-intentional data collection to the teacher.

B. Explicitly describe benchmarks on which you will collect data.

C. Explain the method of data collection.

D. Schedule a follow-up meeting to review and discuss data.

E. Conclude the discussion with words of ongoing regard.

Optional: Print a copy of Reproducible 6.5, Discussion Record, to document your discussion.

Step 4. Monitor progress toward identified benchmarks.

A. Consistently collect data according to schedule.

B. Be overt in your data collection efforts.

C. Engage in frequent, brief conversations with the teacher to report progress.

Step 5. Meet with the teacher to follow up.

A. At the follow-up meeting, determine what further action is necessary.

B. Document the effectiveness of the intervention.

C. Make determination about whether the teacher could benefit from Tier 2 support.

 REPRODUCIBLE 6.6

- A teacher has a deficit in hitting a benchmark that they had been reaching regularly.
- A teacher has an ongoing issue with the ability to hit one or more benchmarks, as part of the comprehensive plan of support in Tier 3.

Teachers struggling to hit benchmarks and who may be exhibiting severe deficits in reaching them may have difficulty doing what is necessary to develop the habits and skills required for success. The gap may seem so wide as to be almost insurmountable. The purpose of goal setting is to instill *hope*. And hope goes a long way toward teacher retention.

Step-by-step instructions for implementing Goal Setting are provided in Reproducible 6.7. This is a general template, and either a coach or administrator may find the need to add or omit steps. This intervention takes the concept of a planned discussion and pairs it with data collection to assess progress toward the goal. While less intensive than the more formal coaching cycle in Tier 2, it is reflective of a true coaching process. Also included are goal-setting documents (Reproducibles 6.8 and 6.9). These tools may be especially helpful as part of the documentation process for the intensive plan of support in Tier 3.

CAUTION

As mentioned at the beginning of this chapter, the C, when used for correction, is always the weakest STOIC variable at your disposal. If the rest of this section hasn't been used to create a well-thought-out system of initial support, the advice provided in this chapter may prove entirely ineffective.

The success of the information provided in this chapter hinges on the idea that, at this point, all the components necessary for change are in place. An overall vision has been developed, and a clear model for classroom management practices has been chosen. You have identified your four cornerstones and created both an initial and an ongoing professional development plan. Data are now being collected on a regular basis through classroom observations, including evaluators, nonevaluative coaches, and a peer-to-peer model. Relational trust between all stakeholders is increasing through effective communication and the use of Partnership Principles.

To assist thinking about these components through the lens of the STOIC Framework, we have provided Reproducible 6.10, STOIC Checklist for Leadership. Leadership teams can use the questions to determine if they have missed any potential steps along the way. While the checklist does not include the specifics of any given plan, it is a helpful reflection for those leading the charge to ensure the basics of good leadership are apparent when guiding any initiative.

Without these precursors, even the most well-designed course correction will veer off over time. With all these items put into place, course corrections will prove far more effective in improving teacher practice and helping a campus reach the overall vision that's been established.

Reproducible 6.7 *Goal Setting Step-by-Step Summary*

Goal Setting
Step-by-Step Summary

Following is a summary of the steps involved in Goal Setting. It is important to use professional judgment, adjusting procedures to meet the needs of the situation and the individual. Engage in Planned Discussion and Data Collection and Debriefing concurrently or prior to the use of this intervention.

Step 1. Plan to meet with the teacher.

A. Schedule the discussion for a time convenient to both you and the teacher.
B. Determine a location where you can meet with the teacher one-on-one.

Step 2. Prepare to work with the teacher to set goals.

A. Review information gathered from previous interventions.
B. Identify at least two teacher strengths using the language of ongoing regard (see Chapter 5).
C. Determine the general outcome you hope to achieve in this meeting.
D. Select a goal-setting format.

Optional: Use Reproducible 6.8, Short-Term Goals, or Reproducible 6.9, Long- and Short-Term Goals, depending on what you judge will work best for the teacher and the situation.

Step 3. Meet with the teacher.

A. Introduce the concept of intentional and specific goal setting to the teacher.
B. Guide the teacher in considering long-range aspirations and/or short-term goals.
C. Help the teacher establish short-term goals.
D. Identify actionable steps that will help the teacher reach their goal.
E. Set a specific, measurable target.
F. Choose a way to monitor progress toward achieving the target.
G. Clarify that the next step would be targeted coaching support within Tier 2.
H. Review responsibilities and sign the Goal Setting agreement (Reproducible 6.8 or 6.9).
I. Schedule a follow-up meeting to review and discuss progress.
J. Conclude the discussion with words of ongoing regard.

Optional: Print a copy of Reproducible 6.5, Discussion Record, to document your discussion.

Step 4. Monitor progress toward identified benchmarks.

A. Consistently collect data according to schedule.
B. Be overt in your data collection efforts.
C. Engage in frequent, brief conversations with the teacher to report progress.

Step 5. Meet with the teacher to follow up.

A. At the follow-up meeting, determine what further action is necessary.
B. Document the effectiveness of the intervention.
C. Make determination about whether the teacher could benefit from Tier 2 support.

 REPRODUCIBLE 6.7

Reproducible 6.8 *Short-Term Goal Setting*

Short-Term Goal Setting

TEACHER ______________________ GRADE/CLASS ______________________

ADMINISTRATOR OR COACH ______________________ DATE AND TIME ______________________

My professional goal is ______________________

____

____

____

____

I can show that I am working on this goal by ______________________

____

____

____

____

Teacher signature ______________________

• • • • •

I can help you reach this goal by ______________________

____

____

____

____

Administrator/Coach signature ______________________

REPRODUCIBLE 6.8

Reproducible 6.9 *Long-Range and Short-Term Goal Setting*

Long-Range and Short-Term Goal Setting

TEACHER ____________________ GRADE/CLASS ____________________

ADMINISTRATOR OR COACH ____________________ DATE AND TIME ____________________

I plan to work on the following goals:

Long Term	*Short Term*

Staff Responsibilities

Things I will do to reach my goals ____________________

Support Responsibilities

Things my administrator and/or coach will do to help me reach my goals ____________________

Progress Monitoring

How we will know if I have reached my goals ____________________

Follow-Up Meeting

We will meet again on _____/_____/_____ to discuss progress.

Teacher signature ____________________ Date __________

Administrator/Coach signature ____________________ Date __________

 REPRODUCIBLE 6.9

Reproducible 6.10 *STOIC Checklist for Leadership*

STOIC Checklist for Leadership

SCHOOL ____________________ DATE ___/___/___

Variables	Questions	Y / N	Comments
Structure for success	1. Have you defined clear expectations through the three-part target?	☐ ☐	
	2. Have you provided staff with any materials and resources they may need for implementation?	☐ ☐	
	3. Have you developed a system for checking in with staff on a regular basis to assess progress or needs?	☐ ☐	
Teach staff clear expectations	1. Have you communicated clear expectations through the three-part target?	☐ ☐	
	2. Have you taught the skills staff need for implementation?	☐ ☐	
	3. Have you taught staff how to use any tools needed for implementation?	☐ ☐	
	4. Have you built in review for skills and tools throughout the year?	☐ ☐	
Observe staff to assess progress and needs	1. Do you check in on individual staff members, interdisciplinary or grade-level teams, and full staff to assess needs?	☐ ☐	
	2. Have you identified data that will be collected to analyze the impact of implementation?	☐ ☐	
	3. Have you identified how trend data will be shared with all staff?	☐ ☐	
Interact positively with staff	1. Do you assess your ratio of positive interactions with staff?	☐ ☐	
	2. Do you intentionally boost your ratio of interactions with reluctant staff members by both verbally and nonverbally reinforcing them?	☐ ☐	
	3. Do you acknowledge and support the efforts of staff?	☐ ☐	
	4. Do you offer incentives, when appropriate, to encourage staff behavior?	☐ ☐	
	5. Do you celebrate the successes of staff when their behavior positively impacts student behavior?	☐ ☐	
Correct and provide support	1. Do you have a plan for how to respond to individual staff who are struggling to effectively implement?	☐ ☐	
	2. Do you have a plan to coach teachers when needed?	☐ ☐	
	3. Do you have a plan for re-teaching all staff if needed?	☐ ☐	

 REPRODUCIBLE 6.10

Wrapping It Up

CHAPTER 6 SUMMARY

The final step in Tier 1 is to create a pathway to Tier 2 coaching support.

What to Know

- A well-designed system of support should be in place prior to engaging in course correction.
- Communication skills and Partnership Principles should be applied throughout the process of course correction and collaboration.
- A process for accessing Tier 2 coaching support for improvement should be clearly communicated to staff.
- A screener should be used as a tool to gauge implementation and save time for all those in a support role on campus.
- Early-stage interventions serve as a bridge between Tier 1 and Tier 2 coaching support.

What to Do

- Ensure that all other variables have been considered to design a comprehensive system of Tier 1 support.
- Identify flags that will signal the need for Tier 2 coaching support.
- Establish a process for teachers to request Tier 2 coaching support.
- Utilize a screener to determine if Tier 2 support is potentially warranted.
- Provide early-stage interventions to teachers who may wish to engage only in Tier 1 coaching support.

Notes

Coaching as Targeted Support for Teachers

Your campus has now put into place a solid Tier 1 system. The leadership team are unified around a model of classroom management and an approach to achieving it. Coaches have been deployed as a resource to which all staff have access. But, even in the best of Tier 1 systems, you will have staff who require additional support. To be clear, this section is not just for teachers who are struggling. This tier is also for teachers who are *thriving* with implementation.

This support could be for a teacher who is demonstrating a lack of skill and needs assistance with implementation. This could be a teacher who has implemented, but hasn't yet achieved efficacy. Another teacher might be exhibiting a deficit in one or more of the Basic 5 Behavior Benchmarks. A teacher who is highly skilled, with an effective classroom management model in place, may also need additional support. Perhaps this teacher has requested or has been chosen to provide a model classroom for the campus or district. Perhaps this is a teacher who aspires to become a coach or an administrator and wants to see the coaching process firsthand.

Tier 2 coaching support is provided through the Improvement Cycle. The Improvement Cycle is a four-part cycle of continuous improvement designed to help coaches and teachers work collaboratively. The cycle is designed to help coaches uphold the Partnership Principles when working with staff on how best to approach changes in practice. The Improvement Cycle embeds the Basic 5 Benchmarks as the target for teachers working to improve their classroom management skills.

The first four chapters of this section discuss how to move through each step of the Improvement Cycle:

> Chapter 7, "Coaching Through a Cycle of Continuous Improvement: Review" discusses how to initiate the Tier 2 coaching process using the Improvement Cycle and the Basic 5 Behavior Benchmarks. During the Review portion of the Improvement Cycle, coaches will collect data centered around the Basic 5 Benchmarks and analyze these data with teachers to identify priorities for improvement. This step includes conducting a preconference with the teacher to discuss which data will be collected and engaging in the data collection and analysis process. While the Basic 5 Observation Tool is the core data collection tool used in Tier 2, other tools for collecting baseline data are also introduced in this chapter.

Chapter 8, "Coaching Through a Cycle of Continuous Improvement: Prioritize" explains how coaches and teachers will use data collected in the Review step to identify aspects of the teacher's classroom management plan that are priorities for improvement. Collaboratively, coaches and teachers use baseline data and identified priorities to set clear, measurable, and impactful goals for improvement.

Chapter 9, "Coaching Through a Cycle of Continuous Improvement: Revise" discusses how the coach and teacher will work collaboratively to identify strategies, policies, and procedures to address goals set in the Prioritize step. This revision plan will include maintaining and preserving aspects of the current management plan that are working and identifying which practices within the STOIC framework should be adjusted or abandoned. The coach will explain and model classroom management strategies as needed to help the teacher incorporate into their daily practice.

Chapter 10, "Coaching Through a Cycle of Continuous Improvement: Implement" reviews how the coach will work with the teacher to implement the classroom management practices that were identified during the Revise step. The coach will monitor implementation of the revised plan by collecting data on each improvement goal and motivate staff and students by highlighting growth and improvement over time.

The last chapter of this section discusses how to integrate each step of the Improvement Cycle into a cohesive model for coaching:

Chapter 11, "Planning Into Practice: The Improvement Cycle in Action" provides an example schedule to demonstrate how the Improvement Cycle looks when put into practice. Use this chapter to reflect on what a coaching process might look like within your own campus and how to schedule and implement each step of the Improvement Cycle when coaching an individual teacher.

In the first section of the book, we were explicit in using the STOIC Framework to design a coaching system as part of Tier 1 universal support for all staff. In the following chapters, the STOIC Framework will be less explicit but no less identifiable in the coaching cycle. The Improvement Cycle itself, as well as the clear benchmarks and data collection process when assessing the classroom, provides *Structure*. When setting priority goals for improvement and developing proposed policies and procedures, coaches will assist in *Teaching* staff new practices. An ongoing system of collaboration blends *Observation* with the chance to *Interact positively* with staff and provide *Correction* if a teacher is off course. Within every system, including coaching as a Tier 2 support, the STOIC Framework should be evident.

CHAPTER 7

Coaching Through a Cycle of Continuous Improvement: Review

Practice the philosophy of continuous improvement. Get a little better every single day. —Brian Tracy

As with all multi-tiered systems, universal strategies will help lead most students down the right path. Others will need more targeted supports. These targeted supports are there to help students who might have specific skill deficits or need further enrichment. Targeted supports can be created for normally high-performing students who are experiencing difficulty in a certain area or who may qualify for gifted and talented support. Targeted supports are also for students who are struggling in many areas.

The same goes for teachers. Targeted Tier 2 supports can be provided for new or struggling teachers. The same supports can be offered to teachers whose overall practice is good but who might be experiencing skill deficits. And teachers who may be serving as exemplars may require additional support as they continue to master an already high skill set.

Targeted Tier 2 coaching in classroom management should be provided in a more structured format than the informal coaching provided to all teachers. While this process can certainly be used with educators at many levels of expertise and under a wide range of conditions in Tier 1, we are introducing this structured cycle as *the* way to coach teachers who have specifically requested or require a higher level of support.

THE IMPROVEMENT CYCLE

Our structured coaching process is a cycle of continuous improvement, which we will refer to as the Improvement Cycle. There are four steps within the Improvement Cycle, as shown in Figure 7.1.

Figure 7.1 *Improvement Cycle*

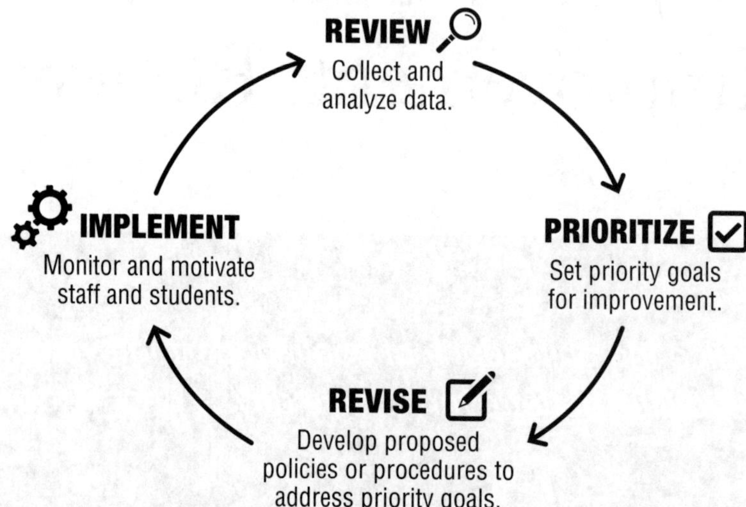

The Improvement Cycle is a way for data to be used to make meaningful decisions and foster improvements in student behavior and success. This directly matches the Improvement Cycle introduced to teachers in *CHAMPS* and *Discipline in the Secondary Classroom* as an ongoing cycle of reflection and growth in the classroom. This cycle is a modified version of that found in the Safe & Civil Schools *Foundations* program, which helps all staff work together to address behaviors at the schoolwide level. In the context of coaching, this cycle will allow coaches and teachers to work collaboratively, yet efficiently, to create classroom environments that help all students reach their highest potential.

The Improvement Cycle embeds the Basic 5 Behavior Benchmarks as the target for teachers working to improve their classroom management skills. The Basic 5 Benchmarks were introduced in Chapter 3 as a way to measure overall effectiveness of your classroom management model (Measure in the three-part target). The Basic 5 Benchmarks are also integral to providing Tier 2 support—they are used to assess classroom functioning and determine the level of structured coaching support needed in Tier 2.

As a reminder, the Basic 5 Behavior Benchmarks include:

- *Ratio of Interactions*—the ratio of positive to corrective interactions between the teacher and students.
- *Opportunities to Respond*—chances given by the teacher for students to engage in teacher-directed instruction.

- *Disruptions*—unwanted or inappropriate behaviors that interrupt the flow of instruction for the teacher or another student or students.
- *On-Task Behavior*—the amount of on-task behavior exhibited by students. (Strictly speaking, on-task is one metric of academic engagement; for simplicity's sake we will use them synonymously.)
- *Alignment With Expectations*—the daily reality of student behavior compared with posted expectations and classroom rules.

Figure 7.2 *Basic 5 Behavior Benchmarks (available for download as Reproducible 3.5)*

Basic 5 Behavior Benchmarks

Level 3 = Stop (do something different)
Level 2 = Caution (intervention recommended)
Level 1 = Keep going (keep doing what you're doing)

BENCHMARK	LEVEL 3	LEVEL 2	LEVEL 1	DATA COLLECTION TOOL
Ratio of Interactions (positive to corrective)	Less than 1:1 or less than 1 interaction per minute	At least 1:1 consistently	At least 3:1 consistently	Ratio of Interactions Monitoring Form (Reproducible 10.1) • 30-minute recording time • Any activity • Use for individual or classwide monitoring
Opportunities to Respond (per 10-minute interval)	Fewer than 10	10 to 40	More than 40	Opportunities to Respond Observation Sheet (Reproducible 10.2) • 10-minute recording time • Use during teacher-guided instruction • Use for individual or classwide monitoring
Disruptions (per 10-minute interval)	More than 10	5 to 10	Fewer than 5	Misbehavior Recording Sheets (Reproducibles 10.3A and 10.3B) • Use for duration of one activity or entire period • Any activity • Use for classwide monitoring
On-Task Behavior	Less than 80%	80% to 89%	90% to 100%	On-Task Behavior Observation Sheet (Reproducible 10.4) • 5-minute recording time • Any independent work time • Use for classwide monitoring
Alignment with Expectations	Less than 80%	80% to 89%	90% to 100%	CHAMPS Versus Daily Reality Scale (Reproducible 10.6) • Use for duration of one activity or entire period • Any activity • Use for classwide monitoring

REPRODUCIBLE 3.5

These major behavior benchmarks have been used to create a tool to gather baseline data (Reproducible 7.1, Basic 5 Observation Tool, shown on the next two pages). This tool casts a net wide enough to identify where one deficit may be creating another. Because these benchmarks are so intertwined and impact one another, a problem that may not be obvious in one area will become apparent within another.

As an example of this, let's say a teacher requests support and academic data show more than 20% of their students are failing a content area or class period. These two flags signal to the system that the teacher may, in fact, be able to access Tier 2 support. The teacher completes the STOIC Classroom Management Screener (Reproducible 6.3B), where implementation of the model is evident. Recent walk-throughs were not able to specifically identify an area in which the teacher is struggling. The coach meets with the teacher and sets up a time to collect baseline data. While opportunities to respond are high, disruptions are also high when measured concurrently. Due to the high number of disruptions, many students aren't on task during teacher-guided instruction. In addition, ratio of interactions shows a high rate of positive attention because the teacher is not redirecting off-task and disruptive behavior. If walk-throughs collected data only on opportunities to respond and/or ratio of interactions, those small snippets of information may miss the larger issues related to classroom management. Collecting data on all five benchmarks may show a very different picture than the briefer snapshot a walk-through provides.

While no professional is ever finished making finer distinctions within each benchmark, mastery of these five will put any teacher well along the path to being an effective classroom manager.

Each benchmark is categorized using three classifications:

- Level 1: Classroom skills are functioning at a high level, and the teacher should proceed with what they already have in practice.
- Level 2: Changing or augmenting current management techniques is recommended.
- Level 3: Immediate change in practice is necessary to secure the learning environment of students.

These levels align somewhat with the idea of tiers, with Level 1 indicating a low need for support in this benchmark and Level 3 indicating a high need for support. If a teacher's performance falls into Level 3 on one benchmark, a coach can gather more specific data regarding this variable and work to help the teacher attain proficiency in that area. If the teacher's scores tend to fall into Level 2 overall, the coach and teacher might choose to focus on one or two skills, or attack all of them directly, using the coach's discretion and relationship with the teacher as a guide.

The column to the far right of the Basic 5 Behavior Benchmarks (Reproducible 3.5), "Data Collection Tool," suggests appropriate monitoring forms to use to explore any one benchmark in more depth. These tools, as well as quick guidelines for their use, are included in Chapter 10 of this book. These benchmarks and monitoring forms are also included as tools in Chapter 10 of both *CHAMPS* and *DSC*.

Reproducible 7.1 *Basic 5 Observation Tool (p. 1 of 2)*

Basic 5 Observation Tool (p. 1 of 2)

TEACHER ____________ CLASS ____________ DATE ________ TIME ______

OBSERVER ____________ ACTIVITY ____________

STEP 1 During a 10-minute observation of teacher-guided instruction, record simple tally marks for each of the following behaviors. ***10 minutes***

BENCHMARK	OBSERVATION PERIOD		TOTAL
	Positive (Appropriate Behavior)	Corrective (Inappropriate Behavior)	
Ratio of Interactions			____:____ Positive:Corrective
Opportunities to Respond			
Disruptions			

STEP 2 **Benchmark: On-Task Behavior**
For the next 5 minutes, focus on a different student every 5 seconds. Record a "+" symbol to indicate on-task or engaged behavior and a "–" symbol to indicate off-task behavior. When each student has been observed, begin the progression again. Continue until 5 minutes have elapsed. ***5 minutes***

1	2	3	4	5	6	7	8	9	10	11	12
13	14	15	16	17	18	19	20	21	22	23	24
25	26	27	28	29	30	31	32	33	34	35	36
37	38	39	40	41	42	43	44	45	46	47	48
49	50	51	52	53	54	55	56	57	58	59	60

Divide the number of on-task (+) marks by the total number of marks (60).

Time on task (percentage of on-task behavior) = ______%.

 REPRODUCIBLE 7.1

Reproducible 7.1 (cont.) *Basic 5 Observation Tool (p. 2 of 2)*

Basic 5 Observation Tool (p. 2 of 2)

STEP 3 **Benchmark: Alignment With Expectations**
Using the rating scale below, rate the degree to which the students met the teacher's expectations for classroom activities or transitions. Identify which activity or transition is being rated in the "Activity" section of each box. ***5 minutes***

RATING SCALE
Percentage of Students Who Met Expectations: **1** = 90% to 100% **2** = 80% to 89% **3** = Less than 80%

Conversation	1	2	3
Help	1	2	3
Activity:			
Movement	1	2	3
Participation	1	2	3
Success!	1	2	3

Conversation	1	2	3
Help	1	2	3
Activity:			
Movement	1	2	3
Participation	1	2	3
Success!	1	2	3

Conversation	1	2	3
Help	1	2	3
Activity:			
Movement	1	2	3
Participation	1	2	3
Success!	1	2	3

Conversation	1	2	3
Help	1	2	3
Activity:			
Movement	1	2	3
Participation	1	2	3
Success!	1	2	3

STEP 4 (Optional) **Anecdotal Notes:** Record any information in this section that may be useful as a springboard for discussion (e.g., data that may be further mined to give a more comprehensive picture of classroom behavior, follow-up questions for the coaching conversation, etc.).

 REPRODUCIBLE 7.1

This chapter will discuss how to initiate the Tier 2 coaching process using the Improvement Cycle and the Basic 5 Behavior Benchmarks. The first step of the Improvement Cycle is Review.

STEP 1: Review

During the Review portion of the Improvement Cycle, data centered around the Basic 5 Benchmarks will be collected and analyzed to identify priorities for improvement. This step includes a series of critical coaching components. To accurately review classroom practice, you must engage in:

- **Preconference.** This is a formal conversation with the teacher to provide full transparency about what data will be collected and for you, the coach, to develop a clear idea of what challenges the teacher currently feels they are facing. This is a critical first step.
- **Preparation.** This step is key to ensuring that both parties are comfortable in what each person's role will be in the process of assessment.
- **Assessment.** In the final step, data are collected and analyzed around specific benchmarks, which were more clearly defined during the preconference.

Preconference

In preparation for this initial formal data collection process, the coach and teacher will engage in a preconference. This preconference will set up the partnership approach outlined in Chapter 5. One of the most effective ways to empower teachers through this coaching process is to interview them about their professional life in school.

When you first seek to understand another's perspective, people will be more interested in listening to what you have to say. Coaches who sit down and listen intently to the challenges, rewards, and concerns teachers experience build trust. Teachers often report that the one-on-one interview with their coach was the first time anyone had ever taken the time to understand fully what goes on in their classrooms. In our experience, most teachers are open to being interviewed because the stated purpose of the interview is to help you, the coach, learn more about the teacher, their needs, and the students they serve.

When possible, the initial preconference should take place in the teacher's classroom. Interviews should last from 30 to 45 minutes. The coach has four objectives:

- To build a relationship with the teacher
- To learn more about the teacher's experiences
- To explain the support that will be provided
- To explain how data will be collected and used

During the interview, the coach should listen authentically, attend to body language, and look for opportunities to build a connection.

Four broad types of questions should be used during the preconference. Ask questions about the teacher's:

- Experience
- Classroom management style
- Past experiences with coaching and consultation
- Specific areas in which they are in need of support

The answer to these questions can widely vary between teachers. By asking questions in these four areas, one can get a fairly comprehensive overview of a teacher's concerns in a short period of time.

For a structured approach to this conversation, consider using the Teacher Interview (Reproducible 7.2) developed by Wendy Reinke (Sprick et al., 2010), which focuses on motivational interviewing to begin the coaching cycle. During the initial conversation with a teacher onboarding to the more formal coaching in Tier 2, this organized format of questioning is particularly useful.

Effective motivational interviewing is about establishing and maintaining collaborative relationships. The goal here is not that the conversation feel so set as to be stiff and impersonal. The goal is to provide a set of guided questions that can help a coach uncover more information, often in a short amount of time. If staff believe that you genuinely accept and understand them, you can trust that you have created the setting for them to move in positive directions.

A big idea in motivational interviewing is the use of *change talk*, which refers to language that conveys a person's desire, ability, reasons, need, or commitment to make a change. Questions are phrased to encourage this talk. The questions offer those in a coaching role a chance to truly practice authentic listening. Motivational interviewing is an especially great way to help teachers who are already highly skilled determine next steps in practice. And it can certainly be used to assist those who may lack drive, for a variety of reasons, to become empowered and motivated.

During the initial conversation, a coach may also consider using the Classroom Ecology Checklist, also created by Wendy Reinke (Sprick et al., 2010). The Classroom Ecology Checklist expands on the STOIC Classroom Management Screener introduced in Chapter 6. It includes a section on instructional management in addition to more specific questions related to the STOIC framework. This checklist can be used as both a baseline and as part of the exit strategy we'll discuss in Chapter 10 to show growth.

As part of the preconference, the coach and teacher will also agree on the time and dates when baseline data will be taken. Ideally, this baseline data should be gathered during teacher-guided instruction over the same 15- to 20-minute span on at least three occasions within a 1–2 week period. This could be during a time of concern identified as a result of an administrator's walk-through. It could also be a time chosen by the

Reproducible 7.2 *Teacher Interview (p. 1 of 2)*

Teacher Interview (p. 1 of 2)

TEACHER ______________ INTERVIEWER ______________ DATE ______________

Preparation Dialogue With Teacher

These questions will allow me to get to know you better and give me an idea of your classroom management style. I will also ask you about your past coaching experience, if any, and provide an opportunity for you to share any difficulties you would like support with. Before we start, do you have any questions?

A. Teacher Experience

1. How long have you been a teacher? Have you always taught this grade level?
2. What do you think it was that made you want to become a teacher?
3. What do you think is the best thing about being an elementary/secondary teacher?
4. What do you think is the most difficult thing about being an elementary/secondary teacher?

B. Classroom Management Style

1. How would you describe your current classroom management style? What are your strengths? What are your weaknesses?
2. Do you have a set of classroom rules? If so, what are those rules?
3. Do you use reward systems in your classroom? If so, what do those systems look like?
4. How do you handle misbehavior in your classroom?

REPRODUCIBLE 7.2

Reproducible 7.2 (cont.) *Teacher Interview (p. 2 of 2)*

Teacher Interview (p. 2 of 2)

5. When working with a student with difficult behavior, what strategies have you found to be most effective? What strategies have you found to be ineffective?

C. Past Consultation Experiences

1. What has been your past experience with coaching or mentoring? What did you find helpful?

2. Ideally, what would you like to have happen when consulting with another professional?

3. How often do you receive feedback on your teaching?

4. What are some of the things you like or dislike about feedback?

5. If given a choice between receiving face-to-face feedback or a printout or email summary of data collected on your teaching, which do you think you would prefer? Why?

D. Specific Areas of Support

1. What are some of the behavioral challenges in your classroom for which you would like support?

2. In your classroom, do you have challenging students who are not currently on a behavior support plan and would most likely benefit from more individualized supports, such as a specialized behavior support plan? How many?

 REPRODUCIBLE 7.2

Reproducible 7.3 *Classroom Ecology Checklist (p. 1 of 2)*

Classroom Ecology Checklist (p. 1 of 2)

This questionnatire assesses your own perception of your classroom. Use it as a starting point for reflecting on what's working, what isn't, and what changes you might like to make. You can ask your partnering coach to complete a separate Classroom Ecology Checklist and then compare notes.

A. Instructional Management

1. How much of your class time is allocated to academic instruction?	☐ Less than 50%	☐ 50%–70%	☐ More than 70%
2. Do you secure student attention at the beginning of a lesson, and are most students engaged during instruction?	☐ Less than 60%	☐ 60%–90%	☐ More than 90%
3. Are academic responses generally accurate when you lead instruction? What would you estimate your students' percentage of correct responses is?	☐ Less than 60%	☐ 60%–85%	☐ More than 85%
4. Do you solicit both group and individual responses to questions, being sure to provide individual opportunities for the majority of students in the classroom (not targeting the same handful of students for every question)?	☐ No	☐ Sometimes	☐ Yes
5. Do you maintain a brisk instructional pace and adjust for complex content, providing students with an optimal number of opportunities to respond (4–6 per minute for new material; 9–12 per minute for drill and practice)?	☐ No	☐ Sometimes	☐ Yes
6. Do you use effective error correction strategies (for example, do you prompt or model rather than say "no" or "wrong")?	☐ No	☐ Sometimes	☐ Yes

B. Classroom Behavior Management

STRUCTURE FOR SUCCESS

1. Does the physical arrangement of desks and furniture allow you to see all parts of the room? Interact with every student individually? Does the layout promote orderly traffic flow?	☐ No	☐ Sometimes	☐ Yes
2. Do you use an attention signal that has been taught directly, practiced, and positively reinforced?	☐ No	☐ Sometimes	☐ Yes
3. Do you secure student attention at the beginning of a lesson, and are most students engaged during instruction?	☐ No	☐ Sometimes	☐ Yes

 REPRODUCIBLE 7.3

Reproducible 7.3 (cont.) *Classroom Ecology Checklist (p. 2 of 2)*

Classroom Ecology Checklist (p. 2 of 2)

TEACH EXPECTATIONS

1. Are classroom routines and expectations clearly defined, stated positively, and posted?	☐ No	☐ Somewhat	☐ Yes
2. Do you have a plan or schedule for teaching classroom expectations?	☐ No	☐ Partial/ Informal	☐ Yes
3. Do transitions between activities occur smoothly and without interruption?	☐ No	☐ Sometimes	☐ Yes

OBSERVE AND MONITOR

1. Do you circulate through all parts of the classroom?	☐ No	☐ Sometimes	☐ Frequently
2. Do you visually scan all parts of the classroom?	☐ No	☐ Sometimes	☐ Frequently

INTERACT POSITIVELY

1. Do you engage in noncontingent positive interactions with every student (for example, greeting each student and demonstrating an interest in student work)?	☐ No	☐ Somewhat	☐ Yes
2. Do you use specific praise—direct, descriptive, and nonattributive—to encourage appropriate behavior?	☐ No	☐ Sometimes	☐ Yes
3. Do you acknowledge expected behaviors regularly? More specifically, is your ratio of positive interactions (the sum of your noncontingent positive interactions and praise) to corrective interactions (reprimands and consequences) 3:1 or better?	☐ No	☐ Sometimes	☐ Yes
4. If misbehavior or lack of motivation is an issue, do you have a system in place for documenting and rewarding appropriate classwide and individual student behavior?	☐ No	☐ Partial/ Informal	☐ Yes

CORRECT FLUENTLY

1. Are disruptions and problem behaviors minimal?	☐ No	☐ Sometimes	☐ Yes
2. Do you use a continuum of consequences to discourage rule violations (for example, ignoring, praising others, proximity, specific reprimand)?	☐ No	☐ Sometimes	☐ Yes
3. Do you have a documentation system for dealing with specific behavioral violations?	☐ No	☐ Partial/ Informal	☐ Yes
4. When you correct misbehavior, are you calm?	☐ No	☐ Sometimes	☐ Always
. . . consistent?	☐ No	☐ Sometimes	☐ Always
. . . brief?	☐ No	☐ Sometimes	☐ Always
. . . immediate?	☐ No	☐ Sometimes	☐ Always

 REPRODUCIBLE 7.3

coach and teacher, potentially during instruction in a particular content area or during a certain class period that is of concern.

One of the main goals of the preconference is to establish rapport; it is important to express empathy and share relevant experiences when appropriate. The willingness of a teacher to open up and express concerns, hesitations, fears, and frustrations is likely to be increased by a positive, friendly, collaborative relationship established at the beginning of the Improvement Cycle.

Preparation

Classroom observations should be as objective as possible. One way to increase objectivity is to separate fact from inference during the observation. A coach's main goal is to collect facts, not to reach conclusions about successes or shortfalls in classroom activities. For example, noting that "students seem to enjoy what is being taught" is an inference, whereas recording each time the teacher provided an academic question and whether the students answered correctly are observed facts.

The coach should arrive in the classroom several minutes before the observation is scheduled to begin and situate themselves where they are inconspicuous but still able to monitor both teacher and student behavior. If possible, the coach should speak briefly with the teacher following the observation. Some teachers may feel anxious about being observed. Coaches can reassure a teacher that their practices are not being judged during data collection.

Classroom observation is a joint process. Both the teacher and the coach have important roles before, during, and after the observation. Collaborating at each stage of the process helps both participants to feel comfortable, making the relationship feel less evaluative and more collaborative from the beginning. Table 7.1 (shown on the next page) lists these roles.

Assessment

Assessment can involve teacher self-evaluation, student feedback, and classroom observation. These baseline data can be used by the coach and teacher to develop a plan to adjust classroom management strategies. During the process of assessment, data are first collected and then analyzed. The following data sources may be collected:

- **Teacher self-evaluation.** The STOIC Classroom Management Screener (Reproducible 6.3B) and the Classroom Ecology Checklist (Reproducible 7.3) can be completed by the teacher to self-reflect on key areas of classroom management. In addition, the teacher can track the occurrence of certain behaviors in the classroom. For instance, a teacher may pick a short period of time during the day, no more than 5 or 10 minutes, when student behavior is most challenging, and

Table 7.1 *Roles in Collaborative Observation*

<table>
<tr><th>If you are the teacher being observed</th><th>If you are the coach observing</th></tr>
<tr><td>Prepare to discuss with the coach:
• Goals for the class.
• What your typical classroom schedule is.
• What you want the observer to notice.
Tell the coach:
• Where you'd like the coach to sit.
• Where the class meets and when.
• Whether and how you'll introduce the observer to the students.</td><td>Clarify the purpose of the observation:
• To guide collaborative development of a classroom management plan.
• To monitor progress over time.
Meet with the teacher to discuss:
• What will happen in class that day.
• What specifically the teacher hopes you'll notice.
• What you'll be doing during the observation.
Schedule a meeting to discuss the information you collect.</td></tr>
<tr><td>If deemed appropriate, introduce the coach to the class and provide a brief explanation of the purpose of the observation to the students. ("Jae is here today to see what we do during math period." "Ms. Patil is visiting to see what kinds of things third graders do in school.")
Afterward, write down your thoughts and reflections on the class and prepare to discuss them with the coach.</td><td>Record observations:
• Use a formal observation tool such as the Basic 5 Observation Tool (Reproducible 7.1).
• Record anecdotal information.
• Jot down questions you want to discuss with the teacher after the observation.
Be sure to enter time intervals of your observations in your notes.
Remain as unobtrusive as possible.</td></tr>
<tr><td>With the coach, reconstruct what happened in class. Think about goals for the class and the specific class session that was observed. Be prepared to describe:
• What you thought went well.
• What you would change.
• What was typical or atypical about the class.
Ask for specific descriptions and constructive suggestions.</td><td>With the teacher, reconstruct what happened in class. Ask the teacher to describe:
• What they thought went well.
• What they would change.
• What was typical or atypical about the class.
Describe rather than evaluate what you saw.
Offer constructive feedback and suggestions.</td></tr>
<tr><td>With the coach, develop a plan of action for improving classroom management.
Develop a time frame for monitoring, reviewing, and revising the plan.</td><td>With the teacher, develop a plan of action for improving classroom management.
With the teacher, develop a plan and specific time frame for monitoring, reviewing, and revising the plan.</td></tr>
</table>

then simply count the number of student disruptions or the number of times they engage in a positive interaction. This information can then be used when working with the coach to establish a goal or show growth.

- **Student feedback.** Involving the students themselves can be one of the most fruitful sources of information in identifying problem areas. When you think about it, asking students what they know about classroom rules or behavioral expectations is the ultimate test of whether the strategies in place are working. When it is developmentally appropriate, involving students in the development and implementation of their own behavior support plan can increase motivation and improve outcomes. However, students should not be interviewed without the coach prearranging it with the teacher and determining that the teacher is comfortable with the initiative. A coach never wants to surprise teachers with any of the actions taken in their classrooms.
- **Classroom observation.** Having a second set of eyes is especially helpful for getting the lay of a whole classroom. Given the multiple, multifaceted, often simultaneous tasks facing a teacher throughout the day, it is highly likely that a few things will go unnoticed from time to time. Simply having another person come into the classroom, such as a coach, mentor, or peer to observe can provide fresh insights. The Basic 5 Observation Tool (Reproducible 7.1), discussed in depth later in this chapter, helps a coach gather baseline data to share with the teacher. We recommend using this tool to collect baseline data and monitor progress throughout the process of providing Tier 2 support to a teacher.

Each tool in this chapter is a means of gathering data that can be used in close cooperation with teachers to set goals, try strategies to improve classroom management, and monitor results. These tools are designed to be collaborative in nature (rather than evaluative). Understanding proactive, data-based strategies will take the guesswork out of managing student behavior, modifying existing classroom management plans, and developing new techniques to deal with complex problems.

As coaches begin to use these forms, keep one thing in mind—they were designed to *improve the classroom environment for the purpose of instruction*, not to dictate or prohibit instructional methods. They do not look for any particular pedagogical approach; rather, they gauge behaviors across a variety of educational activities.

We actively encourage those of you reading and implementing the ideas in this book to modify content as you see fit based on your experience as a coach with behavior management. If you are new to coaching classroom management, we recommend staying true to the process of the Improvement Cycle and the data collection forms introduced in this chapter. This helps avoid the possibility that coaches and teachers may focus on things that have less impact, thereby wasting valuable time. Highly knowledgeable and skillful coaches are encouraged to collaboratively adapt, modify, and tailor definitions and forms freely to meet teachers' individual needs.

BASIC 5 OBSERVATION TOOL

The Basic 5 Observation Tool (Reproducible 7.1) helps you gather preliminary data about a classroom in as little as 60 minutes spread over 3 days. Ideally, this baseline data should be gathered during teacher-guided instruction over the same 20-minute time span on at least three occasions. The three sets of data are then averaged to provide an overall general picture of the classroom, which is then reviewed in the next formal coaching conversation. Check in with the teacher after each observation and schedule the more formal conversation for when you have enough data to engage in a robust dialogue. The two-page format facilitates ease of use, providing a concise measure of the Basic 5 Benchmarks.

Basic 5 Observation Tool (p. 1 of 2)

TEACHER ______ CLASS ______ DATE ______ TIME ______

OBSERVER ______ ACTIVITY ______

STEP 1 During a 10-minute observation of teacher-guided instruction, record simple tally marks for each of the following behaviors. *10 minutes*

BENCHMARK	OBSERVATION PERIOD		TOTAL
	Positive (Appropriate Behavior)	Corrective (Inappropriate Behavior)	
Ratio of Interactions			___:___ Positive:Corrective
Opportunities to Respond			
Disruptions			

STEP 2 **Benchmark: On-Task Behavior**
For the next 5 minutes, focus on a different student every 5 seconds. Record a "+" symbol to indicate on-task or engaged behavior and a "–" symbol to indicate off-task behavior. When each student has been observed, begin the progression again. Continue until 5 minutes have elapsed. *5 minutes*

1	2	3	4	5	6	7	8	9	10	11	12
13	14	15	16	17	18	19	20	21	22	23	24
25	26	27	28	29	30	31	32	33	34	35	36
37	38	39	40	41	42	43	44	45	46	47	48
49	50	51	52	53	54	55	56	57	58	59	60

Divide the number of on-task (+) marks by the total number of marks (60).
Time on task (percentage of on-task behavior) = ______%.

Coaching CHAMPS © 2022 Ancora Publishing REPRODUCIBLE 7.1

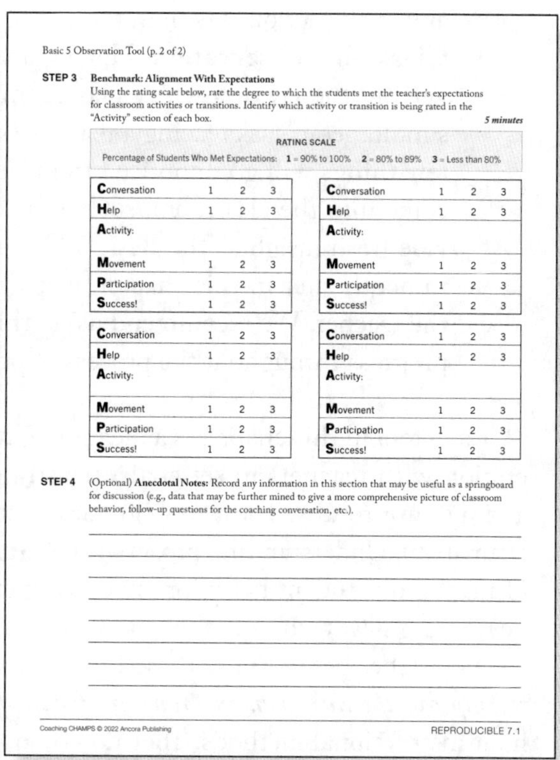

Basic 5 Observation Tool (p. 2 of 2)

STEP 3 **Benchmark: Alignment With Expectations**
Using the rating scale below, rate the degree to which the students met the teacher's expectations for classroom activities or transitions. Identify which activity or transition is being rated in the "Activity" section of each box. *5 minutes*

RATING SCALE
Percentage of Students Who Met Expectations: **1** = 90% to 100% **2** = 80% to 89% **3** = Less than 80%

Conversation	1	2	3
Help	1	2	3
Activity:			
Movement	1	2	3
Participation	1	2	3
Success!	1	2	3

Conversation	1	2	3
Help	1	2	3
Activity:			
Movement	1	2	3
Participation	1	2	3
Success!	1	2	3

Conversation	1	2	3
Help	1	2	3
Activity:			
Movement	1	2	3
Participation	1	2	3
Success!	1	2	3

Conversation	1	2	3
Help	1	2	3
Activity:			
Movement	1	2	3
Participation	1	2	3
Success!	1	2	3

STEP 4 (Optional) **Anecdotal Notes:** Record any information in this section that may be useful as a springboard for discussion (e.g., data that may be further mined to give a more comprehensive picture of classroom behavior, follow-up questions for the coaching conversation, etc.).

Coaching CHAMPS © 2022 Ancora Publishing REPRODUCIBLE 7.1

In the first 10 minutes of the observation, data are gathered simultaneously for three benchmarks: the teacher's ratio of positive to corrective interactions, the teacher's provision of opportunities to respond, and the number of student disruptions. The next 5 minutes are spent gauging students' on-task behavior, or academic engagement. The final few minutes will be used to measure student compliance to a teacher's posted expectations. While the definition and collection method for each of these data points is introduced in Chapter 4 and also discussed in more depth later in this chapter, let's provide some brief guidelines for collecting data on each of the benchmarks within the format of the Basic 5 Observation Tool.

STEP 1 (10 Minutes)

STEP 1 During a 10-minute observation of teacher-guided instruction, record simple tally marks for each of the following behaviors. ***10 minutes***

BENCHMARK	OBSERVATION PERIOD		TOTAL
	Positive (Appropriate Behavior)	Corrective (Inappropriate Behavior)	
Ratio of Interactions			______:______ Positive:Corrective
Opportunities to Respond			
Disruptions			

Ratio of Interactions. When measuring the ratio of interactions for baseline data, we recommend you look at overall interactions without coding for a specific student or behavior. Any time a teacher pays attention to positive behavior, it counts as a positive interaction. This would include when a teacher calls on an individual student to answer a question when the student is on task and engaged. Because the student is engaged in the appropriate, positive behavior, the interaction itself counts as positive. Any time a teacher pays attention to inappropriate behavior, it counts as a corrective interaction. This would include when a teacher calls on an individual student to answer a question when the student is off task and not engaged. Because the student is engaged in an inappropriate behavior when the teacher provides attention, the interaction counts as corrective. So, the same exact teacher behavior could be coded differently because it's the behavior of the student *when* attention is paid that indicates whether the interaction is positive or corrective.

Opportunities to Respond. Each time the teacher asks for a response from the class, tally an opportunity to respond. This response should be academic in nature, may include verbal or nonverbal cues to the students, and may be directed at an individual student or to the class as a whole. An opportunity to respond, or a chance for students to engage in the content, may include a verbal response, a written response (such as being directed to write down quick notes or complete a math problem on a whiteboard), or an action response (such as four corners, thumbs up/thumbs down, etc.). Remember, when a teacher calls on an individual student, that attention will also count as a tally for a positive or corrective interaction. If the student is engaged and on task, ready and willing to answer the question, it counts as a positive interaction. If a student is off task and the teacher calls on them possibly as a way to redirect their attention, count this interaction as corrective. This data point can *only* be collected during teacher-guided instruction. Do not collect data on opportunities to respond during any other instructional activity.

Disruptions. Add one tally each time a student's misbehavior disrupts the flow of instruction or causes another student to become off task. If two students are talking, even if the teacher does not respond, it counts as a disruption because at least two students are off task. If the teacher then responds, it also counts as a corrective interaction. If one student is off task but the teacher is not responding, perhaps using planned ignoring, and no other students are off task, it does not count as a disruption. Don't worry—this is one reason the tool casts a net over all five benchmarks. The student's behavior may not count as a disruption but will show up as off-task behavior when data are collected for that specific benchmark. An outburst by several students at once counts as a single disruption. It also counts as one corrective interaction if the teacher makes a classwide correction and may count as multiple corrective interactions if the teacher responds to a number of specific students.

Prior to using the Basic 5 Observation Tool on a regular basis, we recommend practicing. Collect data on one of these benchmarks, including the practice of calibration with other data collectors, then move on to collecting two of the three before collecting all three of them simultaneously. These practice attempts should *not* be made with a teacher currently receiving Tier 2 support. In fact, we highly recommend practicing on teachers who are consistently meeting benchmarks during administrative walk-throughs within Tier 1.

STEP 2 (5 Minutes)

STEP 2 **Benchmark: On-Task Behavior**

For the next 5 minutes, focus on a different student every 5 seconds. Record a "+" symbol to indicate on-task or engaged behavior and a "–" symbol to indicate off-task behavior. When each student has been observed, begin the progression again. Continue until 5 minutes have elapsed. ***5 minutes***

1	2	3	4	5	6	7	8	9	10	11	12
13	14	15	16	17	18	19	20	21	22	23	24
25	26	27	28	29	30	31	32	33	34	35	36
37	38	39	40	41	42	43	44	45	46	47	48
49	50	51	52	53	54	55	56	57	58	59	60

Divide the number of on-task (+) marks by the total number of marks (60).

Time on task (percentage of on-task behavior) = ______%.

On-Task Behavior. For the next 5 minutes, you will gauge students' connection with instruction, or academic engagement, by measuring on-task behavior. The grid, on the bottom of the first page of the Basic 5 Observation Tool, represents the 60 5-second increments that are found in a 5-minute time period. Determine a pattern that will be followed to see most, if not all, students at least twice during the instructional activity. This measurement grid is best used when students will be relatively stationary. Every 5 seconds, look up at a student and then back at the form. If the student is engaged and on task at the moment you look up, mark a + (plus) symbol. If the student is not engaged, mark a – (minus) sign. When 5 seconds are up, look quickly at the next student in the pattern and make a mark. At the end of 5 minutes, you will have recorded 60 symbols. These snapshots of student behavior at precise moments in time are aggregated to a meaningful average over time. On-task behavior is the percentage obtained by dividing the number of + symbols by the total number of marks (60).

STEP 3 (5 Minutes)

STEP 3 **Benchmark: Alignment With Expectations**

Using the rating scale below, rate the degree to which the students met the teacher's expectations for classroom activities or transitions. Identify which activity or transition is being rated in the "Activity" section of each box. ***5 minutes***

RATING SCALE

Percentage of Students Who Met Expectations: **1** = 90% to 100% **2** = 80% to 89% **3** = Less than 80%

Conversation	1	2	3
Help	1	2	3
Activity:			
Movement	1	2	3
Participation	1	2	3
Success!	1	2	3

Conversation	1	2	3
Help	1	2	3
Activity:			
Movement	1	2	3
Participation	1	2	3
Success!	1	2	3

The remaining few minutes of time will be spent measuring alignment with expectations. For each activity in which the students engage, the teacher should have a set of posted (or at the very least, stated, expectations). Each set of expectations should include directions on how and if students should engage in conversation, how and if students should ask for help, how and if students should be allowed to move within the classroom, and what active participation should look like overall.

Mirroring the idea of tiers, students will be scored on a rubric of 1–3. If more than 90% of students are in alignment with expectations, that variable receives a rating of 1. If 80% of students are in compliance, the variable receives a rating of 2. If fewer than 80%, the rating is 3, indicating a need for intervention of some kind. Measure each variable within each instructional activity that you observed. If a teacher's behavioral expectations aren't visibly posted, it is difficult to accurately determine if expectations are being followed by students or have even been taught at all. And often, a teacher's classroom management may be struggling because the teacher has not clearly defined and taught expectations explicitly to the students in the first place. If expectations are not visibly posted, it may not be possible to gather this portion of the baseline data.

STEP 4 (5 Minutes)

STEP 4 (Optional) **Anecdotal Notes:** Record any information in this section that may be useful as a springboard for discussion (e.g., data that may be further mined to give a more comprehensive picture of classroom behavior, follow-up questions for the coaching conversation, etc.).

____

____

____

____

____

____

____

____

This step is included as a means of recording any anecdotal information that may help springboard dialogue with the teacher. Use this section to record information such as a potential question to ask about a particular practice, an observation of a certain behavior from a specific student, etc.

PRACTICE CALIBRATION FOR CONSISTENCY

Again, prior to using the Basic 5 Observation Tool on a regular basis, we recommend practicing. If the Basic 5 Observation Tool, or an adaptation of this tool, is to be used as standard practice for collecting baseline data in Tier 2, all data collectors in a building should not only be comfortable with the definitions, format, and time frame, but also be reasonably calibrated to one another. Without calibration, the data is largely invalid. Let staff know early in the year that data collectors will be doing walk-throughs using this tool to practice calibration. It has less to do with the teacher (as this data will not be used for formative dialogue) and more to do with getting all data collectors on the same page. Practice should include teachers across the spectrum of classroom management proficiency.

Having accurate baseline data from the outset will help coaches and partnering teachers see eye to eye, set meaningful goals, and improve the teacher's odds of seeing sustained improvement of behavior management in the classroom. Set a date and time to meet with the teacher to analyze any baseline data that has been collected. This may include all of those data sources described above, including teacher self-evaluation, student feedback, and classroom observations.

DATA ANALYSIS

Data analysis is an important part of coaching and, alas, can be a thorny part. If a coach is overly concerned with being "nice" and dances around the truth, they can do a disservice to the teacher (and the teacher's students) by not sharing the specific information that could help the teacher improve. If the coach comes off as judgmental, brusque, or insensitive with their comments, they can irreparably damage their relationships with teachers. As Kegan and Lahey observed, "Many a relationship has been damaged and a work setting poisoned by perfectly delivered constructive feedback!" (2001, p. 128).

How, then, to proceed? We believe coaches can better negotiate this tricky communication challenge by working from the partnership perspective. Thus, discussions with the teacher should be structured as partners collaboratively exploring the data. The goal is to engage the collaborating teacher in conversation about the data, not to "win" by driving home some point. A coach should avoid telling the teacher what the data mean—good or bad. Let the teacher come to their own conclusions.

Data should be introduced as objectively as possible. Data simply give the coach and teacher a departure point for dialogue. Information should be given in specific, observable terms, such as, "The data collected show that students are on task an average of 68%," as opposed to, "Students are off-task quite a bit." Coaches should apply the communication strategies covered in Chapter 5 as well as strive to embed the Partnership Principles within every coaching conversation. An even better approach is to supply the data and begin by asking questions, allowing time for the data to speak directly to the teacher. Following is a sample list of questions to begin dialogue around baseline data:

- What's on your mind?
- How comfortable are you with these data?
- Do you agree or disagree with these data?
- Was this 5-, 10-, 20-minute time period an anomaly or the norm for this class?
- In what ways are the data similar to or different from what you were expecting?
- What do you think went well?
- What do you think could have gone better?
- Given the time we have today, what's the most important thing for us to talk about?
- In your ideal class, what would be different?
- What would be the first signs that your classroom is improving?

My favorite group of questions comes from Steve Barkley, the executive vice president of PLS 3rd Learning and internationally recognized for his ability to facilitate change. "On a scale of 1 to 10, with 1 being the worst lesson you've taught and 10 being the best, how would you have ranked that lesson? Why did you give it that number? What would have to change to move the lesson closer to a 10?" I've found the initial question provides a lot of information. If a teacher says "10" but the data indicate a need for immediate intervention, I know we need to explore practice further. This might be when the idea of video self-reflection is introduced, or a deeper motivational interview done. Either way, the collaborative exploration of data should continue.

QUESTIONS GUIDE REFLECTION

Because the group of questions from Steve Barkley has been so useful to me in my professional life as a coach, I've decided to occasionally use these questions in other areas of my life. And what better place to start looking for areas of improvement than my marriage?

I decided to try it on my husband during a long drive. I said, "Honey, on a scale of 1 to 10, with 1 being this is the worst our marriage has ever been and 10 being this is the absolute best you can imagine marriage to be, where would you rank our relationship right now?" There was a very, very long pause. He said, "This feels like a trick." I assured him it wasn't, but he said any spouse who didn't respond with at least an 11 was an idiot.

While this experiment didn't turn out the way I imagined, it did give me some insight. If a teacher feels the questions being asked are to "trick" them into providing or admitting information they are not ready to give, this is a clear indicator the coaching relationship is in trouble. Perhaps trust has been fractured or eroded over time; perhaps the teacher is simply overwhelmed. Either way, this served as a great reminder that questions should enhance a teacher's ability to reflect, not serve as a guide for them to land on a specific answer for which a coach may be hoping.

When engaged in dialogue, the coach must actively work to avoid top-down feedback (Figure 7.3). Top-down feedback is when data are collected and interpreted by the coach, who decides on a plan of action that is then told to the teacher. Top-down feedback is the belief that the data have given the coach all the answers.

To truly engage in the communication strategies introduced in Tier 1 and embed the Partnership Principles into the coaching conversation, the goal should be to engage in the collaborative exploration of data (Figure 7.4). This is partnership feedback, with the goal to guide teachers through data as they engage in active self-reflection. Partnership feedback is the suspension of the belief that the coach has all the answers. It is, at its core, how coaches truly support teachers.

Have you ever been the recipient of well-intended, perfectly delivered, but completely unnecessary feedback? A while back, I had the opportunity to attend a wedding in Florida. For whatever reason, after I took advantage of the hotel pool, my hair started having problems. That afternoon, I started seeing significant breakage and discoloration.

When I got home, I immediately rushed in to see my stylist for help. I knew to seek her out as an expert. She looked at my hair and, after asking me questions about my

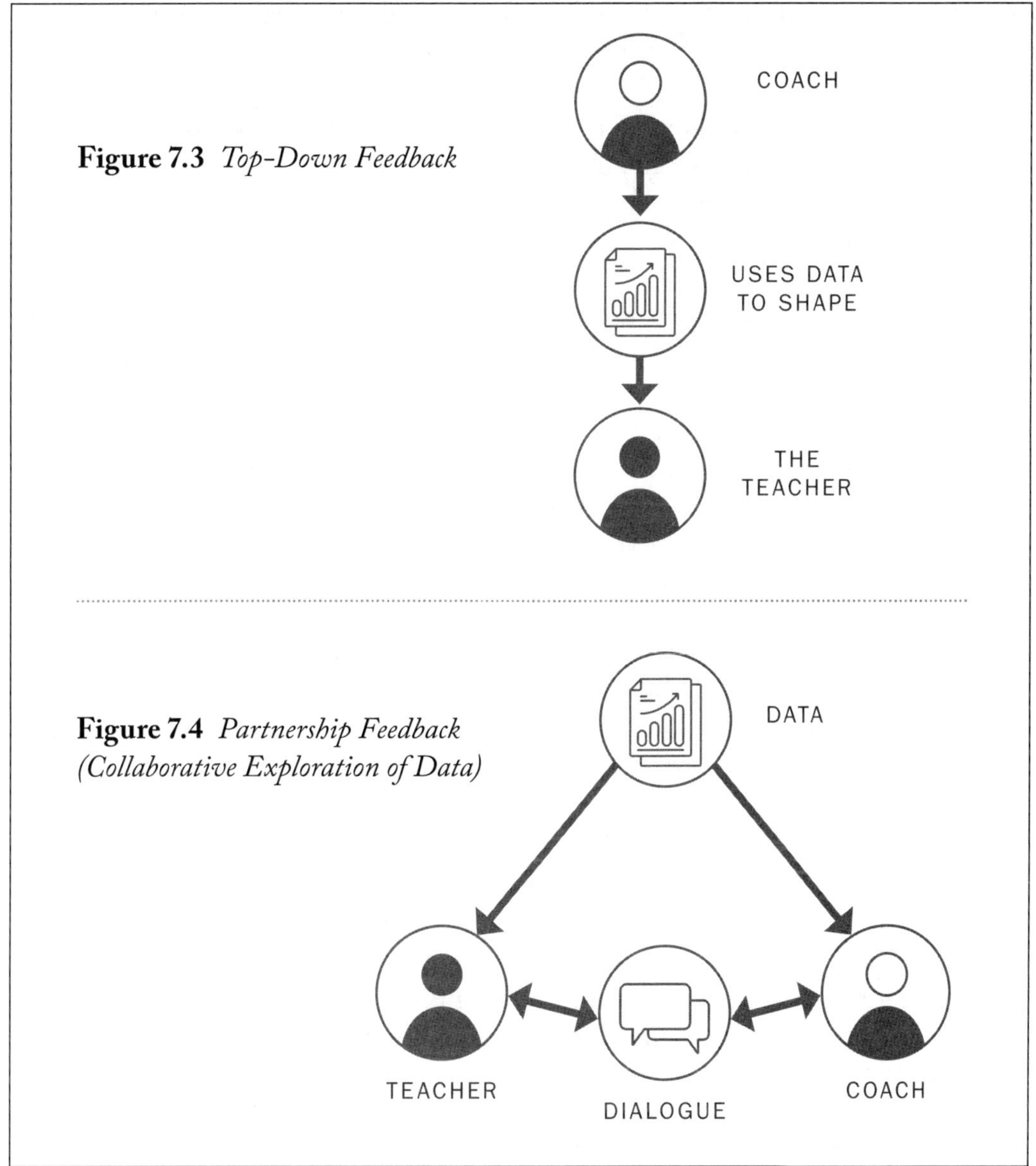

Figure 7.3 *Top-Down Feedback*

Figure 7.4 *Partnership Feedback (Collaborative Exploration of Data)*

upcoming travel and presentation schedule, came up with a plan of action and got to work. She dyed my hair a darker brown to hide the damage, cut some layers into it to mask the breakage, and gave me multiple hair care products to moisturize and smooth the follicles. But the only real solution was going to be the passage of time until my hair simply grew out.

Right after this I had to go to a conference where I was attending as both a participant and a support personnel for the other attendees. We were placed randomly into assigned seats for the week, and I was thrilled that my friend and colleague had also been placed at my table.

My friend had just been to a new stylist, and everyone, including me, was raving about her new cut. It truly did look amazing. Now, I was not telling anyone about the saga of my hair, even though clearly damage was apparent. I was choosing to simply ignore it in both an effort to not appear vain and because I knew there was absolutely nothing more to be done.

The second morning of the conference, as we sat at our table, she asked me if I was coming to her city any time soon. I checked my calendar, super excited at the prospect of perhaps going out to dinner. Then she slid a business card over to me and said she thought I might benefit from going to her stylist.

Let's examine this exchange.

My friend had collected some observational data. My hair did not look good. Then she came up with a plan and delivered it in my lap. This is top-down feedback at its finest. Her intention was pure, and her plan of action was sound. But—the only thing I heard was that she believed I wasn't smart enough to recognize I had a problem, and I was certainly unable to fix it. This may seem silly, but the interaction hurt because she'd missed a critical component of the coaching conversation.

One simple question would have changed the trajectory of our conversation. "Hey, I noticed your hair looks different than it usually does. Do you want to tell me about it?" I would've immediately opened up to my friend, telling her what happened and what I was currently doing to improve it. I would've been more than willing to hear her suggestion because I would have already been given a voice. The violation of partnership principles is inherent in top-down feedback, and even the most carefully worded constructive feedback has the power to damage even the strongest of relationships.

Even the best people trained in the practice of the collaborative exploration of data will fall prey to the instinctual rush to provide top-down feedback. When we aren't allotted enough time or when we truly believe the person being coached has nothing to bring to the table, we will run roughshod over others, forgetting the very real fact that we actually don't have all the answers.

Engaging in the collaborative exploration of data requires two distinct mindsets. One, you must be willing to suspend the belief that you have all the answers. That may feel difficult, but ultimately, it not only empowers staff, but also removes the burden from your shoulders that the coach must be the expert in all things. Two, you must be authentically curious and want to both hear and learn from the teacher's perspective. By applying the communication strategies and partnership principles from Chapter 5, you can do so with sincerity, forming a true collaborative process.

The job of a coach is not to use data as a tool for judgment; it's to help teachers get a clear picture of their current reality. Without a clear picture of current reality, coaching support will be largely ineffective. How can a teacher feel moved to set a goal if they don't believe change is necessary? And how can a coach help if there's no target toward which to work? Once a teacher is comfortable looking at the data simply as information that will be used to guide decision-making, the coach and teacher can begin to look at setting priority goals for improvement, revising strategies to improve classroom management, and implementing those strategies in earnest.

Wrapping It Up CHAPTER 7 SUMMARY

Collecting and reviewing data is the first step in the Improvement Cycle.

What to Know

- The Improvement Cycle is a formal, intentional coaching cycle.

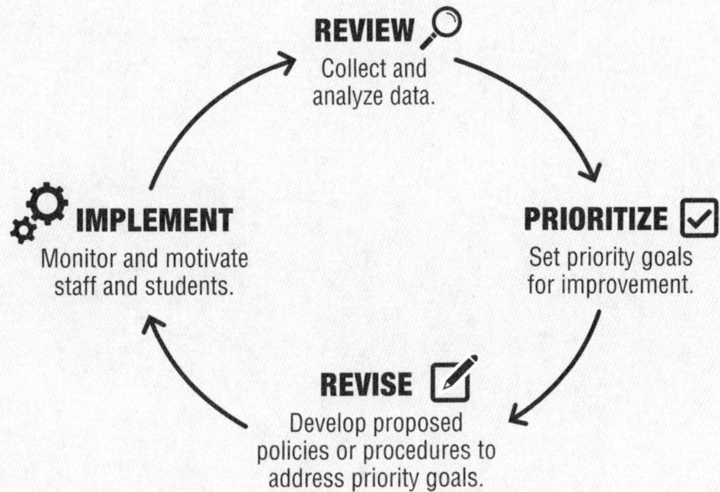

- The first step of the Improvement Cycle is Review. Data are collected and analyzed using the Basic 5 Behavior Benchmarks:
  - Ratio of interactions
  - Opportunities to respond
  - Disruptions
  - On-task behavior
  - Alignment with expectations

What to Do

- Ensure all coaches tapped to work with teachers in Tier 2 understand the Improvement Cycle as a continuous coaching cycle.
- Practice data collection of the Basic 5 Benchmarks with all data collectors to ensure calibration.
- Use the collaborative exploration of data to help teachers gain an accurate picture of current reality.

Notes

CHAPTER 8

Coaching Through a Cycle of Continuous Improvement: Prioritize

Coaching is not about what's wrong; it's about what's next. –Eric Sandberg

The Improvement Cycle, introduced in the last chapter, is a four-part cycle of continuous improvement designed to help coaches and teachers work collaboratively. The cycle is designed to help coaches uphold the Partnership Principles when working with staff on how best to approach changes in practice. In this chapter, coaches and teachers will use the data collected in the Review step to identify aspects of the teacher's classroom management plan that are priorities for improvement, giving the teacher a voice in where to begin. The Prioritize step involves:

- Rank ordering priorities to determine which classroom management aspects are most important and urgent to address with the teacher
- Constructing PEERS goals to clarify what the teacher will be working on.

STEP 2: Prioritize

Determining where to begin can often be the hardest part of this process. Maybe a teacher has several benchmarks that show deficits, and many changes in practice are warranted. Perhaps a teacher is doing relatively well but is finding it difficult to make an assessment on which skill to hone first. And, often, the need for short-term pain reduction makes us blind to the long-term changes in practice that should be explored.

Rank Order Priorities

This process serves to continue the dialogue started when reviewing data. Potential needs are listed, in no particular order. These needs are based on the objective data that were gathered and analyzed in the first step of the Improvement Cycle and may also include more subjective assessment based on a coach and teacher's anecdotal perceptions of the classroom. This should be the free brainstorming of ideas based on not just the Basic 5 Benchmarks but also on other assessments of the classroom management plan, including both teacher and student perceptions.

After needs are listed, two scores will be attached to each. The first score is a rough assessment of how much of an impact the teacher believes this change in practice would have in the classroom. This score is based largely on what we call the educator's cardiac assessment—how staff *feel* about the need listed and the impact it might have. While any scoring rubric could be used, we recommend a rubric of five to determine the impact on how the classroom operates:

5 – Very high impact
4 – Fairly high impact
3 – Moderate impact
2 – Fairly low impact
1 – Very low impact

The second score analyzes how easy it would be to change practice to address this need. Again, we recommend a rubric of five to determine ease of revision and implementation:

5 – Very easy
4 – Fairly easy
3 – Moderately easy
2 – Fairly difficult
1 – Very difficult

An example of how this might look is found in Table 8.1.

Table 8.1

Prioritized Need	Impact	Ease	Total Score
Improve ratio of positive to corrective interactions	5	5	10
Increase opportunities to respond using engagement strategies	5	3	8
Decrease disruptions of an individual student	4	2	6
Motivate students to stay on task	3	3	8
Decrease office referrals overall	3	3	6
Improve students' perception of how they feel about the classroom	5	2	7

Looking at this example, you can now see, based on the teacher's perception of impact and ease, which prioritized needs scored highest. Rank ordering priorities gives coaches a way to provide voice, a critical Partnership Principle, to the teacher. While the nature of this conversation is more subjective in nature, this process asks the teacher to analyze the objective data presented and reconcile that information with their perceived needs and abilities. Choosing those needs that prompted the highest scores is more likely to engage staff in writing collaborative goals that they will truly strive to meet.

This process can also be repeated in the next step of the Improvement Cycle, when coaches and teachers begin to Revise policies and procedures and are determining which strategies to introduce into the teacher's classroom management plan.

Set Goals

The Prioritize step asks coaches and teachers to construct clear, measurable goals based on the data analysis in the Review step and, potentially, the rank order task in this chapter. Here, we want to describe the goal for improvement in a way that the teacher or any other third-party observer can easily make judgments about progress toward the goal. These observations may occur as part of the teacher's self-assessment, an administrative walk-through, or the nonevaluative coach's data collection process. The goal should relate to specific behaviors that can be seen or heard, with measurable outcomes.

> *"The goal should relate to specific behaviors that can be seen or heard, with measurable outcomes."*

Teachers are often asked to set SMART goals as part of their ongoing professional growth. SMART goals are generally understood to be Specific, Measurable, Attainable, Relevant, and Timely. Another variation, which often helps teachers set more meaningful goals, is the PEERS framework (Knight, 2011). With PEERS, teachers will often land on goals that have more impact, and coaches will find helping teachers reach those goals is often easier.

- **Powerful.** A goal should be worth the time the teacher will invest and should make a real difference in students' lives.
- **Easy.** A simple goal provides a destination and the simplest path to it. Complex goals, no matter how powerful, are often abandoned early on.
- **Emotionally compelling.** Goals should invoke an emotional response along with a rational process. A goal that will compel people to act is one that people understand and feel (Heath & Heath, 2010).
- **Reachable.** The best goal is the one that engenders hope—the belief that the goal can be reached through a clear, precise description and strategies to reach it.
- **Student focused.** A goal should make an unmistakable impact on students by focusing on student achievement, behavior, or attitude outcomes.

The Basic 5 Behavior Benchmarks measured through the Basic 5 Observation Tool (Reproducible 7.1) can be used to create SMART or PEERS goals or a multitude of other improvement frameworks. The Basic 5 Benchmarks can also serve as a way of measuring progress toward those goals, essential when considering the Reachable part of the PEERS framework. It can help to create incremental progress goals. It can do any and all of these things. Let's look at an example of a PEERS goal based on the collection of baseline data centered on the Basic 5.

> **Goal:** At least 90% of students will be on task (academically engaged) during teacher-guided instruction.

Perhaps baseline data indicated a rather large deficit in on-task behavior. It may be that students were highly disruptive during instruction; it could be that students were compliant with most behavioral expectations but completely nonparticipatory. The coach and teacher have discussed the data and come to this decision based on the PEERS framework.

- **Powerful.** If students are academically engaged 90% of the time, they will access more instructional content and increase student achievement.
- **Easy.** Ninety percent provides a simple, objective measurement, and the application of engagement strategies is the way to reach it.
- **Emotionally compelling.** The teacher wants students to leave their class having closed the learning gap as much as possible.
- **Reachable.** Ninety percent provides a specific description, and there are multiple strategies available through campus resources that can assist in reaching that goal.
- **Student focused.** This goal clearly focuses on the behavior of students, which will require changing teacher behavior to reach it.

Perhaps this was a PEERS goal set by the teacher as part of the Tier 1 system of support in which teachers were required to set a goal for professional growth using the PEERS framework and to articulate that goal to the administrator and within their smaller learning communities. Based on the baseline data collected as part of Tier 2 support, the coach and teacher see a deficit between current reality and the goal. The original PEERS goal may stay static, but an incremental goal is also developed, still keeping that framework in mind:

> **Incremental PEERS goal:** On-task student behavior by students during teacher-guided instruction will increase by 20%.

The power of incremental goals is that, without them, the original PEERS goal may seem unreachable. It's easy to believe a goal can be reached if you aren't fully aware of your current reality. Once current reality is introduced into the picture, the deficit may be so wide that the goal feels impossible to reach.

Weight Watchers figured out this phenomenon years ago, and many weight-loss companies have followed suit. If a person has many pounds to lose, the ultimate goal may seem unreachable. But if you set an incremental goal—for example, that a person will lose 5% of their body weight—that goal appears attainable no matter how far from the final goal a person is. And when hitting those milestones involves fanfare and accolades for that accomplishment, people are much more likely to stick with it.

Weight loss is an interesting phenomenon on its own. Often, even when people reach their ultimate goals, they gain all those pounds back. Why? Going back to the Change Puzzle at the beginning of this book, many people inadvertently remove components of support before they hit Prochaska's last step in the stages of change, Termination.

Setting a specific, measurable goal and reaching it doesn't mean a teacher won't revert to prior practice. Keep in mind that for a goal to truly be reachable and *sustained*, a teacher and coach will also have to consider what components need to be put in place and kept there even after the goal is reached.

Reproducible 8.1, Prioritize for Improvement (shown on p. 237), is designed to help the coach document the move from data analysis into prioritization. Step 1 assists with rank ordering priorities. We recommend identifying no more than 3–6 priorities at a time so as not to overwhelm the process. Step 2 assists in writing PEERS goal based on the top-ranked priority. This form is completed by the teacher and coach together and should be developed using the communication skills, including the Partnership Principles, introduced in Chapter 5.

Wrapping It Up — CHAPTER 8 SUMMARY

What to Know

- The Improvement Cycle is a formal, intentional coaching cycle.

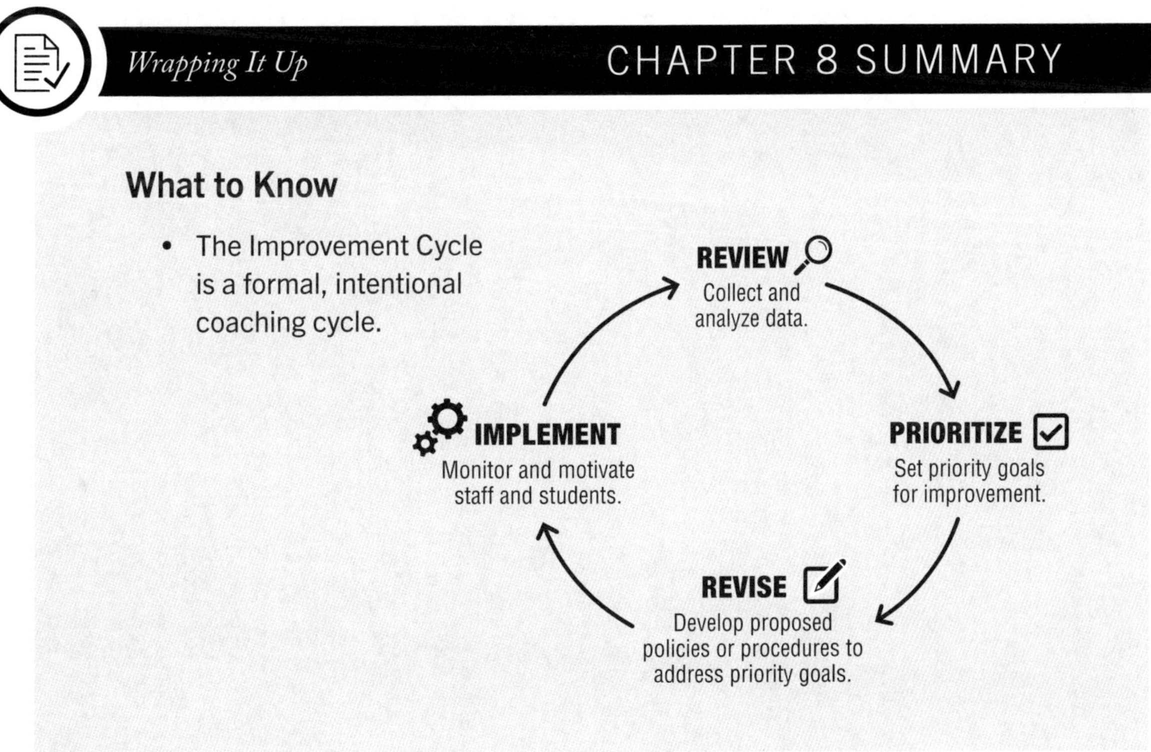

- The second step of the Improvement Cycle is Prioritize. Teacher and coaches identify priorities for improvement and collaborate on the construction of a PEERS goal:
  - **Powerful.** A goal should be worth the time the teacher will invest and should make a real difference in students' lives.
  - **Easy.** A simple goal provides a destination and the simplest path to it. Complex goals, no matter how powerful, are often abandoned early on.
  - **Emotionally compelling.** Goals should invoke an emotional response along with a rational process. A goal that will compel people to act is one that people understand and feel (Heath & Heath, 2010).
  - **Reachable.** The best goal is the one that engenders hope—the belief that the goal can be reached through a clear, precise description and strategies to reach it.
  - **Student focused.** A goal should make an unmistakable impact on students by focusing on student achievement, behavior, or attitude outcomes.

What to Do

- Use the collaborative exploration of data to help teachers set meaningful goals.
- Be able to rank order prioritized needs.
- Be able to construct goals using the PEERS language.

Reproducible 8.1 *Prioritize for Improvement*

Prioritize for Improvement

Step 1: Rank Order Priorities

List 3–6 potential needs. Attach two scores to each.

Impact: *How much impact do you believe a change in practice would have in the classroom?*

5 = Very high impact
4 = Fairly high impact
3 = Moderate impact
2 = Fairly low impact
1 = Very low impact

Ease: *How easy would it be to change practice to address this need?*

5 = Very easy
4 = Fairly easy
3 = Moderately easy
2 = Fairly difficult
1 = Very difficult

POTENTIAL NEED	IMPACT	EASE	TOTAL SCORE

Step 2: Set a PEERS Goal

Based on the need with the highest score, write a PEERS goal. This goal should be *powerful*, *easy*, *emotionally compelling*, *reachable*, and *student focused*.

____
____
____
____
____
____
____

REPRODUCIBLE 8.1

Notes

CHAPTER 9

Coaching Through a Cycle of Continuous Improvement: Revise

Nothing is ever so good that it can't stand a little revision, and nothing is ever so impossible and broken down that a try at fixing it is out of the question. —Rebecca Solnit

In the Revise step, the coach and teacher work collaboratively to revise the teacher's classroom management plan, addressing priorities that were identified in the previous step of the Improvement Cycle. During this step, if data indicate that things are going well, the plan will include maintaining and preserving aspects of the current management plan and identifying which practices can be taken from good to great. If there are one or more problems that were chosen as priorities, the coach and teacher will make decisions about whether to make minor tweaks, major adjustments, or a complete overhaul of aspects of the management plan.

STEP 3: Revise

The Revise step asks coaches and teachers to work collaboratively in developing proposed policies or procedures to address the goals set in the Prioritize step. This process involves working together to:

- **Identify strategies.** Based on the both the teacher's and coach's knowledge and experience, strategies to directly impact the teacher's goal are brainstormed here.
- **Explain strategies.** The coach's role is to break down and teach any strategy or strategies in which the teacher may not be well versed.
- **Model strategies.** In this step, coaches model both the strategy itself and the process of being actively observed.

IDENTIFY STRATEGIES

Before diving headlong into changing everything about a teacher's current classroom management plan, brainstorm some possible options with the teacher. What might the teacher try? How could the teacher address each benchmark? Can you think of an appropriate strategy or strategies for each of the five STOIC variables covered in the CHAMPS resource?

What you come up with might be called a Menu of Strategies, a sample of which is shown in Table 9.1. Make this palette of options an ongoing and collaborative effort. Strategies can be added, discarded, or revised based on their palatability to the teacher and their impact in the classroom. Remember that to be considered, a strategy must be humane and respectful of all students. Treating students with dignity is a prerequisite if they are to feel connected to school, and treating students with respect provides the foundation for lasting positive relationships as well as a far richer classroom environment.

NOTE: In some cases, the coach and teacher may opt to go back to collect more data for Review. Always ask if there are enough data to allow the teacher to understand *why* the class is or is not hitting the Basic 5 Behavior Benchmarks. If, during the collaborative coaching conversation, there is not enough evidence based on existing data to determine *why*, more data collection may be warranted. Use different types of data sources, such as perception data (anecdotal notes, surveys, interview, rating scales, etc.), observation data, and historical data, to obtain a better understanding of the conditions in the classroom. These clarifying data are critically important to avoid making changes to classroom practices based on incorrect assumptions or subjective judgments alone.

This next section provides information on specific behavior management strategies within STOIC that can improve classroom behavior. These high-leverage strategies are a sample of what can be found in *CHAMPS* and *DSC*. These strategies can be used to create or further expand the menu of options a teacher might adopt. Grade-level and content area teams can create their own menus of strategies, or a dialogue can be opened up among teachers who work with the same students.

Behavior is largely driven through environmental design. Developing orderly and productive classroom environments is the foundation of good classroom management (Evertson et al., 2003). The key word here is *productive*. Never forget that the reason we work to revise practice related to behavior is to improve the classroom for the purpose of instruction. Keep this in mind as you choose strategies in relation to the teacher's identified goal.

Both *CHAMPS* and *DSC* are organized around the STOIC acronym, often referred to as the STOIC Framework. The STOIC Framework reminds teachers of the variables over which they have some control in their classrooms. Within each variable are a bevy of strategies that teachers can implement to design an effective behavior management plan autonomous to their classroom.

The goal is to have those staff who are receiving Tier 2 support use this framework to fully engage in the Revise step of the Improvement Cycle. As a reminder, in the Revise step, the coach and teacher collaboratively *identify strategies* to help the teacher

Table 9.1 *Menu of Strategies*

Ratio of Interactions	• Greet students. • Correctly identify students by name. • Show an interest in student work and other interests. • Learn more about student cultures and personal identities. • Identify students' strengths. • Invite students to ask for assistance. • Have conversations with students. • Make a special effort to interact with students with whom you interacted regarding misbehavior. • Provide specific, positive feedback when a student engages in a new or challenging behavior.
Opportunities to Respond	• Give students option to "pass" gracefully. • Have students use "lifelines" to get help from other students. • Begin with questions most students know through review. • Let students know that each will have to answer at least *x* number of questions. • Use "No Opt Out" so students have the opportunity to correct answers when needed (Lemov, p. 28). • Create response cards. • Use write-on/wipe-off boards.
Disruptions	Teacher publicly takes data on own response to disruptions (such as blurting out) with the goal to decrease response to inappropriate behavior and increase response to positive behavior.
On-Task Behavior	• Use content enhancement routines, a set of teacher-focused interventions that are part of the Strategic Instruction Model. • Use Explicit Instruction routines from Anita Archer. • Use High-Impact Instruction techniques from Jim Knight. • Create lesson plans with specific engagement strategies tied to content delivery.
Alignment With Expectations	• Use three-step teaching process (teach > monitor > feedback) to explain expectations. • Use visual display to cue expectations. • Try using precorrections.

reach their goal, the coach *explains strategies* that may need to be broken down for staff, and the coach *models strategies* for the teacher to observe.

Once you internalize the STOIC Framework, it's difficult *not* to engage in systems analysis even outside the campus or classroom. Any time you find yourself in a space or situation that seems poorly managed or destined to result in socially inappropriate behavior, you'll mentally begin to manipulate the variables and implement strategies you believe would improve the system.

Take Louisiana, one of my favorite states. Just based on their food and hospitality alone, I enjoy any time I get to work with groups in the Pelican State. The first time I visited Louisiana, however, my life in the Midwest had not prepared me for what I saw in almost every parish I went—drive-through daiquiri huts. I know these have migrated to other states now, but at the time this was a very new thing to me. My first thought, as a systems analyst who cannot help herself, was to identify the potential problematic behavior that seemed inherent in this situation.

The group that I was with was shocked that I had never been to a drive-through daiquiri hut, but they were willing to answer my question, "Doesn't this increase the likelihood that drinking and driving will occur?" They decided the best way to answer this question was with some action research—so off to the daiquiri hut we went. We sat so I could see the drive-through window, with a daiquiri in hand, and let my curiosity take over.

It is illegal to drink and drive in Louisiana (T in STOIC). Customers were handed a large, unmarked Styrofoam cup through the drive-through. The structure (the S in STOIC) seemed to support the opposite of the law. My group pointed out that this location had attempted a structural intervention to mitigate for that possibility. There was *tape* over the hole in the lid. That did not seem to be a big deterrent, as I watched each person get their drink, drive to the exit, peel the tape off, and take a big swig. I then wondered if that was how Louisiana, as a state, made some money. Were there police observing (the O in STOIC), watching for this to happen? The group laughed and said, "Oh, no, no, if you have Louisiana plates, no one's going to pull you over leaving the daiquiri hut."

Let me get this straight. Louisiana has a law that has been taught to all people of driving age, yet the structure seems antithetical to that law being followed. That is then paired with zero observation of the behavior. What do you think happens in Louisiana? As of this writing, car insurance in Louisiana is roughly 55.9% higher than the national average. Gaps in the framework have often-unintended consequences. And hidden norms lead to huge chasms that even our most compliant students can fall into.

When someone asks me what I do for a living, I tell them I'm a systems analyst. That's exactly what we want those in leadership and our classroom teachers to be—systems analysts in relation to the STOIC Framework to recognize and remove any gaps that lead to hidden norms. It's those gaps that often lead to an inability to hit one or more of the Basic 5 Benchmarks. This chapter will help coaches remind teachers they work with about strategies found in good, research-based classroom management models that can help close any gaps in practice and create an environment better suited to student (and teacher) success.

P.S.: Remember, Louisiana, I love you!

Reminder

The CHAMPS and DSC books discuss each of these variables in more depth and include a more comprehensive selection of strategies. This is a snapshot, or summary, of our recommended model for classroom management that would already be put in place at Tier 1.

We suggest that you use STOIC as a problem-solving framework for identifying strategies that you can manipulate within each variable. Work through each variable and try to list multiple strategies for each category. When each of the five STOIC variables is systematically addressed and incorporated into the partnering teacher's classroom management plan, the pieces are in place for vastly improved student behavior.

- *Structure.* Can you modify structural elements of the setting? Can you modify the organization, orchestration, or predictability brought to behavioral or academic considerations in your classroom?
- *Teach.* Can you modify how you teach behavioral expectations to students? Do you need to re-teach expectations or bring effective instructional techniques to how you teach your behavioral expectations?
- *Observe.* Can you modify supervisory elements within your classroom, such as how you circulate, scan, or collect and present data to students?
- *Interact positively.* Can you modify how you interact with students—by building intentional positive relationships with them and increasing the amount of positive feedback you provide when they are meeting expectations or demonstrating growth?
- *Correct fluently.* Can you modify how you correct misbehavior in the moment, correcting fluently? Can you begin planning simple strategies when individual students require individualized supports?

The goal when identifying strategies is not only to get teachers to implement the practices within the STOIC framework, but to help them be "stoic" in their approach—showing patience and endurance in the face of adversity. It's a perfect description of how the most skillful classroom managers operate.

Structure for Success

The first step is to evaluate the need for structural intervention. The coach and teacher will identify any changes in physical, procedural, or scheduling arrangements that may have a positive effect on behavior.

The necessary level of structure for the classroom can be identified in several ways. The appropriate level of teacher orchestration required for various activities will depend largely on the risk factors of students in the classroom. If, for example, a significant number of immature or emotionally needy children are present, these risk factors suggest a more tightly structured classroom management plan. A less-structured plan may be more conducive to a high-functioning class that comprises primarily mature and independent students. Involve the teacher, conduct observations, and ask students for their take on classroom climate. Consider having others observe the class. More information leads to more effective behavior support plans.

Teachers can determine the appropriate level of structure for their classrooms by completing the Classroom Support Needs Assessment (Reproducible 9.1). This form is designed to help teachers assess risk factors for the student composition in a classroom, allowing them to determine the optimal level of structure. This questionnaire can be offered at any time during the year to help increase a teacher's awareness of factors that influence the level of structure and determine the best way to allow student autonomy while providing enough structure to circumvent discipline problems.

To determine areas of weakness and strength in classroom structure, the coach or another observer should evaluate the following components of structure, both physical and logistical, in an objective manner.

1. **Daily schedule.** Does the schedule maximize instructional time by minimizing wasted time and disruptive behavior? For instance, does the teacher use a balance of activities (teacher directed, independent, and group) immediately following teacher-led instruction? Has the teacher taken proactive steps to address the times of day when students are more likely to misbehave (for example, after recess, on returning from lunch, or when school lets out)?
2. **Physical space.** Does the physical arrangement of the classroom maximize positive teacher-student interaction while minimizing the possibility of disruptions? For instance, can the teacher easily navigate the classroom for active monitoring? Are desks arranged to optimize the most common types of instructional tasks? Do any areas of the room appear cluttered, or do objects obscure the teacher's view?
3. **Attention signal.** Does the teacher use an attention signal to gain the full attention of all students in the classroom? Does the signal have both auditory and visual components?
4. **Beginning and ending routines.** Does the teacher use efficient and effective procedures for beginning and ending the school day or class period? For instance, does the teacher have a routine opening activity for the students each day? Are procedures in place for dealing with students who do not have the required materials or who have been absent? Does the teacher have a specific wrap-up routine for the end of the day or class period?
5. **Classroom rules.** Has the teacher posted, in an easily visible area of the room, three to six positively stated rules that describe specific, observable behaviors students are expected to exhibit? Does the teacher have specific corrective consequences in place if classroom rules are violated?
6. **Student work.** Has the teacher designed easy-to-grasp procedures for assigning classwork and homework? Is a similar procedure in place for turning in completed work? Is there a way students can get questions answered during independent work periods?

It is unlikely that one classroom observation will provide complete insight into all these structural components. If possible, complete at least three observations. It may

Reproducible 9.1 *Classroom Support Needs Assessment (p. 1 of 3)*

Corresponds to *CHAMPS* Repro 1.3, *DSC* Repro 1.2

Classroom Support Needs Assessment (p. 1 of 3)

Part 1. Teacher Needs

Read each question and assign yourself a score from 0–20, with 0 representing the answer on the left of the scale and 20 the answer on the right.

Score

1. What is your tolerance for **background noise**?

I love to have conversations in crowded, noisy restaurants. — Holiday music in department stores drives me crazy after about 30 minutes.

0 1 2 3 4 5 6 7 8 9 10 11 12 13 14 15 16 17 18 19 20 _____

2. What is your tolerance for **individual voices** (volume, pitch, whining, mumbling, etc.)?

No style of voice seems to bother me—even when there are several at once. — Some voices are like fingernails on a chalkboard.

0 1 2 3 4 5 6 7 8 9 10 11 12 13 14 15 16 17 18 19 20 _____

3. What is your tolerance for **interruption**?

I would be fine working as a receptionist—managing phones, people, and equipment. — When the phone rings twice during dinner, I want to scream.

0 1 2 3 4 5 6 7 8 9 10 11 12 13 14 15 16 17 18 19 20 _____

4. What is your tolerance for **background movement**?

I thrive on the hustle and bustle of downtown in a large city. — I prefer to relax by the side of a quiet lake.

0 1 2 3 4 5 6 7 8 9 10 11 12 13 14 15 16 17 18 19 20 _____

5. What is your ability to **multitask** without becoming flustered?

I love to do 3 things at once. — I do not like to talk to anyone while I am collating papers.

0 1 2 3 4 5 6 7 8 9 10 11 12 13 14 15 16 17 18 19 20 _____

Teacher Needs Total Score _____

0–33 LOW SUPPORT NEEDS	34–66 MEDIUM SUPPORT NEEDS	67–100 HIGH SUPPORT NEEDS
You don't require much structure and will probably be content with a Low, Medium, or High Support classroom management plan.	For you to stay calm and positive, your classroom management plan should involve Medium or High Support.	For you to stay calm and positive, your classroom management plan should involve High Support.

 REPRODUCIBLE 9.1

Reproducible 9.1 (cont.) *Classroom Support Needs Assessment (p. 2 of 3)*

Classroom Support Needs Assessment (p. 2 of 3)

Part 2. Student Risk Factors

For each question, circle the number under the statement that best answers the question. If you are unsure about or do not know the answer to a question, circle the middle choice. Add all the numbers circled and enter the total.

Questions 1–6 relate to the population of the entire school.

1. How would you describe the overall **behavior of students** in your school? Score

Generally quite irresponsible. I frequently have to nag and/or assign consequences.	Most students behave responsibly, but about 10% put me in a position where I have to nag and/or assign consequences.	Generally responsible. I rarely find it necessary to nag and/or assign consequences.
10	5	0

____

2. What percentage of students in your school **qualify for free or reduced lunch**?*

60% or more	10% to 60%	Less than 10%
10	5	0

____

3. What percentage of students typically **move in and/or out of the school** during the course of the year?

50% or more	10% to 50%	Less than 10%
10	5	0

____

4. How would you describe the overall **attitude of students** toward school?

A large percentage hate school and ridicule the students who are motivated.	It's a mix, but most students feel OK about school.	The vast majority of students like school and are highly motivated.
10	5	0

____

5. How would you describe the overall nature of the **interactions between students and adults** in your school?

There are frequent confrontations that include sarcasm and disrespect.	There is a mix, but most interactions are respectful and positive.	The vast majority of interactions are respectful and positive.
10	5	0

____

6. How would you describe the **level of interest and support provided by parents** of students in your school?

Many parents are openly antagonistic, and many show no interest in school.	Most parents are at least somewhat supportive of school.	The majority of parents are interested, involved, and supportive of what goes on in school.
10	5	0

____

*While poverty levels tell you nothing about an individual student, the percentage of students from poverty has an influence on your initial decision about level of support. Notice that this is weighted the same at Item 8, the number of students in the class.

 REPRODUCIBLE 9.1

Reproducible 9.1 (cont.) *Classroom Support Needs Assessment (p. 3 of 3)*

Classroom Support Needs Assessment (p. 3 of 3)

Questions 7–10 relate to students in your class this year. Use your most difficult class, or if you are doing this before the school year begins, simply give your best guess.

7. What **grade level** do you teach? Score

K or 1	6, 7, or 8	Other	Score
10	**5**	**0**	___

8. **How many students** do you have in your class?

30 or more	23 to 30	22 or fewer	Score
10	**5**	**0**	___

9. How many students in your class have been identified as **eligible to receive special education services under the categories of Emotional Disturbance or Autism**? *Note:* This label varies from state to state (e.g., ED, EBD, BD, etc.).

Two or more	One	Zero	Score
10	**5**	**0**	___

10. Not including students eligible to receive special education services, how many students in your class have a reputation for **chronic discipline problems**?

Three or more	One or two	Zero	Score
10	**5**	**0**	___

Student Risk Factors Total Score ☐

Interpretation: Use the scale below to interpret student risk factors and determine the most appropriate level of support for your classroom.

0–33 LOW SUPPORT NEEDS	**34–66** MEDIUM SUPPORT NEEDS	**67–100** HIGH SUPPORT NEEDS
Your students can probably be successful with a classroom management plan that involves Low, Medium, or High Support.	For your students to be successful, your classroom management plan should involve Medium or High Support.	For your students to be successful, your classroom management plan should involve High Support.

 REPRODUCIBLE 9.1

help to meet with the teacher and ask about any components that could not be directly observed. In addition, you may want to complete a Classroom Ecology Checklist (Reproducible 7.3 shown on p. 215–216) after observing the class and reconvene with the teacher later to discuss what you observed. If the teacher has also completed a Classroom Ecology Checklist, the two can be compared and any discrepancies discussed.

Students, of course, can provide information about ways in which classroom structure can be increased or decreased. For instance, the coach or teacher might ask students about the structural components listed—daily schedules, the attention signal, beginning and ending routines, classroom rules, and student work routines. Ask the whole class or a representative group of about six students (some of whom are academically above average and some who struggle or sometimes misbehave) what they know about the classroom structure. If disruptions are frequent and the students are unclear about the structure or rules of the classroom, the level of structure needs to be increased and expectations clarified. Anything students find to be ambiguous or unclear with regard to classroom structure is itself a clear target for improvement.

If the data indicate that structure could be improved, the coach and teacher should work together to start building a menu of strategies. Review what's been collected by direct observation, from the teacher, and in talking with students. Pick a few areas to target. The strategies developed should be specific to the needs of the students in the classroom; in other words, choose what will work for *that* teacher and *those* students. Always individualize strategies as a classroom's needs dictate to allow autonomous decision-making on the part of the teacher.

Following are suggestions for improving structure in several areas. Use them as a point of entry for further discussion, individualization, and experimentation.

Daily schedule. If, after you gather information from multiple sources, data show the daily class schedule is not maximizing instructional time or responsible student behavior, the teacher should write down the schedule of daily subjects. For each subject, develop a list of activities. Note the amount of time spent on each activity. Indicate whether the learning activity is teacher-directed instruction (lecture, discussion, question-and-answer session), independent work (seatwork, lab activities), or a cooperative group task. When finished, a measure of the balance of activities within each subject might look something like this:

Daily schedule for math (9:15–10:15 A.M.)

5 minutes	Teacher-directed review of previously taught concepts
10 minutes	Teacher-directed instruction of new concepts
10 minutes	Teacher-directed guided practice
25 minutes	Independent work/cooperative tasks
10 minutes	Teacher-directed corrections/guided practice to identify student errors or misunderstandings

Looking at the daily schedule created, estimate the percentage of class time students spend in various types of tasks:

- 40% teacher-directed instruction
- 35% independent work
- 25% cooperative groups

Using this information, try any of the following:

1. Construct a schedule that balances the types of activities (teacher-directed instruction, independent work, cooperative groups) within and across subjects during the day.
2. Avoid focusing on any one type of activity for too long. One indication that a class segment is running too long is lack of student engagement. When teacher-directed instruction runs too long, students tend to become fidgety and inattentive. When independent work goes too long, students can become bored and stop working, leading to a rise in disruptive behavior.
3. Follow teacher-directed instruction with independent work and cooperative or peer group tasks. Teacher-led instruction is usually the best way to begin class. Starting class with long periods of independent work should be avoided. (There are exceptions—for example, many teachers ask students to work on brief quizzes or challenge problems upon entering the classroom while attendance is taken.)
4. Preemptively address those times of day and specific tasks during which students exhibit the most misbehavior (for instance, immediately following recess, upon entry into the classroom, and during the last 5 minutes of class or the last hour of the day). For problematic times or activities, the teacher may need to precorrect and re-teach expectations, emphasizing how to meet them (see the suggestions under "Teach Expectations" later in this chapter).

A well-designed schedule provides students with a varied, balanced range of activities within subjects. The level of structure in the schedule can flex with the students' needs. As a general principle, teachers should start with a higher level of structure and then relax it as the year progresses and students demonstrate an ability to handle increased autonomy. Lowering the level of structure in a classroom always comes off as a compliment; raising it may be viewed by students as punitive.

Work with the teacher to identify when to shift gears and move on to a new type of task. When the teacher notices students becoming restless during independent work, they can dive into teacher-directed guided practice. When students become inattentive during teacher-led instruction, the teacher might switch to cooperative groups.

Physical layout of the classroom. Arranging the physical space in a classroom to promote positive teacher-student interactions can yield surprising benefits by reducing the possibility of disruption in the first place. Not all teachers have control over the physical layout of the space in which they teach. Team up with the teacher to change what can be changed and make the best of what cannot be changed. Try the following:

- Arrange student desks to optimize the most common types of instruction and level of structure students in the classroom require to remain successfully engaged. For instance, students in need of high structure may be most successful if their desks are separated by enough space to allow them to interact but discourage off-task conversation.
- Arrange the layout to ensure that the teacher has access to all parts of the classroom.
- Minimize disruptions caused by high-traffic areas in the classroom. Think about what tasks students might need to perform away from their desks (getting supplies, sharpening pencils, turning in work, using learning centers, and so forth) and then arrange the room so that students who are moving around will be less likely to distract students who are working at their seats. When it is not possible to organize student desks to avoid high-traffic areas, devise a plan to teach students directly how to move in the areas without distracting other students.
- If necessary and appropriate, set aside an unobtrusive timeout space in the classroom. Timeout is most effective for students in grades K–3. Avoid locating the timeout space where the detained student is on display to other students.

Attention signal. Getting and holding the undivided attention of students in a classroom is an important management skill. All teachers should use some form of attention signal to transition smoothly from animated, noisy activities to focused attention. A signal that includes both visual and auditory components is especially effective. If the teacher has not already settled on a classwide attention signal and taught it to students, develop a plan for teaching students a signal of the teacher's choice and indicate how they should respond when it occurs.

Beginning and ending routines. If students have difficulty focusing at the beginning of the day or end of a class period, devising ways to be more efficient may help. Discuss what routines and procedures might be altered or tweaked:

1. *Entering the classroom.* To make students feel welcome and immediately take their seats and start on a productive task, the teacher might greet each student individually and have ready a short (3- to 5-minute), instructionally relevant activity or quiz that students can work on at their desks. Once students are seated and attendance is taken, the teacher can provide feedback and responses to the entry task.
2. *Addressing tardiness.* A teacher might keep handy a tardy notebook in which students are required to write their names before quietly taking their seats. This procedure prevents a tardy student from diverting attention or interrupting a lesson. Schoolwide policies for excused and unexcused tardies can be invoked by the teacher based on the notebook.

3. *Responding to students who do not have materials or are not prepared.* Be sure that the teacher's expectations for required materials have been communicated clearly. Then help the teacher develop procedures that ensure that students who do not have the required materials can get them in a way that does not disrupt instruction. Suggest a mild consequence (for example, students "owe" the teacher 30 seconds after class or off recess) that will reduce the likelihood of students forgetting materials in the future. Explore ways to reduce the amount of time and energy the teacher spends dealing with the problem (for example, have students fill out a hall pass to go to their lockers for materials). Above all, have the teacher impress upon the students what is expected of them whenever they come to class unprepared.
4. *System for students returning after an absence.* Decide how students who have been absent can determine what assignments they missed and obtain handouts and returned work in a way that does not tie up a large amount of the teacher's time and energy. The teacher might set up two baskets in the classroom—one labeled "Absent—What You Missed" and one labeled "Absent—Assignments to Hand In." Any assigned materials that were missed can be placed in a dated folder and put in the first basket. Any returned or graded papers can be placed in the second basket, in a folder with the student's name on it.
5. *Wrap-up/cleanup.* Teachers should allow enough time at the conclusion of an activity, period, or school day to ensure that things end on a relaxed note, setting aside a few minutes at the end of the day to make sure the classroom is clean and to make last-minute announcements. After the students have cleaned up and organized their materials, the teacher can provide the class with feedback about things they are doing well and things they can work toward improving. If time for these activities is not built into the teacher's current classroom management plan, consider working with the teacher to amend it.
6. *Dismissal.* The teacher should teach and practice the expectation that students will not leave the classroom until they are dismissed by the teacher. To explain this dismissal expectation to students, the teacher can say that the bell is the signal for the teacher, and students will be excused when they are quiet and all wrap-up tasks have been completed.

Classroom rules. Posted classroom rules communicate to all students the specific behaviors expected by the teacher. With the teacher, give some thought to misbehaviors most likely to occur considering students' grade level and development. Develop three to six positively stated rules that are specific and refer to observable behaviors. For instance, "Keep hands, feet, and objects to yourself" is positively stated, specific, and observable, whereas "Do your best" is not specific or observable. After rules are developed, post them in a prominent place that is visible from all parts of the classroom.

In addition, help the teacher identify consequences for each rule infraction, making sure the corrections are mild enough that the teacher will not find it difficult to follow through with them consistently. Finally, develop a plan to teach the students the rules and how they can demonstrate adherence.

Student work. When assignments are repeatedly not completed or turned in, collaboratively review and revise procedures for assigning, monitoring, and collecting student work. Teachers might work with the coach to bolster their procedures in the following areas:

1. *Assigning classwork and homework.* Use a permanent place in the classroom or on an assignment sheet where students can look to determine what needs to be completed. Create a plan for students to keep their own records of assigned homework, such as having them copy the assignment to a sheet of notebook paper to be put in a specific place in their folders.
2. *Managing independent work periods.* If students are having difficulty remaining on task during independent work times, check in with the teacher to make sure that the work is not too difficult for the students to complete independently. Maximize on-task behavior by keeping the length of independent time within the practical limits of the students' attention spans. Schedule independent work following teacher-directed instruction and not during times of the day when students find it difficult to focus.
3. *Determining how students can get questions answered during independent work periods.* If independent work time has not been structured in such a way that students can get questions answered when necessary, higher rates of apparent off-task behavior may result. A teacher can ask students to indicate they would like help in ways other than raising a hand (which apart from being tiring, precludes the use of that hand for schoolwork): by setting a book upright, placing a flag or marker on the corner of their desk, or writing their name on the board with the question.
4. *Collecting completed work.* There are a number of good methods for collecting classwork and homework. Recommend that work be collected personally from each student whenever possible. This allows the teacher to provide immediate feedback to individual students about their work and builds in an extra layer of accountability. Less time-intensive ideas include collecting work by rows or tables, in designated baskets, or through student helpers. Note, however, that none of these methods allow for instant, personalized feedback.

For classrooms in which students are struggling to turn in assigned work, discuss whether it would be helpful for the teacher to show the class the percentage of schoolwork being turned in. One way would be to display a graph showing the overall percentage of homework turned in by students in the classroom over a period of days. To calculate the percentage of assignments turned in on a particular day, divide the number of completed work assignments by the number of students present that day. The teacher can then discuss the importance of being responsible and how completing work fits in with that. Additionally, the teacher can set a goal for work completion, promising a class reward once the goal has been met. Sometimes just the challenge of increasing the percentage of work turned in is motivation enough for students.

For high school educators, one structural consideration is the appropriateness of their current grading practices. With the teacher, evaluate the quality of the current grading system and discuss whether refreshing the grading system might be helpful in that classroom.

Teach Expectations

To function successfully within the structure the teacher has established, students must be taught the teacher's expectations. This can be as simple as a goal discussion or as involved as daily modeling and rehearsal of responsible behavior. An effective classroom management plan must address when, where, and how these positive expectations will be taught to the students. As with structure, there are three avenues by which to identify and determine the need for support within this variable.

The teacher can gauge whether the behavioral expectations of the classroom have been sufficiently communicated by listing all the major types of classroom activities and transitions in which students engage on a regular basis—settling in, attendance routine, teacher-directed instruction, independent work, test taking, cleaning up after activities, handing in work, putting materials away, and leaving the classroom. Review the list and determine what activities or transitions seem to coincide with increases in problem behavior.

If, during independent work times, many students are socializing with peers, using the restroom without permission, and not completing their assigned work, it is likely that classroom expectations for the activities and transitions involved are not clear.

A second set of eyes—the coach's or a peer's—can be helpful during activities or transitions in which student behavior is most challenging. An observer can mark a structured observation instrument or objectively record the verbal and nonverbal behaviors of the teacher and students as an anecdotal record of classroom events. The observation should begin a few minutes prior to the difficult transition or activity being targeted and continue for at least a few minutes afterward. If using a structured observation instrument, the observer should take some notes during or immediately afterward for illustrative purposes. Anecdotal notes (for instance, "See 6 students walking around the room, 4 students talking with one another, 2 students at the teacher's desk waiting for help") can provide the teacher with information about the amount and types of problem behavior occurring. Use the information with the teacher to draft lesson plans for teaching the correct behavioral expectations to the students.

Re-teaching expectations. Develop questions to ask students about behavioral expectations in the classroom. The CHAMPS acronym can be a useful guide to this (Table 9.2). Ask the whole class or a representative group of about six students about their knowledge of the behavioral expectations across a few activities. Pick a time to talk to the students and explain why you are asking them questions. If the students provide different answers or don't have a response, this could indicate that the activity in question should be considered a point of intervention.

Table 9.2 *CHAMPS Expectations*

C	Conversation	May students engage in conversation during this activity or transition? If yes, about what? With whom? How many students can be involved? How long can the conversation last?
H	Help	How can students get questions answered or the teacher's attention? If students have to wait for help, what should they do while they wait?
A	Activity	What is the expected end product of this activity? What should be different after this transition? How long will the activity or transition last?
M	Movement	Can students leave their seats and move about during this activity or transition? If so, what are acceptable reasons?
P	Participation	What should active participation in this activity or transition look and sound like? What behaviors show that the students are participating fully and responsibly? What behaviors show they are not participating?
S	Success (or Special)	Are there any rules unique to this activity or transition that do not fit into any of the other CHAMP categories?

Use these suggestions as a starting point, allowing them to become individualized through collaborative discussions with the teacher.

To increase the clarity of behavioral expectations in the classroom, first list all the major activities and transitions that occur on a daily or regular basis in the classroom, creating a separate entry for every activity for which the teacher has a different behavioral expectation. Help the teacher identify whether any important activities or transitions have been omitted from the list.

Once major classroom activities and transitions have been identified, use the CHAMPS acronym as a guide to important issues. Each activity and transition with different behavioral expectations should have a written plan that defines in detail the behavioral expectations for students, answering potential questions such as those in Table 9.2.

After spelling out behavioral expectations for each activity and transition, the coach and teacher can prepare lessons for teaching these expectations to the students. Each lesson should be taught immediately before the activity or transition is to occur. The goal is for the teacher to explain expectations clearly to the students and to verify that the students understand them. Work together to find ways of getting the message across. Discuss the following:

- Will the CHAMPS acronym be presented to the students?
- Will visual displays be used within the lesson (wall projections, flip charts)?

- Will modeling or role-playing be used, and will students have an opportunity to practice the expectations?
- Will the lesson be taught more than one time? If so, how often?
- Will you teach the first lesson as a model for the teacher?
- How will the teacher reinforce students for meeting the behavioral expectations?

Before teaching students behavioral expectations, the teacher should develop, post, and teach three to six positively stated rules at the beginning of the school year, reviewing them as needed throughout the term. Having classroom rules in place makes it easier for a teacher to communicate situational behavioral expectations, as they can flow naturally from the established classroom rules. Discuss how expectations can be presented and reinforced by referencing the classroom rules.

Teaching behavioral expectations is as important as teaching academic subjects. Depending on the amount of structure needed to successfully support students in the classroom, the teacher may find it helpful to create a lesson plan that includes a step-by-step guide for how behavioral expectations will be taught. Any lesson plan template the teacher is comfortable with will work. The plan can include explicit teaching of the expected behavior, how to model expected behavior—positive and negative, how to provide multiple opportunities for students to practice, and how the teacher will monitor and provide feedback to students, or positive reinforcement procedures—incentives or contingent attention when students display behavioral expectations.

Observe Student Behavior

Observe in STOIC has two levels of connotation, short term and long term. In the short term, Observe indicates the need for teachers to continuously circulate and scan the classroom. This hearkens back to the hard-to-define (but easy to grasp) quality of Withitness first enunciated by Jacob Kounin. Teachers who possess Withitness systematically scan the classroom looking toward the behaviors of individual students or groups of students, responding to any sign of inappropriate behavior immediately. The teacher also circulates to check student work, providing immediate feedback to students and determining which students need more guided practice with academic material. This type of systematic scanning and monitoring of student behavior can be observed by an outside observer or self-monitored by the teacher and easily increased through coaching when necessary.

In the long term, Observe involves collecting objective data to monitor student behavior and provide students with feedback. These data should be collected, perhaps using tools introduced in *CHAMPS*, for ongoing reflection even after exiting Tier 2 support. Every teacher, regardless of tier, should have a procedure to collect and use data as part of an ongoing process of refining their classroom management plan.

Finding ways to increase a teacher's systematic observation of student behavior can create big change with comparatively little effort. For instance, if a class shows a high number of disruptions and low on-task behavior, developing a plan to increase circulating and scanning requires little extra preparation on the classroom teacher's part; the teacher need only make a conscious attempt to move around more and notice everyone in the room. A collaboratively designed plan could specify how often the teacher will circumnavigate the room during independent work and cooperative groups. It might also include utilizing *proximity* when the teacher notices that a student is having difficulty staying on task. In some cases, it might be helpful to model the use of systematic monitoring for the teacher.

Interact Positively

All teachers should provide noncontingent attention by greeting and showing an interest in students. Work with the partnering teacher to provide frequent positive feedback on behavioral and academic effort. When students are meeting the teacher's expectations, following procedures, and engaging appropriately in academic tasks, age-appropriate positive feedback should be provided. Positive feedback should be specific, contingent, and nonembarrassing. It can be verbal, written, or, to a limited extent, nonverbal. In particular, the teacher should look for opportunities to praise students for exhibiting the expectations that have been taught.

When observing the class, pay attention to whether students are getting at least three times more attention when exhibiting expected behaviors than when violating expectations and share the data, formal and anecdotal, with the teacher.

Increasing noncontingent attention. All students like to feel noticed and that their teacher regards them positively. One simple strategy to improve teacher-student interactions is for the teacher to commit to saying hello to all students as they enter the classroom. The teacher can show an interest in students' progress during independent work periods, invite students to ask for assistance, and strike up conversations with one or more students. A special effort should be made to greet or converse with a student with whom the teacher recently had to interact due to misbehavior, showing that what happened is in the past.

> *"All students like to feel noticed and that their teacher regards them positively."*

When the teacher makes an effort to engage with every student individually, the students learn and internalize that they are valued, reducing the likelihood that they will misbehave in that classroom. While data can certainly be collected on noncontingent interactions, teachers also can devise their own self-monitoring plan to track whether they greet their students as they enter the classroom and to identify students, if any, with whom they are less likely to have a conversation.

When thinking about increasing noncontingent positive attention in the classroom, discuss what the teacher might do when a student does not respond positively to a greeting. Consider ignoring inappropriate comments, following up with the student after class, or trying more subtlety (whispering a greeting rather than making a production of it to avoid potential embarrassment). Having a plan and not being caught off guard are proactive ways to avoid conflict. Some students may seem harder to reach than others. Occasional gruff or negative responses go with the territory. Encourage teachers to avoid taking dismissive student behavior personally; the student may be having a bad day, may treat most adults the same way, or may not have had many opportunities to interact with an adult in this manner.

Many students simply need to be presented with further opportunities to learn that their teacher values them and is genuinely interested in them. Building relationships takes time. When a teacher is gently persistent, allowing each STOIC variable a chance to come into play, even many hard-shelled students will in time come to see their teacher as *stoic* in the way we've appropriated the word—unflappable, admired for showing patience and endurance in the face of adversity. Ideally, your teacher's approach may show "tough" students a different way of being in the world—calm instead of confrontational, approachable rather than antagonistic, showing strength through sincerity rather than cynicism.

One note of caution: Noncontingent positive attention has a place and time in the classroom. Typically, noncontingent attention will occur on entry into the classroom, outside of the classroom, or at the end of class. Brief interjections of noncontingent attention from the teacher can be inserted into instructional time ("Louis, great answer. By the way, I noticed you were absent the last 2 days. We missed you."). Teachers should avoid long discussions on tangential topics during teacher-led instruction or when monitoring student independent work. If this becomes a habit, the students may go out of their way to lead the teacher off topic. While it is important to have positive relationships with students, the main purpose of class time is learning! Noncontingent attention should not encroach dramatically upon or disrupt the flow of instruction and learning.

Improving the ratio of positive to corrective interactions. When corrective interactions occur more frequently than positive interactions, there are two points of strategic planning: 1) increase the amount of praise or positive feedback issued to students in the classroom, and 2) decrease the number of reprimands or corrective feedback issued to students in the classroom. These can be done in tandem.

Increasing use of praise. Increasing the amount of praise or positive feedback in the classroom seems like a simple strategy, but it takes some planning and effort. It is always easier to catch students misbehaving than it is to catch them behaving as expected. Following are several suggestions for increasing the use of positive feedback in the classroom:

1. *Catching good behavior.* Have the teacher identify a specific problem behavior that they would like to see less of in the classroom (for example, students calling out answers). Once the problem behavior is identified, define the opposite of this behavior (students should raise their hand to be called on before answering). Next, devise a plan in which the teacher will first teach the expected behavior (raising a hand to be called on), ignore the problem behavior (calling out answers), and "catch" and provide specific positive feedback to students meeting expectations ("Josh, thank you for raising your hand").

2. *Reminder to praise.* Develop a plan for reminding the teacher to use more praise in the classroom. For instance, if the teacher uses a smart board or other technology on a regular basis, the teacher may write "Look up and praise a student" on a colorful paper and stick this reminder to the corner of her device. Then, each time the teacher looks down at her device, she is reminded to look up and provide praise to any student who is meeting expectations. These types of reminders can be placed anywhere they will catch the teacher's eye (for example, next to the clock, on the corner of the desk, on the side of the whiteboard).
3. *Double up on praise.* Every time the teacher provides praise to one student, the teacher will find another student who is also behaving appropriately and provide praise to that student as well (for example, "Keith raised his hand. Juan raised his hand. Nice job not blurting out the answer, you two.").
4. *Increase the number of opportunities to respond provided to students.* Along with each opportunity a teacher provides to the class or a student to answer an academic question comes an opportunity to praise. For instance, if a student provides the correct answer, the teacher can praise the student for answering correctly. If the student does not answer correctly but thought out the problem and made a good attempt, the teacher can praise that student's effort, creating a win-win situation out of a potentially corrective interaction.
5. *Use varied forms of positive reinforcement.* With the teacher, list a variety of forms of positive reinforcement. Have the teacher review the list and identify several to use each day. Teachers can effectively acknowledge appropriate student behavior through specific praise, gestures (thumbs up, clapping, a nod of the head), tangibles (gold stickers), points toward a reward, contacting a parent or caregiver to report student success, and many other creative means of motivation. Time spent thinking of ways to interact positively with students is often time saved from less effective (and less enjoyable) badgering, chiding, and correcting.
6. *Prominently display student work in the classroom.* Publicly posting examples of student work demonstrates to students that the teacher is proud of what they have done and increases their sense of belonging.

Tips for planning positive interactions. Of course, these are only a few suggestions for increasing praise in the classroom. Brainstorm with the teacher and devise a plan tailored to the needs of the classroom. Consider the following tips:

- *Feedback should be accurate and related to a behavior or set of behaviors that did in fact occur.* When a student receives positive feedback for something they did not actually do, it is meaningless.
- *Feedback should be specific and descriptive.* For example, "Great job—you raised your hand" rather than "Great job." Specific descriptive feedback lets students know which aspects of their behavior are worth commenting on. Descriptive feedback also teaches all students in the classroom what is expected. If one

student receives praise for raising their hand, others will know that this behavior is expected and appreciated by the teacher.

- *Feedback should avoid simple, repetitive phrases.* Frequently saying things like "Good job," "Nice work," or "Yes" does not provide specific feedback. When overused, pat phrases become background noise—and students cease to hear them.
- *Feedback should not make judgments or draw conclusions.* Such statements as "You are so smart" and "You are such a well-behaved student" do not provide specific feedback—and can imply that, had the student answered the problem incorrectly or behaved differently, they would not be smart or likable.
- *Feedback should not focus attention on the teacher rather than the student.* For instance, starting praise with "I like the way you . . ." may be specific, but it can inadvertently be taken by students to mean that they should behave to "please" the teacher or that they are liked by the teacher only when they do something the teacher likes.
- *Feedback should be contingent, indicating that the behavior for which feedback is provided has some level of importance.* While noncontingent positive attention has an important role in classroom management, feedback should be based on behaviors that are observable and repeatable. Feedback is contingent when it occurs while someone is learning a new skill or behavior, when it refers to a behavior that requires effort, and when it concerns a behavior of which the student is proud. Providing positive feedback about overly simple behavior can be meaningless and in some instances insulting.
- *Feedback should be age appropriate.* The vocabulary and type of feedback used to describe behavior should be developmentally appropriate and pertain to relatively advanced behavior skills for the students' age and abilities. Keep in mind that older students may be embarrassed by overt teacher attention. For these students, use discreet gestures or a quiet voice, be brief and somewhat businesslike, and avoid making a public display of praise or pausing and making eye contact after offering it.
- *Feedback should be applied more frequently in certain situations.* There are certain times when focusing on specific, positive feedback is more critical. Any time a behavior is new to a class or student, there should be an intentional increase in the amount of positive feedback in relation to that behavior, for instance, when a kindergarten class is learning to keep hands, feet, and objects to self. Another time is when a behavior isn't necessarily new but is a challenge to a class or student. For instance, a seventh-grade student who struggles bringing needed materials to class may need specific, positive feedback when he does. And another time is when the behavior is a source of pride. A senior in high school who consistently meets deadlines for assignments may be proud of that, and specific, positive feedback can add to her feeling of accomplishment.

"Feedback should avoid simple, repetitive phrases. When overused, pat phrases become background noise—and students cease to hear them."

Tips for decreasing the frequency of corrections. Consider the following suggestions for decreasing the frequency of corrections:

- *Planned ignoring.*

  One way to decrease corrective interactions between the students and teacher is to devise a plan that will allow the teacher to ignore minor misbehaviors—this is called planned ignoring. While some student behaviors should never be ignored, particularly dangerous or aggressive actions, others can safely be ignored. It is important first to determine whether the problem behavior is attention seeking in nature—in other words, whether the student engages in the behavior to gain teacher or peer attention despite the fact that they know the behavior is unacceptable. Chronic calling out, tattling, and asking too many questions are examples of likely attention-seeking behavior. When the behavior is identified, the teacher can try planned ignoring as a strategy for changing student behavior. In conjunction with ignoring the attention-seeking misbehavior, the teacher can provide positive feedback and attention to students who are engaged in appropriate behavior. If a targeted student does engage in appropriate behavior, the teacher should attempt to "catch" the student in the act and acknowledge the good behavior.

- *Teach expectations.*

  A sure way to decrease the number of reprimands or corrections is to make certain that students know the teacher's expectations. Make this approach more targeted by working with the teacher to identify when disruptions are most likely to occur and then devise a plan to teach the behavioral expectations for that activity. Don't assume that the students know how to behave. Help the teacher get in the habit of identifying problem behaviors, directly teaching the behavioral expectations in that area, and providing positive feedback when those expected behaviors occur.

- *Precorrection.*

  After students have learned behavioral expectations, some will still benefit from additional support and structure. *Precorrections* are quick reminders of how students should act given directly prior to an opportunity for their use. This technique is especially helpful when a teacher anticipates that students will have difficulty performing skills correctly. Precorrections can be used with the whole class or with individual students who need more support to be successful. A precorrection for calling out might sound like this: "Be sure to raise your hand and wait for me to call on you if you have an answer. What is 8 + 7?"

If the class seems to need even more structure and positive feedback, explore some of the group reinforcement systems described in Chapter 7 of *CHAMPS* (3rd ed.; Sprick, J., 2021).

Correct Fluently

Depending on the teacher's familiarity and experience, the coach may wish to model fluent correction. Explain or model what it means to correct misbehavior calmly, consistently, briefly, and immediately. Discuss how the teacher plans to keep corrections respectful even when confronted with blatant or apparently intentional misbehavior. Talk through scenarios of each type of misbehavior the teacher faces. The goal is to see the teacher working on automatic pilot when correcting any chronic misbehavior, so the focus stays on instruction and on building positive relationships with all students.

Misbehavior happens. It's a fact in even the most skillfully managed classrooms. One way to increase a teacher's readiness to deal with problem behavior is to develop a list of all the misbehaviors occurring in the classroom, beginning with those that are of greatest concern. Be sure that the behaviors are specific and observable ("talking to peers without permission" is specific and observable; "disrespectful" is not). Next, examine the possible reasons for the behavior. Reasons for chronic misbehavior generally fall into four general categories:

- *Awareness*-type misbehaviors
- *Ability*-type misbehaviors
- *Attention-seeking* misbehaviors
- *Purposeful* and *habitual* misbehaviors

Jot down whether the misbehavior seems to occur because students are not aware that they are exhibiting the behavior, because students are not able (physiologically or psychologically) to perform the behavior, because the students are seeking attention from the teacher or peers, or because the behavior is habitual or serves some other purpose for the students. After one or more hypotheses have been generated about why the behavior is occurring, identify a positive response to each misbehavior. For attention-seeking behavior, consider planned ignoring. For problems with ability or awareness, consider a verbal reminder or redirection. Purposeful or habitual problems may require a consequence. Be aware, however, that many behaviors that appear purposeful (at least on the surface) may actually be occurring because the students are unaware they are exhibiting them or don't know how to exhibit the desired behavior. This discussion may be refreshed if a teacher seems to be jumping too readily to consequences when one of the other responses discussed here might yield better outcomes.

The coach can help in the process of determining the types of misbehavior as well as in developing an appropriate response to the misbehavior. In an effective classroom management plan, the focus is on teaching expectations, positively reinforcing expected behavior, and structuring the environment for success. Corrective feedback is necessary, but it's the weakest of the tools in any teacher's kit and as such should be used sparingly.

The strategies outlined here are simply a starting point. One of the key things you as a coach should remember when engaging in dialogue with the teacher about strategies is to not allow your teaching style to overtly influence the direction the conversation takes.

It is sometimes difficult to remember that we, as coaches, are not at the helm of this educator's classroom, and for very good reason. It is ultimately their domain. A coach must always respect that and allow for professional autonomy when asking teachers to put new practices into place.

EXPLAIN STRATEGIES

Planning to implement new practices doesn't simply mean identifying a strategy to help reach the goal. It also involves planning for how a teacher will learn the strategy and wield it effectively. First, a coach must fully understand that of which they speak. If coaches do not fully understand the strategies they are describing, they run the risk of doing a great job of teaching someone *the wrong information!* In our experience, a coach who knows a small number of strategies very well is better prepared than the coach who knows a large number of strategies superficially. Thus, coaches need to read and reread, paraphrase, underline, take notes, create mind maps, flag, highlight, deplete the school's supply of sticky notes—use every strategy that will enhance the comprehension and retention of behavior management methods. Coaches should spend considerable time writing down their thoughts, knowing that what they write, they retain. Coaches should create summaries, paraphrases, presentations, and scripts for conversations. Coaches should be able to use a well-turned phrase, metaphor, or story that captures what's been learned and makes it palpably real to others.

If you can't explain it simply, you don't understand it well enough. *—Albert Einstein*

A coach should be relentless in pursuing the best ways of explaining information. Conversation should be cleared of clichés, buzzwords, and jargon. Instead use language that is *nontranslatable* and *actionable*. Nontranslatable conversation is language immediately understood by the listener. Actionable language impresses clearly upon the listener what must be or might be done. For example, saying "You'll decrease the number of disruptions in your class if you increase the number of praise statements you make" is more actionable than the statement "Creating a positive learning community is an important part of behavior management."

Coaches should weave stories, analogies, and mnemonic devices into the presentation of information. Think about professors or mentors from your own experience. Which ones made things come alive? What inner resources did they draw on that made an impression? The power of anecdote and archetype to frame ideas connects potentially cold-sounding research to warm-blooded stories and practical application.

Consider creating "Strategies at a Glance." Consider Strategies at a Glance for Ratios of Interactions (Reproducible 9.2). This one-page sheet provides specific ideas and strategies teachers can use to increase positive interactions in the classroom. We've also

Reproducible 9.2 *Ratio of Interactions (Strategies at a Glance)*

Ratio of Interactions

STRATEGIES AT A GLANCE

Include:

- A positive interaction marked when a student behaves appropriately and the teacher responds.
- A corrective interaction marked when a student behaves inappropriately and the teacher responds.
- A calculated ratio totaling the number of positive to corrective teacher interactions.

Goals:

- Ratio of positive to corrective interactions of 3:1 or better.
- More specific praise (direct, descriptive, and nonattributive) than general praise.

STRATEGIES

Increase noncontingent positive attention.

- Commit to saying hello to every student who enters the classroom (verbal greeting, handshake, welcoming gesture).
- Show an interest in students' progress during independent work periods.
- Invite students to ask for assistance.
- Engage in conversation with students.
- Plan to greet or talk to any student you recently had to interact with around misbehavior, showing that what happened is in the past.
- Avoid long discussions on tangential topics during teacher-led instruction or when monitoring independent work.

Increase the amount of praise or positive feedback.

- Identify a specific problem behavior that you would like to see less of in the classroom and define the opposite of this behavior. Teach the expected behavior, ignore the problem behavior, and "catch" students meeting expectations by providing specific positive feedback.
- Post a visual reminder to praise students in an area viewed frequently, such as the overhead projector, the clock, the corner of the desk, or the side of a whiteboard.
- After praising one student, find another student who is exhibiting similar behavior and praise that student as well.
- Provide more opportunities to respond.
- Acknowledge appropriate student behavior by creatively using gestures (thumbs up, the "OK" sign, clapping, a nod of the head), tangibles (stickers, stars), points toward a whole class or individual reward, calling a parent to report student success, and other systems of motivation.
- Publicly post examples of positive work, demonstrating pride in what students have done and increasing their sense of belonging.

Decrease the number of reprimands or corrections.

- Ignore minor misbehavior if the behavior is attention-seeking in nature. In conjunction with the planning ignoring, provide positive feedback and attention to students who are engaged in appropriate behavior. Actively attempt to "catch" the students being purposefully ignored when they do engage in appropriate behavior.
- Ensure that students know the expectations. Identify problem behaviors, teach behavior expectations, and provide positive feedback when expected behaviors occur.
- Provide precorrections—quick reminders of how to behave appropriately for an activity—when you anticipate that certain students may have difficultly behaving appropriately.

 REPRODUCIBLE 9.2

Reproducible 9.3 *Opportunities to Respond (Strategies at a Glance)*

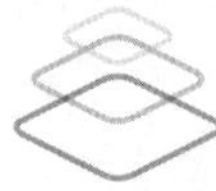

Opportunities to Respond

STRATEGIES AT A GLANCE

Include:

- The number of instructional questions, statements, or gestures seeking an oral response.
- An academic response component.

Do Not Include:

- Directives related to behavior.

Goals:

- 4–6 OTRs per minute of instruction on new material with 80% accuracy.
- 9–12 OTRs per minute of instruction on drill-and-practice material with 90% accuracy.
- Increased academic engagement.

STRATEGIES *(If the number of OTRs provided by the teacher per minute is less than optimal)*

- Break complex problems down into smaller chunks and have students provide answers to each chunk in the problem.
- Ask drill-and-practice questions from note cards and have students provide brief choral or individual answers. Mix individual student responses with classroom choral responses.
- Provide a question and have the students:
  - Quickly write the answer on a small whiteboard, holding it up to show the teacher when they have the answer.
  - Turn to a neighbor and share their answer.
  - Hold up a "response card" (a two-sided visual aid using yes/no, true/false, agree/disagree, etc).
  - Display the thumbs-up or thumbs-down signal.
  - Stand up if they believe the answer is true and stay seated if the answer is false.
- Mix into every lesson brief, fast-paced teacher-directed review of previous material, being sure to ask for responses from both the class as a whole and individual students.
- Use a seating chart. Each time a student is called on individually to answer an academic question, place a check next to their desk.
- Ask a question, allow wait time, and then call on a specific student without having students raise hands.
- Ask a question and then draw students' names from a jar. Once the question has been answered, place the names back in the jar.
- If a student called upon does not know the answer, allow wait time before asking for a classroom choral response. Then return to the student in a few minutes and ask the same question.
- Provide questions that have relevance—that is, the answers are important for the students to learn.
- Craft questions that have the appropriate level of rigor for the students in the class—problems that are not too easy and are academically challenging.

REPRODUCIBLE 9.3

included Strategies at a Glance for Opportunities to Respond (Reproducible 9.3). This provides a clear breakdown of strategies that a teacher can use to increase the opportunities for students to respond and engage in teacher-directed instruction. Summaries like this can serve two distinct purposes. They fulfill the knowledge portion of a smaller target for the teacher, and they force the coach to know the strategy well enough to provide a summary.

Remember that respecting the teacher means that when data show that the classroom is not working well, you can't just jump in with the strategies you feel would work best. What works well for your style may be completely antithetical to your partnering teacher's style. If a strategy isn't one the teacher can get behind, the chances of that strategy's sustained implementation is significantly decreased. A coach must work through the Partnership Principles, described in Chapter 5, to set the stage for the partnering teacher to choose strategies that addresses the student's needs, align with the teacher's personal style, and moves the class toward the goal for improvement.

MODEL STRATEGIES

One of the most powerful ways coaches can affect teacher practices is to go into the classroom and present a model lesson using the strategies that have been identified. Modeling gives the teacher a firsthand look at how best practices can look and sound in the classroom. The teacher can see, in context, how to teach expectations, offer frequent praise, and practice fluent correction. Many teachers report that experiencing just this single component greatly improves their classroom results.

Following are comments from real teachers after seeing strategies modeled in their classrooms:

- *It wasn't until my coach came in my room and showed me how to do it that I realized this could work for me.*
- *I think it was very important for her to come in and model it. I think the value of actually seeing it happen is you get to see how it works and how she interacts with certain kids that have real problems. . . . It also instills confidence in myself. If we had just sat down and talked, I might have understood, but seeing it in practice is a whole different thing.*

Modeling lessons increases teachers' fidelity to research-based teaching practices, bolsters their confidence about implementing new teaching practices, makes introducing new teaching practices easier, and facilitates the learning of new and unfamiliar techniques.

Although modeling is an important, perhaps an essential, component of coaching (if not most learning), coaches should be prudent about when and how they choose to model a lesson. It's best to model classroom management techniques while demonstrating other instructional practices that you know well. For example, a coach who understands principles in Anita Archer's *Explicit Vocabulary Instruction* (used to help students define and master key terms and concepts) might demonstrate how to provide sufficient praise or fluently correct misbehavior while also demonstrating explicit vocabulary instruction.

Before giving a model lesson, the coach should prepare the teacher to get the most out of watching it. Identify the data the teacher should collect while observing the coach, and collaboratively discuss what data might be collected when observing the teacher during this stage (the Implement step of the Improvement Cycle, discussed in the next chapter). A coach who's willing to have data or benchmarks collected on their lesson and engage in a collaborative exploration with the teacher of their own practice can put a teacher at ease about progress monitoring during implementation.

The coach should ensure the teacher understands exactly how to record targeted data. Construct lists of examples and non-examples of particular behavior benchmarks. The coach and teacher could watch a video-recorded lesson, tallying instances of the benchmarks that might be looked at and then comparing notes.

Preparing teachers to gather data while observing a model lesson serves at least three purposes. First, when teachers are intent on gathering specific data, they focus attention on the most important parts of the lesson. Second, the task of gathering data ensures that the teachers do not become distracted by other tasks, such as checking their email, grading papers, or slipping out of the classroom to make copies. Third, when teachers gather data, they are engaging in the same activity that coaches will be involved in later on. After actively observing and gathering data on a coach, teachers are much more open to being observed by the coach—the whole business of coaching ends up being more of a partnership rather than an expert-novice or mentor-protégé relationship.

When coaches present a model lesson, they should be forthright with students. Put students at ease by talking informally with them as they enter the room prior to the lesson. Before beginning, describe the expectations for the lesson explicitly. Explain to students that even though another teacher is in the classroom, their teacher is still the primary authority. To emphasize this, we suggest involving the teacher in the model lesson in some way.

Embrace modeling as more than a means to teach teachers—it is a great opportunity to learn from the collaborating teacher's observations. Working from the partnership perspective allows the collaborating teacher to serve in the role of a coach after the lesson. Such a stance increases the trust between the coach and teacher, and it's a great way for the coach to learn and improve, too.

Coaches should do their best to make modeling as nonthreatening as possible for the teacher. This is a reciprocal partnership, where both the coach and teacher are learning, and modeling is a perfect place for the coach to emphasize that principle. Normalize failure—not all model lessons will go as planned. Coaches should demonstrate what to do and how to respond when a lesson falls flat. For teachers who are hesitant to implement new practice because of a fear of failure, seeing a coach work through this very real possibility may give them the inspiration to try. As coaches, we shouldn't be afraid of failure when modeling either. After all, coaching isn't about making sure *we* are always excellent classroom managers; it's about making sure those we coach become excellent examples themselves.

Wrapping It Up CHAPTER 9 SUMMARY

In the Revise step of the Improvement Cycle, the coach and teacher work collaboratively to address those issues identified as priorities.

What to Know

- The Improvement Cycle is a formal, intentional coaching cycle.

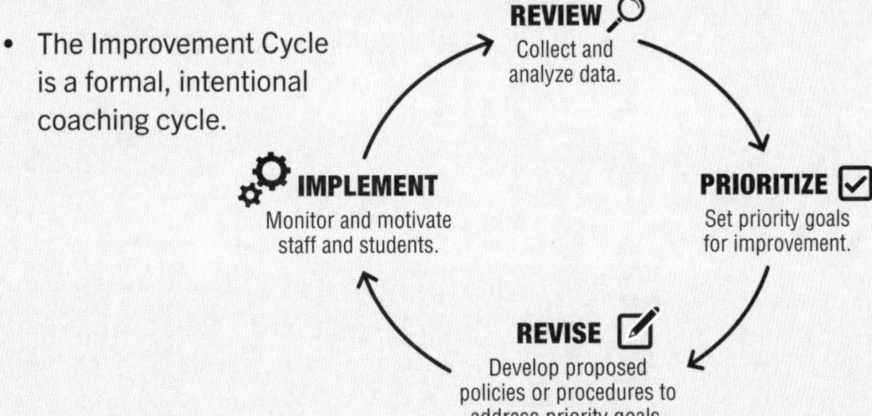

- The third step of the Improvement Cycle is Revise. Coaches and teachers work collaboratively to develop proposed policies and procedures that will address the goal(s) created.
  - **Identify strategies.** Based on the both the teacher's and the coach's knowledge and experience, strategies to directly impact the teacher's goal are brainstormed here.
  - **Explain strategies.** The coach's role is to break down and teach any strategy or strategies in which the teacher may not be well versed.
  - **Model strategies.** In this step, coaches model both the strategy itself and the process of being actively observed.

What to Do

- Learn the strategies based around the STOIC Framework that will best help teachers meet their prioritized goal.
- Be able to explain strategies simply enough that teachers can easily summarize and apply the strategy in the classroom.
- Be prepared to model those strategies in the classroom and engage in collaborative feedback about what was observed.

Notes

CHAPTER 10

Coaching Through a Cycle of Continuous Improvement: Implement

Knowledge is of no value unless you put it into practice. –Anton Chekhov

This step is truly where the rubber meets the road. Up until this point, the coaching process of the Improvement Cycle has included gathering data for review, prioritizing needs in the classroom, and revising policies and procedures. The teacher, however, hasn't yet put any new practice into action. This is often what prohibits change in our own lives. We can see what needs to change personally; we may even choose a goal and determine strategies to help us attain that vision. But we often stop short, continuing to admire our challenges long before we put knowledge into practice. According to Prochaska's stages of behavior change from Chapter 1, this puts us right back into contemplation and, for our teachers, the Improvement Cycle can stop turning. We can't just work with teachers to choose strategies—we must work to ensure that the coaching process helps the teacher put those plans into action.

In the Implement step, a teacher will launch strategies chosen during the Revise step of the Improvement Cycle. Proving this coaching process is indeed cyclical, the coach and teacher will also evaluate the effectiveness and review data to determine what practices should be adjusted or maintained (Review step). This chapter includes data collection tools to monitor for individual benchmarks and ways to motivate both the teacher and students when engaging in new practice. We will identify the role of evaluators, our administrators, and the role of support personnel, our coaches, in this cycle. With both parties actively monitoring progress during the Implement step, a decision to continue ongoing collaboration through the Improvement Cycle or exit the teacher into Tier 1 or 3 will also be made.

STEP 4: Implement

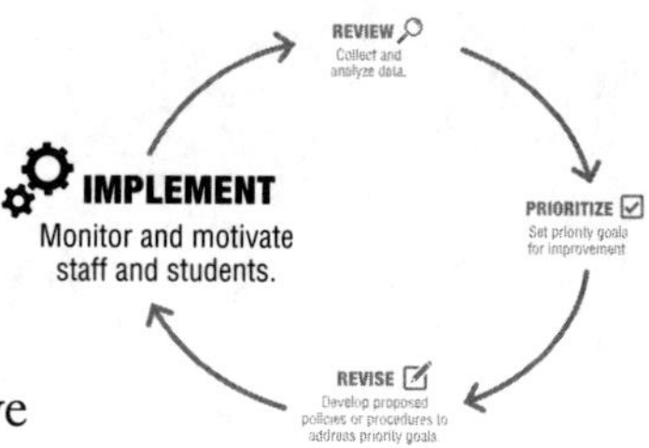

The fourth step in the Improvement Cycle, Implement, will monitor and motivate both staff and student behavior as new practices are put into place. This step is a process that informs and guides revisions to classroom management plans over time. To ensure the best chance at effective implementation, coaches must:

- **Monitor implementation.** In this step, objective data are collected to determine the effectiveness of the strategy or strategies that have been put in place as new teacher practice.
- **Motivate staff and students.** Growth toward the prioritized goal, improvement in teacher practice, and improvement in student behavior should be celebrated.

This process, and specifically the continuation of data collection, loops back into the start of the Improvement Cycle, highlighting the ongoing and continuous nature of improvement.

MONITOR IMPLEMENTATION

Once one or more strategies have been set in motion, objective data should again be collected to determine whether new practices are working. At this point in the cycle, ideally, just like baseline data, progress data should be collected at least three times during the same time over a period of one or two weeks. Bear in mind that behaviors that have become automatic often worsen at first when challenged by a new practice.

The coach and teacher may also choose to monitor progress on two (or more) of the benchmarks concurrently. For example, on-task behavior and opportunities to respond are so often correlated (and frequently influence each other) that the impact is often more pronounced if both areas are looked at for improvement. Opportunities to respond gives a teacher more chances to engage in positive interactions, so looking at these benchmarks together makes sense as well.

At this point, the coach's role shifts slightly. The teacher is putting new strategies into practice—a more active role—while the coach is now monitoring those practices—a more passive role. Collecting baseline data on all Basic 5 Behavior Benchmarks during the Review stage of the Improvement Cycle is a much more intensive process. Monitoring during the Implementation stage, while no less important, will be centered on specific data points tied to the teacher's PEERS goal and on the efficacy of newly revised strategies chosen to help reach that goal.

The following data sources and data collection tools align with the Basic 5 Behavior Benchmarks and the Basic 5 Observation Tool that was used to collect baseline data.

These data collection tools somewhat mirror what can be found in Chapter 10 of both *CHAMPS* and *DSC*. Review these options and select tools that will allow you to monitor progress toward specific improvement goals.

Ratio of Interactions

Along with proactively teaching expectations, the single most effective step teachers can take to connect with their students and improve overall classroom climate is to increase the number of positive interactions they have with each student relative to corrective interactions—their *ratio of interactions*. A teacher who is fixated too much on misbehavior could be inadvertently perpetuating it.

We recommend that teachers maintain at least a 3:1 ratio of positive to corrective interactions. While there is no definitive tipping point for building optimal relationships between teachers and students, new research points to even higher ratios of positive to corrective interactions depending on the exhibition of challenging behavior. The more challenging the behavior or the more frequent inappropriate behavior may be, the higher the ratio.

The Ratio of Interactions Monitoring Form (Reproducible 10.1) can be used to monitor positive and corrective interactions. In its simplest incarnation, the sheet is filled out by making simple tally marks in one of two boxes. The determination of whether an observed interaction is positive or corrective depends entirely on *when* it occurs. It does not depend on what is said, who says it, or the tone of voice. If the student is engaged in a behavior that meets the teacher's expectation and the teacher pays any attention, the interaction is positive. If the student is engaged in a behavior that does not meet the teacher's expectations and the teacher responds, the interaction is corrective. Corrective interactions are not bad or wrong. *Corrective* simply means that at that point in time the teacher is paying attention to a behavior that needs correction. Indeed, corrective interactions can be used as a springboard to positive interactions. A teacher may use a reprimand or correction as a reminder to look for opportunities to engage in positive interactions with other students who are engaging in the appropriate behavior.

The Ratio of Interactions Monitoring Form also includes an optional coding system for capturing more-specific information regarding a teacher's ratios. The alternate coding system can be phased in or used from the beginning of the data collection process. For teachers who consistently average more than three positive interactions for each corrective interaction, the coding system can be used to draw out patterns of interactions. For instance, a teacher may have more positive interactions with female students and primarily corrective interactions with male students. A teacher may show a tendency toward general praise (good, but not as motivational as it might be) instead of specific praise (better—teaches and reinforces positive expectations for the whole class as it motivates and validates the target student). Collecting data and providing feedback in this way allows the coach to continue refining and improving classroom management with teachers who have already reached the highest benchmark.

Reproducible 10.1 shows a filled-in example of the Ratio of Interactions Monitoring Form. Spot the valuable information it reveals. The data show the teacher's overall ratio to be about 1:1, with positive interactions occurring as frequently as corrective interactions. An enhanced coding system was used to indicate a particular student, Nick, for whom the teacher wanted to gather information. The teacher had two positive interactions with Nick and six corrective interactions. When Nick's data are taken out of the calculation, her ratio improves to 8:3. This tells the teacher that she may need to provide Nick with more noncontingent attention and positive feedback whenever possible. It tells the coach that the teacher's general trend with most students is approaching the target ratio of 9:3 (3:1). Moving away from the generality of baseline data into the specificity of singular data points helps pinpoint trends in both teacher and student behavior relatively quickly.

Opportunities to Respond

Increasing students' opportunities to respond academically correlates to an increase in on-task behavior as well as opportunities for the teacher to provide positive feedback (see Appendix). An opportunity to respond (OTR) is defined as an instructional question, statement, or gesture made by the teacher seeking a verbal, written, or action response from students. Each OTR must have an academic response component; it does not include statements or directives concerning behavior. An OTR occurs whenever the teacher directs an academic request to an individual student, a group of students, or the entire class.

Taking up where the Basic 5 Observation Tool leaves off, the Opportunities to Respond Observation Sheet (Reproducible 10.2) analyzes OTRs by students and categories of responses.

The plan here is to focus on four specific students, preferably four who represent different ability levels, so you can see them making verbal, written, and action responses. Record the start time of the lesson, mark a V on the observation sheet each time any of the targeted students makes a verbal response, a W each time any of the targeted students makes a written response, and an A each time a target student makes an action response.

At the end of the lesson, record the stop time and length of the lesson. First, calculate the average number of responses per student by adding the total number of Vs, Ws, and As and dividing by four. Then, divide the average number of responses per student by the total number of minutes observed. This figure is the average responses per minute.

Research with primary-level students determined that learning was maximized when students were responding between 4–6 times per minute with 80% accuracy during instruction on new material and between 9–12 times per minute with 90%–95% accuracy during drill and practice work (Council for Exceptional Children, 1987; Stichter et al., 2009). There is little research, however, on what represents optimal response rates for intermediate and middle school students with more complex tasks and with different types of activities, such as discussion and lecture, embedded into teacher-guided instruction. Therefore, the coach and teacher need to determine whether the number of student responses is optimal for the class and results in a high percentage of student engagement.

Reproducible 10.1 *Ratio of Interactions Monitoring Form*

Corresponds to *CHAMPS* Repro 10.4, *DSC* Repro 10.5

Ratio of Interactions Monitoring Form *(20 minutes)*

TEACHER ______ CLASS ______ DATE ______ TIME ______

OBSERVER ______ ACTIVITY ______

CODING SYSTEM (if used)

M = Male F = Female C = Classwide I = Individual

Additional Codes: N = Nick

___ = ___

___ = ___

___ = ___

POSITIVE INTERACTIONS	CORRECTIVE INTERACTIONS
F, C, F, N, F, M *C, M, N, F*	*N, N, M, N, F* *N, N, C, N*

Ratio of Interactions *1* : *1* *Ratio of Interactions with Nick's data removed: 8:3 (2.667:1)*

The goal is 3:1 or better.

It is the student behavior that is occurring at the time the interaction is initiated, *not the tone of the interaction*, that determines whether an interaction is positive or corrective.

- When a teacher interacts with a student who is exhibiting appropriate behavior, count the interaction as positive.
- When a teacher interactions with a student who is exhibiting inappropriate behavior, count the interaction as corrective.

 REPRODUCIBLE 10.1

Reproducible 10.2 *Opportunities to Respond Monitoring Form*

Corresponds to *CHAMPS* Repro 10.13, *DSC* Repro 10.12

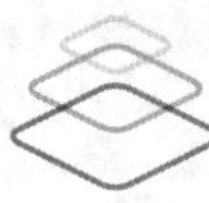

Opportunities to Respond Observation Sheet

Opportunities to respond (OTRs) are instructional questions, statements, or gestures made by the teacher that seek an oral response from one or more students. OTRs must have an academic response component to them and do not include directives related to behavior. Record an OTR for every opportunity to respond, even if the teacher repeats the same question.

TEACHER ______________________ ACTIVITY ____________________________ DATE __________

OBSERVER ______________________ START TIME _______ END TIME _______ OBSERVATION LENGTH _______

Directions: Mark a "V" for each verbal response, a "W" for each written response, and an "A" for each action response.

STUDENT 1	STUDENT 2	STUDENT 3	STUDENT 4

Total number of responses ______ divided by 4 equals ______ (average number of responses)
Average number of responses divded by number of minutes equals ______ (average responses per minute)

Notes on subjective perception of the degree of student engagement in the lesson:

Analysis and plan of action:

 REPRODUCIBLE 10.2

GOING DEEPER: PERCENTAGE OF CORRECT RESPONSES

In conjunction with OTRs, tracking accurate student responses to academic questions can yield important information about a class. A correct academic response occurs when an opportunity to respond directed toward a student or group of students is answered correctly. A coach may choose to collect this data if a teacher's OTRs are high but academic achievement through classroom, district, or state assessment is low.

To calculate the PCR (percentage of correct responses), divide the number of correct academic responses by the number of OTRs. This will help you determine if the content of instruction matches the current ability of students. If student accuracy is below 80% for new material or below 90% for drill-and-practice work, a review of the material may be in order. In more open-ended class activities, a lower rate of correct responses may be healthy as long as students are actively engaged with the lesson—brainstorming sessions, creative writing, problem solving, "extra credit" concepts, and other types of nonlinear instruction. On the other hand, should correct responses consistently hover near 100%, it may be time to take a fresh look at the curriculum, particularly if students are showing signs of restlessness or boredom.
—Wendy Reinke, in *Coaching Classroom Management* (2nd ed., Sprick et al., 2010)

Disruptions

Coaches and teachers can get a pretty good fix on whether a behavior management strategy is working by monitoring the number and types of disruptions that occur in the classroom. Disruptive behavior can be defined as a statement or action by one or more students that interferes with an ongoing class activity. You can count general disruptions using the Basic 5 Observation Tool. To get a more refined picture of misbehavior, use the Misbehavior Recording Sheet, which appears in two configurations on the following pages. Reproducible 10.3A is arranged by seating chart. Reproducible 10.3B is arranged by days of the week. Either form will help isolate and illustrate patterns of individual or group misbehavior. Use and adapt the sample coding system to the differing needs of particular classrooms. As specific misbehaviors are recorded (or other misbehaviors are identified), the goal might be to identify strategies to address one or more of the most troublesome issues and then track the plan's effectiveness in improving the situation.

During a set activity or over an entire class period, mark a tally or code representing a particular behavior in the box corresponding with each student's seat or name. Be crystal clear on which behaviors will be tallied. If the teacher usually ignores verbal outbursts from students, should these be tallied? If the teacher doesn't mind students laying their

Reproducible 10.3A *Misbehavior Recording Sheet (by seating chart)*

Corresponds to *CHAMPS* Repro 10.9, *DSC* Repro 10.9

Misbehavior Recording Sheet (by seating chart)

TEACHER ______________ CLASS ______________ DATE ________ TIME ______

OBSERVER ______________ ACTIVITY ______________

CODING SYSTEM

N = Noncompliance/defiance ______ = ______________

T = Talking out ______ = ______________

O = Out of seat ______ = ______________

H = Hands/feet/objects bothering others ______ = ______________

Name:	Name:	Name:	Name:	Name:
Name:	Name:	Name:	Name:	Name:
Name:	Name:	Name:	Name:	Name:
Name:	Name:	Name:	Name:	Name:
Name:	Name:	Name:	Name:	Name:
Name:	Name:	Name:	Name:	Name:

 REPRODUCIBLE 10.3A

Reproducible 10.3B *Misbehavior Recording Sheet (daily by student name)*

Corresponds to *CHAMPS* Repro 10.7, *DSC* Repro 10.8

Misbehavior Recording Sheet (daily by student name)

TEACHER ______________________ CLASS ________________ DATE __________ TIME ______

OBSERVER ______________________ ACTIVITY ________________________________

CODING SYSTEM

N = Noncompliance/defiance ______ = ____________________

T = Talking out ______ = ____________________

O = Out of seat ______ = ____________________

H = Hands/feet/objects bothering others ______ = ____________________

NAME	1ST HOUR	2ND HOUR	3RD HOUR	4TH HOUR	5TH HOUR	TOTAL

REPRODUCIBLE 10.3B

heads down on the desks, will this be marked as an off-task behavior? Decide collaboratively. As a general starting point, a *disruption* is any behavior that causes the teacher to pause or stop the flow of instruction in order to respond and any behavior that disrupts the learning environment of another. Tally or code a disruption even when the teacher's response is nonverbal.

If a single student precipitates several disruptions simultaneously (for instance, leaves her seat, talks out loud, and knocks a neighboring student's books off his desk), enter three tally or coded marks. If a frequent misbehavior that has not been previously assigned a code becomes apparent, another code representing this behavior can be added, or simply revert to tally marks for all misbehaviors not included in the code.

NOTE: Before using one of the Misbehavior Recording Sheets, ascertain whether student misbehavior stems from a lack of clear expectations. The coach or teacher might simply ask students questions regarding specific expected behaviors for activities and transitions: "While the teacher is giving a lesson, can you sharpen your pencil?" "When you're supposed to be working by yourself at your desk, can you visit with your neighbor?" These are examples of simple yes-or-no questions. More in-depth questions may also be asked: "When you're working with other kids in a group, what are three things you might do that would show you are participating appropriately?" A simple quiz can also be devised to check student understanding of appropriate conduct. Use the informally gathered data to glean which kinds of misbehaviors arise from a lack of understanding and which may be purposeful choices.

If students seem unclear about some of the expected behaviors, the teacher should revisit and refresh them. If the teacher is using the CHAMPS model, it might be a good idea to review and reemphasize the Guidelines for Success for the whole class. If most of the students do understand what is expected of them, work to identify the underlying cause of the occasional misbehaviors more precisely.

On-Task Behavior (Academic Engagement)

If on-task behavior has been identified as a priority for improvement, more in-depth data should be gathered using the On-Task Behavior Observation Sheet (Reproducible 10.4). Data for this form are collected similarly to the Basic 5 Observation Tool. Follow a set pattern to observe each student in turn for 5 minutes. Every 5 seconds, look up at a student in the pattern and then look back at the form. If the student appears engaged and on task at the moment they are observed, mark a + (plus) symbol. If the student is not engaged or at least does not *appear* to be (remember, the reliability of this observation is built on the average of many time slices), mark a – (minus). After the mark is made, wait for the remainder of the 5 seconds and look at the next student in the pattern. As before, divide the number of + symbols by the total number of marks (60) to arrive at a percentage for students' time on task.

Written comments should be specific, observable, and objective. For instance, when copying information on the board, students are mostly on task, but during class discussion

Reproducible 10.4 *On-Task Behavior Observation Sheet*

Corresponds to *CHAMPS* Repro 10.12, *DSC* Repro 10.11

On-Task Behavior Observation Sheet

TEACHER ______________ CLASS ______________ DATE __________ TIME ______

OBSERVER ______________ ACTIVITY ______________

For the next 5 minutes, focus on a different student every 5 seconds. Record a "+" symbol to indicate on-task or engaged behavior and a "–" symbol to indicate off-task behavior. When each student has been observed, begin the progression again. Continue until 5 minutes have elapsed.

1	2	3	4	5	6	7	8	9	10	11	12
13	14	15	16	17	18	19	20	21	22	23	24
25	26	27	28	29	30	31	32	33	34	35	36
37	38	39	40	41	42	43	44	45	46	47	48
49	50	51	52	53	54	55	56	57	58	59	60

Divide the total number of on-task (+) marks by the total number of marks (60).

Time on Task (academic engagement) = ______%

Notes:

REPRODUCIBLE 10.4

of the topic, a pattern develops of many students drifting off-task. This provides a vital clue regarding the effectiveness of the current plan. This should be used to guide the teacher in determining the next step.

Again, it's important that the coach and teacher have clarified and coordinated definitions of on-task versus off-task behavior *before* beginning the data collection process. Various and sundry "misbehaviors" the coach may witness while collecting data may be the product of expectations previously taught by the teacher. Every teacher's preferred personal style is respected in CHAMPS, meaning that what's appropriate engagement for one class may be considered off-task in another. The challenge, then, is knowing whether a student is truly engaged and on task during a particular teacher's lesson.

Even when clear on the expectations, making a snap judgment about small behaviors can be far from easy. From across the room, a student may appear to be focused on the teacher but is in fact daydreaming, or may appear to be concentrating on an assignment when actually writing a personal note. Fortunately, small errors tend to cancel out when a general picture comprising many such snapshots is formed. Results should be reliable to the extent that the evaluation from student to student is consistent, and valid to the extent that the understanding of on-task and off-task behavior has been harmonized with the teacher.

GOING DEEPER: CLASSROOM ACTIVITIES OBSERVATION LOG

This data collection tool is designed to provide more information for teachers who need to increase instructional minutes and improve student engagement. A coach may choose to use this if on-task behavior for a class is low and primarily due to a lack of both instructional minutes and a variety of academic activities. Originally created by Lynn Barnes (Sprick et al., 2010), this tool measures how time is allocated in the classroom for various instructional activities.

It is not the time in class, but what we do with the time we have, that matters. —John Hattie

Effective classroom management is the goal—transitions between activities should be efficient, housekeeping minutes should be kept to a minimum, and reinforcement activities should be simple and quick, yet effective. Charles Payne (2008) found in his Chicago Public Schools research that teachers who received the best academic gains averaged 14% noninstructional classroom minutes. The group of teachers with the least academic gains averaged 29% noninstructional classroom minutes (Sprick et al., 2014, Module A, p. 165).

Long transitions between learning activities and chaotic beginning and ending routines can lead to a loss of instructional minutes. And any time not spent learning becomes down time for students, time for students to engage in behaviors that may require a correction, eating up even more of a teacher's precious instructional minutes in the classroom. It can become a perpetual cycle of despair.

Classroom Activities Observation Log. Reproducible 10.5 is designed for use during a single class period in which there may be multiple instances of certain elements of instruction (transition periods, for example). As you observe the class, note the starting and ending time for routines, activities, and transitions that occur. The total minutes should add up to equal the class length. Then calculate the percentage of time spent in transitions and routines versus the time spent engaged in instructional activities.

The Classroom Activities Observation Log is an excellent tool you can use to observe activity distribution within class periods and provide teachers with a clear visual representation of how their class time is distributed among different activities.

Alignment With Expectations

Many students in our public school system today do not respond to *role-bound authority* (automatic respect for the role of authority figures in society, such as principals, clerics, and parents). Most have been exposed to a variety of teachers, sometimes in a variety of buildings and districts, and have experienced a wide range of "what is expected" in their individual classrooms along the way. These students, especially those who have struggled, are therefore at a disadvantage when a teacher assumes they know what conduct is expected—to figure out each teacher's expectations and hit the mark every time may simply be unachievable. A coach should patiently and persistently work with the teacher to describe to students (many of whom may have only a foggy notion) what appropriate behavior looks and sounds like for each instructional activity and transition in the teacher's classroom.

Because the need for clear expectations is so critical to managing any classroom effectively, we've created a special worksheet to track the ups and downs of student compliance with them. This fifth and final Basic 5 Benchmark is alignment with expectations. The Expectations Versus Daily Reality Rating Scale (Reproducible 10.6) rates the degree to which students have met the teacher's posted expectations. This worksheet can be used by the coach, the teacher, or even students as a self-assessment of behavior. It can also be a powerful communication tool. After an activity, the teacher might display the Daily Reality Scale and ask students to assess themselves. This not only encourages dialogue, but helps students understand that behavior counts and that following expectations is not optional.

Reproducible 10.5 *Classroom Activities Observation Log*

Classroom Activities Observation Log

TEACHER ______________ SUBJECT ______________ PERIOD ___ CLASS LENGTH ________

OBSERVER ______________ SCHOOL ______________ DATE ________

Daily Elements of Instruction	Start Time	End Time	Start Time	End Time	Start Time	End Time	Start Time	End Time	Total Minutes
ROUTINES AND TRANSITIONS									
Beginning Routine									
Minutes -->									
Transitions									
Minutes -->									
Ending Routine									
Minutes -->									
Routines and Transitions Total Minutes -->									
TEACHER-LED INSTRUCTION									
Whole Group Instruction									
Minutes -->									
LEARNING ACTIVITIES									
Small Group Instruction									
Minutes -->									
Independent Work									
Minutes -->									
Centers/Lab									
Minutes -->									
Cooperative Learning									
Minutes -->									
Tests/Quizzes									
Minutes -->									
Learning Activities Total Minutes -->									

Total Class Time ______

REPRODUCIBLE 10.5

Reproducible 10.6 *Expectations Versus Daily Reality Rating Scale*

Corresponds to *CHAMPS* Repro 10.3, *DSC* Repros 10.3A and 10.4A

Expectations Versus Daily Reality Rating Scale

TEACHER ______ CLASS ______ DATE ______ TIME ______

OBSERVER ______ ACTIVITY ______

Directions: Using the rating scale below, rate the degree to which the students met expectations for classroom activities or transitions. Write which classroom activity in which students were engaged in each Activity box. This self-assessment tool should be completed at least three times for the same class during the week.

RATING SCALE

Percentage of Students Following Expectations: **1** = 90% to 100% **2** = 80% to 89% **3** = Less than 80%

Conversation	1	2	3
Help	1	2	3
Activity:			
Movement	1	2	3
Participation	1	2	3
Success!	1	2	3

Conversation	1	2	3
Help	1	2	3
Activity:			
Movement	1	2	3
Participation	1	2	3
Success!	1	2	3

Conversation	1	2	3
Help	1	2	3
Activity:			
Movement	1	2	3
Participation	1	2	3
Success!	1	2	3

Conversation	1	2	3
Help	1	2	3
Activity:			
Movement	1	2	3
Participation	1	2	3
Success!	1	2	3

Data review:

- If all variables within the activity or transition are rated a 1, keep doing what you're doing. The fact that over 90% of your students are meeting expectations indicates that your classroom management plan for the particular activity or transition are working at a Tier 1 level.
- If some of the variables were rated a 2, it may be a good idea to implement one or more classwide motivation systems appropriate for a medium-support classroom. Analyze aspects of the STOIC Framework and the STOIC Classroom Management Screener to determine if minor adjustments are needed in your management plan during the problematic activity or transition.
- If some of the variables were rated a 3, you should probably implement one or more classwide motivation systems appropriate for a high-support classroom. Also analyze aspects of the STOIC Framework and the STOIC Classroom Management Screener to determine what adjustments are needed in your management plan during the problematic activity or transition. Consider whether students require more structure and support to be successful.

 REPRODUCIBLE 10.6

MOTIVATE STAFF AND STUDENTS

To motivate staff to remain on this path of continuous improvement and to continue the implementation of practices that work, we must analyze and look for any evident successes. The coach's role here is to help teachers use data to recognize when newly implemented strategies are leading to the desired results and to use data to inform practice when strategies aren't working . When data show teachers are making improvements in the Basic 5 Benchmarks and drawing closer to their PEERS goal, this should be a cause for celebration. When student behavior is improving, this provides the perfect opportunity for a teacher to engage in an intermittent celebration with their students. Often a strategy that has had a significant impact on student behavior is abandoned simply because no one paid enough attention to its success. To look for both areas of success and explore what may be potentially needed for continuous improvement, we offer the CHAMPS Status Check.

The CHAMPS Status Check (Reproducible 10.7) is a tool for a more reflective approach on implementation. While it can be used collaboratively by a coach and teacher during the Revise step, we recommend its use as part of an after-action report on implementation. Often, asking the right questions while planning new practices or analyzing implementation yields better solutions than skipping ahead to the diagnosis and treatment of a complex set of behaviors that may not yet be fully understood.

Based on the collection of progress-monitoring data, which may include one or more of the behavior benchmarks, a teacher can use this information to decide on next steps with the help of the coach. Specifically, does the teacher want to:

- Keep the goal and strategy or strategies currently in place?
- Revise the goal and/or choose a new strategy?
- Create a completely new goal and/or choose a new strategy to put into practice?

The Improvement Cycle isn't a one-shot deal. It's cyclical for a reason. Because growth occurs over time in a continuous cycle of improvement, we've designed this process to act in the same way. Once a teacher has determined whether to keep, revise, or create a new goal or strategy, assessment begins anew.

By engaging in the collaborative exploration of data, be it baseline or progress monitoring, coaches and teacher re-enter the Review step of the Improvement Cycle. This continuous cycle of improvement allows for the continued autonomy of teachers working toward improving classroom management. Yes, a teacher may be receiving targeted coaching support through the more formal Improvement Cycle, but Tier 2 does not preclude a teacher from pursuing their own professional growth. In reality, it should engage them even further as they look to change and improve practice.

Even when data show us the classroom is performing well, a difficult scenario may occur. Maybe a coach was called in because an administrator observed a classroom that seemed "out of control," but the classroom was simply run in a manner different from the administrator's own teaching style. Coaches should remember the adage, "If it ain't

Reproducible 10.7 *CHAMPS Status Check*

CHAMPS Status Check

TEACHER ______________________ CLASS ____________________ DATE __________ TIME ______

OBSERVER ______________________ ACTIVITY ______________________________

Key question: What are we looking at or for in student behavior?

Expected Performance	Demonstrated By

What lesson, activity, or strategy will we try next, and what will we use to analyze its effects?

broke, don't fix it." When and if this disconnect occurs, the teacher or coach should ask for clarification on how the administrator will objectively measure growth. Without a clear target, there will be no viable way to show progress. If students are actively engaged, behaving respectfully, complying with expectations, given ample opportunities to respond, and responding accurately, that classroom must be allowed to carry on if students are academically achieving.

We all believe that the way we set up and run our classroom is the morally, ethically correct way to run a classroom, but research shows us time and again that the only truly effective classroom is one that meets the Basic 5 Behavior Benchmarks while allowing for the personal style of the teacher to shine through. Educational consultant Mike Booher once said, "Data are vital, but in the end the data's meaning and influence are dependent on the strength of the partnership between teacher and coach." When coaches can work with an educator to create an environment that's both conducive to student success and a showcase of that teacher's professional skills, this level of support is poised to build something truly magnificent.

ONGOING COLLABORATION

The Improvement Cycle is circular, continuing until the classroom teacher and coach determine that the classroom management plan has been effectively and successfully incorporated into the day-to-day flow of the classroom. Even then, periodic observations to establish that progress has been maintained may be profitable, offering an additional opportunity to salute the classroom teacher who has successfully implemented and sustained changes in classroom management. Celebrating success by providing positive feedback is at least as important to teachers, coaches, and administrators as it is for positive student outcomes.

Whether the Improvement Cycle is being used for the first time or as an ongoing process of collaboration, the purpose is to provide the appropriate support for a teacher to learn and master a new teaching practice. Here we identify the role of two cornerstones in providing that ongoing support.

The Role of Nonevaluative Coaches

Because every instructor, and every teaching situation, is unique, coaches quickly learn that they must modify their approach to best meet the specific needs of each teacher. Ongoing collaboration may involve many model lessons or very few. Coaching sometimes involves extensive data collection and debriefing afterward. But it can just as easily take place through brief discussions supplemented by the teacher's own private work and initiative.

The coach needs to provide as much support as necessary, but no more. A coach should do everything they can to help teachers master new ways of teaching as efficiently as possible. Presenting a model lesson or two is an excellent way to accomplish this; however, a coach must guard against taking over and teaching the teacher's class. Ultimately, the teacher must master the new practice on their own. A masterful coach reshuffles the deck as often as needed to meet the needs of each teacher.

"*A coach should do everything they can to help teachers master new ways of teaching as efficiently as possible.*"

The Role of the Evaluator

The administrator does not take a back seat once a teacher has been moved into Tier 2. Whether for support or enrichment, the administrator is still engaging in walk-throughs with the full staff and with teachers who are receiving more targeted coaching. Walk-throughs for staff in Tier 2 can and should be a mix of both 5-minute snapshots of practice and potentially longer data pulls based on the administrator's schedule.

At this point, the administrator is also meeting with any teachers who receive Tier 2 support. They, too, will engage in the collaborative exploration of data, with briefer but no less powerful coaching conversations. The administrator needs to continue to communicate support for the more formal coaching cycles in play and provide the gentle pressure that only an evaluator can.

Without the evaluator as warm demander, a teacher may simply choose not to put new ideas into practice, not out of any malicious intent but because they don't believe it really matters. A staff member may feel even more disconnected from the process, as if their boss, the ultimate pillar of support on a campus, has simply handed them off to be fixed by another. When an evaluator is not part of the ongoing process of support, this becomes analogous to teachers sending students off to the principal, hoping the principal will solve the problem with little involvement from the classroom teacher.

The administrator also needs to make decisions on whether a teacher who is continuing along an exemplary path may serve as a model classroom to other teachers on a campus or perhaps to an entire district. They are looking at ways to further extend the learning and growth of master teachers. The administrator is also making decisions about whether a staff member may need to move into Tier 3 with a formal plan of assistance and if a possible conversation regarding insubordination may be required. These are things only an evaluator can decide; it should never be left up to a nonevaluative coach to make these calls.

EXIT STRATEGY

At this point, based on objective data collection between the coach and teacher and based on data collected by administration via continued walk-throughs during the coaching process, a decision as to whether a teacher continues to receive Tier 2 support must be made.

One of the most common questions asked when working to prepare coaches to support teachers, in both informal cycles as Tier 1 support personnel or the more formal Improvement Cycle, is whether coaches and teachers should identify a date by which the teacher will meet a goal (Knight, 2017, p. 95). Others ask how long it should take for a teacher to hit a goal.

Setting a deadline for a teacher to hit a goal can actually be counterproductive. While the coach and teacher should carefully plan when their coaching conversations will take place and what they hope to accomplish, each coaching session is so unique that the cycle rarely conforms to a set schedule.

In terms of how long it will take to meet a goal, on average, coaching from start to finish typically requires 5–6 hours, but the crucial words here are "on average." Sometimes the timeline is much faster and at other times it takes much longer. Deciding on a set amount of time for coaching with an arbitrary goal date may make scheduling a coach's time easier. However, for a coaching cycle to be truly effective, trying to squeeze coaching into a set time period or stretching it out after the goal has been met isn't as sensible as simply continuing the cycle until the goal is consistently being hit.

Once data show a goal is consistently being hit (through the coach's collection of data, administrative walk-throughs, and perhaps the teacher's self-assessment) and any skill deficit has been largely eliminated, it's safe to assume the formal coaching cycle can be abandoned. The teacher can move back into Tier 1 support, where the coach can provide ongoing collaboration as needed. Or a teacher looking to create a model classroom or serve in the capacity of a coach or administrator one day may turn to extending their skillset even further through repetition of the Improvement Cycle with a focus on another goal.

Keep in mind, it's not that the Improvement Cycle *can't* also occur for a teacher seeking more support within Tier 1—it's that it *must* occur as an intentional part of the plan for teachers in need of more targeted support within Tier 2.

If the goal is not being met, it may be time to determine if it's a matter of skill or will. If it's a matter of skill, the coach and teacher may opt to engage in a more comprehensive collection and assessment of data. If improvement in a certain skill has been prioritized but not met, a coach and teacher may attend additional professional development together, with coaching happening in real time during the session. If a deficit has become a matter of will, meaning the teacher is not invested in the coaching process or the application of strategies to improve classroom management, it may be time for the staff member to move into Tier 3, where a formal plan of assistance may be utilized.

A move into Tier 3 should only happen if the support team in Tier 2, consisting of both evaluators and nonevaluative coaches, has done everything possible to provide for this teacher the six components of change introduced by the Change Puzzle in Chapter 1. We cannot have unrealistic expectations for staff and a poor system of support and expect miracles. Tier 3 should always be looked at as a last resort. If collaborative coaching is effectively put into practice at the campus level, with a solid system of Tier 1 support for all practitioners, the number of teachers who need to move beyond Tier 2 support should be minimal.

One teacher in an at-risk ninth-grade reading classroom, after receiving classroom management training and the opportunity to engage in a formal coaching cycle exclaimed, "This process makes me really self-conscious!" And that is exactly the point. The Improvement Cycle is designed to create, intentionally and collaboratively, a higher level of awareness. The observation tools, specifically designed to measure the Basic 5 Behavior Benchmarks, when used collaboratively between coaches and teachers, are meant to make teachers more aware of how they respond to classroom management and more purposeful in the way they respond to students in a behavioral context. Over time, as teachers learn to trust the coach as a peer, any perception of threat or danger during the coaching cycle will dissipate. The eventual goal, for the coach and for the teachers they serve, is to become self-conscious in the most positive sense: more conscious of self, which is an essential step to becoming a lifelong learner in the art and science of classroom management.

Wrapping It Up **CHAPTER 10 SUMMARY**

The Implement step of the Improvement Cycle is when a teacher launches new strategies and practices in their classroom. The coach helps evaluate the effectiveness of implementation and celebrate improvements.

What to Know

- The Improvement Cycle is a formal, intentional coaching cycle.

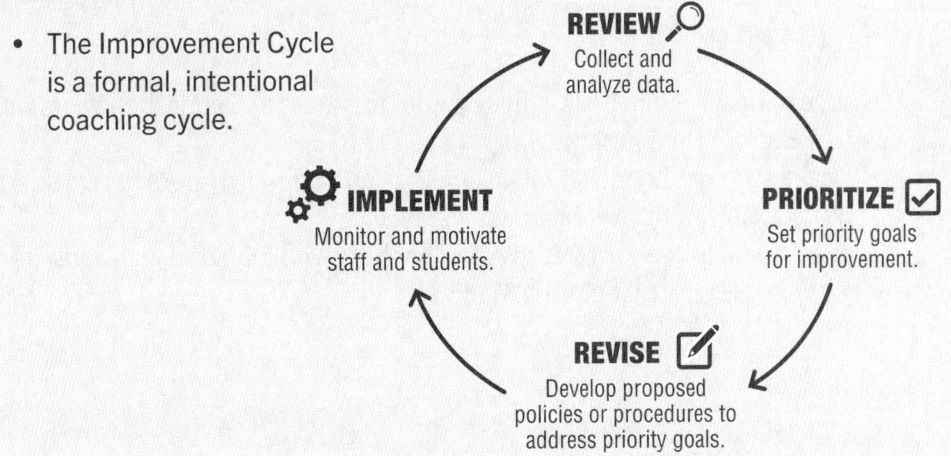

- The fourth step of the Improvement Cycle is Implement. To ensure the best chance at effective implementation, coaches must:
  - **Monitor implementation.** In this step, objective data is collected to determine the effectiveness of the strategy or strategies that have been put in place as new teacher practice.
  - **Motivate staff and students.** Growth toward the prioritized goal, improvement in teacher practice, and improvement in student behavior should be celebrated.

- Ongoing collaboration should be provided, but never used to supersede a teacher's instructional practice.
  - **Nonevaluative coaches.** The nonevaluative coach needs to provide as much support as necessary, but no more. A coach should do everything they can to help teachers master new ways of teaching as efficiently as possible.
  - **Evaluator.** Whether for support or enrichment, the administrator is still engaging in walk-throughs with teachers who are receiving more targeted coaching and making decisions on what ongoing support may be required.

- An exit strategy should be put into place for staff receiving Tier 2 support.
  - Once the goal is being consistently met, a teacher can exit Tier 2, receiving ongoing collaboration as part of the campus Tier 1 support plan.
  - If the goal is not being met, through skill or will, a teacher may receive additional support within Tier 2 or be placed into Tier 3 with a more formal plan of assistance.

What to Do

- Use data collection tools in this chapter to assess individual behaviors within the Basic 5 Benchmarks.
- Make sure both nonevaluative coaches and administrators have a specific role to play in this formal coaching cycle.
- Determine a clear exit strategy for teachers who meet the goal consistently or who will now be entering Tier 3.

CHAPTER 11

Planning Into Practice: The Improvement Cycle in Action

Coaching is unlocking a person's potential to maximize their own performance. —John Whitmore

One thing that distinguishes great teachers is a continual drive to improve aspects of their classroom from day to day and year to year. The best teachers do this by using an ongoing cycle that involves reviewing data, prioritizing goals for improvement based on that data, revising aspects of their classroom management plan to address those goals, and implementing new plans while monitoring the efficacy of those plans (Sprick, J., et al., 2020, p. 253). Any teacher *can* put this continuous cycle of improvement into practice as part of a Tier 1 plan of growth. If a teacher has been placed into Tier 2, whether working to close a deficit or striving to become an exemplar, this Improvement Cycle *must* be put into practice.

In the medical community, the phrase "bench to bedside" describes a process of taking research from a laboratory setting and moving it into clinical application to directly benefit patients. It is a short phrase for a long and complex process. The same can be said for the term *Improvement Cycle*. The preceding chapters in this section have introduced administrators and coaches to the Improvement Cycle, breaking down each step into its critical components. Chapter by chapter, we've walked through this cycle from the initial preconference and data collection with a teacher to deciding how a teacher might exit from Tier 2 support.

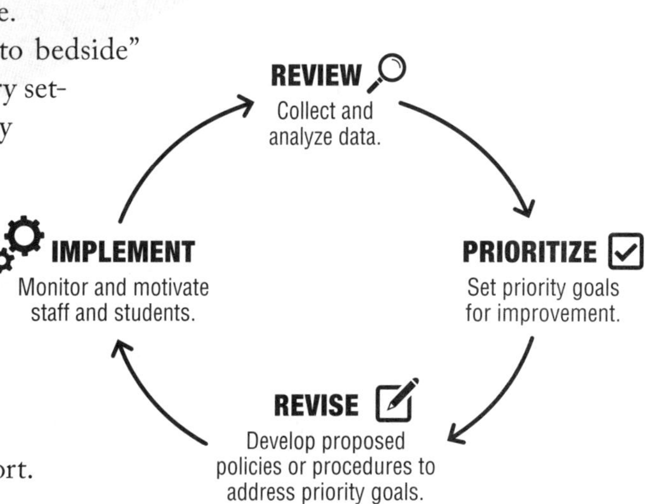

But what might this cycle look like when put into practice? How does this complex process become a manageable tool for coaches and administrators to support staff?

In this chapter we'll take the Improvement Cycle from bench to bedside by walking through a schedule of the coaching process. This schedule serves *only* as an example. Please note, as discussed at the end of Chapter 10, there is no prescribed set of hours or days to help a teacher reach a goal. Because coaching sessions are so unique, the cycle will rarely conform to a set schedule from start to finish. For a coaching cycle to be effective, trying to squeeze coaching into a set time period can be counterproductive and antithetical to the growth of a teacher. Read through this schedule with the intent to reflect on what a coaching process might look like within your own campus, based on your role and the time you have allotted to coach teachers.

A SCHEDULE OF THE PROCESS

This example of the coaching process takes place using approximately ten days spread across time. These days do not have to be sequential but should be scheduled relatively close together. Keep in mind that this is just one example of how the coaching process *can* be put into practice using the Improvement Cycle. At the end of this chapter, we'll also look at when and how an administrator might also engage throughout this sample schedule.

Day 1: *Preconference with teacher*
Day 2: *Collect and summarize data*
Day 3: *Collect and summarize data*
Day 4: *Collect and summarize data*
Day 5: *Collaboratively explore data and set goal(s)*
Day 6: *Revise practice*
Day 7: *Plan for implementation*
Day 8: *Model in the classroom*
Day 9: *Monitor implementation*
Day 10: *Post-conference with teacher*

DAY 1: PRECONFERENCE WITH TEACHER

Arrange for a meeting with the teacher to get to know them as a professional and how they approach classroom management. Consider using the Teacher Interview (Reproducible 7.2) and the Classroom Ecology Checklist (Reproducible 7.3), developed by Wendy Reinke (Sprick et al., 2010).

During this preconference, determine when you might collect data. You may ask the teacher to identify which classes are the least challenging and the most challenging to teach, and then have the teacher choose one other average class. Starting with the most challenging class will give you a look into what may be creating problems for the teacher. Baseline data from all *three* classes can give a valid snapshot of the teacher's entire day. Your observations may take place over a few days or a week, as class schedules and time available for data collection allow.

Introduce the teacher to the Basic 5 Observation Tool (Reproducible 7.1). Make sure the teacher has a shared understanding of how each behavior is defined. While the teacher should have had exposure to the Basic 5 Behavior Benchmarks (Reproducible 3.5) from the support offered in Tier 1, you may choose to take an additional look at them here.

Make sure the teacher understands that any data you collect are confidential. Explain that you are an advocate for the teacher and their students. Print a copy of your confidentiality agreement, review it with the teacher, sign it, and give it to the teacher.

DAYS 2–4: COLLECT AND SUMMARIZE DATA

For each class you will observe, prepare the necessary data collection tools. The Basic 5 Observation Tool (Reproducible 7.1) will help you gather data about an individual classroom in as little as 60 minutes spread over these three days. These data should be gathered during teacher-guided instruction over the same 20-minute time span on at least three occasions. The three sets of data are then averaged to provide an overall general picture of the classroom. On Day 5, this data will be analyzed and used to prioritize a teacher's needs. Check in with the teacher informally after each observation and schedule the more formal collaborative exploration for when you have enough data to engage in a robust dialogue.

Other factors play into the data that will be collected and summarized. You are in no way obligated to use or limit yourself to the Basic 5 Observation Tool. For instance, based on why a teacher was referred to Tier 2, you may use this time to collect additional data in the form of student feedback surveys and perhaps ask the teacher to engage in some level of self-evaluation. If you are new to coaching classroom management, we recommend relying on the Basic 5 Observation Tool as a logical starting point in the Improvement Cycle. Highly knowledgeable and skillful coaches are encouraged to collaboratively adapt and modify how and what data are collected beyond the Basic 5 with the teacher during the preconference.

DAY 5: COLLABORATIVELY EXPLORE DATA AND SET GOAL(S)

Arrange a time to engage in partnership feedback (collaborative exploration of data) as shown in Figure 11.1 (p. 294).

The goal is to engage the collaborating teacher in conversation about the data, not to move the teacher toward some preconceived idea of what to improve. A coach should avoid telling the teacher what the data mean—good or bad. Let the teacher come to their own conclusions.

Figure 11.1 *Partnership Feedback (Collaborative Exploration of Data)*

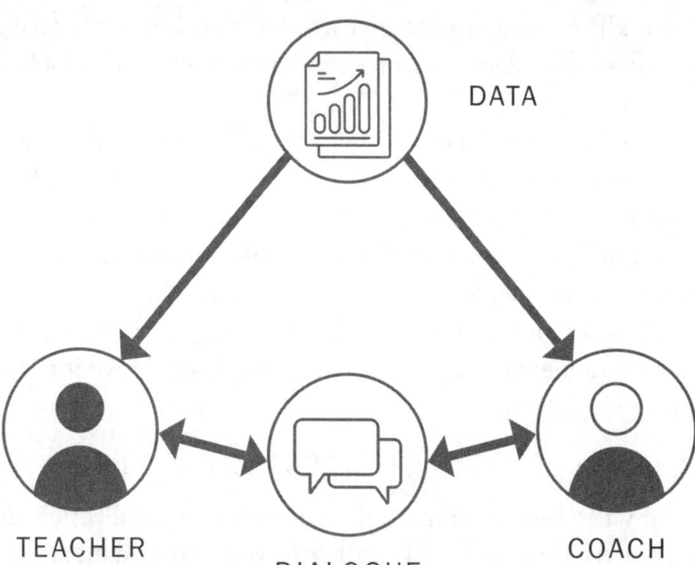

Data should be introduced as objectively as possible. Data are there to provide the coach and teacher a departure point for dialogue. Information should be given in specific, observable terms, such as "The data collected shows that students are on task an average of 68%" as opposed to "Students are off-task quite a bit." During this conversation, coaches should apply the communication strategies covered in Chapter 5 as well as strive to embed the Partnership Principles. One approach is to supply the data and begin by asking questions, either your own or pulled from the sample list introduced in Chapter 7 and shown below:

- What's on your mind?
- How comfortable are you with these data?
- Do you agree or disagree with these data?
- Was this 5-, 10-, 20-minute time period an anomaly or the norm for this class?
- In what ways are the data similar to or different from what you were expecting?
- What do you think went well?
- What do you think could have gone better?
- Given the time we have today, what's the most important thing for us to talk about?
- In your ideal class, what would be different?
- What would be the first signs that your classroom is improving?

Remember, the job of a coach is not to use data as a tool for judgment; it's to help teachers get a clear picture of their current reality. With a clear picture of their current reality in hand, teachers will be better able to prioritize needs and construct a clear, measurable goal for improvement.

On this day, coaches will assist teachers in using data to set a PEERS goal and communicate that goal in a way that they and any third-party observer can easily make judgments about progress. If multiple areas for improvement exist, consider engaging in the rank order activity first to help teachers prioritize challenges. Based on this rank order, teachers will choose one or two challenges on which to focus. As a reminder, a PEERS goal should be:

- *Powerful:* The goal should be worth the time the teacher will invest and should make a real difference in students' lives.
- *Easy:* The goal provides a destination and the simplest path to it. Complex goals, no matter how powerful, are often abandoned early on.
- *Emotionally compelling:* Goals should invoke an emotional response along with a rational process. A goal that will compel people to act is one that they understand and feel (Heath & Heath, 2010).
- *Reachable:* The best goal is the one that engenders hope—the belief that the goal can be reached through a clear, precise description and strategies to reach it.
- *Student focused:* A goal should make an unmistakable impact on students by focusing on student achievement, behavior, or attitude outcomes.

DAY 6: REVISE PRACTICE

Study the teacher's goals and be prepared to assist in designing a plan to help the teacher meet those goals. In addition to brainstorming ideas to address each goal with the teacher, the coach should also be prepared with a list of strategies. If the teacher is newer to the field of education, with less experience and potentially less knowledge of behavior management, having a list of predetermined strategies may be beneficial. Always putting the teacher in the role of the decision maker, urge the teacher to choose those strategies that best suit their instructional style.

Follow the STOIC acronym to assist in identifying strategies the teacher might try:

- *Structure/organize* all school settings for success.
- *Teach* students how to behave responsibly in those settings.
- *Observe* student behavior.
- *Interact positively* with students.
- *Correct* misbehavior fluently.

You and the teacher can use the STOIC acronym to create a menu of strategies. To see an example of this menu and a host of strategies a teacher might consider, you may return to Chapter 9, where the Revise process is explained more in-depth.

The coach should be able to both clearly explain and model those strategies that a teacher selects. If the strategy comes from a coach's own list, this should be a given. If a teacher is choosing a strategy that is new to both the coach and teacher, the coach may have to take a day or two to research the strategy further and practice using it prior to modeling in the classroom. Coaches do not need to be an expert in all strategies—they simply need to be fully transparent with teachers when a practice is new to them.

DAY 7: PLAN FOR IMPLEMENTATION

Meet with the teacher to more formally plan out how strategies will be used during the model lesson. If there are tools that go along with any of the chosen strategies, introduce these and thoroughly explain how each is used. For example, the CHAMPS Transition Worksheet (Reproducible 2.3 in *CHAMPS*) and CHAMPS Activity Worksheet (Reproducible 3.2, *CHAMPS*) can help clarify student expectations. Using the No Assignment Form (Reproducible 3.6, *CHAMPS*) may address challenges that stem from student failure to complete work.

At this point, a lesson plan may be created with an accompanying checklist of teacher practice for the classroom teacher to use when observing the coach's model lesson. Introduce specific data tools that will be used to monitor implementation, with the idea that the teacher will use this tool to collect data on the coach during the lesson. Ensure the teacher knows how to use the selected tools to maximize effectiveness. Discuss how you will model in the classroom any strategies identified. Regardless of the strategy, it is important to model so the teacher can observe the impact of selected strategies in real time.

DAY 8: MODEL IN THE CLASSROOM

Ideally, the coach should model in the most challenging class as identified by baseline data. If the teacher desires, and if time allows, the coach can model in additional classes. Regardless of other strategies, both instructional and behavioral, that have been chosen, the coach should begin the lesson by teaching the students expectations for behavior. This is a perfect opportunity for the coach to model use of the CHAMPS acronym and how to clearly communicate behavioral expectations. For Participation, consider using an additional acronym, SLANT:

- **S**it up straight.
- **L**ean forward.
- **A**ctivate your thinking.
- **N**ote key ideas.
- **T**rack the talker.

The coach should ensure that students see them as a true partner with their classroom teacher. Build the teacher up at the beginning of the model lesson.

> *You have a wonderful math teacher. In fact, [mention another nonattributive and authentic detail about the teacher]. I'm here today because we are working together on some new strategies to help all of you succeed in this classroom.*

SLANT SPECIFICS

SLANT, which comes from Edwin S. Ellis's book *SLANT: A Starter Strategy for Class Participation* (1991), is now used in thousands of classrooms across the country. Occasionally, you will see variations on the acronym. For instance, I used to teach middle school students that the A stood for "Act like you're listening," and I enticed them into compliance by providing the rationale that it might one day fool their parents. (Seventh graders love the opportunity to potentially "fool" anyone.)

When we were researching what tools might be useful when collecting data for effective classroom management , each of us, as coaches, worked with two randomly selected teachers. We couldn't move on to coach the next teacher in the study until one or both of our teachers were hitting the Basic 5 Behavior Benchmarks consistently in Levels 1 and 2.

One of the first teachers with whom I worked was a sixth-grade math teacher. She was an exceptional math teacher, but, unfortunately, the class period (also randomly selected) was the last period of the day. Even the most well-behaved sixth-grade student will often struggle during the last period of the day in a content area that intimidates many. For all our coaching, we could *not* increase on-task behavior. Kids weren't misbehaving—they simply had grown apathetic that late in the day.

After everything we had tried, we finally landed on a simple solution. Teach the students to SLANT, and prompt that behavior when the extrinsic data collector, a graduate student, came in to assess. The teacher taught SLANT and the class agreed on a signal she would use to prompt them to engage in these behaviors when being assessed. She even used my old rationale—let's "fool" the data collector.

Immediately, on-task behavior increased. But the joke was on the students. As much as they thought they were "fooling" the data collector, engaging in SLANT prompted them to pay more attention—possibly even against their will. Not only did on-task behavior improve, but student achievement increased.

She, an already exceptional teacher, used a simple approach—another tool to add to her kit—to improve behavior and impact student achievement. As a reminder, the goal is never to simply improve student compliance; it's to increase motivated behavior to impact student achievement.

Strategies should be embedded into the context of academic instruction. For example, a strategy such as applying the ratio of positive interactions should be done within the academic lesson. While engaging in teacher-guided instruction in a math classroom, be willing to teach the math lesson for that day while also modeling a high ratio of positive to corrective interactions.

Coaches should be modeling how to hit all of the Basic 5 Behavior Benchmarks in addition to other academic and behavioral strategies that may have been selected during the Revise step. For instance, the coach should offer plenty of opportunities to respond when engaged in teacher-guided instruction.

The model lesson should be explicit enough that the teacher will be able to mirror those strategies and methods when teaching the classes that will be observed by the coach.

At the end of the model lesson or lessons, meet with the teacher to share and discuss their observations. Consider making modifications to the strategies, if needed, and help the teacher prepare to put the plans into action.

DAY 9: MONITOR IMPLEMENTATION

Monitoring implementation will most likely not be limited to a single day and will be determined by the teacher's need for support and time available to the coach to engage in additional observations. This, however, is a good place to begin—with the expectation that the coach will be collecting data on the teacher to see if any growth is being made toward that teacher's identified goal.

This can happen using the same monitoring forms used by the teacher on the coach during the model lessons, it can be any single one or all of the Basic 5 Behavior Benchmarks, or it can be any combination of those. Any data collected now should have been agreed upon when planning for implementation.

As another option, and again largely dependent on both time available and need, plan to collect postdata on the same classes that were observed when gathering the predata. Follow the same steps as outlined in Days 2–4 for collecting and summarizing the data in preparation for the post-conference.

DAY 10: POST-CONFERENCE WITH TEACHER

Meet with the teacher and engage once more in partnership feedback (Figure 11.1). Analyze data to look for any evident successes. Plan for an intermittent celebration with the teacher and possibly the class related to growth. Use the CHAMPS Status Check (Reproducible 10.7, p. 285) to reflect on implementation. Based on both the data and reflection, which may include one or more of the behavior benchmarks, use this information to help the teacher decide on next steps. Specifically, does the teacher want to:

- Keep the goal and strategy or strategies currently in place?
- Revise the goal and/or choose a new strategy?
- Create a completely new goal and/or choose a new strategy to put into practice?

By engaging in the collaborative exploration of data once more, coaches and teacher re-enter the Review step of the Improvement Cycle. This sample schedule, with the cycle embedded, is a way for data to be used in the classroom to make meaningful decisions and improvements in student behavior and success. Through this process, whether it takes 2, 10, or 20 days, teachers will understand that effective classroom management is an ongoing cycle of reflection and growth with coaches and teachers working collaboratively to help both them and their students maximize their potential.

THE ROLE OF THE EVALUATOR

Although the nonevaluative coach will be largely responsible for orchestrating the steps and activities outlined in the sample schedule above, the evaluator is still very much involved in the Improvement Cycle. The role of the evaluator within the cycle was introduced in Chapter 10. Here, we look at how this involvement might fit into this sample schedule of the process.

Core to Tier 1 implementation of your classroom management model, the administrator should still be engaging in walk-throughs with the whole staff. For those receiving more targeted Tier 2 support, an administrator may engage in walk-throughs more frequently. We recommend that all teachers in Tier 2 should have an administrative walk-through at least once a week. These walk-throughs can be a mix of both 5-minute snapshots of practice and potentially longer data pulls based on the administrator's schedule. In this sample schedule, at least two administrative walk-throughs should be planned.

The administrator should also meet one-on-one with any teachers receiving Tier 2 support. They, too, will engage in collaborative exploration of data with briefer but no less powerful coaching conversations. The administrator needs to continue to communicate support for the more formal coaching cycles in play and provide the gentle pressure that only an evaluator can. Biweekly one-on-one conversations are recommended; at least once during this sample schedule the administrator should sit down with the teacher to discuss and assess progress.

These one-on-one conversations paired with regular weekly walk-throughs will assist the administrator when eventually making the decision to exit the teacher into Tier 1 or refer the teacher to Tier 3. While there is no gold standard, every 2–3 cycles the administrator should meet with the teacher directly to discuss data collected through teacher self-evaluation or walk-throughs to determine next steps. If the teacher is improving, sustaining a teacher within the Improvement Cycle or placing the teacher into Tier 1 is reasonable. However, if there remains a considerable skill deficit or if deficits appear to be a matter of will, it may be time for the staff member to move into Tier 3, where a formal plan of assistance begins.

Back to Tier 1

If an administrator is having to engage in predetermined walk-throughs because more than 20% of staff need Tier 2 support, this is a clear indication that what's provided for staff in Tier 1 may need to be revisited. We recommend going back to the first section of this book to analyze what may be missing from the system.

Coaches will likely not be able to support more than 20% of staff in formal coaching cycles either effectively or efficiently. The best Tier 2 is always an effective Tier 1. This is true for both our students and staff.

Moving a teacher into Tier 3, deciding a teacher needs to be put on a formal plan of assistance, and engaging in these intensive conversations takes moxie. But moxie alone won't get you very far. Honesty and respect must accompany the will to have these crucial conversations. For a staff member who hasn't met success, be it skill or will or a combination of the two, those in a position of authority must be committed to leading thoughtful, response-driven conversations. You must avoid the *fundamental attribution error*, where you believe that staff are engaging in contrary behavior because that's simply their makeup or they enjoy being the rebel on the campus. If our classroom management model is predicated on the belief that behavior can be changed, we must apply this principle across all stakeholders—students, staff, and even ourselves.

Wrapping It Up

CHAPTER 11 SUMMARY

The Improvement Cycle in action will look different in different environments, and work with individual teachers will rarely follow a predetermined schedule. The 10-day example provided here is just one example of how the coaching process might play out.

What to Know

- Plan to adapt the coaching process to meet the needs of each teacher you coach.
- Partnership Feedback helps teachers reach their own conclusions about what the data show.
- The teacher should be the decision maker in choosing the goals and strategies to adopt.
- The evaluator should be involved in the Improvement Cycle.

What to Do

Include in the process all four steps in the Improvement Cycle:

- Review: Collect and review data
- Prioritize: Meet with the teacher to review the data, set PEERS goals, and prioritize those goals.
- Revise: With the teacher, identify strategies to adopt.
- Implement: Help the teacher learn and launch the new strategies.

Use partnership feedback in your meetings with teachers—let teachers come to their own conclusions.

Coaching as Intensive Support for Teachers

This section is designed to provide an intentional plan of assistance for teachers who have not made significant improvement in Tier 2. The decision to place a teacher in Tier 3 should be an administrative decision based on both objective data and anecdotal notes from the evaluator.

In Tier 3, we are moving to a remarkably higher level of accountability. At this stage, the evaluator becomes much more involved in the process. The nonevaluative coach will still play a role, similar to what was provided in Tier 2, but increased pressure comes from the administrator and, hopefully, the teacher's desire to change.

There is one chapter in this section.

> Chapter 12, "A Formal Plan of Assistance" discusses what the research says (or doesn't say) about the use and creation of formal plans of improvement, lays out the role both the administrator and nonevaluative coach(es) will play in the process, and leads you through construction of an intentional plan of assistance.

A plan of assistance represents a formal, legal, and procedural case for requiring teachers to change practices and improve in accordance with the details outlined in the plan in order to remain at their job. We recognize that the components of teacher performance improvement plans vary widely across states and districts. Use the resources that follow accordingly, being mindful of your own state and district requirements and directives.

CHAPTER 12

A Formal Plan of Assistance

People are remarkably open to criticism when they believe it's intended to help them. —Adam Grant

Disclaimer: This chapter deals with helping teachers through a formal plan of assistance. This process is a suggested format. A formal plan of assistance should always be approved through district human resources or district legal representatives. Please ensure that you are following all district guidelines before proceeding with any portion of this process.

In Tier 3, we are moving to a remarkably higher level of accountability. Once a teacher is placed into Tier 3, their career is on the line. We encourage administrators to weigh the information provided in this chapter against their district human resources department to follow district guidelines and local laws.

The effectiveness of this process assumes that everything leading up to this chapter has been intentionally and well thought out. A Tier 1 system of support for all staff shows:

- Drivers of change are actively being used to overcome any barriers or resistance.
- A classroom management vision has been crafted and clearly communicated schoolwide.
- A plan for initial and ongoing implementation has been set in place.
- Data collection is common practice.
- Effective communication skills and Partnership Principles are regularly applied.
- Staff, administration, and coaches are engaged in early course correction and collaboration.

Leadership has been transparent in how teachers may receive Tier 2 support, either as enrichment or to improve skill deficits. Coaches are engaged with staff in the Improvement Cycle. And teachers know that if they are receiving support in Tier 2 due to a skill deficit and cannot or choose not to improve, there is a more intensive plan of support accessed in Tier 3. If Tiers 1 and 2 are in place and effective, and a teacher has progressed to this point, the Tier 3 process may need to be initiated.

The Tier 3 process is an approach to a formal plan of assistance. Teachers who reach this point have shown either inability or unwillingness to improve their teaching practices. The teacher's skill deficits are leading to a low level of student learning or are creating unsafe classroom practices. Employee feedback at this level is so often focused on what *not* to do. This is probably the case in many teacher plans of improvement. One advantage to the process we introduce in this chapter is that, if done correctly, it focuses on discrete and measurable skills for a teacher to improve.

Similar to a behavior management plan for an individual student, a formal plan of assistance should help the administrator figure out what is missing or should be added to practice, instead of just focusing on what a teacher should *not* be doing. A good improvement plan should also address the underlying reasons for student misbehavior in the classroom. For example, a teacher is experiencing high levels of disruption during teacher-guided instruction. Through observation, an administrator sees that the teacher's ratio of positive interactions is flipped, showing that more attention is paid to inappropriate behavior than to appropriate behavior in the classroom. This is identified as the probable cause of student misbehavior. The teacher's plan of assistance should not focus on reducing misbehavior, but rather on improving the teacher's ratio of interactions.

While still embedded in the partnership approach, this level of coaching deploys more top-down feedback, blending both urgency and support. The evaluator is much more involved in the process, engaging in coaching conversations with much higher stakes. The nonevaluative coach will still play a role, similar to what was provided in Tier 2, but the increased pressure comes from the administrator and the teacher's desire to change. The nonevaluative coach is there in a supporting role only.

The authors of *Crucial Accountability* (Patterson et. al., 2013) found that supervisors typically fall into two camps. There are individuals who may create high levels of morale but do very little to hold others accountable, achieving mediocre results at best. And there are those who can solve problems but often in ways that are demeaning and threatening, eventually leading to poor results (p. 10). To find a balance between these two extremes, evaluators must continue to be what we've been referring to as *warm demanders*.

A formal plan of assistance, if done well, should offer *hope*. Without hope, Tier 3 is no longer a level of *support*, but instead a *threat*. A few years ago, I received a call from a Director of Educator Effectiveness with whom I've been working for a while. She had a single question, "How do you know when to let a teacher go?"

She was mildly kidding, but also a little frazzled by trying to figure out how to best help a teacher when things seemed bleak. While there is never a simple answer to a complex problem, we can determine a central theme—data, and lots of it: data used to identify the correct challenge, data used to determine current reality, and data used to show growth. Data is the key to driving all the decisions made in creating, implementing, and maintaining a formal plan of assistance.

And we cannot forget the power of relationships, another central theme throughout Tiers 1 and 2 and integral to the partnership approach. Returning again to an earlier quote:

> ***We have found that the single factor common to every successful change initiative is that relationships improve. If relationships improve, things get better.*** —*Michael Fullan*

Data and relationships—what we provide for students at this level of intervention is also critical to provide for staff. Data should not be subjective. Data must be something that is measurable, and used objectively. The objective nature of data will help develop and maintain trust through a difficult but necessary process. Without data, teacher improvement plans are built around a perceived notion of improvement, making the target ambiguous and difficult to attain. Data-based decisions should surround an increased effort to build meaningful connections for the staff member—with students, with colleagues, and with campus leadership.

We revisit this Director of Educational Effectiveness, and the teacher, at the end of this chapter. We first look at what the research says (or doesn't say) about the effectiveness of formal plans of improvement. Then we lay out the roles each person plays in the process and lead you through an intentional plan of assistance. Specifically, we focus on:

- Research
- Role of the evaluator
- Role of the coach
- Process of accountability
- Plan of assistance
- Exit strategy

RESEARCH

Estimates suggest that between 5% to 15% of teachers in *any given school* are considered underperforming (Kraft & Gilmour, 2017; Tucker, 2001). Remarkably, there exists no universally agreed-upon definition of what underperforming teachers or marginal performances look like. We do know the research literature points to the following characteristics:

- Sporadic and weak instructional approaches that do not match content and learning goals (Smith, 2008)
- Difficulties teaching statewide content standards (Darling-Hammond, 2012)

- Incessant classroom management issues (Jackson, 1997; Lawrence, 2005)
- Inadequate preparation for instruction (Fuhr, 1990)

We urge administrators to consider the Basic 5 Behavior Benchmarks as the agreed-upon criteria for under- or marginal performance in the area of classroom management.

Teachers designated as marginal in any of the areas listed above are often put on a formal plan of remediation, often without any clear system of support in advance, and the areas of remediation can be subjective. To combat this, we've laid out specific directions for administrators to funnel teachers into support prior to Tier 3. Ideally, administrators are conducting walk-throughs in Tier 1, identifying challenges that impact more than 20% of their staff as topics for schoolwide professional development, and placing teachers who need the Improvement Cycle into Tier 2. A formal plan of assistance should be employed only when the data gathered in Tier 2 clearly show an ongoing deficit through skill or will. Evaluators, fully engaged in their supportive role in Tier 2, will have a clear picture of which teachers need this most intensive intervention.

The intent of a plan of assistance should be twofold. First, a plan of assistance "reflects the school system's concern for its teachers' professional development . . . [and] helping each teacher do so is an integral part of an instructional leader's role" (Tucker, 2001, p. 53). Second, a plan of assistance represents a formal, legal, and procedural case for requiring teachers to change practices and improve in accordance with the details outlined in the plan in order to remain at their job. While the components of teacher performance improvement plans vary widely across states and districts, these plans typically specify areas of concern, objectives and goals for improvement, strategies for achieving improvement, support and resources required, and defined timelines for meeting improvement goals (Lawrence, 2005; Zepeda, 2016).

There is no gold standard of a formal plan of assistance by any name. And there doesn't appear to be any kind of scripted format that might be typically used in approaching these conversations. In this chapter, we attempt to provide such a format. The roles of both the evaluator and the nonevaluative coach are both carefully considered in relation to this format. As with everything else in this book, please feel free to tailor the contents in this section to your and your teacher's individual needs. If you rely on a district standard for determining and creating formal plans of improvement for staff, by all means, use the district plan of assistance and look at this resource potentially as an attached plan of action.

Placing a teacher on a formal plan of assistance has significant legal and human resources implications. Before moving into a plan of assistance, the process should be reviewed and approved by your district's human resources department. We encourage you to find a way to apply some of the principles and components included here only if you find it may be helpful in improving the effectiveness of Tier 3 support.

> "*Before moving into a plan of assistance, the process should be reviewed and approved by your district's Human Resources department.*"

ROLE OF THE EVALUATOR

As mentioned earlier, in Tier 3 we are moving to a much higher level of accountability. As the evaluator, you are much more involved in the process. You are now engaging in a more formal process, outlined later, with teachers. And the stakes for teachers to move to action are much higher. As a whole, this chapter is geared mainly toward you, the evaluator. While we provide our recommendations for the role of the nonevaluative coach, you hold sway over how much and what kind of involvement they will have in the plan.

Ultimately the role of the evaluator includes everything to come in this chapter: determining the role of the coach and any other ancillary support, engaging in the process, creating the formal plan of assistance, and determining when and if a teacher exits Tier 3 support. Teachers exit Tier 3 support based on data and adherence to the plan of assistance. Some teachers will exit Tier 3 because they've improved. And some teachers may exit Tier 3 by being let go. That is a decision only the evaluator can make. And the evaluator must make that decision based on their own active collection of data and engagement in both the process and planning.

When a teacher moves into a formal plan of assistance, they will understand that their job may be on the line. At this stage, your role has become more evaluative and directive. You are communicating that the teacher must change their practices, and that change has to occur within a specified timeline. This will inherently break down some of the trust the teacher may have with you as their leader. However, because trust is vital to a coaching role and the process of improvement, it is important that you communicate your confidence in the teacher's ability to make the necessary changes and your willingness to provide the teacher with requisite resources to support these changes. We strongly suggest that any teacher in Tier 3 receive the support of a nonevaluative coach, who is never required to provide data on the teacher's progress or lack thereof. As the administrator, clearly communicate to the teacher that you are investing in them because you believe in them: "We know how successful you can be, but [this issue] is getting in the way of your ability to fully reach your students. Because we believe in you, we are investing additional resources to help you become the teacher we know you can be."

ROLE OF THE COACH

Knowing how and when to use nonevaluative coaches at this point becomes more complex. Coaches can continue to be deployed using the Improvement Cycle, engaged in the same process in which they were in Tier 2. They are lending support, now with a much more stringent set of goals and guidelines handed down by the evaluator.

Evaluators should check district and state guidelines, as well as with any union representatives, about how much information from the plan of assistance can be shared with nonevaluative coaches and how communication flows between evaluators and nonevaluators regarding the teacher's performance. We recommend that nonevaluative coaches be aware of whether they can continue working with a staff member who is on a formal plan of assistance, and, if so, the specific goals for improvement and expectations for sharing data.

We strongly suggest that data collected by a nonevaluative coach still be treated as confidential. However, we are also fully aware that many plans of assistance call for data collection from a variety of sources, often including the nonevaluative coach. In these cases, we urge coaches to collect data and leave the data with the teacher. The teacher can then provide those data directly to their administrator.

To be clear, the inclusion of a coach as part of Tier 3 support should be with *the intent to keep the teacher in the profession and show authentic improvement.* If the intent becomes solely to collect documentation for the removal of the teacher, nonevaluative coaches should be taken out of the process. First, it is a waste of a good resource—why have your coach work with someone for the intent of termination when they could be working with staff who could, and most likely want to, improve? Second, it may become widely known that coaches have the power to provide information that may lead to someone being removed. Coaches should never be used to coach a teacher *out* of the profession. It dilutes the power of a coach to truly connect with staff and help them improve.

PROCESS OF ACCOUNTABILITY

Administrators need a way to approach and navigate conversations involving high-stakes accountability. This is not an easy task, nor one in which all leaders are highly skilled. There are amazing books out there that go into much more detail about these tough but critical conversations. Here we lay out a simplified plan that may be useful in taking all that has been laid out to this point and extending it into a much more complex situation.

At the core of the process of accountability is a conversation. A conversation where the stakes are higher, yes, but still a caring and collaborative conversation. Simply put, an accountability process includes the following steps:

- Identify the challenge.
- Examine your mindset.
- Frame the conversation.
- Prepare for follow-up.

Identify the Challenge

Identifying the primary challenge a teacher is facing in regard to improvement is one of the most critical, and often most complicated, parts of the process. Problems are rarely simple and singular, often arriving in complex bundles. This makes it difficult to know which challenge or set of challenges to address first.

> *Identifying the primary challenge a teacher is facing in regard to improvement is one of the most crucial, and often most complicated, parts of the process.*

Let's look at an example. A new teacher in your middle school is struggling in the classroom. Based on walk-through data, she has low academic engagement and ambiguous and inconsistent expectations for students. This has resulted in a high number of office referrals. Her STOIC Classroom Management Screener shows she has put the classroom management model into place, but the way she is using the model isn't with fidelity and is largely ineffective. During Planned Discussion, as part of the course correction process outlined in Chapter 6, she agreed to work with the campus coach on implementation and improving on-task behavior through the Improvement Cycle. But the teacher is overwhelmed, angry that the administration isn't punishing the students harshly enough when sent to the office, and resentful at having to take her planning time to meet with the coach when there is so much on her plate. After she meets with the coach for a few weeks, the administrative walk-throughs are showing no signs of improvement, and the teacher has self-reported that she isn't meeting with the coach anymore.

Which challenge do you focus on first? There are so many ways to look at this:

- She isn't fully implementing the model.
- She broke a promise to work with the coach.
- She isn't using any of the engagement strategies brought by the coach to increase on-task behavior.
- She's continuing to depend on the administration to solve what is largely a system problem within the classroom.
- Her mindset and actions aren't consistent with the campus vision.

If you choose the wrong challenge to address, the teacher might get stuck in a loop of poor practice that could eventually lead to termination.

In *Crucial Accountability* (Patterson et al., 2013), the first step is to unbundle the problem. "If you can't reduce a violation to a clear sentence before you talk, the issue almost never becomes more understandable and focused as a conversation unfolds" (p. 24). But how do you unbundle the problem? How do you figure out the real challenge when human beings are such emotional and complex creatures?

The answer lies in looking at the real consequences of the teacher's behavior. The teacher in the example promised to work with the coach to improve on-task behavior but didn't apply any of the strategies offered. First, this resulted in a continued lack of academic engagement. This lack of engagement resulted in students misbehaving. Their misbehavior created a series of office referrals, whereby students were removed from the learning environment. But ultimately, all these together, and perhaps most of all the removal of students from the classroom, are increasing the achievement gap. Her actions are resulting in students falling further and further behind. That may be the most egregious violation, and the one most inconsistent with the campus vision. Connecting the teacher's actions to the vision of the school is a good place to start the conversation.

Examine Your Mindset

As the person leading the conversation, the evaluator must predetermine how the climate will be set. The climate of the conversation determines if trust is strengthened and a relationship maintained or lost. It takes only a few seconds to lose ground, and days and weeks to make it up once gone. Thinking about the context of the conversation, from where and when it will be held to the initial sentence that communicates the identified challenge, sets the tone for creating the plan of assistance and will greatly improve the chances that support will be effective. The climate is driven by the mindset of the person leading the accountability conversation.

The mindset, or perception, of the evaluator toward staff must be examined in advance. Earlier we mentioned the *fundamental attribution error*, which may lead us to believe that a staff member is simply choosing not to change practice, perhaps because they dislike students or to spite leadership. We encourage you, if at this point you have fully bought into the idea of partnership coaching, to think of any other motivational forces that may be contributing to a teacher's lack of improvement.

In the example given earlier of the teacher who didn't improve in Tier 2, would it make a difference if you knew more about her current placement? That she had started out as a primary teacher but was forced to take a middle school position when she moved? That she was hired only a few days before school started and is able to keep ahead of the prescribed curriculum by only a day or two? Knowing the answers to those questions might change your perception of her intent. It certainly did for me. That teacher is not an arbitrary example—she is a teacher I worked with, as a coach, and a rather ineffective coach at that. I'm ashamed to admit this now, but at the time, I believed she wasn't fully committed to changing practice because she didn't prioritize the learning of students. That simply wasn't it. Looking back, I was in violation of so many Partnership Principles—and I hadn't learned to apply what we know about students to what we need to understand about staff.

We are taught that students who engage in chronic misbehaviors do so for a variety of reasons. Often, these reasons boil down to things like lack of ability, lack of awareness, and attention-seeking behaviors, to name a few. If our classroom management model is predicated on the belief that behavior can be changed, we must apply this principle across all stakeholders—students, staff, and even ourselves. Had I realized much earlier that her bundle of challenges really boiled down to an inability to break down a very complicated curriculum for a class level in which she had no experience, I would've spent much less time on things like teaching engagement strategies and much more time on breaking down the curriculum into manageable lessons tied to those strategies.

To create the right climate for a conversation about accountability, you have to presume positive intent—that each person is doing the best they can with what they have. This may turn out not to be true, but at the beginning of Tier 3, this assumption will serve both the administrator and the teacher well.

Frame the Conversation

I have a friend in San Antonio who is an expert in behavior management. People often ask her opinion on their own practice, and she always begins the conversation the same way: "Do you want me to be nice? Or do you want me to be honest? Because sometimes they're the same thing and sometimes they aren't." I've been the recipient of this conversation starter, and there are times, with a laugh included, that I realize I just want her to be nice—I'm seeking validation, not constructive feedback.

Being nice keeps the peace, but it certainly doesn't lead to change when change is needed. To hold the conversation, you must be willing to be honest and apply the lens of the evaluator—the person who can hire and fire staff. We established earlier that this willingness to be upfront and honest, alone, does not necessarily result in a process that will lead to change. There are plenty of leaders out there who put the "brutal" in "brutal honesty." This level of honesty and accountability is much more nuanced. Skillful communication is key, and if you're lacking in this skillset, revisiting the ideas in Chapter 5 and possibly extending your knowledge through other resources may be useful.

NICE VERSUS KIND

There is often a difference between *nice* and *kind*. Sometimes being kind by being honest about teacher practice so they can truly improve does not feel nice. But having the difficult conversation to help the teacher keep their job is the kind thing to do, even though it has the potential power to hurt their feelings in the short run.

Adam Grant (2021) boils down the principles of constructive feedback in three simple steps. One, before you give it, ask if they want to receive it. Now, as an administrator, you don't always have that luxury. And once a teacher is found in need of more intensive support, they must be put in a position to hear feedback. His second step—be clear that you believe in their potential and care about their success—can be demonstrated by using language consistent with the Partnership Principles and presuming positive intent. It's the third step—be as candid as possible in what you say and as thoughtful as possible in how you say it—that should be your mantra when engaging in this level of conversation.

Make the challenge known. This conversation takes a departure from Planned Discussion (see p. 191 in Chapter 6) in that when introducing the primary challenge, you more accurately describe the gap between practice, promise, or intent and the daily reality revealed through data. In this step, you state what is expected compared with what has been observed. Keep the statement clear, simple, and free of judgment.

The following example of how to communicate a judgment-free statement provides two different sentences, each based on what challenge is primary. Once you identify the challenge, this format gives you a simple construct to bring it to light. The language is clear and concise, and doesn't lay blame. It's honesty without the brutality. This strategy can be used from the first accountability conversation to the last, from a conversation involving skill to a conversation involving will or insubordination.

> *Tammy, you agreed to strive for a rate of 80% on-task behavior in your classroom. The current rate is 65%.*
>
> *Clay, you agreed to work with a coach through the Improvement Cycle each week. You've met with the coach only once in the last 4 weeks.*

Whatever the distance between expectation and observation, one or two sentences can communicate it clearly without placing you in an initially adversarial position. By communicating the primary challenge in simple language, you open the floor for honest and productive dialogue during the next stage of the process—designing the plan of assistance.

Motivate the practitioner. Once the primary challenged has been communicated, the staff member must be motivated to solve it.

> ***People begin to become successful the minute they decide to be.*** —Harvey Mackay

We desire for others to be successful, but that desire is meaningless until they desire it for themselves. You can argue that when it comes to the role of evaluator over subordinate, you can motivate someone to change in a variety of ways; some we cautioned against earlier, such as threats (losing a job and income) or humiliation (being ostracized from staff). Certainly, that may result in change, but whether that change in practice will lead to authentic improvement and an increased impact on student learning is questionable at best.

We can't simply decide someone must change—they must feel an emotionally compelling reason to even consider it, and then believe they have the skills and resources to do it. If you want staff to *want* to change, you must make the change both *attainable* and *powerful.*

An important concept in moving people toward a goal has to do with the relationship between a person's motivation to engage in a task and that person's proficiency at that task (Sprick, J., 2021, p. 298). In *CHAMPS*, we call this the Expectancy times Value theory of motivation. This theory explains a person's motivation on any given task as a function of the formula:

Expectancy x Value = Motivation

Let's unpack this theory within the idea of making changes both attainable and powerful.

Attainable. The first variable, *Expectancy*, is how successful a person thinks they will be at a given task. In his seminal work, *Flow: The Psychology of Optimal Experience* (2008), Mihaly Csíkszentmihályi introduces the state of *flow*—an optimal state of intrinsic motivation. Also known as being "in the zone," these moments are characterized by a feeling of great engagement, fulfillment, and skill. To achieve this state of flow, a balance must be struck between the challenge of the task and the skill of the practitioner. For staff, this means that any action steps outlined must be just challenging enough to be only slightly above their current skill level. If the task is too challenging, staff may be in a state of anxiety when asked to change practice. However, if a task is so easy as to be below their skill level, apathy results. It's entirely possible that a teacher has been unsuccessful in the Improvement Cycle of Tier 2 because in reality or perception, they viewed the changes in practice as too difficult to master.

Adopting any new practice is not necessarily easy; in the context of Tier 3 coaching, the term *attainable* is better used. If a teacher is currently operating at a 1:9 ratio of positive to corrective interactions, achieving a 3:1 ratio may not necessarily be attainable. Setting incremental goals may be more realistic (e.g., first striving for a 1:5 ratio, then a 1:1 ratio, then a 2:1 ratio, and then finally a 3:1 ratio). Attainable goals also make it more likely that the teacher experiences success, and these incremental successes can be a powerful motivator for continued improvement.

Think of a time you learned to master a new game app on your phone. The first few levels are always instructive and rewarding, with lots of accolades for learning the first few skills needed (very analogous to the initial implementation of the classroom management model). Each level requires a bit more skill than the last, and the completion of each level includes a bit more celebration. This happens over and over until you're hooked and suddenly an expert at controlling salty warblers or squashing sweets. My guess is if you've engaged in this behavior, at some point you reached a level where your skill set was outstripped by the level of difficulty. Some of you may have engaged in self-talk to convince yourself to play on, mastering it out of repetition or simply sheer luck. And others may have been stuck on a certain level so long you closed the app altogether, either deleting it from your screen or revisiting it only occasionally with no expectation of success. For any one of us to adopt anything new and sustain it for any length of time, we must see the goal as attainable.

Powerful. The second variable, *Value*, is how much a person wants something. Value relates to the question, "Does this person want to do the task, and why?" (Schunk et al., 2012). Value can be intrinsic—a sense of accomplishment for a job well done—or extrinsic—how much a staff member wants to stay in their current position. Many times, it is a combination of both.

To increase the value for staff, a change in practice must then be seen be powerful. Staff must experience some level of intrinsic or extrinsic benefit to what they are being asked to do. This comes from ensuring that any strategy included in a plan of assistance must have a powerful impact on both student learning and teacher growth. For instance, if a staff member is directed to engage in a 3:1 ratio of positive interactions, they may initially view it as trivial. But, if the application of the 3:1 ratio of positive interactions unmistakably improves student behavior, increases student engagement, and dramatically reduces the amount of time the teacher spends correcting misbehavior, resulting in an increase in instructional minutes, it becomes very powerful indeed.

To motivate staff during this conversation, you must assure them that any tasks within the plan of assistance will be broken down to be easily mastered. And you must ensure that what you ask them to do will have a powerful impact on addressing the primary challenge for improvement.

Move to action. From this point forward, the weight of both administrator and teacher input on the path toward improvement is based on factors specific to their relationship, the presumed intent on the part of the evaluator toward the staff member, the amount and quality of support that has been offered prior to Tier 3, and state and district mandates related to teacher improvement.

As you look ahead in this chapter, we include a section that lays out a recommended plan of assistance. Again, we urge you to tailor this plan to your specific needs as well as any formal directives by which you must abide when making decisions regarding teacher retention.

Looking at whatever documentation you will now use to draft a plan of action, determine what things must be filled out in advance of the conversation. Identify which items or actions are rigid and nonnegotiable and which might be more flexible, including those items that might be drafted with the teacher during discussion.

Regardless of how the plan of assistance might be framed and what might be included, when covering these items continue to demonstrate unconditional positive regard. Even though you are meeting with the teacher due to ongoing challenges in their classroom, it is important to demonstrate that you are a safe, caring, and reliable evaluator and that the teacher is accepted and part of the school community regardless of where they are in terms of practice. Take the time to communicate these sentiments to the teacher directly.

At this time, clearly communicate the role of the nonevaluative coach and include this in the written plan of assistance, as well as any additional support (inservices or trainings, additional data collections by outside observers, etc.). The teacher is certainly not isolated from other means of support presented in the first two tiers. They will still be engaged in the ongoing professional development provided in Tier 1, and also have access to a coach through the more formal Improvement Cycle in Tier 2. Coaching as an evaluator is always a complex task, and it becomes even more difficult at this level. You may become even more reliant on the nonevaluator to provide room for growth and support, while you continue to be the main point of pressure.

Remember, the clearer you are during this part of the process and the more specific tasks and timelines become, the greater the likelihood that all parties will follow through. We can't communicate and plan with a language of ambiguity. Holding people accountable to do something, sometime, somehow is analogous to trying to nail jello to the wall (Patterson et. al., p. 198).

Prepare for Follow-Up

The administrator will engage in regular walk-throughs, both scheduled and unannounced. Just as in Tier 2, these should be a mix of both 5-minute snapshots of practice and longer data pulls based on the administrator's schedule. Time should be scheduled for the teacher to engage in regular check-ins with the evaluator. These check-ins can take different forms. Some may be a more formal collaborative exploration of data. Some may check for compliance with the plan of assistance. Some may even involve tweaking the primary challenge. And, at some point, a follow-up will include the decision to retain or dismiss the teacher.

Each follow-up conversation should conclude with a list of tasks, each paired with who is responsible and the deadline by which the task will be completed. Record who does what by when and then follow up to ensure these tasks were accomplished. Identifying whether or when these tasks were accomplished can be the first item on the agenda of each follow-up conversation. Alternatively, you can check at the passing of each deadline on whether the task has been completed.

In addition to follow-up conversations between the administrator and the teacher, you should establish early on whether the support team as a whole will meet on a regular basis. In addition to the administrator, members of the support team might include the nonevaluative coach assigned to work with the teacher and someone at the district level, such as a human resources officer or union representative. If the support team has meetings already scheduled, it may be prudent to add an agenda item to discuss all teachers being served in Tier 3. Be mindful of the confidentiality agreement still intact between staff and nonevaluative coaches and agree in advance what information can and cannot be shared among team members. Decide if and when the teacher should be part of these meetings or if the evaluator continues to serve as the conduit between the staff member and what's discussed by the team.

It cannot be said enough: The purpose of this stage of Tier 3 is to provide a more intensive, intentional level of support for the teacher that results in authentic improvement. The goal should be for the teacher to be *retained*, not *removed*.

PLAN OF ASSISTANCE

We believe that behavior, or teacher practice, can be changed through system design. The STOIC Framework is a reminder of the variables over which we have control that can be used to design these systems of support in any tier. In Tier 3, we created the plan of assistance to include a section for each variable to decrease the likelihood that gaps will exist within the plan itself. Reproducible 12.1 shows an example of a completed plan of assistance. General names and job titles have been used in place of any actual names for this example. Reproducible 12.2 is a template that includes bulleted highlights from

Reproducible 12.1 *Plan of Assistance (p. 1 of 3)*

Plan of Assistance (p. 1 of 3)

FOR: *Jane Doe*

STRUCTURE

PURPOSE OF THE PLAN OF ASSISTANCE

The purpose of this plan is to give you the opportunity to correct deficiencies in current practice as outlined below. It is developed as a cooperative effort between you, your principal, the nonevaluative coach (Learning Coach), the director of educator effectiveness, and the director of human resources. This plan is intended to meet the school district and state performance and conduct standards for elementary teachers. You are directed to follow this Plan of Assistance. Adherence to this Plan of Assistance will be monitored and assessed on a regular basis as outlined on the included schedule.

DATA-DRIVEN STATEMENT OF DEFICIENCY

The current classroom environment fails to support individual and collaborative learning, encourage positive social interaction, provide active engagement in learning, and encourage self-motivation.

On Friday, October 22, 2021, and again on Friday, December 10, 2021, administration met with you to discuss data of concern. Over the past 2 school years, there has been a deficiency in classroom management as reflected in your summative evaluation for 2021–2022 and in evidence from this year's classroom observations by administration. These include both a "Not effective" rating for Standard 3.1 and "No" for Standard 3.3 for 2021.

- *3.1: Develops learning experiences that engage and support students as self-directed learners who internalize classroom routines, expectations, and procedures*
  - *Classroom procedures are unclear or not evident. Students are regularly punished to drive behavior. There are more corrective interactions with students than positives. The daily schedule isn't posted on a regular basis. Students appear unaware of the classroom rules and procedures. Students are hostile to one another.*
- *3.3: Uses positive classroom management strategies, including the resources of time, space, and attention, effectively.*
  - *Uses punishment rather than positive interventions to get student attention. Students are regularly punished to drive behavior. There are more corrective interactions with students than positives.*
- *After three administrative walk-throughs and two collections of the Basic 5 Benchmarks by administration, data collected show, on average:*
  - *7 positive interactions:20 corrective interactions / 20 minute period*
  - *Daily schedule posted 20% = 1 day / week*
  - *Students in compliance with expectations at a rate of 56%*
  - *Disrespectful statements from student to student 5–10 / 20-minute period*
  - *65% of students have been given at least one disciplinary referral in a 9-week period*
  - *40% of students have been given at least two disciplinary referrals in a 9-week period*

PREVIOUS SUPPORT PROVIDED

- *CHAMPS training provided by Learning Coach during 2021 pre-school inservice dates*
- *CHAMPS classroom management district training provided by Title I department on September 25, 2021*
- *Ongoing weekly professional development provided by Learning Coach during 2020–2021 and 2021–2022 school years*
- *Member of the CHAMPS schoolwide adoption committee*
- *Kagan classroom engagement training provided on October 10, 2021*
- *At the end of 2020–2021 school year, you asked for reassignment from fifth grade to first grade. You stated this would be a better placement for you. Request was granted.*

SUPPORT TEAM

- *Principal X: Will do weekly 5 minute walk-throughs to check for progress toward each of the Basic 5 Benchmarks. Biweekly check-ins will be done to monitor adherence to the Plan of Assistance.*
- *Learning Coach (nonevaluative): Will continue to engage in the Improvement Cycle and meet with you weekly. Coach will not be turning over any data to any other member of the support team. You will share the CHAMPS Status Check in biweekly check-ins with Principal X.*
- *Director of Educator Effectiveness: Has been informed of the start date of the Plan of Assistance and the projected date when the retention decision will be made.*
- *Director of Human Resources: Has been informed of the start date of the Plan of Assistance and the projected date when the retention decision will be made.*
- *Principal X, Director of Educator Effectiveness, and Director of Human Resources will meet to determine progress at the midpoint of the plan and again at the projected end date to determine next steps.*

 REPRODUCIBLE 12.1

Reproducible 12.1 (cont.) *Plan of Assistance (p. 2 of 3)*

Plan of Assistance (p. 2 of 3)

TEACH

PERFORMANCE REQUIREMENTS

Expected Performance	Demonstrated By
Create a performance improvement portfolio that you will use to document training and improvement. *Update the portfolio as you work through the plan so that your progress may be checked and feedback given.*	*Completed performance improvement portfolio, in which you document training and keep artifacts required below:* • *Organizational style that clearly demonstrates what you have accomplished.* • *Sections for each major performance requirement. Include sections for each of the five STOIC variables from the* CHAMPS *book and other sections that are appropriate for your objectives.* • *Include photos, documents, training certificates, and notes that you take.* • *Both principal and learning coach should have access to this portfolio.*
Meet weekly with Learning Coach. In this meeting, you and the coach will discuss what's working in the classroom, current challenges and concerns, next steps, and support that you need.	*Each week, you and the coach will complete the CHAMPS Status Check (Reproducible 10.7).* *The CHAMPS Status Check will be put into your performance portfolio and shared with the principal during biweekly check-ins.*
The goals that you set and track must focus on improving your ability to create an environment that supports individual and collaborative learning, encourages positive social interactions, provides active engagement in learning, and encourages self-motivation.	*As referenced below in the section labeled "Observe," you must meet four of the Basic 5 Benchmarks* consistently between Level 1 and 2. Students must:* • *Demonstrate on-task behavior 90%–100% of the time.* • *Have between 10–40+ opportunities to respond in a 10-minute time period of teacher-directed instruction.* • *Be reinforced with a ratio of 3 positives:1 corrective over a 20-minute time period.* • *Meet classroom expectations 90%–100% of the time.* **See attached Basic 5 Behavior Benchmarks (Reproducible 3.5) and Basic 5 at a Glance (Reproducible 3.6).*
Systematically study and work through the CHAMPS *book provided. Section 2 of* CHAMPS *(3rd ed.) is divided into chapters based on each variable of the STOIC Framework.* *Each variable is covered in one or more chapters, and each chapter has tasks to complete.* *You will need to study the book and thoughtfully complete and keep a record of what you have done for each task in the book.*	*Keep track of what you do for each chapter's tasks in your portfolio:* • *Each reproducible form is available as a download and can be printed or completed electronically. If printed electronically, please print out and include in the appropriate section of your portfolio.* • *This plan for improvement gives you 9 weeks. There are 7 chapters in* CHAMPS *Section II.* • *Utilize the Learning Coach to assist you in working through tasks as needed.*

REPRODUCIBLE 12.1

Reproducible 12.1 (cont.) *Plan of Assistance (p. 3 of 3)*

Plan of Assistance (p. 3 of 3)

Each week, you will either observe a lesson with the Learning Coach or be observed. *In each lesson, you will be keeping track of a specific skill that you and the Learning Coach have determined earlier.* *Use the data from the observation for your weekly meeting with the Learning Coach.* *You will video record your lesson biweekly to engage in self-assessment. Self-assessment data should be shared with the Learning Coach.*	*Document each observation tracking sheet in your portfolio:* • *Observations will not indicate that goals have been met, but should show progress toward meeting those goals.* • *Videos of lessons and self-assessment should also indicate progress towards meeting your goals.* • *Over the 9-week period, you will submit two 10-minute clips of videos to the portfolio and include a description of the video's context—lesson objective, your reflection of the lesson, and goals for improvement.*

OBSERVE

SCHEDULE OF OBSERVATIONS

Principal X will conduct both random and preannounced drop-in observations throughout the 9-week plan period. The purpose of the drop-in observations is to monitor your performance efforts, the results of your collaboration efforts with the Learning Coach, and your accuracy and attention to detail on the requirements listed above.

TYPES OF DATA COLLECTION

- *A full document of the formal evaluation criteria and process can be downloaded at the district website.*
- *Individual tracking sheets for each of the Basic 5 Benchmarks (see Reproducibles 10.1–10.6) are attached to this plan*
- *Self-assessment data can be collected using any of the tools from Chapter 10 in* CHAMPS
- *Video self-assessment on a biweekly basis, with two video clips to be shared with the evaluator*

INTERACT

HOW DATA WILL BE SHARED

Principal X will complete weekly 5-minute walk-throughs to check for progress toward each of the Basic 5 Benchmarks.

The Learning Coach will not be turning over any data to any other member of the support team.

You will share the CHAMPS Status Check (Reproducible 10.7) in biweekly check-ins with Principal X.

WHEN FOLLOW-UPS WILL OCCUR

Biweekly check-ins between the teacher and principal will be done in the teacher's classroom. These biweekly check-ins are to monitor adherence to the Plan of Assistance and discuss progress.

The Learning Coach will continue to engage in the Improvement Cycle and meet with you at least weekly.

CORRECT

INDICATORS OF UNSATISFACTORY LEVELS OF IMPROVEMENT

If goals are not met and distinct progress has not been measured based on teacher evaluation criteria or the Basic 5 Benchmarks, your performance will be determined to be unsatisfactory.

This Plan of Assistance will be assessed over the next 9 weeks, from January 3, 2022, to March 7, 2022. At the end of these 9 weeks, the principal and teacher will meet again. If progress has been made, but you, the teacher, in collaboration with the Learning Coach, feel that this has not been enough time to work through and document each of the performance tasks, we will discuss extending the time, not to exceed an additional 6 weeks.

CONSEQUENCES OF NONCOMPLIANCE AND/OR LACK OF IMPROVEMENT

This plan serves as notice that you must comply with the expectations outlined. If adherence to the plan is not evident, paired with unsatisfactory improvement as noted above, it will result in your dismissal from employment.

 REPRODUCIBLE 12.1

Reproducible 12.2 *Plan of Assistance : Bulleted Plan (p. 1 of 3)*

Plan of Assistance (p. 1 of 3)
Bulleted Plan

STRUCTURE

PURPOSE OF THE PLAN OF ASSISTANCE

- Identify the purpose of the plan for the teacher.
- List each person involved in the construction of the plan.
- State the intent of the plan to meet specific district and state standards.
- Give a directive to follow the plan.
- State that adherence will be monitored.

DATA-DRIVEN STATEMENT OF DEFICIENCY

- State the primary challenges.
- Include dates when the administration and teacher met prior to this plan.
- Make connections to district or statewide teacher evaluation systems.
- Include anecdotal observations.
- Include data that support any anecdotal observations.
- Keep the language as neutral as possible.

PREVIOUS SUPPORT PROVIDED

List previous professional developments and other support, including coaching, that has been used prior to this plan to address the primary challenges.

SUPPORT TEAM

- List all support team members who will be working with the teacher.
- Identify the role that each team member will play in providing support.

 REPRODUCIBLE 12.2

Reproducible 12.2 (cont.) *Plan of Assistance: Bulleted Plan (p. 2 of 3)*

Plan of Assistance: Bulleted Plan (p. 2 of 3)

TEACH

PERFORMANCE REQUIREMENTS

Expected Performance	Demonstrated By

Create a table of expected performances and how each performance will be demonstrated.

REPRODUCIBLE 12.2

Reproducible 12.2 (cont.) *Plan of Assistance: Bulleted Plan (p. 3 of 3)*

Plan of Assistance: Bulleted Plan (p. 3 of 3)

OBSERVE

SCHEDULE OF OBSERVATIONS

Schedule evaluative observations.

TYPES OF DATA COLLECTION

- List the types of data tools that will be used.
- Attach data tools to the plan.
- Provide instructions for video self-assessment.

INTERACT

HOW DATA WILL BE SHARED

- Identify who collects data.
- Describe data that will pass, if at all, between support team members.
- Identify data that the teacher will share in the portfolio and during check-ins.

WHEN FOLLOW-UPS WILL OCCUR

- Set the schedule for when observations and meetings will occur.
- Set the schedule for when the evaluator will meet with the teacher.
- Set the schedule for when the learning coach will meet with the teacher.

CORRECT

INDICATORS OF UNSATISFACTORY LEVELS OF IMPROVEMENT

Provide a summary or reference to measurements or standards that will be used to determine if progress is satisfactory or unsatisfactory.

CONSEQUENCES OF NONCOMPLIANCE AND/OR LACK OF IMPROVEMENT

State the result of noncompliance or lack of progress.

 REPRODUCIBLE 12.2

the explanations in this section. Consider downloading Reproducible 12.1, then filling it out as you look at the reference template in Reproducible 12.2.

Let's break down each section of the plan.

Structure

Purpose of the plan of assistance. The purpose of this plan is to give the teacher an opportunity to correct deficiencies in current practice. It may or may not be developed as a cooperative effort. If it is a cooperative effort, list each person involved in the construction of the plan. Clarify that the intent of the plan is to help the teacher meet specific district and state performance standards. Also include a general directive to follow the plan and an explicit statement that adherence will be monitored.

> *"The purpose of this plan is to give the teacher an opportunity to correct deficiencies in current practice."*

Data-driven statement of deficiency. This section should begin with the primary challenges. It should include dates on which the administration and teacher met to look at any concerning data and actions on the part of the teacher. If using a district or statewide evaluation system, connections to those criteria should be made. List district policy violations and any statewide violations of effective teaching standards. As much as possible, stick to statements of fact. If anecdotal evidence pulled from walk-through observations are used, there may be some statements of perception. These perception statements should be backed up by the inclusion of objective data. When you engage the teacher in the process, language included in documentation should be as neutral as possible. Let the data speak.

Previous support provided. List any previous training, staff development, and targeted coaching support from Tier 2 that the teacher has received. Also include any requests by the teacher for additional support that have been granted (additional professional development, reassignment to another grade level, pairing with a mentor teacher, etc.).

Support team. List all support team members who will be working with the teacher and the role each will play. Support team members could include both the administrator and the nonevaluative coach. Beyond those two members, the support team may also include someone at the district level, a human resources officer, a union representative, and any other staff who will be working directly with the teacher. While these are just a few people who *may* be part of the process, the actual team will be determined by the resources you have specific to your building and district. The roles each team member play should be spelled out clearly, including when observations and coaching meetings will be scheduled.

Teach

Performance requirements. This table includes both a list of performances the teacher is expected to do and how each performance will be demonstrated. Performance requirements may include procedural requirements, changes in teacher practice, and measurable benchmarks. Be as specific as possible with your descriptors in each column. We strongly encourage that this be a collaborative process; include the teacher in brainstorming *what* they can do and *how* they can do it. To motivate the teacher, choose goals and practices that are both *attainable* and *powerful.* If performance standards are knowingly above the teacher's skill level and/or won't result in a powerful payoff relatively soon, it will be difficult to support the teacher for retention. If retention and improvement for the teacher are not the true intent of the plan of assistance, other documentation and an alternative process for coaching should be followed. Here are some examples of what might be included in the performance requirements:

Procedural requirements:

- Create a performance portfolio to track progress.
- Meet weekly with nonevaluative coach.
- Video record lessons for self-reflection.
- Study and work through the *CHAMPS* book.
- Post CHAMPS expectations for each learning activity in the classroom.

Changes in teacher practice:

- Increase the number of minutes used for instruction in the classroom.
- Increase positive interactions with students.
- Teach and reinforce expectations for each learning activity in the classroom.

Measurable benchmarks:

- 10–40+ opportunities to respond for every 10 minutes of teacher-guided instruction
- 3:1 Ratio of Interactions (positive to corrective)
- 90%–100% of students in alignment with posted expectations

An effective set of performance requirements should focus on teacher practices that are most likely to impact student outcomes. This is best accomplished by understanding the context of the teacher's classroom and identifying the teacher behaviors that may be contributing to behavior management issues. For example, if a teacher is experiencing high levels of off-task behavior during independent work, it is important to first identify the underlying cause of off-task behavior. Are expectations for student behavior during independent work unclear? Do students require more structure and support for this period? Does the teacher pay more attention to negative behavior than positive behavior? For any of these causes, performance requirements would not focus on reducing student misbehavior, but instead on the teacher behaviors that are most likely to reduce off-task behavior, such as clarifying and re-teaching expectations, restructuring procedures for independent work periods, and improving the teacher's ratio of interactions.

Observe

Schedule of observations. This section should include a plan for the schedule of observations by the evaluator. Keep in mind the intent of observations is to monitor progress and adherence. But these observations also serve as a visual reminder to the teacher to put plans into practice. This is important work. As the evaluator, you should be the biggest cheerleader. After all, the plan of assistance is for the purpose of retention. The support therein, including regular progress monitoring, is to communicate that the support team is truly on the teacher's side and cares about their growth.

Types of data collection. In this section, record the types of data that will be collected. The benchmarks are often listed in the performance requirements and largely translate to this section. The teacher should have full transparency on what data will be used to determine progress.

We recommend including a list of any tools that will be used to collect data and/or attaching these tools to the plan itself.

We strongly recommend that this section include the nonnegotiable directive that teachers engage in video self-assessment. Teachers can have full control over the videos and device used to record (smartphone, tablet, laptop, etc.), but if video has not been used to this point, it should absolutely be included now. In Jim Knight's *Focus on Teaching* (2014), he provides a complete look at how video can be used to help teachers grow in every tier. Using video makes the unseen *seen*. It is a powerful tool that changes practice.

> *Using video during coaching is like the gas in a car. Video helps you move forward, and it's easier and quicker. If you don't have gas in the car, you can't move forward at all. Video is like stepping on the accelerator.*
>
> — Amanda Trimble, Instructional Coach

Interact

How data will be shared and discussed. This includes a summary of who will collect data and who will review data. Some of this information will be transferred from the table of Performance Requirements.

When follow-ups will occur. A schedule should be set for observations and meetings. You can set dates on the calendar or indicate daily, weekly, monthly, etc., intervals. Keep in mind the sometimes already overwhelming calendars of staff, support personnel, and administration. When possible, work to set this schedule collaboratively with the support team and include the teacher.

Correct

Indicators of unsatisfactory levels of improvement. Include here a summary or reference to measurements that will be used to determine progress as they relate to unsatisfactory progress. In this section, also note timelines and deadlines for making satisfactory progress.

Consequences for noncompliance and/or lack of improvement. If adherence to the plan is not evident, paired with unsatisfactory improvement as noted above, state the result in regard to teacher retention.

How can we work collaboratively as partners on something that will have an unmistakable impact on the life of the teacher and the lives of the many students they reach? I live the collaborative exploration of data (Figure 7.4 on p. 227). You, as the evaluator, are now in a place many find uncomfortable—holding people accountable and using top-down feedback (Figure 7.3 on p. 227) to begin drafting a meaningful plan of assistance.

An evaluator shouldn't shy away from top-down feedback. It's a necessary part of the job when it comes to making decisions about teacher retention. But just as the Correct variable from the STOIC Framework cannot be used alone with students, neither can this process or plan, which often hinges on top-down feedback. At its core, this entire chapter would be considered the Correct part of the framework for staff. Building some form of collaboration tied to a proactive plan in which the teacher is involved is critical in upholding the partnership coaching model as best we can in Tier 3. Look to the Partnership Principles in Chapter 5—give the teacher the opportunity to continue reflection and to have a voice and choice over their formal plan of assistance.

TROUBLESHOOTING LACK OF PROGRESS

Sometimes you may find a teacher who has complied with the requirements of their assistance plan. If they have followed all the procedural requirements (observations and meetings with their coach) and have successfully worked to integrate the required teacher skills, but have not shown improvement in student behavior, then it is time to try something new. A teacher in this scenario has proven that they are willing to work with the plan of assistance to enhance their teaching practices. When a teacher is willing and has made changes, but student outcomes have not improved, the process should begin again. The planning team will need to determine new teacher improvement skills. Simply put, the solution did not match the challenge. Just like within a multi-tiered system for students, if the plan did not meet the challenge, it is time to try a new intervention.

With these teachers, the team should acknowledge and celebrate the improvements the teacher has made. Make sure that the teacher knows how much their hard work is appreciated and that you see their willingness to grow.

Observations should be done again in order to correctly identify the challenge within the process of accountability. As a reminder, challenges are often wrapped in complex bundles and must be fully unpacked. Look at the teacher's changes in both behavior and implementation and the corresponding impact on student outcomes.

EXIT STRATEGY

At the end of the timeline attached to the plan of assistance, a decision must be made based on objective documentation as well as the overall assessment from the evaluator.

If the teacher is making distinct progress or has reached their goals, they may exit into either Tier 2 support, continuing to work with the nonevaluative coach through the Improvement Cycle, or into Tier 1, with support occurring on an as-needed basis.

If goals are not met, distinct progress has not been demonstrated, and there has not been evident adherence to the plan, the teacher's performance will be determined to be unsatisfactory. If the plan states that this results in dismissal, the administrator then follows through. Dismissal should occur only if all other levels of support are in place and have clearly been utilized. Remember that this is a last-ditch answer, with high stakes, that requires you to continually reflect on whether your systems are adequate to truly support your staff.

The purpose of this chapter, however dismal the thought of possible termination may be, was not to bring down those of you reading this book. On the contrary, this is to show we can create an intentional plan of assistance, even when things look grim and overwhelming. We can walk confidently knowing we have implemented strong systems of support for all staff, and we do not give up. We do not give up on students, and we certainly don't give up on staff. Plans of assistance should always be about hope. With enough support and with the right resources, even in the direst of circumstances, we can see teachers grow exponentially.

STORY OF HOPE

Let's revisit our Director of Educator Effectiveness and the teacher at the heart of this chapter. The following contains excerpts from our interview about a first-grade teacher in need of support interspersed with my background knowledge of working with the district. What follows is a story about hope—a story about growth when growth seemed impossible.

I had been working with this district for a number of years—working with staff on *CHAMPS* and *Discipline in the Secondary Classroom*, working with coaches, and working with administrators and the district team on schoolwide reform efforts. At one point, I heard from the Director of Educational Effectiveness about a situation with a veteran teacher. This teacher had taught a long time in the district. According to the director, she was one of those teachers who everyone knows is not doing well in the classroom, but no one knows how to fix it.

This was a tough teacher to work with. She was a veteran teacher who had average evaluations. According to the director, "That's the worst possible place you can be because she has a lot of protections in place, as a teacher should. But, you know, she's never gotten any feedback so that's kind of what brought us to this place."

The director went on to describe the situation: "This was a teacher who had about twelve students in her class because so many kids had dropped her class. The only kids left in her class were kids whose parents weren't advocating or didn't know any better, and that was quite common for her. When we first started coaching, we pointed out some major issues, like classroom procedures that were unclear or inconsistent, kids not knowing what to do or when to do it, and student behavior that was really out of control. But mainly, it was also just about a lack of positive classroom experiences. We received a lot of feedback from parents about their kids just not feeling any connection to this teacher, and so that was also a big one. Parents weren't requesting her. They didn't want their kids around her."

So, the director called me. I consider the director a friend as well as a colleague and, as the true professional she is, she never shared names, including those of the campus, the principal, and the teacher. But she was asking a legitimate question—when should the decision be made to dismiss a teacher based on the gravity of the current situation? Please keep in mind, I am not giving any kind of legal advice. This director was well aware of any standards of protocol from the human resources department. She wasn't asking for my recommendation of whether to dismiss the teacher—she was asking in general what might you look for and do in a situation where a teacher is struggling so dramatically?

In my work with this district, I knew they had a lot of information and a lot of people deployed as support personnel, including an incredible group of coaches to support classroom management. But, as is typical with the knowing-doing gap, there wasn't a concrete, consistent plan of action from campus to campus for how teachers implemented the CHAMPS classroom management model. When there's no action plan, as pointed out in the Change Model (Figure 1.2 on p. 28), you'll suffer a lot of false starts, with some people implementing, and others, perhaps those most in need, choosing not to implement at all. This is not to indict anyone in a position of leadership. They, too, have a lot on their plate and multiple competing initiatives vying for their attention. It's to point out that when pieces of the Change Model are missing, it's often difficult to hold someone to account.

I asked the director to describe what support had already been provided to the teacher. The director told me that the principal had arranged for the teacher to participate in classroom management training and recruited her as a member of the CHAMPS schoolwide adoption committee. According to the director, "The principal thought that maybe if the teacher is attending and participating in these meetings, she'll just, you know, pick up on the fact that her teaching and behavior management practices are out of line with what the rest of the school is working on. They were sending her all kinds of indirect messaging about the need to change."

At this point, my recommendation was to really look at whether the support the teacher had received was adequate. If she hadn't been given any directive to improve and no target to hit, based on a lifetime career of average evaluations, it didn't seem fair to lay all the blame for poor classroom management at the feet of the teacher.

The director and I reflected on when we would recommend that teachers give up on students. Of course, the obvious answer is never. Districts and campuses are supposed to have clear systems of support for all students. We create a strong system of policies and procedures on the campus and in our classrooms to ensure that 80%–95% of students at any given time can successfully navigate our systems to engage in instruction. We have an intentional plan of support in Tier 2 for those students who needs aren't met by the current system we have in Tier 1. And, finally, we provide more intensive support, sometimes even with outside agencies, for students who are most in need.

We know that's an effective system for students; shouldn't we have the same system in place for staff? Recognizing that the onus for student behavior isn't solely on their shoulders, we should feel the same for staff. If it's a matter of poor systems that omit categories from the Change Model, if targets use ambiguous language, if there's no clear path to improvement or provision of support personnel, if evaluators haven't committed to measuring clear benchmarks for every teacher, some of the fault for a teacher's ongoing poor performance lies with leadership.

The director agreed. Some campuses had all those things in place, but some campuses were still developing those pieces. Everyone was doing the best they could with what they had. It was time to add to their toolbox. Knowing the somewhat amorphous support that had already been provided, the team recognized that the teacher needed clear, objective targets and a distinct path toward improvement. Thus began the building of a more intentional and comprehensive plan.

The director described this process: "We actually started with another plan of assistance. Our HR director had given us a few plans. But, again, knowing how difficult this would be, what we recognized is that often plans are very hard to monitor. One of the goals that we started out with was to have the teacher develop a classroom management plan. Well, she can give you that in 20 seconds and then how do you monitor that? How do you ever give feedback with it? It was also really important to us that she have some incremental learning along the way so that she's seeing success. So, eventually, we came back to the Basic 5 Benchmarks and the Improvement Cycle, and that's really what we used. We said these things are so important that they must happen, but we didn't want to overwhelm her."

The Basic 5 Observation Tool is used to show baseline performance and growth. Highly skilled teachers who have excellent classroom management and high levels of student achievement have typically mastered all five benchmarks. A teacher who is need of intensive support may show significant deficits in all benchmarks. The goal may not be to hit all five through this formal process, but you must have a starting point. You need something powerful and attainable to motivate the practitioner, especially a teacher who may be defensive and overwhelmed.

The director continues, "As a starting point, we went looking at what she really needed to work on and going back to research and what Tricia had taught us. The relationship and the ratio of interactions, we decided, was the most important. In other words, if good teacher-student relationships don't exist, you can't build anything else off of it. How do you get more engagement? How do you get more opportunities to respond? All of those things were predicated on the relationships that we're building, and that's where we started with her."

Once you identify a starting point, you must begin with data collection. This is to help the evaluator, the nonevaluative coach, and the teacher get a clear picture of current reality, which is the first step in any coaching cycle. This is also to ensure that all those collecting data are in sync, calibrating and discussing any points of contention and what to look for to accurately assess each benchmark. With this teacher, the principal did a baseline observation and recorded seven positives to 21 correctives in a 20-minute lesson. This ratio was a far cry from the 3:1 positive to corrective ratio we were striving for.

Once data have been collected and the plan of assistance has been created, it's time to bring in a nonevaluative coach as part of the process. The director describes this introduction: "The teacher already had clear expectations. These are the targets you must hit, here's what needs to be done, and so that part was already discussed. Then we brought the coach in. We made sure the coach was not part of the evaluation process. But they were involved, after we set the benchmarks, in the coaching piece and in the professional development piece. When we introduced the coach to the teacher, the conversation went something like this: 'We want you to be successful. There is no place, ever, that we would want a teacher to fail. We are always looking in observations for what you are doing well, what's happening, and how we can help you grow.' The principal was monitoring the teacher's performance efforts and their collaboration efforts with a coach. That was nonnegotiable. She had to have these sessions with the coach, make sure she had the time to do so, and I think that also protected the coach. It's not that the coach is coming in, doing a creeper visit where she's just sliding in and watching what you do. Those expectations were set up in advance and this is how many coaching sessions you'll have. But what happened within the coaching session was absolutely confidential."

Setting up a system of dialogue in advance also helps move progress forward. Dialogue can and must happen, but it shouldn't ever be a foregone conclusion that it will. If things are seen as being done to them and not with and for them, the process will inevitably stall. The stakes are too high for that to happen. We must involve the teacher in the process of improvement.

Every time the coach and the teacher met, they completed a collaborative assessment log (similar to Reproducible 10.7, the CHAMPS Status Check) and that was put in the portfolio. The log laid out the dialogue between a teacher and a coach. What's working? What needs work? What are your next steps? What support can we provide? Those "must-dos" created a way to have conversations. The teacher was also responsible for her own learning, so there were specific chapters that she had to read and specific things that she needed to have in her portfolio. This new learning naturally guided coaching conversations, and these conversations were aimed at building the teacher's skill set, not just her compliance factor.

Based on these conversations and the data collected, adjustments can and should be made along the way. Just like you would for students, as the primary challenge becomes clearer, you adjust both your approach and the target, if needed. This is why administrative check-ins are critical.

The director describes one of these check-ins: "She could not hit a 3:1 ratio of interactions to save her life. She nearly lost her job because she could not pay attention to kids doing the right thing. She was constantly scanning for threats, and those kids were a threat every second of every day to her. We had a meeting with her, and she was extremely overwhelmed and really, really frustrated. So we allowed her to deselect one of the other benchmarks. I think this was another thing that made it work—there was give and empathy. But then we made it clear that she had to focus on the remaining benchmarks. I think that was the turning point for her where she knew this was serious business and she wasn't going to be let off the hook."

Once the teacher was fully invested and continued to receive new learning with coaching support and regular administrative check-ins, true growth began. This isn't to say there weren't obstacles along the way. During the interview, the director shared that, just as we see with students, sometimes behavior gets worse before it improves. There was a huge amount of resistance to begin with. But the plan of assistance created a consistent and clear means of support. And the team was tireless in their efforts.

According to the director, "I do know, for the coach, it was a really hard role to play, just because the teacher was so resistant initially. As we walked through it, it got easier and easier, but there was a big hill to go over. You have to give teachers data that they trust and that they know is coming, and, in time, show that they can make a difference. She trusted in the tool, and then we gave her feedback on her improvement. Once she started to see that feedback increasingly got better, what we naturally do, as humans, is want to get better and better."

The director recounts this change process: "I get emotional talking about her because this changed her life. It changed her relationship with her husband. And it changed her relationship with the adults in the building. She was constantly scanning for threats in her life, but the last time we met with her, she found joy, and it was just such a transformation.

"You just never know what people can do until you set a goal and a target and you help them achieve it. Had she not made improvements, we would've released her. We didn't release her from those expectations, and that's where the magic started to happen. Just like a resistant kid, asking, 'Are you going to believe in me enough that you're going to stick with me? Will you still love me enough as a teacher? Do you still believe in me that I can improve?' That's the other thing when I think of this teacher is, just, riding it out with her. We will stick with you. We are still going to hold you to those high expectations. Because you're worth it."

CONCLUSION

Tier 3 support isn't intended to invoke fear in the hearts of staff. It should be seen as a lifeline for those teachers who need support the most. A lack of skills doesn't have to mean the end of the line. Truly effective districts and campuses have thoughtfully implemented plans of assistance to increase teacher retention, teacher improvement, and student achievement. By providing tailored, one-on-one support and empowering teachers to increase skills, support teams deliver hope, just as we ask teachers to deliver hope to students.

As of the writing of this book, we are living in unprecedented times, with a mass exodus of teachers from the workforce. We must create strong systems of support within Tiers 1 and 2. And we must be ready to implement a constructive plan of assistance when warranted. Our purpose must be positive and intentional—we want our teachers to thrive so that students can do the same.

Wrapping It Up

CHAPTER 12 SUMMARY

The Tier 3 process is an approach to a formal plan of assistance. Teachers who reach this point have shown either inability or unwillingness to improve their teaching practices. A formal plan of assistance should always be approved through your district human resources or district legal representatives.

What to Know

- The Research
  - No universally agreed-upon definition of what marginal performance or underperforming teachers look like exists.
  - Very little research has been conducted on the effectiveness of performance improvement plans in meaningfully impacting and improving student achievement, nor on the components of performance improvement plans that are most important and effective in changing teacher practice.
  - There is no gold standard of a formal plan of assistance by any name.
- Role of the Evaluator
  - The evaluator becomes much more involved in the process at the Tier 3 level.
  - Administrative decisions are based on active data collection and engagement in both the process and planning.

- Role of the Coach
  - The coach continues in a role of support but should not be seen as an arm of the evaluator.
  - The inclusion of a coach as part of Tier 3 support should be with *the intent to keep the teacher in the profession and show authentic improvement*.

- Process of Accountability
  At the core of the process of accountability is a conversation, including:
  - The challenge—where the primary challenge is identified.
  - The mindset—or perception—of the evaluator toward the staff member should be examined in advance.
  - The actual conversation, where the evaluator helps the teacher confront the reality of current classroom management practices, works to motivate the teacher, and determine the move to action.
  - The follow-up—where the administrator determines a schedule of regular walk-throughs and check-ins as part of the plan of assistance.

- Plan of Assistance

  Using the STOIC Framework to design an intentional plan of assistance will make it less likely that gaps will exist in a formal plan of assistance.

- Exit Strategy

  The evaluator must make the decision on what constitutes improvement that would place them in a less intensive tier of support and what would lead to a dismissal from contract.

What to Do

- Be clear on the research surrounding current plans of improvement.
- Check to see if there are certain district- and state-level criteria that must be included in a teacher's formal plan of assistance.
- Identify the role the evaluator will play in the process and plan of assistance.
- Identify the role the nonevaluative coach or coaches will play in the process and plan of assistance.
- Practice and engage in accountability conversations.
- Use the STOIC Framework along with district- and state-level mandated components to create a comprehensive plan of assistance.
- Determine what would place a teacher in a less intensive tier of support and what would lead to a dismissal from contract.

REFERENCES

Abramowitz, A. J., O'Leary, S. G., & Futtersak, M. W. (1988). The relative impact of long and short reprimands on children's off-task behavior in the classroom. *Behavior Therapy, 29*(2), 243–247.

Acker, M. M., & O'Leary, S. G. (1988). Effects of consistent and inconsistent feedback on inappropriate child behavior. *Behavior Therapy, 19*(4), 619–624.

Aguilar, E. (2020). *Coaching for equity: Conversations that change practice.* John Wiley & Sons.

Alberto, P., & Troutman, A. C. (2012). *Applied behavior analysis for teachers.* Pearson.

Amato-Zech, N. A., Hoff, K. E., & Doepke, K. J. (2006). Increasing on-task behavior in the classroom: Extension of self-monitoring strategies. *Psychology in the Schools, 43*(2), 211–221.

Archer, A. L., and Hughes, C. A. (2010). *Explicit instruction.* Guilford.

Baer, G. (1998). School discipline in the United States: Prevention, correction, and long-term social development. *School Psychology Review, 27*, 14–32.

Barbetta, P., Norona, K., & Bicard, D. (2005). Classroom behavior management: A dozen common mistakes and what to do instead. *Preventing School Failure, 49*, 11–19.

Beaman, R., & Wheldall, K. (2000). Teachers' use of approval and disapproval in the classroom. *Educational Psychology, 20*, 431–446.

Berends, M., Bodilly, S. J., & Kirby, S. N. (2002). *Facing the challenges of whole-school reform: New American schools after a decade.* Rand Corporation.

Block, P. (2013). *Stewardship: Choosing service over self-interest.* Berrett-Koehler Publishers.

Borich, G. (2004). *Effective teaching methods* (5th ed.). Pearson/Merrill Prentice Hall.

Brafman, O., & Brafman, R. (2009). *Sway: The irresistible pull of irrational behavior.* Doubleday.

Brophy, J. (1981). Teacher praise: A functional analysis. *Review of Educational Research, 51*, 5–32.

Brophy, J. (1986). Classroom management techniques. *Education and Urban Society, 18*(2), 182–194. https://doi.org/10.1177/0013124586018002005

Brophy, J. E., & Good, T. L. (1986). Teacher behavior and student achievement. In M. C. Whitrock (Ed.), *Handbook of research on teaching* (3rd ed., pp. 328–375). Macmillan.

Caldarella, P., Larsen, R. A., Williams, L., Downs, K. R., Wills, H. P., & Wehby, J. H. (2020). Effects of teachers' praise-to-reprimand ratios on elementary students' on-task behaviour. *Educational Psychology, 1–17.* https://doi.org/10.1080/01443410.2020.1711872

Cameron, J., & Pierce, W. (1994). Reinforcement, reward, and intrinsic motivation: A meta-analysis. *Review of Educational Research, 64*, 363–423.

Chesley, G. M., & Jordan, J. (2012). What's missing from teacher prep. *Educational Leadership, 69*(8), 41–45.

Christenson, S., Reschly, A., Appleton, J., Berman-Young, S., Spanjers, D., & Varro, P. (2008). Best practices in fostering student engagement. In A. Thomas & J. Grimes (Eds.). *Best practices in school psychology V* (pp. 1099–1119). National Association of School Psychologists.

Colvin, G., Kame'enui, E., & Sugai, G. (1993). Reconceptualizing behavior management and schoolwide discipline in general education. *Education and Treatment of Children, 16*, 361–381.

Colvin, G., Sugai, G., Good, R. H., III, & Lee, Y. (1997). Using active supervision and precorrection to improve transition behaviors in an elementary school. *School Psychology Quarterly, 12*, 344–361.

Cook, C. R., Grady, E. A., Long, A. C., Renshaw, T., Codding, R. S., Fiat, A., & Larson, M. (2017). Evaluating the impact of increasing general education teachers' ratio of positive-to-negative interactions on students' classroom behavior. *Journal of Positive Behavior Interventions, 19*(2), 67–77.

Council for Exceptional Children (1987). *Academy for effective instruction: Working with mildly handicapped students.* Author.

Covey, S. (1989). *The seven habits of highly effective people.* Simon and Schuster.

Crone, D., & Horner, R. (2003). *Building positive behavior support systems in schools: Functional Behavioral Assessment.* Guilford Press.

Csikszentmihalyi, M. (1994). *The evolving self: A psychology for the third millennium.* Harper Collins.

Csikszentmihalyi, M. (2008). *Flow: The psychology of optimal experience.* Harper Perennial Modern Classics.

Curwin, R. L., Mendler, A. N., & Mendler, B. D. (2018). *Discipline with dignity for challenging youth* (4th ed.). ASCD.

Darch, C., & Kame'enui, E. (2004). *Instructional classroom management: A proactive approach to behavior management.* Pearson/Prentice Hall.

Darling-Hammond, L. (2012). *Creating a comprehensive system for evaluating and supporting effective teaching.* Stanford Center for Opportunity Policy in Education.

Darling-Hammond, L., Wise, A. E., & Klein, S. P. (2019). *A license to teach: Building a profession for 21st-century schools.* Routledge.

De Pry, R. L., & Sugai, G. (2002). The effect of active supervision and pre-correction on minor behavioral incidents in a sixth grade general education classroom. *Journal of Behavioral Education, 11*, 255–264.

Downs, K. R., Caldarella, P., Larsen, R. A., Charlton, C. T., Wills, H. P., Kamps, D. M., & Wehby, J. H. (2019). Teacher praise and reprimands: The differential response of students at risk of emotional and behavioral disorders. *Journal of Positive Behavior Interventions, 21*(3), 135–147.

Ducharme, J. M., & Shecter, C. (2011). Bridging the gap between clinical and classroom intervention: Keystone approaches for students with challenging behavior. *School Psychology Review, 40*(2), 257–274.

Eisler, R. (2000). *Tomorrow's children.* Westview Press.

Ellis, E. (1991). *SLANT: A starter strategy for class participation.* Edge Enterprises.

Emmer, E. T., Evertson, C. M., & Anderson, L. M. (1980). Effective classroom management at the beginning of the school year. *The Elementary School Journal, 80*, 219–231.

Evans, G., & Lowell, B. (1979). Design modification in an open-plan school. *Journal of Educational Psychology, 71*, 41–49.

Evertson, C. M., & Anderson, L. M. (1979). Beginning school. *Educational Horizons, 57*, 164–168.

Evertson, C., Emmer, E., & Worsham, M. (2003). *Classroom management for elementary teachers* (6th ed.). Allyn & Bacon.

Evertson, C. M., & Harris, A. (1999). Support for learning-centered classrooms: The classroom organization and management program. In H. J. Freiberg (Ed.), *Beyond behaviorism: Changing the classroom management paradigm* (pp. 59–74). Allyn & Bacon.

Ferrara, N. C., Vantrease, J. E., Loh, M. K., Rosenkranz, J. A., & Rosenkranz, J. A. (2020). Protect and harm: Effects of stress on the amygdala. In *Handbook of Behavioral Neuroscience* (Vol. 26, pp. 241–274). Elsevier.

Freeman, J., Simonsen, B., Briere, D. E., & MacSuga-Gage, A. S. (2014). Pre-service teacher training in classroom management: A review of state accreditation policy and teacher preparation programs. *Teacher Education and Special Education, 37*(2), 106–120.

Freire, P. (1970). *Pedagogy of the oppressed.* Continuum.

Fuchs, L. S., Fuchs, D., & Deno, S. L. (1985). Importance of goal ambitiousness and goal mastery to student achievement. *Exceptional Children, 52*, 63–71.

Fuhr, D. (1990). Supervising the marginal teacher. *Here's How, 9*(2), n2.

Fullan, M. (2001). *Leading in a culture of change: Being effective in complex times.* Jossey-Bass.

Gage, N. A., Scott, T., Hirn, R., & MacSuga-Gage, A. S. (2018). The relationship between teachers' implementation of classroom management practices and student behavior in elementary school. *Behavioral Disorders, 43*(2), 302–315.

García, E., & Weiss, E. (2019). The teacher shortage is real, large and growing, and worse than we thought. The First Report in *The Perfect Storm in the Teacher Labor Market Series.* Economic Policy Institute.

Gettinger, M., & Ball, C. (2008). Best practices in increasing academic engaged time. In A. Thomas & J. Grimes (Eds.), *Best practices in school psychology V* (pp. 1043–1058). National Association of School Psychologists.

Goldsmith, M., Lyons, L., & Freas, A. (Eds.) (2000). *Coaching for leadership: How the world's greatest coaches help leaders learn.* Pfeiffer.

Good, T., & Brophy, J. (2000). *Looking in classrooms.* (9th ed.). Allyn & Bacon.

Grant, A. (2021). *Think again—The power of knowing what you don't know.* Viking.

Greenwood, C. R., Hops, H., Delquadri, J., & Guild, J. (1974). Group contingencies for group consequences in classroom management: A further analysis. *Journal of Applied Behavior Analysis, 7,* 413–425.

Greenwood, C. R., Horton, B. T., & Utley, C. A. (2002). Academic engagement: Current perspectives on research and practice. *School Psychology Review, 31,* 328–349.

Greer-Chase, M., Rhodes, W. A., & Kellam, S. G. (2002). Why the prevention of aggressive disruptive behaviors in middle school must begin in elementary school. *The Clearing House, 75*(5), 242–245.

Gresham, F. M. (1998). Social skills training with children. In T. S. Watson & F. M. Gresham (Eds.), *Handbook of child behavior therapy* (pp. 475–497). Plenum.

Guardino, C. A., & Fullerton, E. (2010). Changing behaviors by changing the classroom environment. *Teaching Exceptional Children, 42*(6), 8–13.

Hall, R. V., Lund, D., & Jackson, D. (1968). Effects of teacher attention on study behavior. *Journal of Applied Behavioral Analysis, 1,* 1–12.

Hattie, J. (2012). *Visible learning for teachers: Maximizing impact on learning.* Routledge.

Haydon, T., Macsuga-Gage, A. S., Simonsen, B., & Hawkins, R. (2012). Opportunities to respond: A key component of effective instruction. *Beyond Behavior, 22*(1), 23–31.

Heath, C., & Heath, D. (2010). *Switch: How to change things when change is hard.* Crown Business.

Hudson, P., & Miller, S. P. (2006). *Designing and implementing mathematics instruction for students with diverse learning needs.* Allyn and Bacon.

Ingersoll, R. M., Merrill, E., Stuckey, D., & Collins, G. (2018). *Seven trends: The transformation of the teaching force* (CPRE Research Report# RR 2018-2). Consortium for Policy Research in Education.

Jackson, C. M. (1997). Assisting marginal teachers: A training model. *Principal, 77*(1), 28–29.

Jenson, W. R., Rhode, G., & Williams, N. A. (2020). *The Tough Kid tool box.* Ancora Publishing.

Kame'enui, E. J., & Simmons, D. C. (1990). *Designing instructional strategies: The prevention of academic learning problems.* Macmillan.

Kegan, R., & Lahey, L. (2001). *How the way we talk can change the way we learn.* Jossey-Bass.

Klem, A. M., & Connell, J. P. (2004). Relationships matter: Linking teacher support to student engagement and achievement. *Journal of School Health, 74*, 262–273.

Knight, J. (2012). *High-impact instruction: A framework for great teaching.* Corwin.

Knight, J. (2014). *Focus on teaching.* Corwin.

Knight, J. (2015). *Better conversations.* Corwin.

Knight, J. (2017). *The impact cycle.* Corwin.

Kraft, M. A., & Gilmour, A. F. (2017). Revisiting the widget effect: Teacher evaluation reforms and the distribution of teacher effectiveness. *Educational Researcher, 46*(5), 234–249.

Kretlow, A. G., & Bartholomew, C. C. (2010). Using coaching to improve the fidelity of evidence-based practices: A review of studies. *Teacher Education and Special Education, 33*(4), 279–299.

Lawrence, C. E. (2005). *The marginal teacher: A step-by-step guide to fair procedures for identification and dismissal.* Corwin Press.

Lawrence, S., & Tatum, B. (1997). Teachers in transition: The impact of anti-racist professional development on classroom practice. *The Teachers College Record, 99*(1), 162–178.

Lewis, T., & Sugai, G. (1999). Effective behavior support: A systems approach to proactive schoolwide management. *Focus on Exceptional Children, 31*, 1–24.

Maister, D. H., Green, C. H., & Galford, R. M. (2000). *The trusted advisor.* Touchstone/ Simon & Schuster.

Marshall, M. (2001). *Discipline without stress, punishments or rewards: How teachers and parents promote responsibility and learning.* Piper.

Marzano, R. J. (2003). *Classroom management that works: Research-based strategies for every teacher.* Association for Supervision and Curriculum Development.

Marzano, R. J., & Marzano, J. S. (2003). The key to classroom management. *Educational leadership, 61*(1), 6–13.

Mayer, G. O. (1995). Preventing antisocial behavior in the schools. *Journal of Applied Behavior Analysis, 28*(4), 467–478.

McAllister, L., Stachowiak, J., Baer, D., & Conderman, L. (1969). The application of operant conditioning techniques in a secondary school classroom. *Journal of Applied Behavior Analysis, 2*, 277–285.

McKenzie, K. B., & Scheurich, J. J. (2004). Equity traps: A useful construct for preparing principals to lead schools that are successful with racially diverse students. *Educational Administration Quarterly, 40*(5), 601–632.

Millar, M. (1942). *The weak-eyed bat.* Doubleday, Doran.

Murray, S., Mitchell, J., Gale, T., Edwards, J., & Zyngier, D. (2004). *Student disengagement from primary schooling: A review of research and practice.* Report to the CASS Foundation.

Niebuhr, K. (1999). An empirical study of student relationships and academic achievement. *Education, 9*, 679–681.

Oliver, R. M., Wehby, J. H., & Reschly, D. J. (2011). Teacher classroom management practices: Effects on disruptive or aggressive student behavior. *Campbell Systematic Reviews, 7*(1), 1–55.

O'Neill, R. E., Horner, R. H., Albin, R. W., Sprague, J. R., Storey, K., & Newton, J. S. (1997). *Functional assessment and program development for problem behavior: A practical handbook* (2nd ed.). Brooks/Cole.

Partin, T. C. M., Robertson, R. E., Maggin, D. M., Oliver, R. M., & Wehby, J. H. (2009). Using teacher praise and opportunities to respond to promote appropriate student behavior. *Preventing School Failure: Alternative Education for Children and Youth, 54*(3), 172–178.

Patterson, K., Grenny, J., McMillan, R., Switzler, A., & Maxfield, D. (2013). *Crucial accountability: Tools for resolving violated expectations, broken commitments, and bad behavior* (2nd ed.). McGraw Hill Professional.

Payne, C. M. (2008). *So much reform, so little change: The persistence of failure in urban schools.* Harvard Education Press.

Pedota, P. (2007). Strategies for effective classroom management in the secondary setting. *Clearing House, 80*, 163–166.

Pianta, R., Hamre, B., & Stuhlman, M. (2003). Relationships between teachers and children. In W. M. Reynolds & G. E. Miller (Eds.), *Handbook of child psychology: Vol. 7. Educational psychology* (pp. 199–234). Wiley.

Pink, D. (2011). *Drive: The surprising truth about what motivates us.* Riverhead Books.

Prochaska, J. O., Norcross, J. C., & DiClemente, C. C. (1994). *Changing for good.* Avon.

Rames-LaPointe, J., & Hixson, M. D. (2021). On-Task in a Box as a classwide intervention: Effects on on-task behavior and academic productivity. *Psychology in the Schools, 58*(8), 1655–1668.

Reeves, D. (2006). *The learning leader: How to focus school improvement for better results.* ASCD.

Reinke, W., Lewis-Palmer, T., & Martin, E. (2007). The effect of visual performance feedback on teacher behavior-specific praise. *Behavior Modification, 31*, 247–263.

Reinke, W. M., Stormont, M., Herman, K. C., & Newcomer, L. (2014). Using coaching to support teacher implementation of classroom-based interventions. *Journal of Behavioral Education, 23*(1), 150–167.

Rosenshine, B. (1971). *Teaching behaviours and student achievement.* National Foundation for Educational Research.

Scheuermann, B., & Hall, J. A. (2008). *Positive behavioral supports for the classroom.* Pearson Education.

Schon, D. A. (1983). *The reflective practitioner: How professionals think in action.* Basic Books.

Schuldheisz, J. M., & van der Mars, H. (2001). Active supervision and students' physical activity in middle school physical education. *Journal of Teaching in Physical Education, 21*, 75–90.

Schunk, D. H., Meece, J. R., & Pintrich, P. R. (2012). *Motivation in education: Theory, research, and applications.* Pearson Higher Ed.

Senge, P. (1993). *Fifth discipline.* Doubleday Currency.

Shinn, M. R., Ramsey, E., Walker, H. M., Stieber, S., & O'Neill, R. E. (1987). Antisocial behavior in school settings: Initial differences in an at-risk and normal population. *The Journal of Special Education, 21*, 69–84.

Shores, R., Gunter, P., & Jack, S. (1993). Classroom management strategies: Are they setting events for coercion? *Behavioral Disorders, 18*, 92–102.

Shores, R. E., Jack, S. L., Gunter, P. L., Ellis, D. N., DeBriere, T. J., & Wehby, J. H. (1993). Classroom interactions of children with behavior disorders. *Journal of Emotional and Behavioral Disorders, 1*, 27–39.

Silberman, C. E. (1970). *Crisis in the classroom: The remaking of American education.* Random House.

Simonsen, B., Fairbanks, S., Briesch, A., Myers, D., & Sugai, G. (2008). Evidence-based practices in classroom management: Considerations for research to practice. *Education and Treatment of Children, 31*, 351–380.

Smith, R. E. (2008). *Human resources administration: A school-based perspective* (4th ed.). Routledge.

Solomon, B. G., Klein, S. A., & Politylo, B. C. (2012). The effect of performance feedback on teachers' treatment integrity: A meta-analysis of the single-case literature. *School Psychology Review, 41*, 160–175.

Sprick, J., & Sprick, R. (2018). *School leader's guide to tackling attendance challenges.* ASCD.

Sprick, J., Sprick, R., Edwards, J., & Coughlin, C. (2021). *CHAMPS: A positive and proactive approach to classroom management* (3rd ed.). Ancora Publishing.

Sprick, R. S. (2012). *The teacher's encyclopedia of behavior management: 100+ problems, 500+ plans.* Ancora Publishing.

Sprick, R. S., Booher, M., Isaacs, S., Sprick, J., & Rich, P. (2014). *Foundations: A proactive and positive behavior support system* (3rd ed., Modules A–F). Ancora Publishing.

Sprick, R., Coughlin, C., Garrison, M., & Sprick, J. (2019). *Interventions: Support for individual students with behavior challenges.* Ancora Publishing.

Sprick, R. S., Knight, J., Reinke, W., Skyles, T., & Barnes, L. (2010). *Coaching classroom management* (2nd ed.). Ancora Publishing.

Sprick, R., Sprick, J., Coughlin, C., & Edwards, J. (2021). *Discipline in the secondary classroom* (4th ed.). Jossey Bass.

Sprick, R. S., Sprick, J., Sprick, M., & Coughlin, C. (2020). *Early-stage interventions.* Ancora Publishing.

Stichter, J. P., Lewis, T. J., Whittaker, T. A., Richter, M., Johnson, N. W., & Trussell, R. P. (2009). Assessing teacher use of opportunities to respond and effective classroom management strategies: Comparisons among high-and low-risk elementary schools. *Journal of Positive Behavior Interventions, 11*(2), 68–81.

Stone, D., Patton, B., & Heen., S. (2000). *Difficult conversations: How to discuss what matters most.* Penguin.

Sugai, G., & Lewis, T. (1996). Preferred and promising practices for social skill instruction. *Focus on Exceptional Children, 29*, 1–16.

Sutherland, K., Wehby, J., & Copeland, S. (2000). Effect on varying rates of behavior-specific praise on the on-task behavior of students with EBD. *Journal of Emotional and Behavioral Disorders, 8*, 2–8.

Thomas, D., Becker, W., & Armstrong, M. (1968). Production and elimination of disruptive classroom behavior by systematically varying teacher's behavior. *Journal of Applied Behavior Analysis, 1*, 35–45.

Tucker, P. (2001). Helping struggling teachers. *Educational Leadership, 58*(5), 52–55.

Udvari-Solner, A. (1996). Examining teacher thinking: Constructing a process to designing curricular adaptations. *Remedial and Special Education, 17*, 245–254.

Voltz, D. L., Brazil, N., & Scott, R. (2003). Professional development for culturally responsive instruction: A promising practice for addressing the disproportionate representation of students of color in special education. *Teacher Education and Special Education, 26*(1), 63–73.

Walker, H., Horner, R., Sugai, G., Bullis, M., Sprague, J., et al. (1996). Integrated approaches to preventing antisocial behavior patterns among school-age youth. *Journal of Emotional and Behavioral Disorders, 4*, 193–256.

Walker, H. M., Ramsey, E., & Gresham, F. M. (2004). *Antisocial behavior in school: Evidence-based practices*. Wadsworth Publishing Company.

Weinstein, C. (1977). Modifying student behavior in an open classroom through changes in the physical design. *American Educational Research Journal, 14*, 249–262.

Wolfgang, C. H., & Glickman, C. D. (1986). *Solving discipline problems: Strategies for classroom teachers* (2nd ed.). Allyn & Bacon.

Wood, S. J., Murdock, J. Y., Cronin, M. E., Dawson, N. M., & Kirby, P. C. (1998). Effects of self-monitoring on on-task behaviors of at-risk middle school students. *Journal of Behavioral Education, 8*, 263–279.

Zepeda, S. J. (2016). Principals' perspectives: Professional learning and marginal teachers on formal plans of improvement. *Research in Educational Administration & Leadership, 1*(1), 25–59.

APPENDIX

The Research

In the realm of educational research, effective classroom management is tied to student success with a confidence approaching absolute, the kind of certainty usually reserved for scientific "theories" like evolution and black holes. We know that strong classroom management practices increase student engagement, reduce student misbehavior and disruptions, and improve academic achievement (e.g., Brophy, 1986; Christenson et al., 2008; Gage et al., 2018; Gettinger & Ball, 2008; Marzano & Marzano, 2003; Simonsen et al., 2008).

However, there is the ideal of top-notch training in effective classroom management practices, and then there is the reality. States differ greatly in licensing standards and the extent to which they invest in teaching classroom management (Darling-Hammond et al., 2019; Freeman et al., 2014). In some states, new teachers do not need a single credit of coursework in classroom management or teaching strategies to receive certification. It is entirely possible and not unusual for a beginning teacher to enter the field with little or no training in classroom management.

When teachers do not receive adequate classroom management training and support, they frequently report feel unprepared for the demands of managing student behaviors in their classrooms and ongoing frustration with a perceived lack of support in managing misbehavior (Chelsey & Jordan, 2012). The end result for a sizable number of teachers is burnout. Nearly half of new teachers leave the profession within 5 years, citing discipline problems and lack of administrative support for dealing with discipline issues as the two most common reasons (Ingersoll et al., 2018). Given the growing teacher shortage crisis in America, teacher retention has become a national policy concern (Garcia & Weiss, 2019). It's clear that we need to do a better job of supporting teachers, and focusing more professional development resources on classroom management can have an unmistakable impact on teachers' skill levels, job satisfaction, and retention.

Teachers need behavioral support in the classroom now more than ever. Professional development and other teacher-training methods in classroom management can improve teacher skills, but one-shot training alone may not always lead to the lasting impact school and district leaders hope to accomplish. Pairing professional development with an effective coaching program can be a highly powerful tool in increasing both the rate and quality of implementation. Given that disruptive student behavior cuts into time teachers might spend teaching and students might spend learning, coaches play an important role in improving outcomes for students—and for the teachers we will otherwise lose.

Proactive Classroom Management: The STOIC Framework

Proactive classroom management does not seek perfect behavior from students as an end in itself, but rather seeks to establish an environment conducive to learning—a perfect climate for fostering learning, mutual respect, and appropriate behavior. In *CHAMPS*, *Discipline in the Secondary Classroom*, and this book, effective classroom management strategies are presented within the STOIC framework, an acronym that is directly linked to research studies that document each component's importance in managing student behavior in the classroom. A summary of the research that underpins this framework follows.

- *Structure your classroom for success.* The way the classroom is organized (physical setting, schedule, routines and procedures, quality of instruction, and so on) has a huge impact on student behavior; therefore, effective teachers carefully structure their classrooms in ways that prompt responsible student behavior (Baer, 1998; Evans & Lowell, 1979; Gettinger & Ball, 2008; Good & Brophy, 2000; Guardino & Fullerton, 2010; Scheuermann & Hall, 2008; Udvari-Solner, 1996; Weinstein, 1977). Well-designed physical space prevents a wide array of potential behavioral problems (Evans & Lowell, 1979; Simonsen et al., 2008; Weinstein, 1977). Research suggests the physical arrangement should allow the teacher to visually scan all parts of the room from any other part of the room (Pedota, 2007; Shores et al., 1993) and allow movement that minimizes distractions for students who are working at their seats (Evertson et al., 2003; Jenson et al., 2020).

- *Teach behavioral expectations to students.* Effective teachers overtly teach students how to behave responsibly and respectfully in every classroom situation and during all major transitions (Brophy & Good, 1986; Emmer et al., 1980; Evertson et al., 2003; Lewis & Sugai, 1999). The research supports the effectiveness of teaching rules (Brophy & Good, 1986; Curwin et al., 2018) using positive and negative examples (Gresham, 1998; Kame'enui & Simmons, 1990; Sugai & Lewis, 1996) with a focus on what teachers expect students to do. This ensures that students know the expected behavior and sets the stage for student success (Barbetta et al., 2005; Colvin et al., 1993; Darch & Kame'enui, 2004; Emmer et al., 1980; Greenwood et al., 1974; Lewis & Sugai, 1999; Marshall, 2001; Mayer, 1995; Simonsen et al., 2008; Walker et al., 1996).

- *Observe and supervise.* Effective teachers monitor student behavior by physically circulating whenever possible and visually scanning all parts of the classroom frequently. One of the most effective behavior management strategies a teacher can implement is to circulate throughout the room as much and as unpredictably as possible (Colvin et al., 1997; De Pry & Sugai, 2002; Gettinger & Ball, 2008; Schuldheisz & van der Mars, 2001). In addition, effective teachers use meaningful data to observe student behavior (particularly chronic misbehavior) in objective ways and monitor trends across time (Alberto & Troutman, 2012; Evertson et al., 2003; Scheuermann & Hall, 2008; Shores et al., 1993).

- *Interact positively with students.* Teachers should focus more time, attention, and energy on promoting and acknowledging responsible behavior than on responding to misbehavior (Beaman & Wheldall, 2000; Brophy & Good, 1986; Rosenshine, 1971; Thomas et al., 1968). Increased positive interactions between teachers and students have been shown to decrease misbehavior and lead to increases in on-task behavior (Beaman & Wheldall, 2000; Brophy & Good, 1986; Caldarella et al., 2020; Cook et al., 2017; Thomas et al., 1968; Walker et al., 2004). Research also suggests that students are more likely to behave well and work hard to meet a teacher's expectations when the teacher-student relationship is positive and respectful (Borich, 2004; Brophy, 1981; Cameron & Pierce, 1994; Hall et al., 1968; Klem & Connell, 2004; Marzano, 2003; Niebuhr, 1999; Pianta et al., 2003; Reinke et al., 2007; Sutherland et al., 2000). Students achieve more when teachers have high expectations for them (Brophy & Good, 1986; Fuchs et al., 1985; Hattie, 2012).

- *Correct fluently.* Teachers are encouraged to preplan their responses to misbehavior to increase the likelihood they will respond in a brief, calm, and consistent manner. This practice helps ensure that the flow of instruction is maintained (Brophy & Good, 1986; Lewis & Sugai, 1999). Research has consistently shown that students learn more efficiently when they receive immediate feedback about their behavior (Gettinger & Ball, 2008; Good & Brophy, 2000; Hudson & Miller, 2006; Kame'enui & Simmons, 1990). The research supports correcting misbehavior by providing instruction about the rule and how to follow the rule (Darch & Kame'enui, 2004; Emmer et al., 1980; Evertson et al., 2003) in a direct, brief, and explicit manner (Abramowitz et al., 1988; McAllister et al., 1969). There is a focus on implementing corrective consequences consistently (Acker & O'Leary, 1988; Alberto & Troutman, 2012; Scheuermann & Hall, 2008) and matching consequences to the severity of the problem (Simonsen et al., 2008; Wolfgang & Glickman, 1986). In addition, with chronic and severe misbehavior, the teacher is prompted to consider the function of the misbehavior and build a corresponding plan to help the student learn and exhibit the appropriate behavior (Alberto & Troutman, 2012; Crone & Horner, 2003; O'Neill et al., 1997).

Together, these five variables capture the essential aspects of any classroom management plan. In *CHAMPS* and in this book, the STOIC framework provides guidance for teachers and coaches to develop and refine management plans that are research based and tailored to fit the unique needs of each classroom.

Critical Indicators of Classroom Functioning: The Basic 5 Behavior Benchmarks

In this book, the Basic 5 Behavior Benchmarks are used to assess classroom teachers and determine the level of structured coaching support across all tiers. The Basic 5 gets its name from the five categories of behavior, or benchmarks, that represent indicators of classroom functioning.

- *Opportunities to respond.* An opportunity to respond (OTR) occurs each time a teacher provides an occasion for a student or group of students to respond to an academic question (e.g., "What is the state capital of Texas?"). The rate at which these OTRs occur has a direct effect on classroom management. High rates of OTR during teacher-led instruction have been shown to decrease problem behavior and increase academic achievement, and off-task behaviors tend to occur when students become disengaged from instruction (Haydon et al., 2012, Sutherland & Wehby, 2001). Increasing the rate of opportunities to respond is one of the most powerful strategies for increasing the likelihood that students will be engaged with instruction and demonstrate appropriate and on-task behavior (Partin et al., 2009; Simonsen et al., 2008). Further, when you increase active student engagement, students have less time to misbehave. According to recommendations from research, the optimal rate of OTRs is four to six per minute of instruction on new material with 80% accuracy, and nine to twelve per minute of instruction on drill-and-practice material with 90% accuracy (Council for Exceptional Children, 1987; Stichter et al., 2009). We have included this research recommendation in the Basic 5 Benchmarks, with the goal being to offer approximately 40+ OTRs per 10-minute block of teacher-directed instruction.

- *Ratio of interactions.* Often forgotten among critical classroom variables are teacher-student interactions. Increased positive interactions between teachers and students can have profound effects on student outcomes. Positive interactions are defined as both noncontingent positive interactions and contingent positive praise that draws attention to students' positive behaviors. Research confirms that high rates of positive interactions can simultaneously increase student engagement and decrease inappropriate behavior (Caldarella et al., 2020; Cook et al., 2017; Downs et al., 2019; Sutherland et al., 2000). Achieving a high ratio of positive interactions means making the conscious effort to interact with every student more frequently when the student is behaving appropriately than when they are behaving inappropriately. At a minimum, effective teachers give at least three times more attention to students for growth, effort, and positive behavior, as well as simply showing interest in students, than for inappropriate behaviors or failure to meet expectations (e.g., Caldarella et al., 2020; Cook et al., 2017). As part of the Basic 5 Benchmarks, we have incorporated this research finding into a recommendation for teachers to interact at least three times more often with each student when they are behaving appropriately than when they are misbehaving (that is, at least a 3:1 ratio).

- *Disruptions.* A disruption is any behavior that causes the teacher to pause or stop the flow of instruction in order to respond. Disruptions cost teachers valuable instructional minutes, and these interruptions can add up to serious losses over the course of the school year. Research has shown that students in classrooms with frequent disruptive behavior experience less academic engagement and lower academic outcomes (Shinn et al., 1987). A lack of effective classroom management skills may also worsen the progression of aggressive behavior for children in classrooms with higher levels of disruption (Greer-Chase et al., 2002). A large body of research demonstrates the direct relationship between classroom management and the reduction of disruptive behavior. In a meta-analysis of this research, Oliver et al. (2011) reported that high-quality classroom management has an average effect of 0.80 ($p < 0.05$), or almost a full standard deviation reduction of classroom disruptive behavior. Effective classroom management strategies that have shown to reduce student disruptions include using a physical arrangement that minimizes disruptions (e.g., keeping student desks away from high-traffic areas); establishing, teaching, reviewing, and monitoring behavioral expectations across all classroom activities; increasing active supervision and monitoring of student behavior; maintaining high rates of student engagement; and using a continuum of strategies to effectively and efficiently respond to disruptions (Simonsen et al., 2008; Sprick, J., et al., 2021; Sprick, R., et al., 2021). In an effort to maximize instruction minutes and minimize the effects of disruptive behavior, one of the Basic 5 Benchmarks focuses specifically on reducing the number of disruptions that occur during time allocated for instruction, with a goal of achieving 5 or fewer disruptions per 10-minute instructional block.

- *On-task behavior.* On-task behavior is defined as a student being academically engaged in the current task of the instructional activity. Student attention to the instructional task at hand results in increased learning and is crucial for the development of life-long learning skills (Greenwood, 2002; Murray et al., 2004). Academic engagement mediates the relationship between school instruction and student outcomes, and is a necessary prerequisite for effective performance and achievement in the classroom (Ducharme & Shecter, 2011). The research literature has shown that improving on-task behavior leads to improvements in academic performance in addition to collateral reductions in problem behavior (Amato-Zech et al., 2006; Rames-LaPointe & Hixson, 2021; Wood et al., 1998). The Basic 5 Benchmarks highlight the importance of achieving high rates of on-task behavior by including a goal that 90% of students should be actively on-task during any given activity,

- *Alignment with expectations.* The need for clear expectations is critical to managing any classroom effectively. Clearly defined behavioral expectations lead to a greater likelihood that students will engage and be successful in relation to instructional content. Posting, teaching, and reviewing expectations and providing feedback are associated with decreases in off-task behavior and disruptive behavior and increases in academic engagement, leadership, and conflict resolution (Simonsen et al., 2008). As research is unequivocal about the importance of teaching behavioral expectations, the Basic 5 Benchmarks include a final variable that captures the degree to which students have met the teacher's posted expectations. During any given activity, the goal for this benchmark should be 90% or more of students in alignment with posted expectations.

In this book, we have singled out these five indicators of classroom functioning because they are important to student outcomes, can be observed in the classroom, are malleable, and are supported by a large body of research. Teachers who understand these indicators and are trained and supported in monitoring and manipulating them shape a better experience for themselves and their students.

Impact of Teacher Coaching

Classrooms play a pivotal role in the lives of children. With the growing number of students exhibiting behavior problems at school, teachers are in need of training and support, particularly those who struggle with adding critical classroom management variables to their repertoire.

Research demonstrates the positive impact that high-quality coaching can have on teacher behavior. When provided with observational data and performance feedback from coaches, teachers improve their use of evidence-based practices, including classroom management practices (e.g., Kretlow & Bartholomew, 2010; Reinke et al., 2014; Solomon et al., 2012). Clearly, improving training and support provided to teachers is one of the most powerful interventions for improving student outcomes and classroom functioning as well as for reducing burnout and retaining teachers within the field.

The concepts and strategies provided in the preceding chapters have antecedents in well-documented research, and in particular studies conducted over the past two decades. We know what works; what remains is the work of raising awareness, making classroom management a sincere priority moving forward, and committing to the most practical solutions that deliver positive results.

Some Additional Resources from the SCS Library

by Dr. Randy Sprick and Colleagues

CHAMPS and *Discipline in the Secondary Classroom*

Student misbehavior has always been a leading cause of teacher frustration. *CHAMPS* and *Discipline in the Secondary Classroom (DSC)* empower teachers to improve student behavior and motivation by creating classrooms where all students can thrive. By reducing misbehavior, teachers focus their time and energy on instruction and student success. Teachers will create a positive classroom community where they help students develop social-emotional skills for life.

Educators discover practical strategies to motivate students to engage in responsible behavior, build positive relationships, manage their work, understand acceptable uses of electronic devices in the classroom, and engage with instruction.

For students who struggle in school related to experiences of trauma, poverty, systemic racism, generational difficulties with the school system, or a disability, purely punitive and reactive approaches will not encourage positive behavioral changes. Teachers will learn proactive strategies to structure for success, reduce misbehavior before it happens, focus on positive behavior and student strengths, and use an instructional approach to correct behavioral missteps.

CHAMPS teachers guide students toward a successful school career and increase their chances for success in work and in life.

The research-based CHAMPS model will help teachers create highly successful classroom management plans that will:

- Include high expectations for all students' success
- Build positive relationships with students
- Create consistent, predictable classroom routines
- Teach students how to behave successfully
- Observe and monitor student behavior and data
- Provide frequent positive feedback
- Correct misbehavior in a calm, consistent, and fluent manner

CHAMPS and *DSC* are companion processes to improve student behavior within the classroom. *CHAMPS* is designed for K–8 classrooms and *DSC* is for 9–12 classrooms.

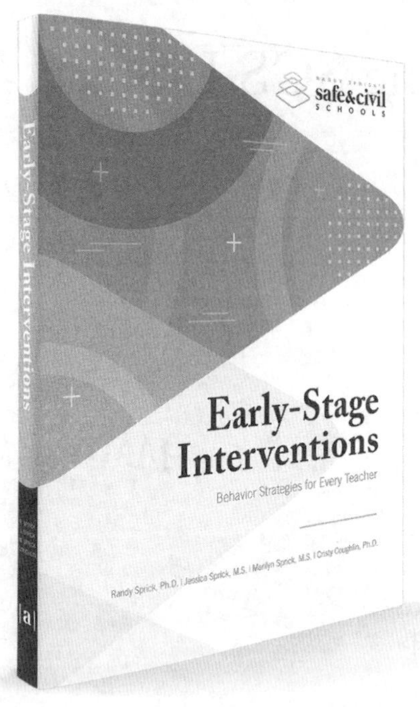

Early-Stage Interventions: Behavior Strategies for Every Teacher

GRADES K–12

Early-Stage Interventions offers a set of simple, teacher-friendly interventions to use as a starting place in addressing an individual student's chronic misbehavior—disrespect, noncompliance, lack of motivation, bullying, aggression, and more. Though every teacher will encounter students who display challenging behavior, many feel unprepared to effectively deal with such behavior in the classroom.

The first section of this book discusses pre-intervention strategies: implementing effective classroom management techniques and assessing and adjusting academic support. With a well-designed classroom management plan, most students will behave appropriately most of the time. However, you are likely to have one or two students who engage in chronic misbehavior.

To help these students, this book presents a continuum of early-stage interventions that are easy for classroom teachers to plan and implement. Start with the simplest one first, and continue on only when the student's behavior doesn't improve. Step-by-step directions guide you through each of these interventions:

- Planned Discussion
- Correction Planning
- Increasing Positive Interactions
- Data Collection and Debriefing
- Goal Setting
- Building a Supportive Relationship
- Function-Based Intervention

When teachers are able to improve misbehavior in the classroom in its early stages, a school's more intensive Tier 2 and 3 resources can be focused on intervening with more intractable behavior problems.

Teacher's Encyclopedia of Behavior Management: 100+ Problems/500+ Plans (2nd ed.)

GRADES K–12

Since 1995, thousands of teachers have come to rely on the effective interventions detailed in *Teacher's Encyclopedia of Behavior Management* to help them create and maintain productive, respectful, PBIS-driven learning environments.

Comprehensive and insightful, the Encyclopedia offers more than 500 easy-to-implement intervention plans that cover over 100 common classroom problems, including:

- Arguing—Students with the teacher and students with each other
- Blaming others/Excuses for everything
- Cliques/Ganging up
- Forgetting materials
- Homework issues
- Transitions, Problems with
- Work completion—Daily work

NEW STREAMLINED, EASY-TO-REFERENCE DESIGN

The second edition includes a more streamlined, easy-to-reference design and 75 ready-to-use reproducible forms to make intervention implementation easy. Among the fourteen new problems are misuse of electronics, cyberbullying, gambling, and skipping class.

For each misbehavior addressed, the Encyclopedia offers an assortment of plans so you can select an intervention tailored to the purpose, duration, and severity of the particular situation. A series of questions guides you through relevant considerations to help you identify the plan that best suits your situation or develop your own custom intervention. As always, you can trust all resources in the Safe & Civil Schools Library to offer strategies and techniques that reflect proven research on best classroom practices.

Interventions: Support for Individual Students With Behavior Challenges (3rd ed.)

GRADES K–12

Interventions helps educators who work with challenging students plan and implement evidence-based, tiered strategies to increase motivation and improve behavior.

This resource gives educators information about how to create a continuum of problem-solving and intervention supports for students who don't respond to universal efforts—or those students who require the higher levels of support, resources, or expertise characteristic of Tier 2 and Tier 3 supports.

This book is designed for school personnel who are responsible for ensuring that students' needs for behavioral, social, and emotional support are met, as well as anyone who will be involved in planning or implementing an individual intervention:

- School psychologists, school counselors, and behavior specialists
- Members of problem-solving and behavior leadership teams
- Building-based administrators
- District personnel such as special education directors/coordinators, directors of school psychology, and supervisors of school counselors

This revised edition provides recommendations for efficient schoolwide coordination for delivery of intervention services—the background tasks administrators and school leaders must complete in order to establish a system for individualized intervention. It also presents an evidence-based model to guide effective and efficient problem-solving for individual students. The framework for building behavior interventions can be used for any stage of a problem, with implementation guidance, sample forms, charts, and data collection tools.

Step-by-step instructions detail how to plan and implement a set of specialized intervention strategies designed to support:

- Students with internalizing challenges
- Students who exhibit escalating, dangerous, or highly disruptive behavior
- Students who may benefit from behavioral contracting, structured reinforcement, or self-monitoring and self-evaluation systems

Some Resources from The Tough Kid Series

by Dr. William Jenson and Colleagues

The Tough Kid Book: Practical Classroom Management Strategies (3rd ed.)

GRADES 1–8

Help Tough Kids succeed in school and in life! Tough Kids combine behavioral excesses such as noncompliance, aggression, and tantrums with less obvious deficits in academic, self-management, and social skills. Tough Kids are a challenge, but you can use proactive, positive techniques to manage and motivate them. *The Tough Kid Book* is for regular and special education teachers, counselors, instructional coaches, and any educator who wants effective and positively focused classrooms.

This book guides you through the process of identifying and assessing Tough Kids. It provides suggestions for structuring your classroom to ensure success for all kids—including the most difficult. Step-by-step instructions explain how to implement both positive and corrective strategies for classrooms, groups, and individual students. Advanced behavior strategies are designed specifically for Tough Kids. For Tough Kids currently in special placements, the Tough Kid Generalization Model offers a detailed plan for returning them successfully to the general education classroom.

All techniques presented in *The Tough Kid Book* have been shown to be effective by rigorous research. The newly updated third edition includes:

- Advanced strategies such as Tootling and Clean Your Plate to teach and encourage Tough Kids to demonstrate positive behaviors such as praising classmates and completing their independent work
- Techniques to improve academic engagement and performance
- Tips for using a functional behavior assessment to uncover the function of a misbehavior
- Executive functioning skills and the Tough Kid
- How to select and teach classroom rules

The companion book, *The Tough Kid Tool Box*, provides ready-to-use reproducibles and detailed directions for implementing many of the behavior management strategies presented in *The Tough Kid Book*.